W9-BLX-409

NATIONALISM AND RELIGION IN AMERICA

1774—1789

NATIONALISM AND RELIGION IN AMERICA

1774—1789

BY
EDWARD FRANK HUMPHREY, Ph.D.

NEW YORK / RUSSELL & RUSSELL
1965

FIRST PUBLISHED IN 1924
REISSUED, 1966, BY RUSSELL & RUSSELL
L.C. CATALOG CARD NO: 65–17902
PRINTED IN THE UNITED STATES OF AMERICA

TO

Christine Vera

AND

John James Humphrey

Carissimi liberi erepti
Quasi flores aratro tacti

"Of all the dispositions and habits which lead to political prosperity, religion and morality are indispensable supports." George Washington, *Farewell Address*, 1796.

"*Pro Ecclesia et Patria.*" Motto of Trinity (Washington) College, 1823.

"There is no country in the world where the Christian religion retains a greater influence . . . . . than in America . . . . . It must be regarded as the foremost of the political institutions of that country." Alexis de Tocqueville, *Democracy in America*, 1835.

"Christianity is in fact understood to be, though not the legally established religion, yet the national religion . . . . . Religion and Conscience have been constantly active forces in the American Commonwealth . . . . . by which moral and political evils have been held at bay, and in the long run generally overcome." James Bryce, *American Commonwealth*, 1888.

TABLE OF CONTENTS

PART III

THE STATE AND RELIGION

NATIONALISM AND RELIGION IN AMERICA

CHAPTER I

INTRODUCTION

What part did religion play in the creation of American nationalism, — not merely in the formation of an American state but more in the moulding of the still deeper spirit of American unity which underlies nationalism? The following study, *Nationalism and Religion in America, 1774 to 1789*, is undertaken with the hope that it may throw some light on that subject.

A nation may be defined as a group of free people held together by ties such as race, language, religion, manners and customs, traditions, history, geographical surroundings, commerce, laws, etc. The elements entering into the compound nationality are numerous and their relative importance varies with each separate nation. Obviously no definite history of the birth of American nationalism can be written until all of the elements which make for nationalism have been listed and evaluated. Religion was one of the more potent factors in the making of The United States of America.

It is to be noted at the outset that we are dealing with the forces of Nationalism and Religion, and that we are in no sense confining ourselves to the narrow limits which would be imposed were we to treat of the usual terms

State and Church. Separation of Church and State in America has tended to divert attention from the more important factors, Religion and Nation. The American nation has limited the powers of its government. For political purposes we have divorced the Church and the State, thereby placing decided limitations upon each. But this is a governmental limitation. In America there is a distinct recognition of the fact that there is a nation above the state; the nation created the state and can make and unmake its laws and government. Quite different was the Teutonic conception of the state as a supreme and all powerful individuality, possessed of a soul which autocratically ruled a subordinate nation.

The American conception allows for national characteristics that are independent of the state. So we are a Christian nation even though Christianity is not a feature of the American state. The adoption of the American concept of the limited state resulted in the ideal of a free church in a free nation, the present American ideal of religious freedom. As a corollary to this we have the ideal of a state freed from ecclesiastical control. Numerous treatises have dealt with the relations of church and state in the formative period of American history, but we purpose to follow the trend of events in connection with nationalism and religion.

The formative period of American nationalism was from 1774 to 1789. During those fifteen years separate colonial institutions were superseded by national ones and the process was accompanied by the awakening of an American national conscience. The first Continental Congress assembled in 1774 to petition for a redress of grievances; its members protested their loyalty as British colonists. These American colonies of Great Britain had existed up to the time of the Revolutionary War as thirteen separate and distinct political units. Nor had they seriously attempted to break down the social, economic, educational or religious barriers which separated them. They seemed to dread unification; they were more afraid of consolidation than was their mother country. So strong was this feeling that even devout members of the Church of England worked against the introduction of an American Episcopacy lest it might prove the beginning of a development which would ultimately produce a complete autocratic hierarchy with centralized authority.[1] The Church of England was at a disadvantage in America just because it possessed a traditional centralized organization; dissenting sects possessed an advantage in organization more in harmony with the American spirit of local autonomy.[2] Anyone or any organization which stood for unification was suspect in America before 1774.

The Second Continental Congress is commonly credited with the creation of an American nation. It did produce the Declaration of Independence, the Articles of Confederation and the Federal Constitution. But these acts, great as they were, did not jointly or separately constitute a nation. The Declaration of Independence did not, as so commonly supposed, "bring forth on this

[1] Hawks, *Efforts to obtain a Colonial Episcopate before the Revolution*, in *Protestant Episcopal Historical Society Collection*, vol. i, pp. 136-357. Cross, *The Anglican Episcopate and the American Colonies*, in *Harvard Historical Studies*, vol. ix.

[2] Henry Caner to the Archbishop of Canterbury, January 7, 1763, "We are a Rope of Sand, there is no union, no authority among us; we cannot even summon a Convention for united council and advice, while the Dissenting Ministers have their Monthly, Quarterly, and Annual Associations, Conventions, Etc., to advise, assist, and support each other in any measures which they shall think proper to enter into." Quoted from Perry, *Historical Collections*, vol. iii, Mass., pp. 489-491.

Continent a new nation." Far from creating new institutions or a new spirit of unity, it merely freed the then existing institutions from British control. The spirit of Thomas Jefferson, its author, was not a creative one. Independence was his mania: "the less government the better" according to his political creed. The Declaration of Independence but cleared the way for the creation of whatever spirit or form of institutions the colonists might elect to produce. The Articles of Confederation and the Federal Constitution represent efforts on the part of the colonists to give political form to their conception of a nascent nationalism.

Where did the spirit of nationalism originate? This study shows that religious forces play an important rôle in the formation of a national spirit and even in the shaping of national institutions according to model furnished by prior American efforts at ecclesiastical organization.

At that time the pulpit was the most powerful single force in America for the creation and control of public opinion. This fact must not be lost sight of when we are trying to trace the development of the growth of a popular consciousness of Americanism. Nobody in America approached George Washington in the early control of public opinion. An important paragraph of his *Farewell Address to the People of the United States*, September 7, 1796, admonishes attention to the forces of morality and religion as political factors in the life of the American people. Washington said:

"Of all the dispositions and habits which lead to political prosperity, Religion and Morality are indispensable support. For in vain would that man claim the tribute of Patriotism who should labor to subvert these great pillars of human happiness, these firmest props of the duties of Men and Citizens. The mere politician, equally with the pious man, ought to respect and to cherish them. A Volume could not trace all their connections with private and public felicity. Let it simply be asked, where is the security for property, for reputation, for life, if the sense of religious obligation desert the oaths, which are the instruments of investigation in courts of justice? And let us, with caution indulge the supposition that morality can be maintained without religion. Whatever may be conceded to the influence of refined education on minds of peculiar structure, reason and experience both forbid us to expect that national morality can prevail in exclusion of religious principles.

It is substantially true, that virtue or morality is a necessary spring of popular government. The rule, indeed, extends with more or less force to every species of free government. Who that is a sincere friend to it can look with indifference upon attempts to shake the foundation of the fabric."

Washington recognized the religious element in the American history of his time but unfortunately the historian of his day was sufficiently skilled neither in historical analysis nor in critical exposition, to chronicle events and forces clearly. The part played by religious forces in the development of American nationalism remains to be written; and it remains to be written in an age which has departed far from Washington's standards of appreciation of religion and morality as historic forces. In fact this essay is undertaken at a time when a foremost American educator has just characterized Washington's *Farewell Address* with the Ten Commandments as "excellent documents in their days."

Separation of church and state early in the development of American nationalism led, perhaps inevitably, to the almost complete elimination of the religious element from works on American political history. Certainly the American historian carefully omits the religious element from our constitutional history from the time of the achievement of independence. And now even the religious element of the earlier periods is being belittled.

A modern review of the Pilgrims finds that they came to America not primarily for religious freedom but for gain;[1] and Puritanism is fast becoming a trade corporation rather than a religious movement.

One searches in vain through the narrowly political histories of the period covered by this treatise for an appreciation of religious events and influences. Yet this very period marked a turning point in the politico-religious history of the world. It gave to the world America's Magna Charta of religious freedom:

"No religious test shall ever be required as a qualification to any office or public trust under the United States." (Article VI, section 3 of the Constitution.)

"Congress shall make no law respecting an establishment of religion, or prohibiting the free exercise thereof." (First Amendment.)

Thus the first great experiment in religious liberty is surely a political event of no lesser magnitude for the state than for the churches of America. It fixed a distinctive character to both, well described by Philip Schaff as, "A free church in a free state, a self-supporting and self-governing Christianity in independent but friendly relation to the Civil Government."[2]

Religion does not disappear in America with the establishment of religious liberty, it is not even eliminated as a political force. Careful observers of American institutions have always found it a powerful element in our political life. Alexis de Tocqueville, one of the most

[1] Usher, *The Pilgrims.*

[2] Schaff, "Church and State in the United States" in *American Historical Association Papers*, vol. ii, no. 4, p. 9. "This relation of Church and State marks an epoch . . . . . I know of no ecclesiastical or secular history or special treatise, which gives a satisfactory account of it; and the works on the Constitution of the United States touch only on the legal aspect of the religious clauses, or pass them by altogether."

philosophical foreign observers that has ever visited America, wrote in the presidency of Van Buren:

"There is no country in the whole world in which the Christian religion retains a greater influence over the souls of men than in America, and there can be no greater proof of its utility, and of its conformity to human nature, than that its influence is most powerfully felt over the most enlightened and free nation of the earth . . . . In the United States religion exercises but little influence upon the laws and upon the details of public opinion, but it directs the manners of the community, and by regulating domestic life, it regulates the state . . . . . Religion in America takes no direct part in the government of society, but it must, nevertheless, be regarded as the foremost of the political institutions of that country, for if it does not impart a taste for freedom, it facilitates the use of free institutions. This opinion is not peculiar to a class of citizens or to a party, but it belongs to the whole nation and to every rank of society. I am certain they hold it to be indispensable to the maintenance of republican institutions."[1]

The ablest analysis and description of American institutions yet written was done by James Bryce in the first administration of Grover Cleveland. He found that:

"It was religious zeal and the religious conscience which led to the founding of the New England Colonies two centuries and a half ago — those colonies whose spirit has in such a large measure passed into the whole nation. Religion and conscience have been a constantly active force in the American commonwealth ever since, not indeed strong enough to avert many moral and political evils, yet at the worst time inspiring a minority with a courage and ardor by which moral and political evils have been held at bay, and in the long run generally overcome.

A perusal of the literature which the ordinary American of the educated farming and working class reads, and a study of the kind of literature which those Americans who are least colored by European influences produce, lead me to think that the Bible and Christian theology altogether do more in the way of forming the imaginative background to an average American view of the world of man and nature than they do in Modern Protestant Europe.

[1] Alexis de Tocqueville, *Democracy in America*, translated by Henry Reeve, N. Y., 1838, vol. i, p. 285 sq.

It is an old saying that monarchies live by honor and republics by virtue. The more democratic republics become, the more the masses grow conscious of their own power, the more do they need to live, not only by patriotism, but by reverence and self-control, and the more essential to their well-being are those sources whence reverence and self-control flow."[1]

The religious element has always been a powerful factor in American history and just at present there exists a special need for its restoration to the pages of historical narratives. We are again awake to the problems of the social organism; the disruptive influences of the World War have made us re-examine the elements of our nationalism; we are asking ourselves, "What is Americanism?" We find countless books descriptive of our constitutional form of government; but they are catalogues of details, descriptions of mechanics, rather than evaluations of the American spirit. Recently a new conception of history has crept into the works of such men as President Lowell, *Public Opinion and Popular Government*, Herbert Croly, *The Promise of American Life*, or Walter Lippmann, *Preface to Politics*. Human society is no longer considered as an organism or a mechanism, but rather as the action of men in association, and the state is no longer power or force, but "the will to live together." Dr. J. N. Figgis' book, *Churches in the Modern State*, has become one of the forces in present-day social theory. And the English Guild Socialist, G. D. R. Cole, finds that at present there are "three live sources of social theory — the Church, industry, and history."[2] Human nature is being restored to our political concepts.

[1] Bryce, *American Commonwealth*, vol. ii, Chapter civ, "Influence of religion," pp. 571-583. Also see "Democracy and Religion," Chapter ix, vol. i. *Modern Democracies*.

[2] Cole, *Social Theory*, p. 10.

A decade ago it had begun to look as though everything human would be eliminated for social consideration and that men must be considered merely as automatons in a mechanistic state. Individuality, morality, patriotism, freedom, and all things spiritual were eliminated in order to prove an economic determinism. Woodburn could write in 1892, *Causes of the American Revolution,* "I have not attempted an appreciation of the deep underlying moral causes of which the Revolution has appeared to many but the natural outcome."[1] This method produced, in 1913, *An Economic Interpretation of the Constitution of the United States,* by Charles A. Beard, which concluded:

> "The movement for the Constitution of the United States was originated and carried through principally by four groups of personalty interests which had been adversely affected under the Articles of Confederation: money, public securities, manufactures, and trade and shipping.
>
> The direct, impelling motive (for the adoption of the Constitution) . . was the economic advantages which the beneficiaries expected would accrue to themselves first, from their actions.
>
> The Constitution was essentially an economic document based upon the conception that the fundamental private rights of property are anterior to government and morally beyond the reach of popular majorities."[2]

In 1918, *The Colonial Merchants and the Revolution,* by A. M. Schlessinger, analyzed with minute care the economic elements which produced the Revolution.[3]

[1] Woodburn, *Causes of the American Revolution,* in *Johns Hopkins University Studies,* tenth series, vol. xii, p. 608.

[2] Beard, *An Economic Interpretation of the Constitution,* pp. 18, 324.

[3] Schlessinger, *The Colonial Merchants and the Revolution,* in *Columbia University Studies,* vol. lxxviii, no. 182. McIlwain, *The American Revolution: A Constitutional Interpretation,* thinks that the economic historians themselves have performed a valuable service in dispelling the view that the colonists were trying to throw off a heavy and oppressive burden. He contends that the economic historians have read themselves out of court and that the Revolution was primarily a political constitutional struggle.

These works by Beard and Schlessinger are invaluable guides for the period of history covered by the present study. There is no intention on the part of the author to minimize the value of the economic factor in determining the early character of Americanism. Its influence was profound, but no more weighty than that of morality, religion, education, patriotism, or countless other elements. Who would estimate the quantitative value of each? Yet in the consideration of relative values several things should be borne in mind. In the first place we are dealing with a period in which the pulpit to a very large extent controlled public opinion; at that time the preacher was the leading politician. Moreover, in the eighteenth century the Industrial Revolution had not yet affected American institutions; and, consequently, the economic forces of 1776 were vastly different from those of the present time, the modern industrial democracy of 1924. In the second place the beginning of a separation of church and state was not made until 1785 and the alliance of church and state was still most powerful, nationalism and religion were everywhere considered as interdependent. "God and Country," "Pro Ecclesia et Partia," were typical slogans. To Washington of that age religion and morality were "the indispensable props" of political prosperity. "With the exception of some parts of Scotland," says Lecky, "no portion of the British Islands was animated with the religious fervor of New England, and no sketch of the American Revolution is adequate which does not take this influence into account."[1]

It will be found that the relation between religious and political movements in America during the Revolutionary and Critical periods, 1774 to 1789, was intimate. This was

[1] Lecky, *History of England in the Eighteenth Century*, vol. iii, p. 484.

the epoch of the appearance of American nationalism. It is true that the germs and origins of most phases of American nationalism may be traced both to the earlier colonial period of American history and indeed even farther back to English habits; yet the fact remains that a consciously open Americanism appears at this time. Independence was the first step toward this Americanism, and we purpose to follow the actions of the various churches of America in their contributions to political independence. This will constitute the first part of the book.

But independence entailed a reorganization of the churches themselves; they were compelled to adopt new national organism, the churches themselves were nationalized, new church constitutions were formed. The second portion of this book deals with the nationalization of the churches. This process counted much in the creation of a national American conscience; just how much, is the difficult question encountered by this study. Church and state undergo a parallel development in the evolution of American unity. For both a necessity for union and centralization sprang from the separation from Great Britain; the threat of anarchy impelled union for self-preservation, for strength, and general welfare.

The enthusiasm with which different denominations undertook the work of reformation and the character of the American institution produced, differ greatly, though the phenomenon appears in every one of them. Some, such as the Congregationalists and the Baptists, were already so "independent" that they took naturally to the new régime. In fact, the state seems to many merely to be following a lead which these denominations had already marked. But with them, even, competition with the other disestablished bodies, so independent too, and stronger in numbers and discipline, compelled a strengthening of the national bonds; mere independence no longer was a guarantee of strength. The Dutch Reformed and the Presbyterian churches had already organized themselves on a quasi-national basis as a means of combating foreign spiritual control; these denominations were obliged to strengthen rather than to alter their form of organization. Some few denominations, the German Reformed, the Moravians and the Quakers, were content to remain for years in a position of subordination to foreign ecclesiastical control. They refused to profit by the lesson of American independence; they missed a part of the spirit of American nationalism and suffered thereby a consequent retardation in their development. Three communions, — Episcopalian, Roman Catholic, and Methodists — found it imperative that they address themselves immediately and seriously to the task of a complete ecclesiastical reorganization. They seem alive to all of the possibilities of the situation and it is not surprising to find that they go even so far in certain instances as to accompany ecclesiastical reorganization with efforts at theological alterations which they feel will be more in keeping with the American spirit. It is the more aggressive denomination that most vitally affects the corresponding political movements for nationalism.

There is no question but that various churches influenced the formation of our political institutions. Republicanism was well established in the institutions of the Presbyterian and Congregational Churches; its roots may be traced to Calvin. Many members of the Federal Constitutional Convention were trained in their practices of government. The Protestant Episcopal

Church and its near relative, the Methodist Episcopal Church, worked out their American Constitutions in advance of the Federal Constitution. The Protestant Episcopal Church was numerically one of the most important churches in America[1] and certainly it was the most important politically. Many of the men who participated in the Federal Convention had just gone through the process of national constitution-making in the conventions of that church. One cannot help being struck with the similarity of its organization to that of our national government. In like manner, it will be clearly evident to anyone who will compare the two institutions that to the Roman Catholic College of Cardinals we owe our system for the election of President and Vice-President, — the electoral college.

American education had a great deal to do with the relative importance of the various denominations in their influence upon institutional development. American colleges had trained a sufficient number of leaders for the American state and for American churches in most denominations. Harvard, William and Mary, King's College, Brown, Rutgers, Princeton, etc., were church colleges, every one of them, their dual task for America

[1] Baird, *Religion in America*, pp. 103-104, gives the following estimate of the number of ministers and churches of each denomination in America at the time of the Revolution:

Episcopal	250 clergy	300 churches
Presbyterian	177	417
Congregational	575	700
Baptist	424	471
Methodist	Not a separate body	
Lutheran	25	60
German Reformed	...	...
Dutch Reformed	30	82
Associate	13	20
Moravian	12	6 or 8
Roman Catholic	26	52

was to train both preachers and statesmen. Some of the American churches were handicapped by not possessing colleges on this side of the Atlantic.

The general character of American ecclesiastical institutions was determined by the development of the period under discussion. All of the churches worked out their national institutions under the stress of mutual jealousies. No one or two sects were strong enough to maintain exceptional pretensions over the others when in combination, and French philosophic thought as interpreted by the searching deistic criticism of such men as Benjamin Franklin and Thomas Jefferson, kept them on their mettle and made them justify every act. All of the churches seem to have felt the effects of the prevalent doctrinaire political theories of Rousseau, Montesquieu, and their contemporaries. So we find American ecclesiasticism, like the American political state, stamped with the contract theory of government, with the doctrine of separation of powers, and with the ideal of the consent of the governed. These theories we find combined with the more distinctive American principles, which had grown from the early independent movement, — equality of all religious communions before the law and non-interference on the part of the state with religion. Above all the Revolution compelled distinctively American churches to a complete independence from foreign ecclesiastical control.[1]

The influence of certain powerfully organized religious bodies, exerting a political influence through the Constitutional Convention, where they forced through certain measures which were being opposed by some of the most

[1] Schaff, "Church and State in the United States or the American Idea of Religious Liberty and its Practical Effects" in *Papers of the American Historical Association,* vol. ii, no. 4.

powerful economic interests in America, demonstrates the power of the church at this period. The Anti-slavery clauses of the Constitution may be attributed to the "religious fanaticism" of Quakers, Methodists, Baptists, and various other church organizations.

It is comparatively easy to recognize religious influences where they have produced tangible institutional results, but we must always hold in mind the more difficult problem of forming an estimation of the influence which they had in the formation of an American spirit. Independence cleared the way for the Americanization of all the forces of American life. Before a real nation could be produced, each of the elements must be brought into harmony with national ideals. Nationalization is the chief feature of all institutional development for the period under discussion. Uncertainty as to its outcome makes of this a "critical period." Possibly the relative importance of the national movement among the American churches is disclosed by the priority of its achievement. Church unity, attained, exerted a great influence, through its almost complete control over public opinion, in inducing nationalization along other lines. Alexander Hamilton was able to produce American financial unity only after he had assisted at the unification of first his church and then his political government.

PART ONE

RELIGIOUS ELEMENTS OF THE AMERICAN REVOLUTION

CHAPTER II

THE PROTESTANT EPISCOPAL CHURCH IN THE REVOLUTION

It is exceedingly dangerous to fix formulae representative of the conduct of the various religious denominations of America with respect to the Revolution. It has been attempted and we read that Quakers were "non-combatant and inactive," that Episcopalians were "pro-English," and that Methodists "imitating John Wesley, denounced the revolting Americans."[1] Such phrases are misleading and true only for certain specific cases. Quakers seceded in order to form a militant party, "Free Quakers," Anglicans accepted positions of danger and responsibility with the revolting colonies and Methodists volunteered in great numbers for active service. Clergy and laity of every denomination were in confusion as to their patriotic and religious duties.

To a Lutheran clergyman, Dr. Helmuth, the situation in Philadelphia, as he observed it, was as follows:

"Throughout the whole country great preparations are making for the war, and almost every person is under arms. The ardor manifested in these melancholy circumstances is indescribable. If a hundred men are required, many more immediately offer, and are dissatisfied when they are not accepted. I know of no similar case in history. Neighborhoods, concerning which it would have been expected that years would be required to induce them voluntarily to take up arms, became

[1] De Witt, *First General Assembly* or Thomson, *The Presbyterian Churches in the United States*, p. 56, "The Congregationalists, Presbyterians, Reformed, Lutherans and Baptists as a whole were on the patriotic side, while the Episcopalians and the Methodists in the main sided with the mother-country, which also possessed the sympathy and quiet cooperation of the majority of the Friends."

strongly inclined for war as soon as the battle of Lexington was known. Quakers and Mennonites take part in the military exercises, and in great numbers renounce their former religious principles. The hoarse din of war is hourly heard in our streets. The present disturbances inflict no small injury on religion. Everybody is constantly on the alert, anxious like the ancient Athenians, to hear the news, and, amid the mass of news, the hearts of men are, Alas, closed against the Good Word of God.

The Lord is chastening the people, but they do not feel it . . . . . In the American army there are many clergymen, who serve both as chaplains and as officers. I know two, one of whom is a colonel, and the other a captain. The whole country is in perfect enthusiasm for liberty. The whole population, from New England to Georgia, is of one mind, and determined to risk life and all things in defence of liberty. The few who think differently are not permitted to utter their sentiments. In Philadelphia the English and German students are formed into military companies, wear uniforms, and are exercised like regular troops. Would to God that men would become as zealous and unanimous in asserting their spiritual liberty, as they are in vindicating their political freedom."[2]

And John Adams wrote to his wife from Philadelphia:

"Does Mr. Wibird preach against oppression and the other cardinal vices of the time? Tell him the clergy here of every denomination, not excepting the Episcopalians, thunder and lighten every Sabbath. They pray for Boston and Massachusetts. They thank God most explicitly and fervently for our remarkable successes. They pray for the American Army."[2]

Among all sects in America there was a religious enthusiasm for Liberty; the religious temper of America was one of the prime causes of the Revolution. Edmund Burke so informed Parliament. The Americans, he said, were not only Protestants, but Protestants against Protestantism itself. They were dissenters from the Church of England; they were Puritans, Congregationalists, Presbyterians, Baptists, and Quakers. Their ancestors, persecuted in England, had fled to America and they hated

[1] Schmucker, *Retrospection of Lutheranism in the United States* quoting a letter in the Hallische *Nachrichten*, pp. 1367-8; Baird, *op. cit.* pp. 102-103.

[2] *Letters of John Adams, Addressed to his Wife*, vol. i, p. 50.

the English Church. In their religious beliefs and practices, they had advanced beyond all other Protestants in the liberty of the Reformation. They had rejected so many dogmas and sacraments that they were more free in their religion than most of the people of Europe. They had trained and accustomed themselves to the freest and most subtile debate on all religious questions, regardless of priests councils, or creeds; and they had encouraged this individualism until even the women thought for themselves, and it was said that every man's hat was his church. Such simple church organization as they possessed was democratic like that of the Baptist and Congregationalists, or republican like that of the Presbyterians. The people had learned to elect their own religious leaders, — called them and also dismissed them when they failed to please the majority. Such religious liberty naturally led to extreme political liberalism; why should the right of private judgment allowed for religious matters be denied in things political?

Perhaps these characteristics applied more uniformly to New Englanders or to Scotch-Irish Presbyterians of the frontier but we find churchmen of Virginia as ardent for independence as the most fiery frontier Scot. Anglican Americans such as Washington, Jefferson, Madison, or Mason had outgrown any religious autocracy, and the Roman Catholics such as the Carrolls had imbibed the same spirit of liberty.[1]

True, there remained in America a party, Tory in the extreme, more reactionary than could be found in the old world, to whom all democratic or republican doctrines were anathema and who would restore religious along with political autocracy. It worked openly for the ad-

[1] Fisher, *Struggle for American Independence*, vol. i, pp. 18-19.

advancement of such policies, and fear that their efforts might be crowned with success was a potent cause in bringing on the war. An ever impending threat of "Ecclesiasticism" was one of the chief grievances of New England.[1] The Agents of France in the colonies of America, such as DeKalb and Bon Vouloir, found in the religious situation such an element of disaffection towards the mother country that they counseled the French government to foster this as *the surest force capable of arousing public opinion* to such a degree as to produce a rupture with Great Britain.[2]

The charge of "Ecclesiasticism" prevented the mass of Americans from understanding the position of the American Anglicans. The colonial branches of the Church of England were without local authority; they were entirely dependent on the Bishop of London and the Society for the Propagation of the Gospel. Consequently at frequent intervals they would agitate the establishment of an episcopate in America. It never seems to have been recognized by their opponents in America that this was in reality a step toward independence, that therein the Episcopalians were indulging the American desire for "Home Rule". Every effort of theirs in this direction met with vigorous opposition from their Presbyterian and Congregational fellow countrymen. In fact we find these two sects held joint conferences between the years 1766 and 1775 with the avowed main object, "to prevent the establishment of an Episcopacy in America."[3]

"Ecclesiasticism," however, to these sects was a real, not a fictitious, peril. The joint assemblies which it

[1] *Supra*, p. 3; Chamberlain, *John Adams*, pp. 17-45.
[2] Cornelis De Witt, *La Vie de Thomas Jefferson*; Abbé Robin, A *New Journey in North America*; *Correspondence* of De Kalb.
[3] *Infra*, pp. 68-71.

instigated did much to forward the union of the colonies, — even indirectly political union. As Pre-Revolutionary national gatherings of colonies, they influenced for union to a greater degree than any other body, not excepting the transient Albany Congress which is so stressed in all our histories. They afforded a training in the utilization of national institutions and they repeatedly asserted that they existed, not for narrowly religious motives, but to oppose the introduction into America through bishops, of those political powers which the clergy in England possessed.

In *A View of the Causes and Consequences of the American Revolution*, by Jonathan Boucher, a reprint of thirteen discourses preached in North America between the years 1763 and 1775, published in London 1797 and dedicated to George Washington, we possess an excellent exposition of the mind of the extreme Anglican Tory clergyman on the eve of the Revolution. To the Reverend Mr. Boucher:

> "A leveling republican spirit in the church naturally leads to republicanism in the State."[1] . . . . "God forbid any of us should live to see the day when we may be convinced of the truth of King James' maxim — 'No bishop, no king' and when this dominion, now the fair image of one of the best governments upon the earth, shall be so degenerate and mean as to become the ape of New England in her civil institutions, and therefore too likely to follow the same wretched model in what the people of New England call the platform of religion. And when it is recollected, that till now, the opposition to an American episcopate has been confined chiefly to the demagogues and independents of the New England provinces, but that it is now espoused with much warmth by the people of Virginia, it requires no great depths of political sagacity to see what the motives and views of the former have been, or what will be the consequences of the defection of the latter."[2]

[1] Boucher, *A View of the Causes and Consequences of the American Revolution*, p. 104.

[2] *Ibid.*, pp. 102-103.

These views were expressed in America in a sermon, "On the American Episcopate," delivered in 1771. In editing this is London in 1797, he added:

"It by no means follows that episcopacy was thus opposed from its having been thought by these trans-Atlantic oppositionists as in any respect in itself proper to be opposed; but it served to keep the public mind in a state of ferment and effervescence; to make them jealous and superstitious of all measures not brought forward by demagogues; and, above all, to train and habituate the people to opposition . . . . .

That the American opposition to episcopacy was at all connected with that still more serious one so soon afterwards set up against the civil government was not indeed generally apparent at the time; but it is now indisputable, as it also is that the former contributed not a little to render the latter successful. As therefore this controversy was clearly one great cause that led to the revolution, the view of it here given, it is hoped, will not be deemed wholly uninteresting.

Hardly was their independence gained before an episcopate was applied for and obtained; an episcopate in every point of view as obnoxious as that which the same men, who were now its chief promoters, and who were also the most forward in the revolution, had just before so violently resisted." [1]

Tiffany thinks that "the sudden collapse of all such opposition after the Revolution . . . . . shows that the popular objection to the introduction of bishops was chiefly political."[2] Certainly it was a widespread opposition. In Parliament Lord Chatham remarked, "Divided as they are into a thousand forms of polity and religion, there is one point in which they all agree: they equally detest the pageantry of a king and the supercilious hypocrisy of a bishop."[3] John Adams wrote to Dr. Jedediah Morse, December 2, 1815:

"Where is the man to be found at this day, when we see Methodistical bishops, bishops of the Church of England, and bishops, archbishops, and

[1]Boucher, *op. cit.*, pp. 149-151; Chamberlain *John Adams*, p. 37; Perry, *American Episcopal Church*, vol. i, p. 425, note 4.

[2]Tiffany, *Protestant Episcopal Church*, p. 277.

[3]Quoted in Perry, *American Episcopal Church*, vol. i, p. 412.

Jesuits of the Church of Rome, with indifference, who will believe that the apprehension of the Episcopacy contributed fifty years ago, as much as any other cause, to arouse the attention not only of the inquiring mind, but of the common people, and urge them to close thinking on the constitutional authority of Parliament over the Colonies? This, nevertheless, was a fact as certain as any in the history of North America. The objection was not merely to the office of a bishop, though even that was dreaded, but to the authority of Parliament, on which it must be founded . . . . . . There is no power or pretended power, less than Parliament, that can create bishops in America. But if Parliament can erect dioceses and appoint bishops, they may introduce the whole hierarchy, establish tithes, forbid marriages and funerals, establish religions, forbid dissenters, make schism heresy, impose penalties extending to life and limb as well as to liberty and property."[1]

Loyal Episcopalian sermons for the period are rare; they were delivered under difficulties and their preservation is hardly to have been expected. The Reverend Boucher informs us of some of the difficulties attending their delivery:

"I received letters threatening me with the most dreadful consequences if I did not desist from preaching at all. All the answers I gave to these threats were in my sermons, in which I declared I could never suffer any human authority to intimidate me from doing what I believed to be my duty to God and His church; and for more than six months I preached, when I did preach, with a pair of loaded pistols lying on the cushion; having given notice that if any one attempted, what had long been threatened, to drag me out of the pulpit, I should think myself justified in repelling violence by violence. Some time after, a public fast was ordained; and on this occasion my curate, who was a strong republican, had prepared a sermon for the occasion, and supported by a set of factious men, was determined to oppose my entering my own pulpit. When the day came, I was at my church at least a quarter of an hour before the time of beginning; but, behold, Mr. Harrison was in the desk, and was expected, I was soon told, to preach. In addition to this, I saw my church filled with not less than two hundred armed men under the command of Mr. Osborne Sprigg, who soon told me I was not to preach. I returned for answer that there was but one way by which they could keep me out of it, and that was by taking away my life. At the proper

[1] *John Adams, Works,* vol. x, p. 185; Morse, *Annals of the American Revolution*, pp. 197-203.

time, with my sermon in one hand and a loaded pistol in the other, like Nehemiah I prepared to ascend my pulpit, when one of my friends, Mr. David Cranford, having got behind me, threw his arms round me and held me fast. He assured me that he had heard the most positive orders given to twenty men picked out for that purpose, to fire on me, the moment I got into the pulpit, which therefore he never would permit me to do, unless I was stronger than himself and some others who stood close to him. I maintained that once to flinch was forever to invite danger; but my well-wishers prevailed, and, when I was down, it is horrid to recollect what a scene of confusion ensued. Sprigg and his company contrived to surround me and to exclude every moderate man. Seeing myself thus circumstanced, it occurred to me that there was but one way to save my life, — this was by seizing Sprigg, as I immediately did, by the collar, and with my cocked pistol in the other hand, assuring him that if any violence were offered to me, I would instantly blow his brains out. I then told him he might conduct me to my house, and I would leave them. This he did, and we marched together upwards of a hundred yards, guarded by his whole company — whom he had the meanness to order to play the rogues' march all the way we went. Thus ended this dreadful day, which was a Thursday. On the following Sunday I again went to the same church, and was again opposed, but more feebly than before. I preached the sermon I should have preached on the Thursday, with some comments on the transactions of the day." [1]

Boucher's sermons thoroughly illustrate the aristocrat's contempt for the American doctrine of equality. He pontificated in opposition thereto as follows:

"that the whole human race is born equal; and that no man is naturally inferior, or in any respect subjected to another; and that he can be made subject to another only by his own consent. The position is equally ill-founded and false; both in its premises and conclusions. In hardly any sense that can be imagined, is the position strictly true; but, as applied to the case under consideration, it is demonstrably not true. Man differs from man in everything that can be supposed to lead to supremacy and subjection . . . . . Without government, there can be no society; nor, without some relative inferiority and superiority, can there be any government." [2] "It surely was something more than ridiculous, when

[1] Boucher, "Autobiography" in *Notes and Queries*, 5th series, vol. i, pp. 103-104; quoted Tyler, *Literary History of the American Revolution*, vol. i, pp. 318-320.

[2] Boucher, A *View of the Causes and Consequences of the American Revolution*, pp. 514-515.

not long since, a popular candidate at one of our elections solicited your suffrages in his favor, on the plea of his being, as to his political tenets, a Whig, and the advocate of revolution principles, and in religion a Low-churchman. If folly can ever excuse audacity, this man's utter ignorance of the terms he used, may be admitted as some apology for his presumption."[1]

The Reverend Boucher was a clergyman of Virginia. Hawkes states of Episcopalians of this colony,

"The clergy were generally friends to the mother country — attached to it by the circumstances of birth, and bound as they were individually by the oath of allegiance. A portion of the laity adopted their opinions; it was, however, very small, for the great mass of the population in Virginia was opposed to England. Nor were all the clergy loyalists; they numbered in their ranks some sturdy republicans, though these formed a minority, including not quite one-third of the whole body . . . . . Bishop Madison, Messers Bracken, Belmaine, Buchanan, Jarratt, Griffith, Muhlenberg, Thurston and Davis. Of the laity were General Washington, Patrick Henry, Richard Henry Lee, F. L. Lee, Mason, Pendleton, Lyons, Grayson, Harrison, Carrington, Fleming, Nelson, Randolph, Meade, Mercer and hundreds of other names, deservedly dear to Virginia."[2]

The clergy of New England and New York were more inclined to loyalty to the mother country than were their Southern brethren. Dr. Leaming wrote from Norwalk, Connecticut:

"The missionaries being placed in this colony, is not only very serviceable in a religious, but in a civil sense. In the north-east of this colony there have been most rebellious outrages committed on account of the Stamp Act, while those towns where the Church has got a footing, have calmly submitted to civil authority. It is said that Mayhew, the day before the mob pulled down the Deputy-governor's house, preached sedition from these words; 'I would they were even cut off that trouble you!' He has abused the Church with impunity, and perhaps he thinks he may escape in abusing the State also."[3]

Mr. Beach wrote from the same Colony:

"I have of late, taken pains to warn my people against having any concern in the seditious tumults with relation to the Stamp-duty, en-

[1] Boucher, *A View of the Causes, etc.*, p. 98.
[2] Hawks, *Ecclesiastical History of the United States*, vol. i, pp. 135-137
[3] Beardsley, *Episcopal Church in Connecticut*, vol. i, p. 240.

joined upon us by the Legislature at home; and I can with truth and pleasure say, that I cannot discover the least inclination toward rebellious conduct in any of the church people here . . . . . I wish I could say the same of all sects in these parts."[1]

While Mr. Lamson sent word from Fairfield:

"In a time of anarchy and disloyalty in this country, the professors of the Church of England have in general, throughout the Province of New England, distinguished themselves by a peaceable submission and quiet deportment. The missionaries have exerted themselves upon the occasion in exhorting their own congregations and others to peace, and a due submission to authority; by which means we have been exposed to the calumny and insult of the enemies of the Church and State. Some of us have been threatened with having our houses pulled down over our heads, though as yet they have kept themselves, in this part of the country, from acts of open violence."[2]

The Memoir of the Reverend John Stuart, D.D., of New York states:

"No class was so uncompromising in its loyalty as the clergy of the Church of England in this State; and they in consequence did not fail to experience the bitter effects of their own unwise resolution."[3]

An illuminating description of the position of the colonial clergy of the Church of England comes from the Reverend Charles Inglis, of Trinity Church, New York, under date of October 31, 1776, in a report submitted to the Venerable Society relative to conditions in the colonies, but with particular reference to Trinity Parish:

"All the Society's Missionaries, without excepting one, in New Jersey, New York, Connecticut, and, so far as I can learn, in the other New England Colonies, have proved themselves faithful, loyal subjects in these trying times; and have, to the utmost of their power, opposed the spirit of disaffection and rebellion which has involved this continent in the greatest calamities. I must add, that all the other clergy of our Church in the above Colonies, though not in the Society's service, have

[1] Beardsley, *op. cit.*, vol. i, p. 241.
[2] *Ibid.*, vol. i, p. 242.
[3] *Documentary History of New York*, vol. iv, p. 508.

observed the same line of conduct, and, although their joint endeavors could not wholly prevent the rebellion, yet they checked it considerably for some time, and prevented many thousands from plunging into it, who otherwise would certainly have done so.

You have, doubtless, been long since informed by my worthy friends, Dr. Chandler and Dr. Cooper, to what an height our violences were risen so early as May 1775, when they were both obliged to fly from hence, and seek protection in England. These violences have been gradually increasing ever since; and this, with the delay of sending over succors, and the king's troops totally abandoning this province, reduced the friends of government here to a most disagreeable and dangerous situation, particularly the Clergy, who were viewed with peculiar envy and malignity by the disaffected; for, although civil liberty was the ostensible object, the bait that was flung out to catch the populace at large and engage them in the rebellion, yet it is now past all doubt that an abolition of the Church of England was one of the principal springs of the dissenting leaders' conduct; and hence the unanimity of dissenters in this business. Their universal defection from government, emancipating themselves from the jurisdiction of Great Britain, and becoming independent, was a necessary step towards this grand object. I have it from good authority that the Presbyterian ministers, at a synod where most of them in the middle colonies were collected, passed a resolve to support the continental congress in all their measures.[1] This and this only can account for the uniformity of their conduct; for I do not know one of them, nor have I been able, after strict inquiry, to hear of any, who did not, by preaching and every effort in their power, promote all the measures of the congress, however extravagant.

The Clergy, amidst this scene of tumult and disorder, went on steadily with their duty; in their sermons, confining themselves to the doctrines of the Gospel, without touching on politics; using their influence to allay our heats and cherish a spirit of loyalty among the people. This conduct, however harmless, gave great offence to our flaming patriots, who laid it down as a maxim, 'That those who were not for them were against them.' The Clergy were everywhere threatened, often reviled with the most opprobrious language, sometimes treated with violence. Some have been carried prisoners by armed mobs into distant provinces, where they were detained in close confinement for several weeks, and much insulted, without any crime being even alleged against them. Some have been flung into jails by committees for frivolous suspicions of plots, of which even their persecutors afterwards acquitted them. Some who were obliged to fly their own province to save their lives have been taken prisoners, sent back, and are threatened to be tried for their lives be-

[1] *Infra.*, p. 76.

cause they fled from danger. Some have been pulled out of the reading desk because they prayed for the king, and that before independency was declared. Others have been warned to appear at militia musters with their arms, have been fined for not appearing and threatened with imprisonment for not paying those fines. Others have had their houses plundered, and their desks broken open under pretence of their containing treasonable papers.

Thus matters continued; the clergy proceeding regularly in the discharge of their duty where the hand of violence did not interfere, until the beginning of last July, when the congress thought proper to make an explicit declaration of independency . . . . .

This declaration increased the embarrassments of the clergy. To officiate publicly, and not pray for the king and royal family according to the liturgy, was against their duty and oath, as well as dictates of their conscience; and yet to use the prayers for the king and royal family would have drawn inevitable destruction on them. The only course which they could pursue, to avoid both evils, was to suspend the public exercise of their function, and shut up their churches.

This, accordingly was done. It is very remarkable that, although the clergy of those provinces I have mentioned did not, and, indeed, could not consult each other on this interesting occasion, yet they all fell upon the same method in shutting up their churches. The venerable Mr. Beach, of Connecticut, only is to be excepted, if my information be right, who officiated as usual after independency was declared . . . . . All the churches in Connecticut (Mr. Beach's excepted . . . . .) as well as those in this province, except in this city, Long Island, and Staten Island, where his Majesty's arms have penetrated, are now shut up. This is also the case with every church in New Jersey; and I am informed by a gentleman lately returned from Pennsylvania, who had been a prisoner there for some times, that the churches in the several missions of that province are shut up, one or two excepted, where the prayers for the king and royal family are omitted. The churches in Philadelphia are open. How matters are circumstanced in the more southerly colonies, I cannot learn with any certainty; only that the provincial convention of Virginia have taken upon themselves to publish an edict, by which some collects for the king are to be wholly omitted in the liturgy, and others altered, the word 'commonwealth' being substituted for the 'king'. For my part, I never expected much good of those clergy among them who opposed an American episcopate. If such should now renounce their allegiance, and abandon their duty, it is no more than what might naturally be looked for. There are, however, several worthy clergymen in those provinces, some of whom I hear have taken sanctuary in England, particularly from Maryland. This province, although the most loyal and peaceable of any of the continent, by a strange fatality is become the scene of war, and suffers most. This city, especially, has a double portion of the calamities brought on by the present rebellion; and perhaps a brief detail of our situation for some months past, may gratify curiosity, and convey to the Society the clearest idea of the state of things here. Upon General Howe's departure from Boston to Halifax, early in the last spring, the rebel army was drawn to this city, which they fortified, in the best manner they could, expecting it would be attacked. . . . Dr. Auchmuty, the rector, being much indisposed during the spring and summer, retired with his family to Brunswick, in New Jersey; and the care of the churches, in his absence, of course devolved on me, as the oldest assistant — a situation truly difficult and trying in such times, especially as the other assistants were young and inexperienced, though very loyal, and otherwise worthy young men.

About the middle of April, Mr. Washington, commander-in-chief of the rebel forces, came to town with a large reinforcement. Animated by his presence, and, I suppose, encouraged by him, the rebel committees very much harassed the loyal inhabitants here and on Long Island. They were summoned before those committees, and, upon refusing to give up their arms and take the oaths that were tendered, they were imprisoned or sent into banishment. An army was sent to Long Island to disarm the inhabitants who were distinguished for their loyalty. Many had their property destroyed, and more were carried off prisoners. It should be observed, that members of the Church of England were the only sufferers on this occasion. The members of the Dutch church are very numerous there, and many of them joined in opposing the rebellion; yet no notice was taken of them nor the least injury done to them . . . . At the present time, there are many hundreds from this city and province prisoners in New England; and among these the mayor of New York, several judges and members of his Majesty's council, with other respectable inhabitants.

Soon after Washington's arrival, he attended our church; but on the Sunday morning, before divine service began, one of the rebel generals called at the rector's house (supposing the latter was in town,) and not finding him, left word that he came to inform the rector that 'General Washington would be at the church, and would be glad if the violent prayers for the king and royal family were omitted.' This message was brought to me, and, as you may suppose, I paid no regard to it.

On seeing that general not long after, I remonstrated against the unreasonableness of his request, which he must know the clergy could not comply with; and told him further, that it was in his power to shut up our churches, but by no means in his power to make 'the clergy depart from their duty.' This declaration drew from him an awkward apology for his conduct, which I believe was not authorized by Washington. Such incidents would not be worth mentioning, unless to give those who are at a distance a better idea of the spirit of the times.

May 17th was appointed by the congress as a day of public fasting, prayer, and humiliation throughout the continent. At the unanimous request of the members of our Church who were then in town, I consented to preach that day; and, indeed, our situation made it highly prudent, though a submission to an authority that was so far usurped was exceedingly grating and disagreeable. In giving notice the preceding Sunday, I only mentioned that there would be a sermon on the ensuing Friday, which was the 17th, without saying anything of the reason, or by what authority. It was exceedingly difficult for a loyal clergyman to preach on such an occasion, and not incur danger on the one hand, or not depart from his duty on the other. I endeavored to avoid both, making peace and repentance my subject, and explicitly disclaimed having anything to do with politics. This sermon, in the composition of which I took some pains, I intend to publish for various reasons, should I be able to recover it from the place where it now is, with all my books and papers, in the country. The several churches in this province (except two, where the clergymen thought they might without danger omit service), and so far as I can learn, through all the thirteen united colonies, as they are called, were opened on this occasion.

Matters became now critical here in the highest degree. The rebel army amounted to near 30,000. All their cannon and military stores were drawn hither, and they boasted that the place was impregnable. The mortifications and alarms which the clergy met with were innumerable. I have frequently heard myself called a Tory, and traitor to my country, as I passed the streets, and epithets joined to each, which decency forbids me to set down. Violent threats were thrown out against us, in case the king were any longer prayed for. One Sunday, when I was officiating, and had proceeded some length in the service, a company of about one hundred armed rebels marched into the church, with drums beating and fifes playing, their guns loaded and bayonets fixed, as if going to battle. The congregation was thrown into the utmost terror, and several women fainted, expecting a massacre was intended. I took no notice of them, and went on with the service, only exerted my voice, which was in some measure drowned by the noise and tumult. The rebels stood thus in the aisle for near fifteen minutes, till, being asked into pews by the sexton, they complied. Still, however, the people expected that, when the collects for the king and royal family were read, I should be fired at, as menaces to that purpose had been frequently flung out. The matter, however, passed over without any accident. Nothing of this kind happened before or since, which made it more remarkable. I was afterwards assured that something hostile and violent was intended; but He that stills the raging of the sea, and madness of the people, overruled their purpose, whatever it was.

In the beginning of July, independency was declared: as this event was what I long had expected, I had maturely considered, and was determined, what line of conduct to pursue. General Howe had arrived some time before from Halifax, as did Lord Howe from England. They had taken possession of Staten Island, where the fleet lay in sight of this city, at the distance of nine miles; and only waited the arrival of the fleet from England, to make a descent and reduce New York. This circumstance pointed out still more clearly what part I should act. However, I thought it was proper to consult such of the vestry as were in town, and others of the congregation, and have their concurrence; and I must do them the justice to say, that they were all unanimous for shutting up the Churches; and chose rather to submit to that temporary inconvenience, than, by omitting the prayers for the king, give that mark of disaffection to their sovereign. To have prayed for him, had been rash to the last degree — the inevitable consequence had been a demolition of the churches, and the destruction of all who frequented them. The whole rebel force was collected here, and the most violent partizans from all parts of the continent. A fine equestrian statue of the king was pulled down, and totally demolished, immediately after independency was declared. All the king's arms, even those on signs of taverns, were destroyed. The committee sent me a message, which I esteemed a favor and indulgence, to have the king's arms taken down in the church, or else the mob would do it, and might deface and injure the churches. I immediately complied. People were not at liberty to speak their sentiments, and even silence was constructed as a mark of disaffection.

Things being thus situated, I shut up the churches. Even this was attended with great hazard; for it was declaring, in the strongest manner, our disapprobation of independency, and that under the eye of Washington and his army. The other assistants now went to their respective friends in the country . . . . . I remained in the city, to visit the sick, baptize children, bury the dead, and afford what support I could to the remains of our poor flock, who were much dispirited; for several, especially of the poorer sort, had it not in their power to leave the city. After we had ceased to officiate publicly, several of the rebel officers sent to me for the keys of the churches, that their chaplains might preach in them; with these requisitions I peremptorily refused to comply, and let them know that, 'if they would use the churches, they must break the gates and doors to get it.' Accordingly, I took possession of all the keys, lest the sextons might be tampered with; for I could not bear the thought that their seditious and rebellious effusions should be poured out in our churches. When those requisitions were repeated with threats, my answer was, 'that I did what I knew to be my duty, and that I would adhere to it, be the consequences what they would.' Upon this they desisted, and did not occupy the churches.

I cannot reflect on my situation at that time, without the warmest emotions of gratitude to Divine Providence for preserving me. I was watched with a jealous, suspicious eye. Besides the imputation of being notoriously disaffected — an imputation which had flung others in jail without any other crime, — I was known and pointed at as the author of several pieces against the proceedings of the congress. In February last, I wrote an answer to a pamphlet entitled, 'Comon Sense,' which earnestly recommended and justified independency. It was one of the most virulent, artful, and pernicious pamphlets I ever met with, and perhaps the wit of man could not devise one better calculated to do mischief. It seduced thousands. At the risk, not only of my liberty, but also of my life, I drew up an answer, and had it printed here; but the answer was no sooner advertised, than the whole impression was seized by the sons of liberty and burnt. I then sent a copy to Philadelphia, where it was printed, and soon went through the second edition. This answer was laid to my charge, and swelled the catalogue of my political transgressions. In short, I was in the utmost danger, and it is to the overruling hand of Providence that I attribute my deliverance and safety. With difficulty I stood my ground till about the middle of August, when almost all who were suspected of disaffection were taken up and sent prisoners to New England. I therefore found it necessary to return to Flushing on Long Island; but I had not sooner left that place, than the committee met, and entered into a debate about seizing me. This obliged me to shift my quarters, and keep as private as possible, till the 27th of that month, when General Howe defeated the rebels on Long Island, which set me and many others at liberty.

On Sunday, the 15th of September, General Howe, with the king's forces, landed on New York Island, four miles above the city; upon which the rebels abandoned the city, and retired towards King's Bridge, which joins this island to the continent. Early on Monday morning, the 16th, I returned to the city, which exhibited a most melancholy appearance, being deserted and pillaged. My house was plundered of everything by the rebels. My loss amounts to near 200 pounds this currency, or upwards of 100 pounds sterling. The rebels carried off all the bells in the city, partly to convert them into cannon, partly to prevent notice being given speedily of the destruction they meditated against the city by fire, when it began. On Wednesday, I opened one of the churches, and solemnized Divine Service, when all the inhabitants gladly attended, and joy was lighted up in every countenance on the restoration of our public worship; for very few remained but such as were members of our Church. Each congratulated himself and others on the prospect of returning peace and security; but alas! the enemies of peace were secretly working among us . . . . . On Saturday . . . . . they set fire to the city . . . . . We had three churches, of which Trinity Church was the oldest and largest. It was a venerable edifice, had an excellent organ, which cost 850 pounds sterling, and was otherwise ornamented. This church, with the rector's house and the charity school, — the two later, large expensive buildings, — were burned. St. Paul's Church and King's College had shared the same fate, being directly on the line of fire, had I not been providentially on the spot, and sent a number of people with water on the roof of each . . . . . The Church corporation has suffered prodigiously, as was evidently intended. Besides the buildings already mentioned, about 200 houses, which stood on the church ground, were consumed; so that the loss cannot be estimated at less than 25,000 pounds sterling. This melancholy accident, and the principal scene of war being here, will occasion the clergy of this city to be the greatest sufferers of any on the continent by the present rebellion.

Upon the whole, the Church of England has lost none of its members by the rebellion as yet, — none, I mean, whose departure from it can be deemed a loss; on the contrary, its own members are more firmly attached to it than ever. And even the sober and more rational among dissenters, — for they are not all equally violent and frantic — look with reverence and esteem on the part which Church people here have acted. I have not a doubt but, with the blessing of Providence, his Majesty's arms will be successful, and finally crush this unnatural rebellion. In that case, if the steps are taken which reason, prudence, and common sense dictate, the church will indubitably increase, and these confusions will terminate in a large accession to its members. Then will be the time to make that provision for the American Church which is necessary, and place it on at least an equal footing with other denominations by granting it an episcopate, and thereby allowing it full toleration. If this opportunity is let slip, I think there is a moral certainty that such another will never again offer; and I must conclude, in that case, that Government is equally infatuated with the Americans at present . . . . And I may appeal to all judicious persons, whether it is not as contrary to sound policy, as it certainly is to right reason and justice, that the king's loyal subjects here, members of the national Church, should be denied a privilege the want of which will discourage and diminish their numbers, and that merely to gratify the clamors of dissenters, who have now discovered such enmity to the constitution, and who will ever clamor against anything that will tend to benefit or increase the Church here." [1]

This Reverend Inglis, whose report to the Venerable Society we have just followed, was one of the chief propagandists for the Tory party in America. He is supposed to have written the *Letters of Papinian*, addressed to John Jay and to the people of North America, setting forth "the conduct, present state and prospects of the American Congress." These denounced what the author considered:

"The tremendous assumption of power made by the Revolutionary leaders; the gross tyrannies practised by them upon the common people, the fallacious hopes with which they had fed their credulous followers, and the delusions which they had spread through the land respecting the character and purpose of the co-called movement for American rights and liberties." "You will find," he continued, "these pretended enemies of oppression the most unrelenting oppressors and their little fingers heavier than the king's loins." [2] "There is more liberty in Turkey than in the dominions of the Congress . . . . . The rebellion, begun by unprincipled and selfish men, has been without justification in any public necessity; it is therefore wicked; it is without prospect of success; it is destined to bring disaster upon all who continue to support it." [3]

Dr. Inglis had also, as he informs us, replied to Paine's *Common Sense*, with a pamphlet entitled, *The True Interest of America Impartially Stated in Certain Strictures on a Pamphlet entitled Common Sense*, by An American, Philadelphia, 1776. [4]

The Dr. Chandler of Elizabeth, New Jersey, mentioned by Dr. Inglis in the above report to the Venerable Society, had published in 1774, *A Friendly Address*, to point out the dangerous consequences of resisting Parliament, and

[1] Hawkins *Historical Notices of the Missions of the Church of England in the American Colonies Previous to the Independence of the United States*, pp. 328-341; *Ecclesiastical Records of the State of New York*, vol. vi, pp. 4292-4300; *Documentary History*, vol. iii, pp. 637-646.

[2] Inglis, *Letters of Papinian*, p. 6; Tyler, *op. cit.*, vol. ii, p. 73.

[3] Inglis, *op. cit.*, p. 21.

[4] Inglis, *The True Interest of America Impartially Stated.*

another pamphlet under the title *What Think Ye of The Congress Now?* At one time he was erronously thought to be the "Westchester Farmer." It is not surprising that he found it expedient to leave the country.[1]

The Venerable Society was also in receipt of a similar report of about the same date December 29, 1776, from the Reverend Samuel Seabury, of New York. This ran (in part):

"I hope my conduct will be approved by the Society. I assure them I have done everything in my power to retain the people in their duty, nor did I shut up the church, or leave the Mission, while it was practicable for me to do duty in either. I must also observe, that but few of my congregation are engaged in the rebellion. The New England rebels used frequently to observe, as an argument against me, that the nearer they came to West Chester, the fewer friends they found to American liberty—that is, to rebellion; and, in justice to the rebels of East and West Chester, I must say, that none of them ever offered me any insult, or attempted to do me any injury, that I know of. It must give the Society great satisfaction to know that all their Missionaries have conducted themselves with great propriety, and on many occasions with a firmness and steadiness that have done them honor. This may, indeed, be said of all the clergy on this side the Delaware, and, I am persuaded, of many on the other. But the conduct of the Philadelphia clergy has been the very reverse. They not only rushed headlong into the rebellion, themselves, but perverted the judgment, and soured the tempers, and inflamed the passions of the people, by sermons and orations, both from the pulpit and the press. Their behavior hath been of great disadvantage to the loyal clergy. Messers. Babcock, Townsend and James Sayre were seized by the rebels some time in October, and I have not heard of their being discharged.

Mr. Veits is a close prisoner in Hartford jail, and has been in irons. He is to be tried for his life, some say for assisting the royalists, who were confined in Simsbury mines, in breaking out; others for concealing those unhappy people after they had broke out, and for helping them to make their escape.

Mr. Beardsley has been obliged to leave his Mission . . . . Mr. Leaming has been taken up by the rebels, but was dismissed in a few hours."[2]

[1] Hawkins, *op. cit.*, pp. 160-161.

[2] Seabury's *Original Letters*, vol. xix, 1, 190; Hawkins, *op. cit.*, pp. 303-308.

No Tory minister in America had a stormier career than did this Reverend Samuel Seabury. He exonerates the rebels of Chester, East and West; but he does not relate the experiences of the preceding year. November 22, 1775, while engaged in his pastoral duties, he had been suddenly seized by a band of armed men, who, first having pillaged his desk and house, forced him to mount and accompany his captors to New Haven. He was borne through the street of that city in triumph and committed to prison under heavy guard and denied visits from friends or the use of pen, ink or paper, except for the purpose of writing to his family and then only under inspection. The principal charge against him was that he had written the pamphlets of the "Westchester Farmer," a charge undoubtedly true but which at that time could not be substantiated. At the end of more than a month's imprisonment, in default of evidence, he was dismissed. Thenceforth he had to avoid public appearance and to have faithful friends constantly on guard to warn him of approaching danger. At one time, under stress of extraordinary danger, he and his friends, Chandler of New Jersey, and Myles Cooper, President of King's College, were forced to flee for their lives; and, for several days and nights, they lay in a secret room. After the battle of Long Island, Seabury fled to the British lines. A troop of cavalry was quartered in his rectory, and consumed all the produce of his glebe; the pews of the church were burned for firewood; the church turned into a hospital. Seabury became a chaplain in the British Army and was assigned to a regiment of American Loyalists.

The series of pamphlets by the "Westchester Farmer" was begun in 1774 with the appearance of *Free Thoughts on the Proceedings of Continental Congress.* "Will you," he asks, "submit to this slavish regulation?" "You must," he replies, "our sovereign lords and masters, the high and mighty delegates, in Grand Continental Congress assembled, have ordered and directed it!" "Will you be the instruments in bringing the most abject slavery on yourselves?" "Do as you will, but by Him that made me, I will not! No, if I must be enslaved, let it be by a King at least, and not by a parcel of upstarts, lawless committeemen . . . . . Renounce all dependence on Congress and committees. They have neglected and betrayed your interests."[1] Other pamphlets from the same "Westchester Farmer" were: *The Congress Canvassed,*[2] *A View of the Controversy between Great Britain and her Colonies,*[3] *An Alarm to the Legislature of the Province of New York,*[4] *and The Republican Dissected.*[5]

The attitude of Inglis and Seabury was offensive to a considerable body of the New York Episcopalians. Dr. Samuel Provoost, who was to become the first bishop of the state, bore arms in the patriotic cause and on patriotic grounds became a bitter enemy of Samuel Seabury.[6] It was an Episcopalian layman, Alexander Hamilton, trained in the Episcopalian King's College (Columbia), who rebutted the Westchester Farmer in the pamphlets: *A Full Vindication of the Measures of Congress from the Calumnies of their Enemies;*[7] and *The Farmer Refuted.*[8] This was the young Hamilton who saved his college

[1] Seabury, *Free Thoughts on the Proceedings of the Continental Congress.*
[2] Seabury, *The Congress Canvassed.*
[3] Seabury, *A View of the Controversy between Great Britain and her Colonies.*
[4] Seabury, *An Alarm to the Legislature of the Province of New York.*
[5] Seabury, *The Republican Dissected.*
[6] Perry, *Bishop Seabury and Bishop Provoost.*
[7] Hamilton, *A Full Vindication of the Measures of the Congress.*
[8] Hamilton, *The Farmer Refuted.*

president, President Cooper, from the fury of the patriotic mob. New York Episcopalianism was to furnish the Revolutionary cause with such leaders as Jay, Duane, and Morris. It should not be judged solely or even primarily by the conduct of Inglis, Seabury or Cooper.

Seabury, however, was quite correct when he stated that the general tone of Philadelphia Episcopalianism was more revolutionary than that of New York. In the ministers, Duché, Coombe, and Smith, Philadelphia possessed three of the most powerful exponents of America's cause. Indeed, Christ Church where they preached has been styled "the cradle of the Country as it is the cradle of the American Church."[1]

The Reverend William Smith, Provost of the College of Philadelphia, long concealed his identity under the simple title, "A Lover of his Country." At the commencement exercises of May 1766, immediately following the repeal of the Stamp Act, he expressed the following sentiments:

> "O happy America! if now we but know how to prize our happiness. The unguarded sallies of intemperate zeal will soon be forgotten; but the steadfast, the noble, the patriotic efforts of cool and good men, in the vindication of native and constitutional rights, will more and more claim the regard of all the free, in every clime and age, and perhaps be consecrated by time into one of the brightest transactions of our story; asserting our pedigree and showing that we were worthy of having descended from the illustrious stock of Britons."[2]

Smith's most notable patriotic utterance was the sermon, *On the Present Situation of American Affairs*, preached in Christ Church, June 23, 1775, two days after the departure of Washington to take command at Cambridge, in the presence of Congress. It contained the

[1] Perry, *Influence of the Clergy in the War of the Revolution*, p. 3.
[2] *Four Dissertations*, pp. 9-10.

boldest words on the question of the day that had as yet been spoken in America from an Anglican pulpit.[1] Perry says of this sermon:

"It would appear that to this discourse more perhaps than to any other printed document, the clear understanding of the position of our fathers in the view of English and American sympathizers was due. The sermon was republished in almost countless editions at home and abroad. It was translated into various languages — German, Swedish, Welsh — and so convincing was its logic, and so lucid was its style, that the chamberlain of the City of London, was at the charge of an edition of ten thousand copies which were circulated broadcast throughout Great Britain."[2]

Smith's sermon for the Public Fast Day of July 20, 1775, was less fiery.[3] He was opposed to independence and under the name of Cato composed a series of eight essays to counteract *Common Sense* and the spirit which it aroused.[4] From 1776 on he ceased to lead in Pennsylvania politics; though he did accept independence as inevitable and though he continued a leader in Episcopalian affairs.

Thomas Coombe, assistant minister at Christ Church and St. Peter's, preached a sermon on the day set apart by Congress for a National Fast Day, July 20, 1775, in which he fully justified the course of the colonies up to that point in their opposition to ministerial encroachments.[5] Coombe, however, was one of the first to refuse to follow the development of the American cause.

So prominent was Jacob Duché in the early American struggle and so profound was the effect of his desertion to

[1] Smith, *Works of*, vol. iii, pp. 252-286.
[2] Perry, *Influence of the Clergy in the War of the Revolution*, pp. 2-3.
[3] Smith, *op. cit.*, vol. ii, pp. 112-126.
[4] *Ibid*, vol. i, p. 575.
[5] Coombe, Thomas Edwin, *A Sermon, preached July 20th, 1775*. Philadelphia, 1775.

the British that he may well be styled "The Benedict Arnold of the American Clergy." Accepting the Chaplaincy of Continental Congress for three years he inspired it with his fiery sermons; no preacher in America exercised greater influence for freedom than did Duché during his tenure of that office, 1774 to 1776. And though he was weak enough to be won back to the British cause during their occupation of Philadelphia, he, nevertheless, left sermons which are classics in the cause of American liberty. *The Duty of Standing Fast in our Spiritual and Temporal Liberties*[1] was also preached in Christ Church, July 7, 1775, before the First Battalion of the City and Liberties of Philadelphia and was dedicated "To His Excellency George Washington Esquire, General and Commander in Chief of all the Forces of the United Colonies in North America." The text was *Galatians*, v. 1, "Stand fast, therefore, in the Liberty wherewith Christ hath made us free!" Duché invoked Deity to "Remove far from his (the king's) Royal Person all those, who would seek to change his government into oppression, and to gratify their own licentious desires at the expense of the blood and treasure of his subjects." This sermon was published both in Philadelphia and in London.

July 20, 1775, marks the first general fast ever kept in America. On that date Continental Congress "in view of the critical and calamitous state . . . . . for all the English colonies on this continent as a day of public humiliation and prayer" assembled at their usual place of meeting at half-past nine and went in a body "to attend divine service at Mr. Duché's church."[2] Mr. Duché took

[1] Duché, Jacob, *The Duty of Standing Fast in our Spiritual and Temporal Liberties. A Sermon, in Christ Church, Philadelphia, July 7, 1775, before the First Battalion, etc.* Philadelphia, 1775.

[2] *Journals of Congress*, vol. ii, pp. 81, 87, 192; *Infra*, p. 412.

for his subject *The American Vine.* He spoke of himself and his countrymen as "injured and oppressed" and as "unmeriting the harsh and rigorous treatment" they were receiving from the mother country; and he thrilled his hearers with fresh indignation and horrors at this unnatural severity. "'Tis not now," he exclaimed, "foreign enemy, or the savages of our own wilderness that have made the cruel and unrighteous assault; but it is even, thou, Britain, that with merciless and unhallowed hands wouldst cut down and destroy this branch of thine own vine."[1]

Duché's influence was great. John Adams listened to him and confessed that he had never listened to better praying, such pronunciation, such fervor, such earnestness and pathos and in language so elegant and sublime "as was delivered by this Episcopalian clergyman for the American cause."[2] It gave this staunch Congregationalist just the lesson he needed and worked for a rapprochement between the two most numerous and influential denominations in America. John Adams was won from a violent opposition to an earnest support of the cause of an American episcopacy. He became one of the leading instruments in the procurement of the consecration of the American bishops White and Provoost, by the British clergy at Lambeth Palace. Later he came to boast of this as one of his most important services to America.[3]

The consistent leader among Episcopalians to champion the American cause was the Reverend William White, later Bishop White. Coolly judicious, he arrived at his conviction slowly and then, quite in contrast to the

[1] Duché, *The American Vine. A Sermon preached before Congress, 20 July, 1775.* Philadelphia, 1775.

[2] *Letter* of John Adams, vol. i, pp. 23-24.

[3] *Infra*, p. 220.

impetuous Duché, he followed through consistently patriotic to the end. He thus recounts his course:

"I continued . . . . . to pray for the king until Sunday (inclusive) before the fourth of July, 1776. Within a short time after, I took the oath of allegiance to the United States and have since remained faithful to it. My intentions were upright and most seriously weighed; and I hope they were not in contradiction to my duty."[1]

At the darkest moment of the Revolution, William White was offered the Chaplaincy of Congress; his brother-in-law, Robert Morris, warned him that to accept was to offer his throat to be cut, yet he accepted. He continued in that office until independence had been fully established.[2]

A friend to Washington and the other patriotic leaders, we shall see later how this consistent Americanism was to aid in fixing upon the American Episcopalian Church an American character.[3]

Dr. Samuel Provoost, first Bishop of New York, was a patriot and bore arms in the strife, as did Dr. John Croes, first Bishop of New Jersey. Madison, first Bishop of Virginia, and President of William and Mary College, stood for the American cause, as did their first bishop-elect, David Griffith. Dr. Edward Bass, the first Bishop of Massachusetts, had his missionary stipend withdrawn by the Venerable Society for the Propagation of the Gospel for alleged sympathy with the "rebellion." Robert Smith, the first Bishop of South Carolina, was an active combatant and this was recognized by his acceptance as an original member of the Society of the Cincinnati in that state.[4]

The most powerful and the most unrelenting of the

[1] Wilson, *Memoir of William White*, p. 51.
[2] *Infra.*, pp. 414-415.
[3] *Infra.*, ch. viii.
[4] Perry, *Influence of the Clergy in the War of the Revolution*, p. 4.

Tory satirists was Jonathan Odell, Rector of St. Mary's parish, Burlington, New Jersey. He fled to the British lines about the beginning of the year 1777, from whence he issued his characterizations of Americans and the American cause. Of Dr. Witherspoon he writes:

> "Known in the pulpit by seditious toils,
> Grown into consequence by civil broils,
> Three times he tried, and miserably failed,
> To overset the laws — the fourth prevailed.
> Whether as tool he acted, or as guide,
> Is yet a doubt — his conscience must decide.
> Meanwhile unhappy Jersey mourns her thrall,
> Ordained by vilest of the vile to fall;
> To fall by Witherspoon! — O name, the curse
> Of sound religion, and disgrace of verse.
> Member of Congress, we must hail him next:
> 'Come out of Babylon,' was now his text.
> Fierce as the fiercest, foremost of the first,
> He'd rail at kings, with venom well-nigh burst.
> Not uniformly grand — for some bye-end,
> To dirtiest acts of treason he'd descend;
> I've known him seek the dungeon dark as night,
> Imprisoned Tories to convert, or fright;
> Whilst to myself I've hummed, in dismal tune,
> I'd rather be a dog than Witherspoon.
> Be patient, reader — for the issue trust;
> His day will come — remember, Heaven is just."[1]

The following lines indict Washington:

> "Hear thy indictment, Washington, at large;
> Attend and listen to the solemn charge;
> Thou hast supported an atrocious cause
> Against thy king, thy country, and the laws,
> Committed perjury, encouraged lies,
> Forced conscience, broken the most sacred ties;
> Myriads of wives and fathers at thy hand
> Their slaughtered husbands, slaughtered sons, demand.

[1] *Loyalist* (*The*) *Poetry of the Revolution*, pp. 17-18.

What could, when halfway up the hill to fame
Induce thee to go back and link with shame?
Was it ambition, vanity or spite
That prompted thee with Congress to unite?
Or did all three within thy bosom roll,
'Thou heart of hero with a traitor's soul'?
Go, wretched author of they country's grief,
Patron of villainy, of villains chief;
Seek with thy cursed crew the central gloom,
Ere Truth's avenging sword begin thy doom;
Or sudden vengeance of celestial dart
Precipitate thee with augmented smart." [1]

All of Odell's work as an Anti-American political satirist is embraced in four poems: "The Word of Congress,"[2] "The Congratulation,"[3] "The Feu de Joie,"[4] and "The American Times."[5]

Up to the very last battle of the Revolution, and while there was a British soldier on American soil, Doctor Odell maintained his confidence that the "rebellion" would be crushed. When America won, he retired to Nova Scotia, where he lived in poverty, an unreconstructed loyalist to the end.

Perry finds that two-thirds of the signers of the Declaration of Independence belonged to the Episcopal Church and that six of them were either sons or grandsons of Episcopalian clergymen,—Francis Lewis, William Hooper, Caesar Rodney, George Ross, George Taylor and Samuel Chase.[6]

Sufficient evidence has been adduced to show that American Episcopalianism was pretty much divided in

[1] *Loyalist (The) Poetry of the Revolution*, pp. 9-12; Tyler, *op. cit.*, vol. ii, pp. 124-125.
[2] *Loyalist (The) Poetry of the Revolution*, pp. 38-55.
[3] *Loyalist (The) Verses of Joseph Stansbury and Doctor Jonathan Odell, relating to the American Revolution*, pp. 45-50.
[4] *Ibid.*, pp. 51-58.
[5] *Loyalist (The) Poetry*, pp. 1-37.
[6] Perry, *The Faith of the Signers of the Declaration of Independence* and *Influence of the Clergy in the War of the Revolution*, p. 6.

its allegiance. As a generalization, we may conclude that the Southern and Middle States were generally patriotic while the North favored the British. Perry finds that "the larger number of the Clergy in the Southern and Middle States" were "patriots," "as well as not a few in the North."[1] While for both laity and clergy, Dean Hodges claims that, "Outside of New England, the leaders of the new nation were mostly of our (Episcopalian) communion."[2]

Perhaps, in retrospect, this denomination is to be censured for not throwing its entire and undivided support to the American cause. Division in its ranks caused it to lose in popular opinion some of that glory which accrued to the Congregationalists of New England and to the Presbyterians of the Middle States for their reputed wholehearted and undivided allegiance. Also Episcopalians can point to no official acts wherein their church came to the support of the Revolution. Here, however, it must be borne in mind that this church was possessed of no official organization of the nature of a synod, conference, or coetus, — the legislative bodies of Presbyterian, Reformed, or Baptist Churches; in fact, they were even deprived of their hierarchy. Possessing no organization for expressing collective opinion, they were thrown back upon individual convictions. And here, the reputations of certain active individual Tory ministers have, quite unjustly, tended to brand American Episcopalians in general as pro-British. This for a sect which counted among its members such sturdy leaders as George Washington, Thomas Jefferson, James Madison, Patrick Henry, John Marshall, Benjamin Franklin, Robert Morris, John Jay, James Duane, and Alexander Hamilton.

[1] Perry, *Influence of the Clergy*, p. 4.

[2] Hodges, *Three Hundred Years of the Episcopal Church in America*, p. 75.

CHAPTER III

THE CONGREGATIONAL CHURCH IN THE REVOLUTION

The importance of Congregationalism in the Revolution was about equal to the weight of the New England influence, minus Rhode Island. In all the New England states except the latter it was the established religion and a Puritan theocracy was waging the Revolution. Ezra Stiles, president of Yale, still taught that religion was the primary concern. In his election sermon of 1783, before the Connecticut Assembly, he remarked:

"It is certain that civil dominion was but the second motive, religion the primary one, with our ancestors, in coming hither and settling this land. It was not so much their design to establish religion for the benefit of the state, as civil government for the benefit of religion, and as subservient, and even necessary, towards the peaceable enjoyment and unmolested exercises of religion — of that religion for which they fled to these ends of the earth." [1]

Ecclesiastical domination on the part of the Congregationalists has done much to distort the New England conception of the Revolution. Thornton concludes from his study, *The Pulpit of the American Revolution*, that "To the Pulpit, the Puritan Pulpit, we owe the moral force which won our independence." But Thornton confines his study almost exclusively to Congregational sermons; for to him "the unanimity and efficient service of the Puritan clergy in the war of the Revolution" was in direct contrast to "the zeal of the Episcopalian ministers and

[1] Thornton, *The Pulpit of the American Revolution, or the Political Sermons of the Period, of 1776*, p. xix.

'missionaries' in their hostility to it."[1] Thornton appreciates only Congregationalism.

Certainly when Boucher remarked that "In America, as in the Great Revolution in England, much execution was done by sermons,"[2] he was not thinking exclusively of the established clergy of New England; he realized the power of the rebellious clergy in the South. A New England loyalist has left us an estimate of the power of the Northern clergy, "what effect must it have had upon the audience to hear the same sentiment and principles which they had before read in a newspaper delivered on Sundays from the sacred desk, with religious awe, and the most solemn appeal to heaven, from lips which they had been taught from their cradles to believe could utter nothing but eternal truths."[3]

The New England clergy were generally consulted by the civil authorities; and not infrequently political suggestions, emanating from the pulpit on election days, days for "fasting and humiliation," "Thanksgiving" days, and the like, were enacted into law. The "Election Sermon" which had been instituted in 1633 was one of the most effective instruments imaginable for the creation of public opinion. Preached before the Governor and the entire law-making body of the colony in solemn assembly, it was immediately published and circulated throughout the colony. No appeal could have been devised which could have reached more directly both the governed and the governors.

William Gordon, the Puritan historian of the Revolu-

[1] Thornton, *op. cit.*, pp. xxxviii, xxxi.

[2] Boucher, "Autobiography" in *Notes and Queries*, 5th series, vol. vi, p. 142.

[3] *Novanglus et Massachusettensis*, p. 51.

tion, gives us the following summary of the character and influence of the New England ministry:

"Ministers of New England, being mostly Congregationalists, are from that circumstance, in a professional way, more attached and habituated to the principles of liberty than if they had spiritual Superiors to lord it over them,[1] and were in hopes of possessing, in their turn, through the gift of government, the seat of power. They oppose arbitrary rule in civil concerns from the love of freedom, as well as from a desire of guarding against its introduction into religious matters. The patriots, for years back, have availed themselves greatly of their assistance. Two sermons have been preached annually for a length of time, the one on general election day, the last Wednesday in May, when the new General Court have been used to meet, according to charter, and elect counsellors for the ensuing year; the other, some little while after, on the artillery election-day, when the officers are selected, or new officers chosen. On these occasions political subjects are deemed very proper; but it is expected that they be treated in a decent, serious, and instructive manner. The general election preacher has been elected alternately by the Council and House of Assembly. The sermon is styled the *Election Sermon,* and is printed. Every representative has a copy for himself, and generally one or more for the minister or ministers of his town. As the patriots have prevailed, the preachers of each sermon have been the zealous friends of liberty; and the passages most adapted to promote the spread and love of it have been selected and circulated far and wide by means of newspapers, and read with avidity and a degree of veneration on account of the preacher and his election to the service of the day. Commendations, both public and private, have not been wanting to help on the design. Thus, by their labors in the pulpit, and by furnishing the prints with occasional essays, the ministers have forwarded and strengthened, and that not a little, the opposition to the exercise of that parliamentary claim of right to bind the colonies in all cases whatever."[2]

Robert Treat Paine called Dr. Jonathan Mayhew, "The Father of Civil and Religious Liberty in Massachusetts and America." To John Adams, Mayhew was "a Whig of the first Magnitude," and Bancroft speaks of him as "the boldest and most fervid heart in New Eng-

[1] On this point see sermon of Rev. John Wise, *Democracy is Christ's Government in Church and State,* republished in 1772.

[2] Quoted by Thornton, *Pulpit of the American Revolution,* p. xxv-xxvi.

land." His sermon of January 30, 1749, *A Discourse concerning Unlimited Submission and Non-Resistance to the Higher Powers* [1] has been spoken of as the "morning gun of the American Revolution."[2] It was Dr. Mayhew who suggested to James Otis the idea of Committees of Correspondence, on the Lord's Day, June 8th, 1766, "Would it not be proper and decorous for our assembly to send circulars to all the rest . . . . . expressing a desire to cement and perpetuate union among ourselves . . . . . cultivating a good understanding and hearty friendship between these colonies appears to me so necessary a part of prudence and good policy."[3] Dr. Mayhew was probably the strongest opponent of the introduction of episcopacy into America. In the very last of his sermons on

[1] Mayhew, *Discourse concerning Unlimited Submission and Non-Resistance to the Higher Powers*, Boston, 1750.

[2] Thornton, *op. cit.*, p. 43. James Truslow Adams, *Revolutionary New England*, pp. 195-196, cites Jonathan Mayhew to establish a thesis that "In the mid-years of the century, commercial and political interests did rapidly supersede those of religion in the minds of the mass of even New England people . . . . . So greatly, indeed, had the situation altered by 1750 that Jonathan Mayhew, when he delivered a political sermon . . . . . felt called upon to defend himself against the possible charge that it was 'out of character for a Christian minister to meddle with such a subject'." Had Mr. Adams quoted more freely from his source such an implication could not have been deduced for Mayhew remarked, "It is hoped that but few will think the subject of it an improper one to be discoursed on in the pulpit, under a notion that this is preaching politics, instead of Christ . . . . . Why . . . . . should not those parts of Scripture which relate to civil government be examined and explained from the desk, as well as others? Obedience to the civil magistrates is a Christian duty; and if so, why should not the nature, grounds, and extent of it be considered in a Christian assembly? Besides, if it be said that it is out of character for a Christian minister to meddle with such a subject, this censure will at last fall upon the holy apostles. They write upon it in their epistles to Christian churches; and surely it cannot be deemed either criminal or impertinent to attempt an explanation of their doctrine." Thornton, *op. cit.*, pp. 47-48.

[3] Bradford, *Life of Mayhew*, pp. 428-430; Tyler, *op. cit.*, vol. i, pp. 139-140.

public questions, Mayhew avowed that he had "learnt from the holy scriptures, that wise, brave and virtuous men were always friends to liberty; that God gave the Israelites a king, or absolute monarch, in his anger, because they had not sense and virtue enough to like a free commonwealth, and to have Himself for their King; that the Son of God came down from heaven to make us 'free indeed'; and that 'where the spirit of the Lord is, there is liberty'."[1] Jonathan Mayhew was the leading representative of those preachers who, in the first years of the Revolution, educated public opinion for its bold doctrines and duties on "freedom" and "liberty."

One of the "purest and most undaunted public characters to confront us on the threshold of this period," is Charles Chauncy, pastor of the First Church in Boston, preacher, author and political monitor for the Revolution. Chauncy brought to its support an invincible confidence in its final triumph. "Our cause is so just," said he again and again, "that if human efforts should fail, a host of angels would be sent to support it."[2] With the Revolutionary movement, in every stage and phase of it, particularly as interpreted by the radical politicians of New England, he was in perfect sympathy. Perhaps his most characteristic contribution to its development was made through the part he took in controversy over the projected introduction of Anglican bishops. From year to year, however, during this whole period, there was scarcely any aspect of the struggle, upon which Chauncy did not utter some notable comment, giving his imperiled country-

[1] Mayhew, *The Snare Broken, A Thanksgiving Discourse, preached at the Desire of the West Church in Boston, N. E., Friday, May 23, 1776, occasioned by the Repeal of the Stamp Act*, p. 35.

[2] Tudor, *Life of James Otis*, p. 148; Tyler, *op. cit.*, vol. ii, pp. 279-281.

men the most ample help in the form of counsel, warning and reproof.

In 1766 he delivered a *Discourse on "The Good News from a Far Country,"* on the day of public thanksgiving for the repeal of the Stamp Act. In this he discussed the whole problem of Anglo-American relations, with the tone of a man of affairs as well as of a cloistered thinker and divine.[1] In 1770 he preached on *Trust in God, the Duty of a People in a Day of Trouble;*[2] in 1774 he published *A Letter to a Friend*, giving an account "of the hardships and sufferings the town of Boston . . . . . must undergo in consequence of the late act of the British parliament."[3] And in 1778 he published his sermon *The Accursed Thing* (*sordid avarice*) *must be taken away from among the people, if they would reasonably hope to stand before their Enemies.*[4]

Samuel Langdon, president of Harvard College, was another of the Congregational leaders of the Revolution. He addressed the provisional government at Watertown, May 31, 1775, on "government corrupted by vice," calling them to their duty. "We have lived to see the time," he said, "when British liberty is just ready to expire; when

[1] Chauncy, *A Discourse on the Good News from a Far Country. Delivered July Twenty-fourth, a Day of Thanksgiving to Almighty God, throughout the Province of Massachusetts-Bay in New England, on occasion of the Repeal of the Stamp Act; appointed by his Excellency, the Governor of said Province, at the Desire of its House of Representatives, with the advice of his Majesty's Council.* Boston, 1766.

[2] Chauncy, *Trust in God, the Duty of a People in a Day of Trouble. A Sermon preached May 30, 1770.* Boston 1770.

[3] Chauncy, *A Letter to a Friend, giving a concise but just Representation of the Hardships and Sufferings the Town of Boston is exposed to, and must undergo, in consequences of the late Act of the British Parliament.* Boston, 1774.

[4] Chauncy, *The Accursed Thing must be taken away from among the People, if they would reasonably hope to stand before their Enemies. A Sermon preached at the Thursday-Lecture in Boston, September 3, 1778.* Boston, 1778.

that constitution of government which has so long been the glory and strength of the English nation, is deeply undermined and ready to tumble into ruins; when America is threatened with cruel oppression, and the arm of power is stretched out against New England, and especially against this colony, to compel us to submit to the arbitrary acts of legislators who are not our representatives, and who will not themselves bear the least part of the burdens which without mercy they are laying upon us."[1] Washington's Army around Boston, not having been properly supplied with chaplains, President Langdon voluntarily for months undertook that work, and was later rewarded by Congress for his patriotic services.

Politically, the most influential of the Congregational preachers was Samuel Cooper, pastor of the Brattle Street Church in Boston. Cooper was on intimate terms with the men of affairs of New England, and was a writer for the press on all matters of current interest. His *The Crisis* published in 1754 was in opposition to a proposed colonial excise.[2] During the Revolution he is said to have written for the *Boston Gazette*, many of the most fearless articles that appeared in that influential journal.

Samuel Cooper was selected from all the preachers of Massachusetts to deliver the sermon before the Governor and Legislature of that state upon the occasion of the inauguration of the new government under its first written constitution in 1780. This sermon is, in reality, a treatise on political philosophy, and pictures the mission of this new nation.[3]

[1] Langdon, *A Sermon before the Congress . . . . . at Watertown, May 31, 1775.* Watertown, 1775, pp. 5-7; Thornton, *op. cit.*, pp. 227-258.
[2] Cooper, *The Crisis.*
[3] Cooper, *A Sermon, October 25, 1780, on the Commencement of the Constitution and Inauguration of the New Government.*

It would be impossible to list all of the Congregational ministers who aided the Revolutionary cause: — all were called to the service of their states. The First Provincial Congress of Massachusetts issued the following appeal in 1774:

"Reverend Sirs: —

When we contemplate the friendship and assistance our ancestors, the first settlers of this province (while overwhelmed with distress) received from the pious pastors of the churches of Christ, who, to enjoy the rights of conscience, fled with them into this land, then a savage wilderness, we find ourselves filled with the most grateful sensations. And we cannot but acknowledge the goodness of Heaven in constantly supplying us with the preachers of the gospel, whose concern has been the temporal and spiritual happiness of this people.

In a day like this, when all the friends of civil and religious liberty are exerting themselves to deliver this country from its present calamities, we cannot but place great hopes in an order of men who have ever dis-distinguished themselves in their country's cause; and do, therefore, recommend to the ministers of the gospel in the several towns and other places in the colony, that they assist us in avoiding that dreadful slavery with which we are now threatened, by advising the people of their several congregations, as they wish their prosperity, to abide by, and strictly adhere to, the resolutions of the Continental Congress, as the most peaceable and probable method of preventing confusion and bloodshed, and of restoring that harmony between Great Britain and these colonies, on which we wish might be established not only the rights and liberties of America, but the opulence and lasting happiness of the whole British Empire.

Resolved, That the foregoing address be presented to all the ministers of the gospel in the province."[1]

If we may judge by the sermons printed and preserved, the ministry of Massachusetts nobly responded. Certain it is that they have left us a notable series of election sermons.

Gad Hitchcock, pastor of a church in Pembroke, Massachusetts, preached in 1774 on the text (*Proverbs*,

[1] Quoted from Thornton, *Pulpit of the American Revolution*, pp. xxxvii-xxxviii.

xxix, 2), "When the righteous are in authority, the people rejoice; but when the wicked rule, the people mourn." It is filled with counsel. "The people are the only source of civil authority on earth." "With respect to rulers of evil dispositions, nothing is more necessary than that they should believe resistance in some cases to be lawful." "All lawful rulers are the servants of the public." "The happy union and similarity of sentiment and measures which take place thro' the continent in regard to our common sufferings, and which have added weight to the American cause, must be cherished by every prudent and constitutional method, and will, we trust, meet with your countenance and cultivation." "If I am mistaken in supposing plans are formed and executing subversive of our natural and charter rights and privileges, and incompatible with every idea of liberty, all America is mistaken with me.[1]

We have already mentioned the sermon of President Langdon, delivered at Watertown in 1775.[2] In that he announced this doctrine, prophetic of the Declaration of Independence. "Every nation, when able and agreed, has a right to set up over themselves any form of government which to them may appear most conclusive to their common welfare." "By the law of nature any body of people, destitute of order and government, may form themselves into a civil society according to their best prudence, and so provide for their common safety and advantage. When one form is found by the majority, not to answer the grand purpose in any tolerable degree, they may by common consent put an end to it, and set up another; only as

[1] Hitchcock, *Election Sermon . . . . . May 25, 1774.* Boston 1774.

[2] *Supra.*, p. 53.

all such great changes are attended with difficulty, and danger of confusion, they ought not to be attempted without urgent necessity, which will be determined always by the general voice of the wisest and best of the community." "It must be ascribed to some supernatural influence on the minds of the main body of the people through this extensive continent, that they have so universally adopted the method of managing the important matters necessary to preserve among them a free government, by corresponding committees and congresses, consisting of the wisest and most disinterested patriots in America, chosen by the unbiased suffrages of the people assembled for that purpose, in their several towns, counties, and provinces . . . . . The judgment and advice of the Continental Assembly of Delegates have been as readily obeyed, as if they were authentic acts of a long established parliament."

William Gordon, pastor of the Third Church in Roxbury, Massachusetts, and historian of the Revolution, preached the sermon in 1775. His text is an abundant exposition of its content . . . . . *Jeremiah* xxx, 20, 21: "Their children also shall be as afore-time, and their congregation shall be established before me, and I will punish all that oppress them: and their nobles shall be of themselves."[1]

Samuel West, from a church in Dartmouth, devoted the greater part of the 1776, May 29, sermon to the question of church and state. Later, in 1788, West was to act as a member of the Convention which ratified the Federal Constitution.

"The law of self-preservation will always justify opposing a cruel and tyrannical imposition, except where opposition is attended with greater

[1] Gordon, *Election Sermon, Preached. . . . . July 19, 1775.*

evils than submission; which is frequently the case where a few are oppressed by a large and powerful majority. This shows the reason why the primitive Christians did not oppose the cruel persecutions that were inflicted upon them by the heathen magistrates; They were few compared with the heathen world and for them to have attempted to resist their enemies by force would have been like a small parcel of sheep endeavoring to oppose a large number of ravening wolves and savage beasts of prey; it would without a miracle have brought upon them inevitable ruin and destruction. Hence the wise and prudent advice of our Saviour to them was, 'When they persecute you in this city, flee to another'."[1]

Samuel Webster of Salisbury preached in 1777 from *Ezekiel* xlv, 8, 9;[2] and Phillips Payson of Chelsea in 1788 from *Galatians* iv, 26, 31, "But Jerusalem which is above is free, which is the mother of us all. So then, Brethren, we are not children of the bondwoman but of the free."[3] In this sermon Payson argues against separation of Church and State, "Let the restraints of religion once be broken down, as they infallibly would be by leaving the subject of public worship to the humors of the multitude, and we might well defy all human wisdom and power to support and preserve order and government in the state." The sermon of 1779 was assigned to a Baptist minister, Rev. Samuel Stillman, pastor of the First Baptist Church of Boston.[4] Simeon Howard, pastor of the West Church in Boston, preached in 1780 from *Exodus* xvii, 21, "Thou shalt provide out of all the people able men, such as fear God, men of truth, hating covetousness; and place such over them to be rulers."[5]

[1] West, *Election Sermon* . . . . . *May 24, 1776*; Thornton, *op. cit.*, pp. 259-322.
[2] Webster, *Election Sermon* . . . . . *May 28, 1777.*
[3] Payson, *Election Sermon* . . . . . *May 27, 1778;* Thornton, *op. cit.*, pp. 323-353.
[4] *Infra.*, pp. 119-120.
[5] Howard, *Election Sermon* . . . . . *May 31, 1780*; Thornton, *op. cit.*, pp. 355-396.

Of more than ordinary interest is the sermon of 1781 by Jonas Clark, pastor of a church in Lexington and author of *A Brief Narrative of the Principal Transactions of that Day* (April 19, 1775),[1] this sermon being for the first General Election after the inauguration of the new government under the new constitution. The text was *Psalms* xlvii, 8, 9, "God sitteth upon the throne of His holiness: The Princes of the people are gathered together; even the people of the God of Abraham; for the shields of the earth belong unto God: He is greatly exalted." The sermon contained the following doctrines:

"It remains with the community, state, or nation, as a public, political body, at any time, at pleasure to change, alter or even totally dissolve the constitution, and return to a state of nature, or to form anew, as to them shall seem meet.

A people have an unalienable right to know the constitution they enjoy, the government they are under, the laws they are subject to, and what is justly expected and required of them as subjects.

A sacred regard to the constitution, a cheerful obedience to the laws, and a reverend submission to the authority of those who are vested with the powers of government, are as much the duty of subjects, even in free states, as it is of rulers to be faithful to the trust reposed in them by the people. The obligations are mutually binding, equally indispensable, and equally necessary to the liberty, safety, prosperity and happiness of society.

The subjection here enjoined is not absolute, or that passive obedience and non-resistance, so absurdly preached up, in the darker ages of the world; but that obedience and subjection to good and faithful rulers, which the social compact and the laws of the land require. And without this, government is at an end . . . . . In a word, religion among a people, in its power, purity and governing influence, is the guardian of liberty, the strength of government, the energy of laws, the bond of society, and both the glory and defence of the state.

The wisdom of the counsels, the firmness of the resolution, and the equity of the measures of the United States, in Congress assembled; and in the states respectively; — The exertions that have been made, in the cause of liberty and mankind; and the success which hath attended: —

[1] Clark, *A Sermon preached at Lexington, April 19, 1776.*

The Articles of Confederation which have been formed and completely ratified by all the states, as the basis of freedom and mutual support; And the glorious revolution, that hath taken place in America; as they do honor to human nature, and engage the attention of an admiring world; being transmitted by the pen of the faithful historian, will be a subject of most pleasing contemplation to all true lovers of liberty and the rights of mankind in succeeding generations.

Standing armies are abhorrent to the first principles of freedom, and dangerous to the liberties of a free Commonwealth. The sword, in the hands of the free citizens, is the protection of society, and the safety and defence of a people truly brave, truly free. — May I be permitted to ask, Whether the sword is in the hands of all the inhabitants of this Commonwealth? — Whether all the people have arms? — Or, Whether, having arms, they are taught the art — military, and the use of their arms, so as to be effectually prepared to oppose an invading enemy, upon the shortest notice?"[1]

Zabdiel Adams of Lunenburg, a cousin of John Adams, preached in 1782 from *Ecclesiastes* viii, 4, "Where the word of a king is, there is power; and who may say unto him what doest thou?"

"Rumors of accommodation are circulating through the air. Great Britain, it is said, holds out the olive branch, and makes overtures of peace. If the terms are not insiduous; if our independence can be secured; and treaties formerly made with our illustrious ally, the King of France, kept sacred, then it must be with the wish of every good man in America to have the horrors of war speedily closed with such a peace. But of this our rulers in Congress must be the judge in the dernier resort. With them it lays to make peace or prolong the war, and in them we should confide. We are now in sight of the promised land. How humiliating it would be to have our Independence, just brought to the birth, fail for want of strength to be delivered.

A few more campaigns will determine the event of the present struggle, and doubtless land us on the rock of independence, security and peace.

The ruling power of every state or kingdom should be elected by the body of the people.

The legislative body is superior in power to the executive."[2]

[1] Clark, *Election Sermon, Preached . . . . . 1781,* Boston, 1781.

[2] Adams, *Election Sermon, Preached . . . . May 29, 1782.* Boston, 1782.

There is the note of triumph and prophecy to be expected in the sermon of Mr. Guming, pastor of the church in Billerica, of 1783, from *Peter* v, 5:

"Yea, all of you be subject to one another, to behold . . . . . the future glory, grandure and magnificance of America! To behold her raised superior to all her enemies; extending her friendly arms for the support and protection of other states and nations against the attacks of restless encroaching ambition; and (while none dare to distrust or affront her) offering a refuge and asylum, in her bosom, to the injured and oppressed of the human race in all quarters of the globe.

Though the land now rests from war and we daily expect to hear that the definite treaty of peace is completely ratified, yet it would be exceedingly unsafe for people to lay by their arms, and neglect all military matters. Our country affords so many objects to excite the ambition of other nations . . . . . that we can have no security of a lasting peace, or of enjoying long the blessings of freedom if we should totally withdraw our attention from the arts of war and be unprovided with the means of defence. Standing armies in a time of peace are indeed dangerous to liberty; but a well furnished and well disciplined militia is of great importance to a state . . . . . The public welfare requires that our militia be kept on such a respectable footing, as shall render us secure at home, and formidable abroad.

In order to preserve the union between the states and establish it upon a permanent basis, whatever is inconsistent with the principles, which upon the maturest deliberation, have been adopted, as the grand cement of it, must be carefully avoided; and a proper attention paid to the interest and welfare of the whole." [1]

The Congregational ministers of Connecticut possessed a central body known as the General Association which illustrates concerted action on the part of Congregationalism. At the session of this body held at Mansfield, June 1774, a committee, the Reverends Waterman, Drummond, and Baldwin, were appointed to draw up a letter of condolence to the ministers of Boston. The following strongly patriotic communication was accordingly

[1] Guming, *Election Sermon, Preached . . . . . May 28, 1783,* Boston, 1783.

forwarded from the General Association of Connecticut to the Boston ministers:

"Reverend and Dear Sirs; —

We your brethren of the colony of Connecticut met by delegation from the several counties in general association, at our annual meeting, cannot but feel deeply impressed with the present melancholy threatened situation of America in general and the distressed state of the Town of Boston in particular, suffering the severe resentment of the British Parliament by which the subsistence of thousands is taken away. We readily embrace this opportunity, to manifest our hearty sympathy with you in your present distresses. We consider you as suffering in the common cause of America; in the cause of civil Liberty, which, if taken away, we fear would involve the ruin of Religious Liberty also. Gladly would we contribute everything in our power for your encouragement and relief; however, our situation enables us to do little more than to express our sincere, affectionate concern, and with fervent addresses to commend your cause, and the cause of America — the cause of liberty and above all of religion, to the Father of Mercies, who can easily afford effectual relief, who hath the hearts of all at his disposal and can turn them as he pleases. We feel deeply sensible what a load must lie upon the minds of the ministers of Boston — enough to sink their spirits unless armed with vigor, Christian fortitude and resolution. In hopes that it may afford you some consolation, we assure you of our sincere condolence and unremitted prayers in your behalf; and we shall in every way suitable to our character and station use our influence with the good people of this Colony to concur in every proper measure calculated to afford relief to America in general, and the distressed Town of Boston in particular. We pray that the ministers of Boston may be inspired by the Great Head of the Church with wisdom sufficient for their direction in such a critical day as the present. And we cannot but hope the united prayers of America may obtain that audience in Heaven which will ensure salvation to us; and that God will give them and their people firmness, unanimity, patience, prudence, and every virtue which they need to support them under their heavy trials, and enable them to stand firm in the glorious cause of liberty, express such a temper and exhibit such an example as shall be well pleasing to God, and recommend them to the compassion and favor of their fellow men. We earnestly pray that God would humble us all under a deep sense of our numerous transgressions and criminal declensions, show us the absolute necessity of repentance and reformation, humble us under his mighty hand and pour out a spirit of fervent supplication on you, on us, and all the people of this Land." [1]

[1] *Records of the General Association, etc.*, pp. 75-78.

This was by no means the first action of a patriotic nature taken by this body in the interest of the struggle with Great Britain. In 1768 the thanks of the body were voted to Dr. Chauncy of Boston and to William Livingston of New York, in the former case "for the good service he had done to the cause of religion, liberty and truth, in his judicious answer to the appeal for an American episcopate and in his defence of the New England church and colonies against the unjust reflections cast upon them in the bishop of Landaff's sermon before the society for propagating the gospel in foreign parts"; in the latter case "for his late vindication of the New England churches and planters against the injurious reflections and unjust aspersions cast upon them in the bishop of Landaff's later sermon . . . . . contained in his manly and spirited letter to his lordship."[1] Copies of these votes were transmitted to the men commended and they were also ordered to be published in the Boston and New York papers respectively.

In 1769 the General Association took "into serious consideration the dark and threatening aspect of divine Providence upon our Nation and Land in regard to their civil liberties and public interest," and held that it would be "desirable that a day be set apart for public fasting and prayer" and accordingly "agree for ourselves and recommend it to the Brethren in the Ministry, to our own churches and the churches throughout the colony to set apart the last Thursday of August next for the purpose aforesaid, earnestly desiring both ministers and people, unanimously to join in the seasonable, solemn and important duty."[2]

[1] *Records of the General Association etc.*, pp. 63-64.
[2] *Ibid.*, pp. 66-67.

Their most important patriotic pronunciamento was issued by the Cornwall meeting, June 18, 1776:

"An Address of the General Association to the Consociated Pastors and Churches in the Colony of Connecticut.

Reverend and Beloved:

Deeply impressed with a sense of the calamitous state in which our Land is involved: reduced by the arbitrary edicts of the British Parliament, and the cruel and inhuman methods used to enforce them to the sad necessity of defending by force and arms those precious privileges which our fathers fled into this wilderness quietly to enjoy: declared rebels by the British King and Parliament: not only the power of Britain, but a large army of foreign mercenaries, hired at a most extravagant price, employed to dragoon us into obedience or rather abject submission to Tyranny: our foreign trade almost annihilated: many of our towns ruined and destroyed: our children, our friends, our dearest connections called from our bosoms to the field of battle: and some of them captivated and enslaved by our cruel and insulting foes: detestable parricides interspersed among us, aiming to give a fatal stab to the country which gave them birth, and hath hitherto fostered them in her indulgent bosom: and in many places both at home and abroad deplorable sickness wasting away the inhabitants of our land: deeply impressed with a view of these dire calamities, we are lead anxiously to enquire what sins and iniquities prevalent in our land have called down these heavy judgments of Heaven upon us."

(Here follows a list of sins; intemperance, profanity, injustice, fraud, exaction, etc. etc.)

"A want of love of our Country, and of a disposition to prefer the great interests of the community to the little private interests of our own—a disposition to anarchy while struggling for Liberty—impatience under lawful and necessary restraint.

"Tenderly concerned for both the temporal and spiritual interests of our dear country, and fully convinced of the necessity of our being deeply humbled under a sense of our sins, and of a general reformation taking place, in order to obtain and secure these invaluable blessings; we hope we shall obtain the serious attention of our brethren in the gospel ministry, and their and our respective churches, while we endeavor to unite our voice with that of our civil fathers in bearing our testimony against these Heaven-provoking sins, and in resolving against them . . .

And as the future hopes both of the temporal and spiritual prosperity of our country are so much founded upon the rising generation, we would be importunate with the youth of our churches and congregations heartily to join in this necessary and important work of reformation —

that they would seriously consider they have a greater interest in the prosperity of their country, than those more advanced in years; That the important betrustment now lodged with their parents of transmitting the blessings of religion and liberty to posterity will soon devolve upon them . . . . . ."[1]

DeWitt says of the Congregational ministers that they "gave to the cause of the Colonies all that they could give of the sanction of religion."[2]

[1] *Records of the General Association etc.*, pp. 89-96.
[2] DeWitt, *First General Assembly*, p. 19.

CHAPTER IV

THE PRESBYTERIAN CHURCH IN THE REVOLUTION

No one should question the loyalty of the Presbyterians to the Revolutionary cause, but it is possible to take exception to the enthusiasm of those who would credit this denomination with a monopoly of patriotism.[1] Their sturdy Republicanism did, however, give them an influence over the course of the Revolution out of all proportion to their numbers. During the colonial era Professor Andrews finds, that "Of all . . . . . denominations the most powerful and influential were the Congregational and the Anglican."[2] The Revolution advanced other sects and preëminently the Presbyterians. They already possessed the most powerful intercolonial organization on the continent in their yearly Synod, — prototype of so many American republican national federal assemblies. To this centralized organism the cause of political republicanism added just that enthusiasm which made American Presbyterians a host of crusaders for independence.[3]

The bed-rock principle of Presbyterianism was constitutional republicanism. The church was a federated Christian commonwealth, not a hierarchy and not an aggregation of petty democracies. In the former respect it differed from Anglicanism and Catholicism; in the latter from Baptists and Congregationalists. The church was

[1] Ford, *The Scotch-Irish in America.*

[2] Andrews, *Colonial Folk-Ways*, p. 163.

[3] Blaikie, *Presbyterianism in New England*, p. 171 sq. notes two Presbyterian ministers of that section who went over to the British lines.

governed by assemblies, — congregational, classical or synodic; not by church officials individually considered. The Presbyterian official possessed no "prerogative."[1] The form of the political organization under which we now live, commonly called constitutional republicanism, has been traced to the social organism instituted by Calvin himself.[2]

The writing and testimonies before Parliament of Joseph Galloway, a loyalist of the province of Pennsylvania, have furnished the chief authority for those who would ascribe a paramount Presbyterian origin to the American Revolution. Galloway enumerates the opponents of the British government in 1774 as "Congregationalists, Presbyterians and smugglers." Testifying before a committee of the House of Commons in 1779 he maintained that not one-fifth of the people of America had independence in view and that in the army established by the Continental Congress "there were scarcely one-fourth natives of America, — about one-half were Irish and the other fourth were English and Scotch."[3]

Galloway's summary is as follows:

"In the beginning of the year 1764, a convention of the ministers and elders of the Presbyterian congregations in Philadelphia wrote a circular letter to all the Presbyterian congregations in Pennsylvania, and with it

[1] Breckinridge, *Presbyterian Government not a Hierarchy, but a Commonwealth.*

[2] Balch, Thomas, *Calvinism and American Independence*, Philadelphia 1909. Laveleye, *Essais et Etudes, Premiere Series*, essays on "*Le Protestantisme et le Catholicisme dans leur rapports avec la liberte et la prosperite des peuples*," and "*De l'influence de la religion sur les formes de gouvernement*," Smith, *Presbyterianism and the Revolution.*

[3] Galloway, *The Examination of Joseph Galloway, Esq., late Speaker of the House of Assembly of Pennsylvania, Before the House of Commons, in a Committee on the American Papers:* O'Brien, M. J., *A Hidden Phase of American History: Ireland's Part in America's Struggle for Liberty;* Hartigan, *The Irish in the American Revolution.*

enclosed the proposed articles of union. The reasons assigned in them are so novel, so futile, and absurd, and the design, of exciting that very rebellion, of which the Congregationalists of New England, and the Presbyterians in all the other Colonies are at this moment the only support, is so clearly demonstrated that I shall make no apology for giving them to the Reader at full length, without any comment:

The Circular Letter and Articles of 'Some Gentlemen, of the Presbyterian Denomination' in the Province of Pennsylvania.

Philadelphia, March 24, 1764.

Sir; —

The want of union and harmony among those of the Presbyterian denomination has been long observed, and greatly lamented by every public-spirited person of our society. Notwith tanding we are so numerous in the province of Pennsylvania, we are considered as nobody, or a body of very little strength and consequence, so that any encroachments upon our essential and charter privileges may be made by evil minded persons who think that they have little fear from any opposition that can be made to their measures by us. Nay, some denominations openly insult us as acting without plan or design, quarreling with one another, and seldom uniting together even to promote the most salutary purposes; And thus they take occasion to misrepresent and asperse the whole body of Presbyterians, on account of the indiscreet conduct of individuals belonging to us.

It is greatly to be wished that we could devise some plan that would cut off even the least grounds for such aspersions, that would enable us to prevent the bad conduct of our members, and that would have a tendency to unite us more closely together; so that, when there may be a necessity to act as a body, we may be able to do it whenever we may be called to defend our civil or religious liberties and privileges, which we may enjoy, or to obtain any of which we may be abridged.

A number of gentlemen in this city, in conjunction with the clergymen of our denomination here, have thought the enclosed plan may be subservient to this desirable purpose, if it be heartily adopted and prosecuted by our brethren in this province, and three lower counties; and in this view we beg leave to recommend it to you. It cannot possibly do any hurt to us,-and it will beyond doubt make us a more respectable body. We, therefore, cannot but promise ourselves your hearty concurrence from your known public spirit, and desire to assist anything that may have a tendency to promote the union and welfare of society, and the general good of the community to which we belong.

We are yours, etc.

The Plan of Articles

Some gentlemen of the Presbyterian denomination having seriously considered the necessity of a more close union among ourselves, in order to enable us to act as a body with unanimity and harmony have unanimously adopted the following plan viz:

1st. That a few gentlemen in the city of Philadelphia with the ministers of the Presbyterian denomination there, be chosen to correspond with their friends in different parts, to give and receive advices, and to consult what things may have a tendency to promote our union and welfare, either as a body, or as we are connected together in particular congregations, so far as it will consist with our duty to the best of Kings, and our subjection to the laws of Government.

2nd. That a number of the most prudent and public-spirited persons in each district in the province, and those lower counties, be chosen with the ministers in said districts, to correspond in like manner with one another, and with the gentlemen appointed for this purpose in Philadelphia; or

3rd. That the same be done in each congregation or district where there is no minister; a neighboring minister meeting with them as often as it is convenient and necessary.

4th. That a person shall be appointed in each committee, thus formed, who shall sign a letter in the name of the committee, and to whom letters shall be directed, who shall call the committee together, and communicate to them what advice is received, that they may consult together what is best to be done.

5th. That one or more members be sent by the Committee in each county or district, yearly or half-yearly, to a general meeting of the whole body, to consult together what is necessary for the advantages of the body, and to give advice in any affairs that relate to particular congregations, and that the stated meetings of said delegates be on the last Tuesday of August yearly.

6th. That the place of the general meeting be at Philadelphia or Lancaster on the last Tuesday of August, 1764.

7th. That each committee transmit to the committee in Philadelphia their names and numbers, with what alterations, may at any time be made in them.

8th. That the committee in town consist of the ministers of the Presbyterian denomination in this city, and Mr. Treat, together with (here follows a list of 27 names).

In consequence of this letter, a union of all the Presbyterian congregations immediately took place in Pennsylvania and the Lower Counties. A like confederacy was established in all the Southern Provinces, in pursuance of similar letters wrote by their respective conventions.

These letters were long buried in strictest secrecy. Their design was not sufficiently matured, and therefore, not proper for publication. Men of sense and foresight, were alarmed at so formidable a confederacy, without knowing the ultimate extent of their views; however, at length, in the year 1769, the letters from the conventions of Philadelphia and New York were obtained and published.

A Union of Presbyterian forces being thus established in each Province, these projectors then took *salutary steps* (as they were called in a letter from one of the Committee at Philadelphia to his friend) to get the whole Presbyterian interest on the *Continent* more firmly united. These steps ended in the establishment of an annual synod at Philadelphia. Here all the Presbyterian congregations in the *Colonies* are represented by their respective ministers and elders. In this synod all their general affairs, political as well as religious are debated and decided. From here their orders and decrees are issued throughout America; and to them as ready and implicit obedience is paid as is due to the authority of any sovereign power whatever.

But they did not stop here; the principal matter recommended by the faction in New England, was a union of the *Congregational and Presbyterian* interests throughout the colonies. To effect this, a negotiation took place which ended in the appointment of a standing committee of correspondence with powers to communicate and consult, on all occasions, with a like committee appointed by the congregational churches in New England. Thus the Presbyterians in the Southern Colonies who while unconnected in their several congregations, were of little significance, were raised into weight and consequence, and a dangerous combination of men, whose principles of religion and polity were equally averse to those of the established Church and Government was formed.

United in this manner throughout the Colonies those republican secretaries were prepared to oppose the Stamp Act, before the time of its commencement, and yet sensible of their own inability without the aid of others; no acts or pains were left unessayed to make converts of the rest of the people, but all their industry was attended with little success. The members of the Church of England, Methodists, Quakers, Lutherans, Calvinists, Moravians, and other dissenters were in general averse to every measure which tended to violence. Some few of them were, by various arts, and partial interests prevailed on to unite with them, and those were either lawyers or merchants, who through their professional business would be affected by the act, or bankrupt planters, who were overwhelmed in debt to their British factors. But the republicans, predetermined in their measures, were unanimous. It was these men who excited the mobs, and led them to destroy the stamped paper; who compelled the collectors of the duties to resign their offices, and to pledge their faith that they would not execute them; and it was those men who promoted, and for a time enforced the non-importation agreement and by their personal applications, threats, insults, and inflammatory publications and petitions, led the Assemblies to deny the authority of Parliament to tax the Colonies, in their several remonstrances."[1]

This report probably afforded the average Englishman of that day his conception of the causes of the Revolution; it certainly raises a clear spectre of Presbyterian Republicanism. But how distorted or glaringly inaccurate are its facts. The organization of a united Presbyterianism for America long ante-dates 1764, for by 1758, we find the amalgamation of the two great synods of Philadelphia and New York. We know that the organization of this national body was primarily for religious rather than for political purposes. The still further union of the Congregationalists with the Presbyterians was not effected until 1766 and then it was to combat, not taxation, but the introduction of an American episcopacy.

No wonder the well informed John Witherspoon remarked, in a letter dated March 20, 1780: "I have read lately your parliamentary enquiry into the causes of your want of success in America. The examination of Galloway in particular is a curiosity. I know that he, and such as he, are blinded and stupefied to an almost incredible degree, by their prejudices; and yet it is hard to suppose that he thought as he said in all points."[2] Regarding his own conduct, Witherspoon declared, in a sermon before his own congregation, May 17, 1776, "You are all my

[1] Galloway, *Historical and Political Reflections on the Rise and Progress of the American Revolution;* Breed, *Presbyterianism and the Revolution*, Philadelphia, 1876. Smith, *Presbyterianism and the Revolution*, 1845; Smith, *The Real Origin of the Declaration of Independence*, Columbia, 1847. Ford, *op.cit.*, pp. 583-587.

[2] Witherspoon, *Works*, vol. iv, p. 382.

witnesses, that this is the first time of my introducing any political subject into the pulpit."[1] And the Synod of 1775 officially went on record as opposing a complete break with the mother country[2] and recorded that "It is well known to you (otherwise it would be imprudent indeed thus publicly to profess) that we have not been instrumental in inflaming the minds of the people, or urging them to acts of violence and disorder. Perhaps no instance can be given on so interesting a subject, in which political sentiments have been so long and so fully kept from the pulpit, and even malice itself has not charged us with laboring from the press."[3]

Galloway's statement does represent the true feeling of British officialdom in America that there was an intimate connection between Presbyterian religion and all things political. From the beginning the agents of the crown noted a Presbyterian opposition to the oppressive measures of the government. John Hughes, the stamp distributor for Pennsylvania, wrote Benjamin Franklin, September 25, 1765, relative to his appointment, "When it is known that I have received my commission, I fancy I shall not escape the storm of Presbyterian rage!" And in his *Report*, October 12, 1765, he records, "Common justice calls upon me to say, the body of the people called Quakers, seem disposed to pay obedience to the Stamp Act, and so do that part of the Church of England and Baptists, that are not some way under Proprietary influence. But Presbyterians and Proprietary minions spare no pains to engage the Dutch and lower class of people, and render the royal government odious."[4]

[1] *Infra.*, p. 90.
[2] *Infra.*, p. 75., for text of this important Pastoral Letter.
[3] *Records of the Presbyterian Church*, pp. 466-469.
[4] Hughes, *Report*, October 12, 1765; Ford, *op. cit.*, p. 466.

That Tory Episcopalian of Trinity Church, New York, whose position we have already noted, wrote on October 31, 1776:

"I have it from good authority that the Presbyterian ministers, at a Synod where most of them in the middle colonies were collected, passed a resolve to support the Continental Congress in all their measures. This, and this only, can account for the uniformity of their conduct; for I do not know one of them, nor have I been able, after strict inquiry, to hear of any, who did not, by preaching and every effort in their power, promote all the measures of the Congress, however extravagant." [1]

Fortunately, the records of the Presbyterian Synods for this period are complete and we can determine the official position of American Presbyterianism relative to each of the various controversies. They show that official action, relative to the Stamp Act, came only after its repeal, but that the spirit of Presbyterianism had been hostile to it from its inception. At the Synod of 1766, an overture was advanced by Dr. Alison, "that an address should be made to our sovereign, on the joyful occasion of the repeal of the Stamp Act, and thereby a confirmation of our liberties," and at the same time he proposed a copy of an address for examination, "Which was read and approved."[2] The following pastoral letter was also prepared: May 30, 1766:

"We think it our indispensable duty, not only in our particular charges, but in this united and more public capacity, to direct you to some suitable reflections upon the late remarkable and merciful steps of Divine Providence, and to inculcate a becoming improvement of an event, the most interesting and important to the people of this continent. For, not only in the word of God should we attend his Divine Will, but also mark his hand in that Providence by which he directs the course of human affairs with invariable wisdom and paternal goodness.

[1] *Documentary History of New York*, vol. iii, pp. 1050-1051; Hawkins, *Historical Notices*, pp. 328-329.

[2] *Records of the Presbyterian Church*, p. 360.

The faithless French, and their savage allies, were lately the rod of Divine displeasure for our many provocations. Under the calamities of war, and the wasting ravages of Indian cruelty, we were repeatedly brought to approach the throne of Grace, with solemn fasting and prayer; and thereby openly professed our resolution to forsake the ways of sin, and turn unto the Lord. But, alas! we rendered not to God according to the multitude of his tender mercies, for no sooner was the rod removed, and the blessings of peace restored, but we became more vain and dissolute than before.

The Almighty thus provoked, permitted counsels of the most pernicious tendency, both to Great Britain and her colonies. The imposition of unusual taxes, a severe restriction of our trade, and an almost total stagnation of business, threatened us with inevitable ruin. A long suspense, whether we should be deprived of, or restored to, the peaceable enjoyment of the inestimable privilege of English liberty, filled every breast with the most painful anxiety. A gloomy cloud thickened over our heads, ready to burst upon us in a desolating storm. Had our gracious Sovereign, the present ministry, and the British Parliament been less wise, just, and good; had they, instead of yielding to a spirit of moderation, unhappily recurred to force, we shudder at the very thoughts of the consequences. We cannot look down the precipice on the brink of which we stood, without horror. We were not without reason apprehensive that the tumultuous outrages, which in some places attended a determined opposition to the disrelished statute, might provoke the resentment of the British legislature.

While we thus call upon you to fear God, you will not forget to honor your king, and pay a due submission to his august parliament. Let this fresh instance of royal clemency increase the ardor of your affection to the person, family, and government, of our rightful and gracious sovereign. This you will manifest by a cheerful and ready obedience to civil authority. A spirit of liberty is highly laudable when under proper regulations, but we hope you will cheerfully distinguish between liberty and licentiousness.

We most earnestly recommend it to you to encourage and strengthen the hands of government, to demonstrate on every proper occasion your undissembled love for your mother country, and your attachment to her true interest, so inseparably connected with our own.

That thus you may become wise and good, as well as free and happy, and that while you enjoy liberty, civil and religious, you may not be the servants of sin and Satan, is the fervent prayer of those who watch for your souls, as men who must give an account."[1]

[1] *Records*, ed. 1904, pp. 362-363.

In 1769 the Synod appointed a day for special prayer and fasting in view of "the threatening aspect of public affairs."[1] The same was repeated in 1771 "in consideration of the aspect which matters both civil and religious, bear."[2] This reappears in 1774 for "the dark and threatening aspect of public affairs, both civil and religious."[3] They would do the same in 1775

"considering the present alarming state of public affairs . . . . . . But as the Continental Congress are now sitting and may appoint a fast for the same purpose, the Synod, from respect to that august body, and for the greater harmony with all other denominations, and for the greater public order, if the Congress shall appoint a day not above four weeks distant from the said last Thursday in June, order that the congregations belonging to this Synod do keep the day appointed by the Congress . . . . and if they appoint a day more distant, the Synod order both to be observed by all our communion. The Synod also earnestly recommend it to all the congregations under their care to spend the afternoon of the last Thursday in every month in public solemn prayer to God, during the continuance of our present troubles."[4]

The Synod of 1775 appointed Dr. Witherspoon, Dr. Rodgers, Messrs. Caldwell, Halsey, Smith, Kerr, and Ogden to draft a pastoral letter which after a few alterations was approved and ordered to be printed, and is as follows:

"Very dear Brethren — The Synod of New York and Philadelphia being met at a time when public affairs wear so threatening an aspect, and when (unless God in his sovereign Providence speedily prevent it) all the horrors of a civil war throughout this great Continent are to be apprehended, were of opinion, that they could not discharge their duty to the numerous congregations under their care, without addressing them at this important crisis . . . . .

"The Synod cannot help thinking that this is a proper time pressing all of every rank, seriously to consider the things that belong to their eternal peace. Hostilities, long feared, have now taken place; the sword has been drawn in one province, and the whole continent, with hardly

[1] *Records*, p. 398.
[2] *Ibid.*, p. 420.
[3] *Ibid.*, p. 460.
[4] *Ibid.*, pp. 464-465.

any exception, seem determined to defend their rights by force of arms. If, at the same time, the British ministry shall continue to enforce their claims by violence, a lasting and bloody contest must be expected. Surely then, it becomes those who have taken up arms, and profess a willingness to hazard their lives in the cause of liberty, to be prepared for death, which to many must be certain, and to every one is a possible or probable event.

We have long seen with concern, the circumstance which occasioned, and the gradual increase of this unhappy difference. As ministers of the gospel of peace, we have ardently wished that it could, and often hoped that it would have been more early accommodated. It is well known to you, (otherwise it would be imprudent indeed thus publicly to profess), that we have not been instrumental in inflaming the minds of the people, or urging them to acts of violence and disorder. Perhaps no instance can be given on so interesting a subject, in which political sentiments have been so long and so fully kept from the pulpit, and even malice itself has not charged us with laboring from the press; but things are now come to such a state, that as we do not wish to conceal our opinions as men and citizens, so the relation we stand in to you seemed to make the present improvement of it to your spiritual benefit an indispensable duty.

Suffer us to lay hold of your present temper of mind, and to exhort, especially the young and vigorous, by assuring them that there is no soldier so undaunted as the pious man, no army so formidable as those who are superior to the fear of death . . . . . .

Let it not be forgotten, that though for the wise ends of his Providence it may please God, for a reason to suffer his people to lie under unmerited oppression, yet in general we may expect, that those who fear and serve him in sincerity and truth, will be favored with his countenance and strength . . . . .

After this exhortation, which we thought ourselves called upon to give you at this time, on your great interest, the one thing needful, we shall take the liberty to offer a few advices to the societies under our charge, as to their public and general conduct; and, ...

First. In carrying on this important struggle, let every opportunity be taken to express our attachment and respect to our sovereign King George, and to the revolution principles by which his august family was seated on the British throne. We recommend, indeed, not only allegiance to him from duty and principle, as the first magistrate of the empire, but esteem and reverence for the person of the prince, who has merited well of his subjects on many accounts, and who has probably been misled into the late and present measures by those about him; neither have we any doubt that they themselves have been in a great degree deceived by false information from interested persons residing in America. It gives us the greatest pleasure to say, from our own certain knowledge of all belonging to our communion, and from the best means of information, of the far greatest part of all denominations in this country, that the present opposition to the measures of administration does not in the least arise from disaffection to the King, or a desire of separation from the parent state. We are happy in being able with truth to affirm, that no part of America would either have approved or permitted such insults as have been offered to the sovereign in Great Britain. We exhort you, therefore, to continue in the same disposition, and not to suffer oppression, or injury itself, easily to provoke you to anything which may seem to betray contrary sentiments: let it ever appear, that you only desire the preservation and security of those rights which belong to you as freeman and Britons, and that reconciliation upon these terms is your ardent desire.

Secondly. Be careful to maintain the union which at present subsists through all the colonies: nothing can be more manifest than that the success of every measure depends on its being inviolably preserved, and therefore, we hope that you will leave nothing undone which can promote this end. In particular, as the Continental Congress, now sitting in Philadelphia, consists of delegates chosen in the most free and unbiased manner, by the body of the people, let them not only be treated with respect, and encouraged in their difficult service — not only let your prayers be offered to God for his direction in their proceedings — but adhere firmly to their resolutions; and let it be seen that they are able to bring out the whole strength of this vast country to carry them into execution. We would also advise for the same purpose, that a spirit of candor, charity, and mutual esteem, be preserved and promoted towards those of different religious denominations. Persons of probity and principle of every profession, should be united together as servants of the same master, and the experience of our happy concord hitherto in a state of liberty should engage all to unite in support of the common interest; for there is no example in history, in which civil liberty was destroyed, and the rights of conscience preserved entire.

Thirdly . . . . . It is with the utmost pleasure we remind you, that the Continental Congress determined to discourage luxury in living, public diversions, and gaming of all kinds . . . . . The greatest service which magistrates, or persons in authority can do, with respect to the religion or morals of the people, is to defend and secure the rights of conscience in the most equal and impartial manner.

Fourthly. We cannot but recommend, and urge in the warmest manner, a regard to order and public peace; and as in many places during the confusions that prevail, legal proceedings have become difficult, it is hoped, that all persons will conscientiously pay their just debts, and to the utmost of their power serve one another, so that the evils inseparable from a civil war may not be augmented by wantonness and irregularity.

Fifthly. We think it of importance, at this time, to recommend to all of every rank, but especially to those who may be called to action, a spirit of humanity and mercy. Every battle of the warrior is with confused noise, and garments rolled in blood. It is impossible to appeal to the sword without being exposed to many scenes of cruelty and slaughter; but it is often observed, that civil wars are carried on with a rancour and spirit of revenge much greater than those between independent states. The injuries received, or supposed, in civil wars, wound more deeply than those of foreign countries, it is therefore, the more necessary to guard against this abuse, and recommend that meekness and gentleness of spirit, which is the noblest attendant on true valor. That man will fight most bravely, who never fights till it is necessary, and who ceases to fight as soon as the necessity is over.

* * * * *

We conclude with our most earnest prayer, that the God of heaven may bless you in your temporal and spiritual concerns, and that the present unnatural dispute may be speedily terminated by an equitable and lasting settlement on constitutional principles.

New York, May 22nd, 1775

N. B. The stated clerk is to insert the pastoral letter from the printed copy. The Synod agree that five hundred copies of said pastoral letter be printed . . . . . Mr. Halsey dissents from that paragraph of said letter which contains the declaration of allegiance."[1]

The first body of clergy in America openly to recognize the Declaration of Independence and identify themselves with the cause of freedom was the Presbytery of Hanover in Virginia. It memorialized the Virginia Assembly as follows, October 24, 1776:

"To the Honorable the General Assembly of Virginia. The Memorial of the Presbytery of Hanover humbly represents:

That your memorialists are governed by the same sentiments which have inspired the United States of America, and are determined that nothing in our power and influence shall be wanting to give success to their common cause. We would also represent that dissenters from the Church of England in this country have ever been desirous to conduct

[1] *Records of the Presbyterian Church,* pp. 463, 466-469; *American Archives,* fourth series, vol. ii, pp. 1846-1847.

themselves as peaceable members of the civil government, for which reason they have hitherto submitted to various ecclesiastical burdens and restrictions that are inconsistent with equal liberty. But now, when the many and grievous oppressions of our mother-country have laid this Continent under the necessity of casting off the yoke of tyranny, and of forming independent governments upon equitable and liberal foundations, we flatter ourselves, that we shall be freed from all the encumbrances which a spirit of domination, prejudice, or bigotry has interwoven with most other political systems. This we are the more strongly encouraged to expect by the Declaration of Rights, so universally applauded for that dignity, firmness, and precision with which it delineates and asserts the privileges of society, and the prerogatives of human nature; and which we embrace as the Magna Charta of our commonwealth, that can never be violated without endangering the grand superstructure it was designed to sustain. Therefore, we rely upon this Declaration, as well as the justice of our honorable Legislature, to secure us the free exercise of religion according to the dictates of our consciences; and we should fall short in our duty to ourselves, and the many and numerous congregations under our care, were we, upon this occasion, to neglect laying before you a statement of the religious grievances under which we have hitherto labored, that they may no longer be continued in our present form of government.

It is well known that in the frontier counties, which are justly supposed to contain a fifth part of the inhabitants of Virginia, the dissenters have borne the heavy burdens of purchasing glebes, building churches and supporting the established clergy, where there are very few Episcopalians, either to assist in bearing the expense, or to reap the advantage; and that throughout the other parts of the country there are also many thousands of zealous friends and defenders of our State, who, besides the invidious, and disadvantageous restrictions to which they have been subjected, annually pay large taxes to support an establishment from which their consciences and principles oblige them to dissent: all which are confessedly so many violations of their natural rights; and in their consequences, a restraint upon freedom of inquiry, and private judgment.

In this enlightened age, and in a land where all of every denomination are united in the most strenuous efforts to be free, we hope and expect that our representatives will cheerfully concur in removing every species of religious, as well as civil bondage. Certain it is, that every argument for civil liberty, gains additional strength when applied to liberty in the concerns of religion; and there is no argument in favor of establishing the Christian religion, but what may be pleaded, with equal propriety, for establishing the tenets of Mohammed by those who believe the Alcoran; or, if this be not true, it is at least impossible for the magistrate to adjudge the right of preference among the various sects that profess the Christian faith, without erecting a claim to infallibility, which would lead us back to the Church of Rome.

We beg leave farther to represent, that religious establishments are highly injurious to the temporal interests of any community. Without insisting upon the ambition and the arbitrary practices of those who are favored by government, or the intriguing, seditious spirit which is commonly excited by this, as well as by every other kind of oppression, such establishments greatly retard population, and, consequently, the progress of arts, sciences, and manufactures. Witness the rapid growth and improvement of the Northern provinces compared with this. No one can deny that the more early settlement, and the many superior advantages of our country, would have invited multitudes of artificers, mechanics, and other useful members of society, to fix their habitation among us, who have either remained in their place of nativity, or preferred worse civil governments, and a more barren soil, where they might enjoy the rights of conscience more fully than they have a prospect of doing in this. From which we infer that Virginia might have now been the capital of America, and a match for the British arms, without depending on others for the necessaries of war, had it not been prevented by her religious establishment.

Neither can it be made to appear that the Gospel needs any such civil aid. We rather conceive that, when our blessed Saviour declares his kingdom is not of this world, he renounces all dependence upon state power; and as his weapons are spiritual, and were only designed to have influence on the judgement and heart of man, we are persuaded that if mankind were left in the quiet possession of their inalienable religious privileges, Christianity, as in the days of the Apostles, would continue to prevail and flourish in the greatest purity by its own native excellence, and under the all-disposing providence of God.

We would also humbly represent, that the only proper objects of civil government are the happiness and protection of men in the present state of existence; the security of the life, liberty, and property of the citizens, and to restrain the vicious and encourage the virtuous by wholesome laws, equally extending to every individual; but that the duty which we owe to our Creator, and the manner of discharging it, can only be directed by reason and conviction and is nowhere cognizable but at the tribunal of the universal Judge.

Therefore, we ask no ecclesiastical establishment for ourselves; neither can we approve of them when granted to others. This, indeed, would be giving exclusive or separate emoluments or privileges to one set of men, without any special public services, to the common reproach and injury of every other denomination. And, for the reasons recited, we are induced earnestly to entreat that all laws now in force in this commonwealth, which contenance religious domination, may be speedily repealed; that all, of every religious sect may be protected in the full exercise of their several modes of worship; exempted from all taxes for the support of any Church whatsoever, farther than what may be agreeable to their own private choice or voluntary obligation. This being done, all partial and invidious distinctions will be abolished, to the great honor and interest of the State, and every one be left to stand or fall according to his merit, which can never be the case so long as any one denomination is established in preference to others.

That the great sovereign of the universe may inspire you with unanimity, wisdom, and resolution and bring you to a just determination on all the important concerns before you is the fervent prayer of your memorialists."[1]

The Synod of 1777 renewed its appointment of a day of public humiliation, fasting, and prayer, considering "the low and declining state of religion among us, and the abounding of iniquity, for which an holy and jealous God yet continues to visit our country with righteous judgements."[2] The year 1778 saw the British in possession of Philadelphia and the Synod was held at Bedminster. It resolved that:

"The Synod, taking into their most serious consideration, that the lamentable decay of vital piety, for which we have had so much reason to mourn for several years past, still continues; that gross immoralities are increasing to an awful degree; and that the calamities of war are yet permitted to afflict our land, do therefore agree to renew the recommendation of last Synod to all our congregations, to spend the last Thursday of every month, or a part of it, in fervent prayer to God, that he would be pleased to pour out his Spirit on the inhabitants of our land, and prepare us for deliverance from the chastenings he hath righteously inflicted upon us for our sins; that he would graciously smile on our arms, and those of our illustrious ally, by land and sea; and grant a speedy and happy conclusion to the present war. And it is earnestly recommended to the several Presbyteries, to take care that this recommendation be complied with . . . . . .[3]

[1] Foote, *Sketches of Virginia*, pp. 323-324.
[2] *Records.*, p. 478.
[3] *Ibid.*, pp. 481-482.

Adjourned to meet at Philadelphia on the third Wednesday of next May at 10 o'clock, A. M. — but if that place be in the enemy's hand, then to meet here."

The Synods of 1779, 1780 and 1781, meeting in Philadelphia, repeated practically the same formula.[1] Official interest in the fate of the American cause was never lacking, and the weight of the Synod was thrown into the scales where it appeared to them it would avail most.

A very large percentage of the individual leaders of the Revolution were Presbyterians. Education for spiritual leadership accounts in large part for the prominence of individual Presbyterians. Their college, The College of New Jersey (Princeton), thus early, clearly recognized the important connection between religious education and politics. It was to furnish a larger number of men to act as leaders in the political movements of the times than any other American college. Nine of its alumni were members of the Federal Constitutional Convention in 1787; namely, Alexander Martin of North Carolina, Luther Martin of Maryland, Oliver Ellsworth of Connecticut, William Patterson of New Jersey, Gunning Bedford of Delaware, James Madison of Virginia, William Davie of North Carolina, and Jonathan Dayton of New Jersey; Edmund Randolph of Virginia had also been a student at the college. Joseph Reed, Washington's Military Secretary, was another alumnus. The college president, John Witherspoon, was closely identified with all the political movements of the times. In fact, Witherspoon's keen interest in things political gave to the College of New Jersey the character of a training school of political science.

But all Presbyterians were interested in politics. Prominent among the non-Princeton Presbyterian element

[1] *Records*, pp. 483, 488, 491.

to be found in the Federal Constitutional Convention were the following:

William Livingston of New Jersey, a member of the First and Second Continental Congresses, and Governor from 1776 to 1780.

James Wilson, a signer of the Declaration of Independence, and later a justice of the United States Supreme Court.

Thomas McKean, a member of the Pennsylvania Assembly from 1765 to 1782.

Charles Thomson, characterized by John Adams as "the Sam Adams of Philadelphia, the life of the cause of liberty," and the secretary to Continental Congress from 1774 to 1789.

The most powerful single "Princeton" influence in the Revolution was President John Witherspoon, styled by John Adams, the "animated Son of Liberty."

Although Witherspoon did not arrive in America until 1768, so quickly did he enter into the spirit of this new world, so completely did he identify himself with its modes and aspirations, and so powerfully did he contribute to its intellectual leadership that we must concede him the foremost place among the leaders of Revolutionary American Presbyterianism.[1] A direct descendant of John Knox, Witherspoon had inherited the militant political ecclesiastical tradition of Scotland; and he was trained for ecclesiastical politics and practiced them until he was called from Scotland to Princeton in 1768. His fame had already been established.

At Princeton he was to gain even greater repute as a statesman and a patriot. He guided with uncommon success the course of education in this institution until the Revolution suspended its functions. His reputation attracted to it some of the brightest and noblest of America's youth. Bancroft tells us, "It was from Witherspoon of

[1] Sprague, *Annals*, vol. iii, p. 289; Sanderson, *The Signers*, vol. v. pp. 116-157. "President Witherspoon in the American Revolution," *American Historical Review*, vol. 1. No. 4, pp. 671-679.

New Jersey that Madison imbibed the lesson of perfect freedom in matters of conscience."[1] At the memorial service for Witherspoon, at Princeton in 1795, Rev. John Rodgers, asserted that "more than thirty members of the Congress of the United States, since the formation of that illustrious body, have been sons of the College of New Jersey."[2] To Witherspoon's instruction America owes many of her most distinguished patriots and legislators. He was the first of that long line of American college presidents who illustrate in a high degree the possibilities of college service for political leadership.

Under Witherspoon's guidance or influenced by his teachings, was formed a large proportion of the early clergy of the Presbyterian Church in the United States. Later we shall note his great influence in shaping the organization of the American Church.[3] Even greater were his achievements as a practical politician, a member of the Continental Congress. The closing of his college transferred the educator to the world of active politics. In 1774 he met with the Committee at New Brunswick and with William Livingston labored to instruct their delegates that the tea should not be paid for. The matter was left to the general congress, but William Livingston was selected as delegate.[4]

The provincial congress of New Jersey in session to frame a new constitution, opened, June 11, 1776, with a prayer by John Witherspoon, a regularly chosen member of that body, and from then until the close of the Revolution, Witherspoon was busy applying the Presbyterian theories of republicanism to the constitution of new civil

[1] Bancroft, *op. cit.*, vol. v, p. 123.
[2] Rodgers, *The Faithful Servant Rewarded*, pp. 1-3.
[3] *Infra*, pp. 260-282.
[4] Bancroft, *History of the United States*, vol. iv, p. 33.

governments. Judge Elmer tells us that, "It has always been understood that the Rev. Dr. John Witherspoon . . took an active part in preparing it (the constitution of New Jersey, adopted July 2, 1776). There were two eminent lawyers, Jonathan Dickinson Sergeant, and John Cleves Symmes, on the committee to draft the constitution, but the chairman was the Rev. Jacob Green, the Presbyterian minister of Hanover, and the instrument bears quite as prominent marks of clerical as of legal authorship."[1] This same provincial congress resolved to reënforce the army of New York with thirty-three hundred of the New Jersey militia.

Five friends of independence were elected to represent New Jersey in Continental Congress; Richard Stockton, Abraham Clark, John Hart, Francis Hopkinson, and John Witherspoon. New Jersey exerted great weight in the final contest for independence. On July 1, 1776, near the end of the debate on the subject, John Witherspoon rose and in a short speech remarked that though he had not heard all the discussion in that body, yet he had not wanted ample sources of information; and that, in his judgment, the country was not only ripe for independence, but was in danger of becoming rotten for want of it, if its declaration were longer delayed.[2] In a letter of March 20, 1780, to a friend in Scotland, Witherspoon remarked, "Were our condition ten times worse than it is, nothing short of the clear independence of this country would be accepted." Witherspoon was a signer of the Declaration of Independence, and continued a member of Congress till 1783.

[1] Elmer, *Reminiscences of New Jersey*; Bancroft, *op. cit.*, vol. iv, p. 431-432.

[2] Bancroft, *op. cit.*, vol. iv, p. 440; Breed *Presbyterians and the Revolution* p. 166; Smyth, *Presbyterians in the Revolution*, p. 31.

Witherspoon signed the Articles of Confederation on behalf of his state, November 26, 1778. In discussing the articles in 1776 he said, "All agree that there must be a confederation for this war; in the enlightened state of men's minds, I hope for a lasting one. Our greatest danger is of disunion among ourselves. Nothing will come before congress but what respects colonies and not individuals. Every colony is a distinct person; and, if an equal vote be refused, the smaller states will be vassals to the larger."[1] But Witherspoon soon came to realize that a stronger union was needed than that provided for by the Article, particularly as to control of Commerce and Revenues. In Congress on February 3, 1781, he proposed to clothe that body with authority to regulate commerce and to lay duties upon imported articles. The idea was accepted and it was agreed that it was indispensably necessary for the states to vest in Congress a power to levy a duty of five per cent on imports of articles of foreign growth and manufacture. But as the separate approval of each of the thirteen states was necessary before this could become a law, it was never adopted.[2]

Witherspoon in Congress was a member of the committee on foreign affairs, a member of the board of war, a member of the secret committee, also of the committees of finance, supplies for the army, and various special committees. In November 1776, one of the darkest periods of war, when our armies had retreated to Jersey, discouraged and poorly supplied, with enlistments expiring, he was made one of a committee of three to repair to the Headquarters of General Washington to consult,

[1] *Secret Journals of Congress,* vol. i, pp. 290-315; Bancroft, *op. cit.,* vol. v, p. 13.

[2] Bancroft, *op. cit.,* vol. v, p. 453.

and to render assistance in recruiting the regiments whose terms had expired or were about to expire, and also to "inquire into and redress to the utmost of their power the just grievances of the soldiers." On December 9, 1776, he was placed on a committee with Richard Henry Lee and Samuel Adams "to prepare an address to the inhabitants of America and a recommendation to the several states to appoint a day of fasting, humiliation, and prayer." In 1778, with three others, he was appointed to prepare a *manifesto* on the brutal treatment of American prisoners by the British. Their report was adopted by Congress.

Perhaps his greatest work was in connection with the finances of the country. In 1778 he was put on the committee on finances with Robert Morris, Elbridge Gerry, Richard Henry Lee, and Gouverneur Morris. Every emission of paper currency, after the first or second, he opposed. He even hazarded his popularity for a time by the vigor of his opposition. Afterwards, at the insistence of some of the very gentlemen who had opposed him in Congress, he published his ideas on the nature, value and uses of money in a most clear and judicious essay, *Essay on Money, as a medium of commerce; with remarks, on the advantages and disadvantages of paper admitted into general circulation, by a citizen of the United States.*[1] Witherspoon's conception of the basis of a sound financial policy for the United States ante-dates those of Alexander Hamilton.

Witherspoon served as a member of the Provincial Assembly of New Jersey in 1776, as a member of the state

[1] Witherspoon, *Essay on Money as a Medium of Commerce; with remarks on the advantages and disadvantages of paper admitted into general circulation; by a citizen of the United States.* Philadelphia, 1786.

senate in 1780, as a member of the state assembly in 1783, and as a member of the Constitutional assembly in 1789.

His literary remains furnish us with a wealth of sound patriotism.[1] Noteworthy are the following:

"For my own part, of property I have some, of reputation more: that reputation is staked, that property is pledged, on the issue of this contest. And although these grey hairs must soon descend into the sepulchre, I would infinitely rather that they should descend thither by the hand of the executioner than desert at this crisis, the sacred cause of my country."[2] (This quotation is inscribed on the Witherspoon monument in Fairmount Park, Philadelphia.)

"There is not a single instance in history in which civil liberty was lost, and religious liberty preserved entire. If, therefore, we yield up our temporal property, we at the same time deliver the conscience into bondage."[3]

"The question then is: Shall we make resistance with the greatest force, — as rebel subjects of a government which we acknowledge or as independent states against an usurped power which we detest and abhor."[4]

"Can any person of a liberal mind wish that these great and growing countries should be brought back to a state of subjection to a distant power? And can any man deny that, if they had yielded to the claims of the British Parliament, they would have been no better than a parcel of tributary states, ruled by lordly tyrants, and exhausted by unfeeling pensioners, under the commission of one too distant to hear the cry of oppression, and surrounded by those who had an interest in deceiving him."[5]

"Is there a probable prospect of reconciliation on constitutional principles? What are those constitutional principles? Will anybody show that Great Britian can be sufficiently sure of our dependence, and yet be sure of our liberties?"[6]

"It ought, therefore, in my opinion, to meet with the cordial approbation of every impartial person, as I am confident it will of posterity,

[1] *Works of John Witherspoon, D.D., LL.D., To Which is prefixed an account of the author's life.* By Rev. Dr. John Rogers. 9 vols. Edinburg, 1815.

[2] *Proceedings and Addresses at the Laying of the Corner-Stone and at the unveiling of the statue to John Witherspoon on Fairmount Park,* Philadelphia. Compiled by the Rev. William P. Breed, D.D., Philadelphia.

[3] *Works,* vol. v, p. 203.

[4] *Ibid.*, vol. ix, p. 92.

[5] *Ibid.*, vol. v, p. 224.

[6] *Ibid.*, vol. ix, p. 97.

that they have united for common defence, and resolved that they will be both free and independent, because they cannot be the one without the other."[1]

"As to American Independence, I mean to show, — 1. That it was necessary. 2. That it will be honorable and profitable. And 3. That in all probability it will be no injury, but a real advantage, to the island of Great Britain."[2]

"I am much mistaken if the time is not just at hand when there shall be greater need than ever in America for the most accurate discussion of the principles of society, the rights of nations, and the policy of the states. For only by making a people 'virtuous' can they be made 'invincible'."[3]

"For what would it signify to risk our possessions and shed our blood to set ourselves free from the encroachments and oppression of Great Britain, with a certainty, as soon as peace was settled with them of a more lasting war, a more unnatural, more bloody, and more hopeless war, among the colonies themselves."[4]

"It is not impossible, that in future times all the states on one quarter of the globe, may see it proper by some plan of union, to perpetuate security and peace: and sure I am, a well planned confederacy among the states of America, may hand down the blessings of peace and public order to many generations."[5]

The greatest of all the Witherspoon utterances in point of influence was the sermon which he preached at Princeton, May 17, 1776, this "Being the General Fast Appointed by the Congress throughout the United Colonies," on the subject *The Dominion of Providence over the Passions of Men.* This sermon gives a calm and striking statement of the reasons for America's demand of the right to control her own affairs. It was much read on both sides of the Atlantic; and at Glasgow it was sent forth embellished with notes of indignation wherein the author was called a rebel and a traitor.[6] The sermon

[1] *Works* of John Witherspoon, vol. v, p. 224.
[2] *Ibid.*, vol. v, p. 224.
[3] *Ibid.*, vol. ix, p. 231.
[4] *Ibid.*, vol. iv, p. 348.
[5] *Ibid.*, vol. iv, p. 351.
[6] Sprague, *Annals*, vol, iii, pp. 293-294.

bears the following dedication: "To the Honorable John Hancock, Esq., President of the Congress of the United States of America; in Testimony of the Highest Esteem for his personal character and public Conduct the following sermon is humbly inscribed by his most obedient humble servant the Author."[1]

"We are now putting on the harness, and entering upon an important contest, the length of which it is impossible to foresee and the issue of which it will perhaps be thought presumptuous to foretell. But as the truth, with respect to God's moral government, is the same and unchangeable; as the issue, in the case of Sennacherib's invasion, did but lead the prophet to acknowledge it; our duty and interest conspire in calling upon us to improve it.

The ambition of mistaken princes, the cunning and cruelty of oppressive and corrupt ministers, and even the inhumanity of brutal soldiers, however dreadful, shall finally promote the glory of God, and in the meantime, while the storm continues, his mercy and kindness shall appear in prescribing bounds to their rage and fury.

What ground there is to give praise to God for his favors already bestowed on us, respecting the public cause. It would be a criminal inattention not to observe the singular interposition of providence hitherto, in behalf of the American colonies. It is, however, impossible for me in a single discourse, as well as improper at this time to go through every step of our past transactions . . . . . How many discoveries have been made of the designs of enemies in Britain and among ourselves, in a manner so unexpected to us as to them, and in such season as to prevent their effect? What surprising successes have attended our encounters in almost every instance? Has not the boasted discipline of regular and veteran soldiers been turned into confusion and dismay before the new and maiden courage of freemen in defence of their property and their right? . . . . . The shameful flight of the army and navy of Britain, was brought without the loss of a man. To all this we may add, that the counsels of our enemies have been visibly confounded, so that I believe I may say with truth, that there is hardly any steps which they have taken, but it has operated strongly against themselves, and been more in our favor than if they had followed a contrary course.

I look upon ostentation and confidence to be a sort of outrage upon

[1] *The Dominion of Providence over the Passions of Men, A Sermon preached at Princeton on the 17th of May, 1776,* by John Witherspoon. Philadelphia, 1776; *Works,* vol. v, pp. 176-216.

providence, and when it becomes general, and infuses itself into the spirit of a people, it is a forerunner of destruction.

I do not mean to speak prophetically, but agreeably to the analogy of faith, and the principles of God's moral government. Some have observed that true religion, and in her dominion, riches, literature, and arts, have taken their course in a slow and gradual manner, from East to West since the earth was settled after the flood, and from thence forebode the future glory of America. I leave this as a matter rather of conjecture than certainty, but observe, that if your cause is just, if your principles are pure, — and if your conduct is prudent, you need not fear the multitude of opposing hosts.

You are all my witnesses, that this is the first time of my introducing any political subject into the pulpit. At this season, however, it is not only lawful but necessary, and I willingly embrace the opportunity of declaring my opinion without any hesitation, that the cause in which America is now in arms, is the cause of justice, of liberty, and of human nature. So far as we have hitherto proceeded, I am satisfied that the confederacy of the colonies, has not been the effect of pride, resentment, or sedition, but of a deep and general conviction, that our civil and *religious* liberties, and consequently in a great measure the temporal and eternal happiness of us and our posterity depended on the issue . . . . *There is not a single instance in history in which civil liberty was lost and religious liberty preserved entire.* If, therefore, we yield up our temporal property, we at the same time deliver the conscience into bondage.

You shall not, my brethren, hear from me in the pulpit, what you have never heard from me in conversation; I mean railing at the king personally, or even his ministers and the parliament, and people of Britain, as so many barbarous savages. Many of their actions have probably been worse than their intentions. That they should desire unlimited dominion if they can obtain or preserve it, is neither new nor wonderful. I do not refuse submission to their unjust claims, because they are corrupt or profligate, although probably many of them are so, but because they are men, and therefore liable to all the selfish bias inseparable from human nature. I call this claim unjust of making laws to bind in all cases whatsoever, because they are separated from us, independent of us, and have an interest in opposing us. Would any man who could prevent it, give up his estate, person, and family, to the disposal of his neighbor, although he had liberty to choose the wisest and the best master? Surely not! This is the true and proper hinge of the controversy between Great Britain and America. It is, however, to be added, that such is their distance from us, that a wise and prudent administration of our affairs is as impossible as the claim of authority is unjust. Such is and must be their ignorance of the state of things here, so much time must elapse before an error can be seen and remedied, and so much injustice and partiality must be expected from the arts and misrepresentation of interested persons, that for these colonies to depend wholly upon the legislature of Great Britain, would be like many other oppressive connections, injury to the master, and ruin to the slave.

The management of the war itself on their part, would furnish new proof of this, if any were needful. Is it not manifest with what absurdity and impropriety they have conducted their own designs? We have nothing so much to fear as dissension, and they have by wanton and unnecessary cruelty forced us into union. At the same time to let us see what we have to expect, and what would be the fatal consequences of unlimited submission, they have uniformly called those acts *Lenity*, which filled this whole continent with resentment and horror. The ineffable disdain expressed by our fellow subjects, in saying, 'That he would not hearken to America, till she was at his feet,' has armed more men, and inspired more deadly rage, than could have been done by laying waste a whole province with fire and sword. Again, we wanted not number, but time, and they sent over handful after handful, till we were ready to oppose a multitude greater than they had to send. In fine, if there was one place stronger than the rest, and more able and willing to resist, there they made the attack, and left the others till they were duly informed, completely incensed, and fully furnished with every instrument of war.

I mention these things . . . . . as decisive proofs of the impossibility of these great and growing states, being safe and happy when every part of their internal polity is dependent on Great Britain. If, on account of their distance, and ignorance of our situation, they could not conduct their own quarrel with propriety for one year, how can they give direction and vigor to every department of our civil constitutions from age to age? . . . . . There is a certain distance from the seat of government, where an attempt to rule will either produce tyranny and helpless subjection, or provoke resistance and effect a separation.

I have said, if your principles are pure. The meaning of this is, if your present opposition to the claims of the British ministry does not arise from a seditious and turbulent spirit, or a wanton contempt of legal authority; from a blind and factious attachment to particular persons or parties, or from a selfish, rapacious disposition, and a desire to turn public confusion to private profit — but from a concern for the interest of your country, and the safety of yourself and your posterity. On this subject I cannot help observing, that though it would be a miracle if there were not many selfish persons among us, and discoveries now and then made of mean and interested transactions, yet they have been comparatively inconsiderable both in number and effect. In general, there has been so great a degree of public spirit, that we have much more reason to be thankful for its vigor and prevalence, than to wonder at the few appearances of dishonesty and disaffection. It would be very uncandid to ascribe the universal ardor that has prevailed among all ranks of men, and the spirited exertions in the most distant colonies to any thing else than public spirit. Nor was there ever perhaps in history so general a commotion from which religious differences have been so entirely excluded. Nothing of this kind has as yet been heard, except of late in the absurd, but malicious and detestable attemps of our few remaining enemies to introduce them. At the same time, I must also for the honor of this country observe, that though government in the ancient forms has been so long unhinged, and in some colonies not sufficient care taken to substitute another in its place; yet has there been, by common consent, a much greater degree of order and public peace, than men of reflexion and experience foretold or expected. From all these circumstances, I conclude favorably of the principles of the friends of liberty, and do earnestly exhort you to adopt and act upon those which have been described, and resist the influence of every other.

Once more, if to the justice of your cause, and the purity of your principles, you add prudence in your conduct, there will be the greatest reason to hope, by the blessing of God, for prosperity and success. I have chiefly in view union, firmness and patience. Everybody must perceive the absolute necessity of union. It is indeed in everybody's mouth, and therefore instead of attempting to convince you of its importance, I will only caution you against the usual causes of division. If persons of every rank, instead of implicitly complying with the orders of those whom they themselves have chosen to direct, will needs judge every measure over again, when it comes to be put in execution; if different classes of men intermix their little private views, or clashing interests with public affairs, and marshal into parties, the merchant against the landowner, and the landlord against the merchant; if local provincial pride and jealousy arise, and you allow yourselves to speak with contempt of the courage, character, manners, or even language of particular places, you are doing a greater injury to the common cause, than you are aware of. If such practices are admitted among us, I shall look upon it as one of the most dangerous symptoms and if they become general, a presage of approaching ruin.

By firmness and patience, I mean a resolute adherence to the duty, and laying your account with many difficulties, as well as occasional disappointment. In a former part of this discourse, I have cautioned you against ostentation and vain glory. Be pleased farther to observe that extremes often beget one another, the same persons who exult extravagantly of success, are generally most liable to despondent timidity on every little inconsiderable defeat. Men of this character are the bane and corruption of every society or party to which they belong, but they are especially the ruin of an army, if suffered to continue in it. Remember the vicissitude of human things, and the usual course of providence. How often has a just cause been reduced to the lowest ebb, and yet when firmly adhered to, has become finally triumphant. I speak this now while the affairs of the colonies are in so prosperous a state, lest this prosperity itself, should render you less able to bear unexpected misfortunes . . . . The sum of the whole is . . . that the blessing of God is only to be looked for by those who are not wanting in the discharge of their duty . . . .

* * * * *

A good form of government may hold the rotten materials together for some time, but beyond a certain pitch, even the best constitution will be ineffectual, and slavery must ensue. On the other hand, when the manners of a nation are pure, when true religion and internal principles maintain their vigor, the attemps of the most powerful enemies to oppress them are commonly baffled and disappointed.

* * * * *

He is the best friend to American liberty, who is most sincere and active in promoting true and undefiled religion, and who sets himself with the greatest firmness to bear down profanity and immorality.

* * * * *

We have sometimes taken the liberty to forebode the downfall of the British Empire, from the corruption and degeneracy of the people. Unhappily the British soldiers have been distinguished among all the nations in Europe, for the most shocking profanity.

* * * * *

I exhort all who are not called to go into the field, to apply themselves with the utmost diligence to works of industry. It is in your power by this means not only to supply the necessities, but to add to the strength of your country. Habits of industry prevailing in a society, not only increase its wealth, as their immediate effect, but they prevent the introduction of many vices, and are intimately connected with sobriety and good morals . . . . . The active farmer who rises with the dawn and follows his team or plow, must in the end be an overmatch for those effeminate and delicate soldiers, who are nursed in the lap of self-indulgence, and whose greatest exertion is in the important preparation for, and tedious attendance on, a masquerade, or midnight ball.

* * * * *

In the last place, suffer me to recommend to you frugality in your families, and every other article of expense. This the state of things among us renders absolutely necessary, and it stands in the most immediate connection both with virtuous industry, and active public spirit Temperance in meals, moderation and decency in dress, furniture and equipage, have I think, generally been characteristics of a distinguished patriot. And when the same spirit prevades a people in general, they are fit for every duty, and able to encounter the most formidable enemy. The general subject of the preceding discourse has been the wrath of man praising God. If the unjust oppression of your enemies, which withholds from you many of the usual articles of luxury, and magnificence, shall contribute to make you clothe yourselves and your children with the works of your own hands, and cover your tables with the salutary productions of your own soil, it will be a new illustration of the same truth, and a real happiness to yourselves and your country.

* * * * *

Upon the whole, I beseech you to make a wise improvement of the present threatening aspect of public affairs, and to remember that your duty to God, to your country, to your families, and to yourselves, is the same. True religion is nothing else but an inward temper and outward conduct suited to your state and circumstances in providence at any time. And as peace with God and conformity to him, adds to the sweetness of created comforts while we possess them, so in times of difficulty and trial, it is in the man of piety and inward principle, that we may expect to find the uncorrupted patriot, the useful citizen, and the invincible soldier . . . . God grant that in America true religion and civil liberty may be inseparable, and that the unjust attempts to destroy the one, may in the issue tend to the support and establishment of both."

Text: *Psalm* lxxvi, 10. "Surely the wrath of Man shall praise thee; the remainder of Wrath shalt thou restrain."

How fortunate it was for the American cause that this clear-headed thinker, this expert in the art of popular expression, this moulder of public opinion was in full sympathy with those deep human currents of patriotic thought and feeling that then swept towards an independent national life for this land. Capable beyond most men of seeing the historic and cosmopolitan significance of the movement, he had the moral greatness to risk even his own great favor with the American people, by telling them that the acquisition of independence was not everything, that even greater perils than Red-Coats and

Hessians were to be met with in the form of shallow and anarchical politics, unscrupulous partnership, incompetence, selfishness, and disregard of moral obligations. Under such leadership the churches of America were the great stabilizers of political institutions during that period of disruption and anarchy which followed the breakdown of British control. Law and order prevailed through the efforts of the moral leadership of the churches.

Another power in Presbyterian Revolutionary leadership was George Duffield, one of the chaplains of Continental Congress, pastor of the Third Presbyterian Church in Philadelphia. His staunch opinions touching the great dispute drew to his church many of the leaders of the Revolutionary movement. John Adams attended, June 11, 1775, and wrote home to his wife, "I have been this morning to hear Mr. Duffield, a preacher in this city, whose principles, prayers, and sermons more nearly resemble those of our New England clergy than any that I have heard. His discourse was a kind of exposition on the thirty-fifth chapter of *Isaiah*. America was the wilderness, and the solitary place, and he said it would be glad, 'rejoice and blossom as the rose.' He labored 'to strengthen the weak hands and confirm the feeble knees.' He said to them that were of a fearful heart, 'Be strong, fear not. Behold, your God will come with vengeance, even God with a recompense; he will come and save you' . . . . . He applied the whole prophecy to this country, and gave us as animating an entertainment as I ever heard. He filled and swelled the bosom of every hearer."[1] About six weeks later, Adams wrote again, "This day I have heard my parish priest, Mr. Duffield, from *2 Chronicles*, xv, 1, 2. This gentleman never fails to adapt his discourse to

[1] *Familiar Letters of John Adams and His Wife*, p. 65.

the times. He pressed upon his audience the necessity of piety and virtue, in the present times of adversity, and held up to their view the army before Boston as an example . . . . . You may well suppose that this language was exceedingly pleasing to me."[1]

On the National Fast Day, May 17, 1776, Duffield drew a parallel between George III and Pharaoh. He joined the army around New York as chaplain for the summer of 1776, remaining with them throughout the whole of that disastrous campaign.[2] Returning to Philadelphia in the fall, just before Trenton, he publicly "rebuked his people because there were so many men in the house, saying there 'would be one less to-morrow, and no lecture on Wednesday evening'."[3]

The Tory satirist, Odell, thus describes Duffield:

> "A saint of old, as learned monks have said,
> Preached to the fish — the fish his voice obeyed.
> The same good man convened the grunting herd —
> Who bowed obedient to his powerful word.
> Such energy had truth, in days of yore;
> Falsehood and nonsense, in our days, have more.
> Duffield avows them to be all in all,
> And mounts or quits the pulpit, at their call.
> In vain 'New Light' displays her heavenly shine,
> In vain attract him oracles divine:
> Chaplain of Congress give him to become,
> Light may be dark, and oracles be dumb.
> It pleased Saint Anthony to preach to brutes—
> To preach to devils best with Duffield suits."[4]

Duffield was a preacher rather than a publicist; only one of his sermons is extant, a sermon preached in his own church on the 11th of December, 1783, the day of national thanksgiving for deliverance and peace.[1]

John Rodgers, pastor of the old Wall Street Presbyterian Church, is another shining example of the patriotic Presbyterian preacher.[2] He served in turn as Chaplain of General Heath's brigade, Chaplain of the Convention of the State of New York, Chaplain of the Council of Safety, and Chaplain of the First Legislature of New York State. This evidences his popularity as a preacher. He was a trustee of the College of New Jersey and was selected to preach the memorial sermon for its late president, in 1795.[3] Next to Witherspoon he was the most notable figure in American Presbyterianism. He numbered among his parishioners:

> Peter Van Burg Livingston, a brother of William Livingston, a founder of the College of New Jersey, a member and president of the First Provincial Congress of New York, 1775, and a member of the Second Provincial Congress, 1775-1776.
>
> Alexander McDougal, author of *A Son of Liberty to the Betrayed Inhabitants of the Colony,* president of the meeting in 1774, that elected the delegates to the first Continental Congress, Colonel, Brigadier General and Major General in the Continental Army, a member of Continental Congress, 1781-1782 and 1784-1785, elected Minister of Marine, thereby becoming our first Secretary of Navy, and New York State Senator, 1783-1786.

Dr. Rodgers's most famous sermon was the one of December 11, 1783, the day of public national thanksgiving, on *The Divine Goodness Displayed in the American Revolution,*[4] from the text, *Psalms* cxxv, 3: "The

[1] Duffield, *A Sermon Preached in the Third Presbyterian Church in the city of Philadelphia, Thursday, December 11, 1783.* Philadelphia, 1784. Reprinted in *The Patriotic Preachers of the American Revolution.* pp. 344-368.

[2] Miller, Samuel, *Memoir of the Rev. John Rodgers,* Philadelphia, 1840.

[3] *Supra,* p. 83.

[4] Rodgers, John, *The Divine Goodness Displayed in the American Revolution, A Sermon preached December 11th, 1783, A Day of public*

Lord hath done great things for us, whereof we are glad." There are two noteworthy features of this sermon, its indictment of the British war on American churches and its vision of the future of America:

"It is much to be lamented, that the troops of a nation that has been considered as one of the bulwarks of the Reformation, should act as if they had waged war with the God whom Christians adore. They have, in the course of this war, utterly destroyed more than fifty places of public worship, in these states. Most of these they burnt, others they leveled to the ground, and in some places left not a vestige of their former situation; while they have wantonly defaced, or rather destroyed others, by converting them into barracks, jails, hospitals, riding schools, etc. Boston, Newport, Philadelphia, and Charleston, all furnished melancholy instances of this prostitution and abuse of the house of God; and of the nineteen places of public worship in this city (New York) when the war began, there were but nine fit for use, when the British troops left it.

It is true, Trinity Church, and the old Lutheran, were destroyed by fire, that laid waste so great a part of the city, a few nights after the enemy took possession of it; and therefore, they are not charged with designedly burning them, though they were the occasion of it; for there can be no doubt, after all that malice has said to the contrary, but the fire was occasioned by the carelessness of their people, and they prevented its more speedy extinguishment. But the ruinous situation in which they had left two of the Low Dutch Reformed Churches, the three Presbyterian Churches, the French Protestant Church, the Anabaptist Church, and the Friends new meeting house, was the effect of design, and strongly marks their enmity to those societies . . . . .

* * * * *

We have under the auspices of his holy providence, risen into existence, and taken our station among the nations, and the empires of the earth. An event of such magnitude, that it forms a new era in the history of mankind.

The eyes of the nations of the earth, and particularly the eyes of all Europe, are upon these States, to see what use they will make of the great things God has done for us . . . . . Would you reap the fruits of your toils, your losses and your blood; it is indispensably necessary that the federal union of these States be cemented and strengthened — that the honor of the Great Council of the nation be supported, and its

thanksgiving. N. Y., 1783. Reprinted in *Patriotic Preachers of the American Revolution*, pp. 312-343.

salutary measures carried into execution, with unanimity and dispatch without regard to partial views, or local interests — that the credit of this new empire be established on the principles of strictest justice and its faith maintained sacred and inviolable, in whatever way, or to whatever description of persons it has been pledged, or may at any time be pledged. Alas! that its glory has suffered so much already, by the failure of our currency. Let us carefully repair this waste of honor, if we cannot repair the waste of property, by the most sacred adherence to our engagements in all future time.

You will please to remember farther, that the virtue I recommend, both political and moral, is essential to the preservation of the clear-earned privilege in which we rejoice this day. This is especially the case in a democratic government and the more democratic the government, the more necessary."

Jacob Green, a graduate of Harvard in 1744, pastor of the Presbyterian Church of Hanover, New Jersey, was an early and fearless champion of independence. He not only preached it from his pulpit, but he is reputed to have published a pamphlet thereon. Green was made chairman of the committee which drafted the constitution of the state of New Jersey in 1776, and doubtlessly influenced the nature of that document considerably.[1]

John Miller of Dover preached, before the Declaration of Independence, from the text "We have no part in David, nor any inheritance in the son of Jesse: to your tents, O Israel!" Robert Davidson of the First Presbyterian Church of Philadelphia, preached from the text, "For there fell down many slain because the war was of God." Other patriotic Presbyterian preachers to be noted are: Patrick Alison of Baltimore, John Blair and James Waddell of Virginia.

Then there were the fighting elders: Generals Morgan and Pickens at Cowpens, and Colonels Campbell, Williams, Cleaveland, Shelby, and Sevier at King's Mountain.

[1] Sprague, *Annals*, vol. iii, p. 138; Tyler, *op cit.*, vol. ii, p. 294; Bancroft, *op. cit.*, vol. iv, p. 432.

Alexander McWhorter of Newark, an alumnus of the College of New Jersey, was chaplain of Knox's brigade and was with Washington at the crossing of the Delaware. He was known as "one of the most able, learned and useful ministers in the American church." James Hall of North Carolina was a captain of cavalry as well as chaplain of a regiment. James Armstrong was of the Second Maryland brigade, Adam Boyd of the North Carolina brigade; and Daniel McCall was with the Canadian expedition.[1]

Among the Pennsylvania troops under Washington was a chaplain, named Hugh Henry Brackenridge, who was of the Class of 1771 of the College of New Jersey, with James Madison and Philip Freneau. He won fame for his patriotic essays:

"The Battle of Bunker Hill," a tragedy written in 1776.
"The Death of General Montgomery," 1777.
"Six Political Discourses Founded on Scripture," 1778, under the following sub-titles:
"The Bloody Vestiges of Tyranny."
"The Nature and Artifice of Toryism."
"The Fate of Tyranny and Toryism."
"The Agency of Heaven in the Cause of Liberty."
"The Blasphemy and Gasconade and Self-dependence in a Certain General."
"The Great Wrath of the Tyrant and the Cause of it."

These essays are choice specimens of imprecation according to the style of the Old Testament:

"Woe unto them, for they have rejected the frequency and humility of our petitions. They have been deaf to all entreaty, and the softest words of soft expostulation. They have pursued, without remorse, the dire intention to destroy us. They have pursued it in a cruel manner. They have warred with a rage unknown to civilized nations. They have mangled the bodies of our heroes on the field of battle. They have burned houses of religious worship. They have stabbed and shed the

[1] Gillette, *op. cit.*, pp. 186 sqq.; Briggs, *op. cit.*, p. 91 sq.; Blaikie, *op. cit.*, p. 175 sq; Smythe, *op. cit.*, p. 32 sq.

blood of unarmed and supplicating clergymen. This they have done to persons of the same language and religion with themselves. Woe unto them, for they have shed a brother's blood. They have gone in the way of Cain."[1]

The supreme knight and the great martyr of Presbyterianism, was pastor James Caldwell of the Presbyterian Church of Elizabeth, New Jersey, "the Rebel High Priest," "the Fighting Chaplain."[2] He has been made famous by the story, "Give 'em Watts!" It is told that at the Springfield engagement when the militia ran out of wadding for their muskets, Parson Caldwell, galloped to the Presbyterian Church, and returning with an armful of hymn-books, threw them on the ground, exclaiming, "Now, boys, give 'em Watts! Give 'em Watts!" Whether or not this legend is authentic, its currency reflects the influence of Caldwell. He was the pastor of one of the leading Presbyterian churches of New Jersey. His congregation was a famous one.

William Livingston was its chief personage.[3] As the editor of the "Watch Tower" section of the New York *Mercury*, he established an organ for the Presbyterian sentiments of America. In opposition to the establishment of an American episcopate, he wrote an open *Letter to the Right Reverend Father in God, John Lord, Bishop of Llandaff* (1768). He edited and in a large measure wrote the "American Whig" columns in the *New York Gazette* (1768-1769). His estate in New Jersey was known as

[1] Brackenridge, *Six Political Discourses*, p. 13.

[2] *Caldwell and the Revolution, a historical sketch of the First Church of Elizabeth prior to and during the war of the Revolution. Being a discourse delivered on Sunday, January 25th, 1880. The Centennial Anniversary of the Burning of the Church Edifice of the First Presbyterian Church of Elizabeth, New Jersey.* By Rev. Everard Kempshall, D.D., Elizabeth, N. J., 1880.

[3] Sedgwick, *Life of William Livingston;* Livingston, The *Livingstons of Livingston Manor*.

"Liberty Hall." He represented New Jersey in the first and second Continental Congresses (1774-1776), and was chosen first governor of the state, which office he filled until his death in 1790. He was a delegate to the Federal Constitutional Convention (1787) and there supported the New Jersey plan.

Elias Boudinot of Caldwell's congregation was deputy to the Provincial Congress of New Jersey from May to August 1775, and from May 1777 to July 1778 he was commissary-general of prisoners, with the rank of colonel, in the Continental Army. He was a member of Continental Congress in 1778, and from 1781 to 1783, — from 1782 to 1783 he was president of that body. For a short time he acted as Secretary of Foreign Affairs. From 1789 to 1795, he was a member of the national House of Representatives, and from 1795 to 1805 Director of the United States Mint at Philadelphia. He was a founder of the American Bible Society and served as a trustee of the College of New Jersey. He published *The Age of Revelation* (1790) in reply to Thomas Paine's *Age of Reason*. As president of the Continental Congress he officially signed the Treaty of Ratification of the Peace of Paris. He was a brother-in-law of Richard Stockton.[1]

Pastor Caldwell's congregation also contained Abraham Clark, a signer of the Declaration of Independence, member of the Provincial Council of New Jersey in 1775, member of Continental Congress, 1776-1778, 1781-1783, 1785-1788, delegate to the Annapolis Convention in 1786, and member of Congress 1791-1794. Then too there was Jonathan Dayton, a graduate of the College of New Jersey, member of the New Jersey Assembly, 1786-1787,

[1] Boudinot, *The Life, Public Services, Addresses and Letters of Elias Boudinot*. *Infra*. pp. 515-516.

member and speaker, 1790, member of the New Jersey Senate, 1789-1790, delegate to the Constitutional Convention, 1787, member of Congress, 1791-1799 and its speaker 1795-1799, and United States Senator, 1799-1805. Fully forty commissioned officers of the Continental Army were from this congregation.

To add to the fame of Caldwell, the British made martyrs of both himself and his wife. General Knyphausen's expedition took Elizabeth in 1780, burning Caldwell's church and shooting his wife. Later they shot Caldwell himself, claiming that it was by mistake.[1]

Dr. Inglis might well say, "I do not know one Presbyterian minister, nor have I been able, after strict inquiry, to hear of any, who did not by preaching and every effort in his power promote all the measures of the colonial congress, however extravagant."[2] The Presbyterians themselves at the close of the war expressed officially their gratification at the part they had played therein. The "Pastoral Letter" of the Synod of 1783, composed by Witherspoon, Spencer and Smith, read:

> "We cannot help congratulating you on the general and almost universal attachment of the Presbyterian body to the cause of liberty and the rights of mankind. This has been visible in their conduct, and has been confessed by the complaints and resentment of the common enemy. Such a circumstance ought not only to afford us satisfaction on the re-review, as bringing credit to the body in general, but to increase our gratitude to God, for the happy issue of the war. Had it been unsuccessful, we must have drunk deeply of the cup of suffering. Our burnt and wasted churches, and our plundered dwellings, in such places as fell under the power of our adversaries, are but an earnest of what we must have suffered, had they finally prevailed. The Synod, therefore, request you to render thanks to Almighty God, for all his mercies, spiritual and temporal, and in particular manner for establishing the Independence of the United States of America."[3]

[1] Bret Harte, *Caldwell of Springfield*, a poem. [2] *Supra.*, p. 29.
[3] *Records of the Presbyterian Church*, pp. 499-500; Briggs, *op. cit.*, p. 357.

CHAPTER V

THE DUTCH REFORMED, GERMAN REFORMED, LUTHERAN, BAPTIST, METHODIST AND ROMAN CATHOLIC CHURCHES IN THE REVOLUTION

The situation of the Dutch Reformed Church during the Revolution was similar to that of its near relative, the Presbyterian Church; its republican principles were the especial target of British hatred. Subjected to a British animus, the like of which had destroyed Presbyterian churches and martyred its ministers the Dutch Reformed Church experienced increased indignities because of its location, chiefly in New York City and the Hudson River Valley, the strategic position which the British sought to gain and to hold.[1] Dutch Reformed congregations were driven from their homes; pastors and flocks were separated and scattered; churches were desecrated and destroyed. New York's most beloved pastor, Archibald Laidlie, died in exile.

Dr. John H. Livingston, that most temperate teacher and the leader of this denomination, tells us in a sermon of July 4, 1790, at the re-opening of the Middle Dutch Church in Nassau Street:

"I dare not speak of the wanton cruelty of those who destroyed this temple, nor repeat the various indignities which have been perpetrated. It would be easy to mention facts which would chill your blood! A recollection of the groans of dying prisoners, which pierced this ceiling; or the sacrilegious sports and rough feats of horsemanship exhibited within these walls might raise sentiments in your mind, perhaps, not

[1] Todd, *Centennial Discourse.*

harmonizing with those religious affections, which I wish, at present, to promote, and always to cherish."

It is not surprising then that the Dutch Reformed Church supported the Revolution in every possible way, enlistments, days of fast, humiliation, thanksgiving and prayer, — a truly patriotic denomination. The Reverend Dr. Miller informs us that: "For a considerable time before this crisis arrived, Dr. Rodgers and several other clergymen of this city (New York), among whom were Dr. Mason and Dr. Laidlie, had been in the habit of holding weekly meetings, for cultivating friendship with each other and for mutual instruction, Toward the close of 1775 the gentlemen concerned, agreed to suspend their usual exercises at these meetings, and to employ the time, when they came together, in special prayers for a blessing upon the country, in the struggle on which it was entering. This meeting . . . . . was kept up, until the ministers composing it, and the great mass of the people under their pastoral care, retired from the city, previous to the arrival of the British forces."[1]

The following minute from the Records of Trinity Church shows that a Dutch Reformed congregation remained in the city:

"October 29, 1779, It being represented to this corporation by one of its members that the Old Dutch Church in this City is at present used as a hospital for His Majesty's troops: The Board impressed with a grateful remembrance of the former kindness of that Ancient Church in permitting the use of their Church to the members of the Church of England, when they had no proper edifice of their own for that purpose, offer to the members of the Ancient Dutch Church the use of St. George's Chapel for the celebrating their worship." [2]

[1] Miller, *Memoir of the Late Venerable Dr. Rodgers*, quoted by Gunn, *Memoir of Rev. John H. Livingston*, pp. 250-251.

[2] *Ecclesiastical Records*, vol. vi, pp. 4304-4305: *Records of Trinity Church*, vol. i, p. 140.

The Rev. Mr. Inglis, Rector of Trinity Church, reported to the Venerable Society, November 26, 1777:

"The members of the Dutch Church in this City have always lived in the utmost harmony with the members of our Church . . . . . The loyal Dutch continued in the City after it was reduced by the King's troops; and a loyal minister (Rev. Garrett Lydekker) officiated for them. But the commandant was under the necessity of taking their Church lately for an hospital, and the Dutch Congregation signified their inclination that we should assist them. I immediately called my vestry and after maturely considering all circumstances we judged it advisable for many reasons to let them have the use of one of our Churches. Accordingly their Minister now officiates . . . . . in St. George's Chapel." [1]

Upon regaining their own church from the British the Ancient Dutch Congregation, April 8, 1780, thanked Trinity Church for the use of St. George's Chapel, saying:

"The Christian-like behavior and kind attention shown . . . . . . in our distress by members of the Church of England will make a lasting impression on the mind of the Ancient Reformed Dutch Congregation, who have always considered the interests of the two churches inseparable." [2]

The General Synod of 1775 records, Article xi, a recommendation "to all the Reformed Churches . . . . . in the two Provinces of New York and New Jersey, to set apart Wednesday, 7th May next, as a day of solemn humiliation, with fasting and prayer . . . . . . taking to heart the present sad state and perilous condition of our land."[3] In the years 1776 and 1777, the Reverend Body was prevented from convening by the war.

The Synod of 1778, held at New Platz, "with sorrowful hearts contemplate the pitiful condition of land and Church: some of our cities being desolated, our villages, and boroughs subverted, many of our houses of worship, and their furniture burned, desecrated, plundered, and cast to

[1] *Ecclesiastical Records*, vol. vi, pp. 4303-4305.
[2] *Ecclesiastical Records*, vol. vi, p. 4305.
[3] *Acts and Proceedings of the General Synod*, vol. i, p. 57.

the ground; many dear pledges of the loving Jesus, together with the faithful ambassadors of His Cross, driven from their peaceful homes and compelled to roam through the land, so that, with respect to those once flourishing congregations, we may, even weeping, take up the lamentation of the Church of old, and say; 'The ways of Zion do mourn because none come to the solemn feasts; all her gates are desolate; her priests sigh, her virgins are afflicted, and she is in bitterness'."[1] November 12 was set apart as a day of humiliation and prayer.

The Synod of 1780, at New Platz, in October, clearly and explicitely recognized the new government in the following address:

"To his Excellency, George Clinton, Esquire, Governor of the State of New York, General and Commander-in-chief of all the Militia, and Admiral of the Navy of the same, and to the honorable the Senate and House of Assembly of the said State:

The Memorial and Petition of the Reverend Synod of the Low Dutch Reformed Church in America humbly sheweth,

That the beneficent Ruler of the Universe has, at divers times and occasions, given the most indubitable proofs of his Divine and benevolent interposition for the good of these United States, and this State in particular . . . . .

That the unwearied exertions of these United States, and of this State in particular, and especially the unparalleled perseverance of the American army exhibited in the prosecution of the *present just and necessary war*, from whatever personal motives it may otherwise proceed, cannot but be considered as national virtues; such as have usually been owned and accepted of by the Deity in the issue.

That the Magistrates and other officers of Government have from time to time exerted their influence and authority for obtaining the end which an overruling Providence so evidently pointed out as worthy of the best efforts of the citizens of those States, which as far as we know have been answered with equal alacrity by a great part of our fellow-citizens being subjects of these States."[2]

The Synod at New Millstone, October 1782, decided that it was time to effect an understanding between church and state, as to their mutual obligations in respect to sins and their punishments. Article ix, section three, enquires

[1] *Acts and Proceedings*, vol. i, p. 68.

[2] *Ibid.*, vol. i, pp. 84-86; *Ecclesiastical Records*, vol. vi, pp. 4307-4308.

"Whether it would not be advisable, in order to prevent further corruption of morals among the rising generation and others, that this Reverend Body, present to the honorable government an exposé, setting forth briefly, but distinctly, the sins and disorders punishable by the civil magistrates, with the accompanying desire, that their Excellencies please to take such order in relation to this point, that the salutary laws of the land may be faithfully executed for the suppression of such evils, and the avoidance of further and greater judgments of the Most High.

This Reverend Body approves the proposition but desiring that the other Particular Bodies also represent their wishes, postpone a decision until the next General Meeting."[1]

At the close of the war the Domine Rubel was deposed for certain immoralities and for his Toryism. Among the sturdy Dutch Reformed patriots we find the names of Schuneman, Hardenbergh, Foering, Romeyn, Westerlo, Du Bois, and Leydt, ministers of their gospel.[2]

The record of the German Reformed Church throughout the Revolution was, on the whole, decidedly patriotic. Several prominent military officers were from its ranks: General Nicholas Herkimer, "the hero of Oriskany," Baron Frederick William Von Steuben; and the ministers appear generally to have been earnest advocates of independence. At the beginning of the war the Reverend John H. Weikel got into trouble for preaching from the text, "Better is a poor and a wise child, than an old and foolish king, who will no more be admonished." The Reverend C. D. Weyberg, of Philadelphia, was imprisoned for his patriotism and his church was occupied by the British soldiers. On the first Sunday after his liberation he preached on the words, "O God, the heathen are come into thine inheritance; thy holy temple have they defiled." The Reverend J. C. A. Helffenstein of Lancaster, preached to the Hessian prisoners there on the text, "Ye

[1] *Acts and Proceedings*, vol. i, p. 198.
[2] Corwin, *Manual of the Reformed Church in America*, p. 66.

have sold yourselves for naught; and ye shall be redeemed without money," and again from, "If the Son therefore shall make you free, ye shall be free indeed." To the American soldiers departing for conflict he preached from, "If God be for us, who can be against us?" Schlatter was imprisoned for his sympathy with the American cause; Hendel was accompanied by armed men when he preached in Lykens Valley, the guards standing at the door to protect him; the Reverend John Conrad Boucher frequently preached to the soldiers in camp.

On the other hand there was considerable British sentiment manifested by German Reformed clergy. The Reverend John Michael Kern of New York, was an enthusiastic loyalist, who believed that in America neither church nor state was prepared for independence. At the close of the war he migrated to Nova Scotia. The most prominent German opponent of the American cause, was Dr. John Joachim Zubly, of Savannah, Georgia, one of the most prominent members of his church. He was granted the degree of Doctor of Divinity by the College of New Jersey in 1770. Early in the struggle he took a prominent part with the Sons of Liberty. In 1769, under the name "A Freeholder of South Carolina," he published a pamphlet entitled, *An Humble Enquiry into the Nature of Dependency of the American Colonies upon the Parliament of Great Britain and the Right of Parliament to lay Taxes on the Said Colonies.*[1] In 1775 in an address to the Earl of Dartmouth, prefixed to a sermon on *The Law of Liberty*, which he had preached at the opening of the provincial congress of Georgia, he discussed the parliamentary

[1] Zubly, *An Humble Enquiry into the Nature of the Dependency of the American Colonies upon the Parliament of Great Britain and the Right of Parliament to lay Taxes on the Said Colonies*, by a Freeholder of South Carolina. N. P., 1769.

position of the right "to bind the colonies in all cases whatsoever." Dr. Zubly asserted:

"My lord, the Americans look upon this as the language of despotism in its utmost perfection. What can . . . . . an emperor of Morocco pretend more of his slaves, than to bind them in all cases whatsoever." [1]

"My lord, the Americans are no idiots, and they appear determined not to be slaves. Oppression will make wise men mad; but oppressors, in the end, frequently find that they were not wise men. There may be resources, even in despair, sufficient to render any set of men strong enough not to be bound 'in all cases whatsoever'." [2]

"The bulk of the inhabitants of a continent extending eighteen hundred miles in front of the Atlantic, and permitting an extension in breadth as far as the South Sea, look upon the claim 'to bind them in all cases whatsoever,' as unjust, illegal and detestable. Let us suppose for a moment, that they are grossly mistaken; yet an error imbibed by millions, and in which they believe the all of the present and future generations lies at stake, may prove a very dangerous error. Destroying the Americans, will not cure them; nor will any acts that condemn them to starve or be miserable, have any tendency to persuade them that these acts were made by their friends." [3]

"My lord, the violence of the present measures has almost instantaneously created a continental union, a continental currency, a continental army; and before this can reach your lordship, they will be as equal in discipline, as they are superior in cause and spirit, to any regulars. The most zealous Americans could not have effected in an age, what the cruelty and violence of administration has effectually brought to pass in a day." [4]

"In this respect, as well as in the strong sense of liberty, and in the use of firearms, almost from the cradle, the Americans have vastly the advantage over men of their rank almost everywhere else. From the constant topic of present conversation, every child unborn will be impressed with the notion — it is slavery to be bound at the will of another 'in all cases whatsoever'. Every mother's milk, will convey a detestation of this maxim. Were your lordship in America, you might see little ones acquainted with the word of command before they can distinctly speak,

[1] Zubly, *The Law of Liberty*: *A Sermon on American Affairs*, preached at the opening of the Provincial Congress of Georgia, Philadelphia, 1775, vi; Tyler, *op. cit.*, vol. i, p. 484.

[2] *Ibid.*, vi-vii.

[3] *Ibid.*, ix-x.

[4] *Ibid*, xiii-xiv; Tyler, *op. cit.*, vol. ii, p. 484.

and shouldering the resemblance of a gun before they are well able to walk."[1]

At the beginning of the Revolution there was no man in Georgia more influential than Dr. Zubly. On the fourth of September, 1775, he, with four others, was selected to represent the colony of Georgia in the Continental Congress. He accepted the appointment with the consent of his congregation which agreed "to spare their minister for a time for the good of the common cause."

Dr. Zubly, like so many others, was working for a redress of grievances and could not accept the idea of independence. He wrote a *Reply* to Paine's *Common Sense* in which occurs the following sentence, "The author looks upon an entire separation not as a last remedy, but as a new and dangerous disease; and earnestly prayeth that America, in that connection, may soon and forever enjoy that constitution and freedom which the representatives so justly claim." As early as June 1766, on the repeal of the Stamp Act, he had said in a sermon in Savannah, with reference to any man who would divide British America from Great Britain, "let him be accursed by both."[2] And in 1775, before the provincial congress of Georgia, he declared:

"The idea of separation between America and Great Britain is big with so many and such horrid evils, that every friend to both must shudder at the thought. Every man that gives the most distant hint of such a wish, ought instantly to be suspected as a common enemy. Nothing would more effectually serve the cause of our enemies, than any proposal of this kind. All wise men, and all good men, would instantly speak, write, and act against it. Such a proposal whenever it should be made, would be an inlet to greater evils than any we have yet suffered."[3]

[1] Zubly, *The Law of Liberty*, xv; Tyler, *op. cit.*, vol. i, pp. 484-485.
[2] Zubly, *The Stamp Act Repealed, A Sermon preached at Savannah, June 25, 1766*, p. 19. South Carolina reprint, Charleston, 1766.
[3] Zubly, *The Law of Liberty*, p. 25; Tyler, *op. cit.*, vol. i, p. 485.

For about four months Dr. Zubly occupied a seat in the Continental Congress; but it soon became evident that his sentiments were objectionable to the majority of that body. Early in 1776, when the question of independence was being debated, Samuel Chase arose and publicly accused Zubly of treasonable correspondence with Sir James Wright, colonial governor of Georgia. Soon thereafter, Dr. Zubly left Congress, and returned home for the purpose of using his influence against separation. But his popularity had vanished and he was treated with great harshness. In 1777 he was banished from Savannah, with the loss of half of his estate. He did later return with the re-establishment of the royal government and he was there at the time of his death in 1781. The Church which he founded is known as the Independent Presbyterian Church.

The official assembly of the German Reformed Church, the Pennsylvania Coetus, resolved at its meeting in 1775, May 10-11:

"In consideration of the great troubles and sad conditions under which we now live . . . . . that on the last Wednesday of next June, a day of general fasting, repentance and prayer shall be held in all our congregations.'[1]

A Coetal letter was despatched to the Synods and Classes on the subject, May 12.[2]

The spirit of this body is well illustrated in the following minute of 1783, May 14:

"It appeared . . . . . as if a special joy and cheerfulness of spirit was to be seen in the ministers and also in the faithful elders, on *account of the blessed times of peace,* whereby the Lord crowned the physical and spiritual struggle of true Republicans. To us, as American ministers,

[1] *Minutes and Letters of the Coetus of the German Reformed Congregations in Pennsylvania, 1747-1792,* p. 350.

[2] *Ibid.*, p. 352.

under the supervision of the Reverend Fathers of Holland, this change of our government must be especially welcome, on account of the closer union with the Reverend Classis of Amsterdam and the Reverend Synods, which can be expected on account of the unrestricted fellowship now open to the two republics, which God may further bless." [1]

In 1775 the Reformed and Lutherans united in the publication of an appeal to the German citizens of New York and North Carolina, urging them to support the measures of Congress and the cause of American freedom. In this the Germans of Pennsylvania are represented as doing everything to substain the measures of Congress, in organizing militia companies and corps of Yeagers ready to march whenever and wherever commanded.[2]

The Germans of America in 1775 were not well organized and in no distinctively German denomination was there unanimity of sentiment relative to the Revolution. This was as true for German Lutherans as for German Reformed. Fortunately for Lutherans they possessed the family of their patriarch Muhlenberg to give them a loyal American complexion. The father, Henry Melchoir Muhlenberg, practically occupied the position of overseer of all the Lutheran churches from New York to Georgia, though unfortunately his contact with the various units was of the slightest. Throughout the war he and his sons occupied prominent positions as patriots. Muhlenberg the elder devoted his time to ecclesiastical affairs; his sons served their country.[3]

The son, John Peter Gabriel Muhlenberg, was pastor of a church at Woodstock, Virginia, at the opening of hostilities. When the news of Bunker Hill reached Virginia, he reminded his congregation that there was a time

[1] *Minutes and Letters*, p. 383.
[2] Seidensticker, *First Century of German Printing*, p. 91.
[3] Mann, William J., *Life and Times of Henry Melchoir Muhlenberg*.

to preach and a time to pray; as for him, the time to preach was past. "It is now," he cried, "the time to fight"; and throwing off his vestments he stood forth in the garb of a Virginia colonel.

His brother having remonstrated with him for his enlistment, he wrote:

> "You may say that as a clergyman nothing can excuse my conduct. I am a clergyman, it is true, but I am a member of society as well as the poorest layman, and my liberty is as dear to me as any man. I am called by my country to its defence. The cause is just and noble. Were I a Bishop . . . . . I should obey without hesitation; and as far am I from thinking that I am wrong, I am convinced it is my duty so to do — a duty I owe to my God and my Country."[1]

In February, 1777, John Muhlenberg became a brigadier-general in the Continental Army; in September 1783, he was breveted major-general. He took part in the battles of Brandywine, Germantown, and Monmouth; at Yorktown he commanded the first brigade. He was a member of the Virginia Convention of 1776; later he was vice-president of the supreme-executive council of Pennsylvania and he represented that state both in the House and in the Senate of the United States.[2]

A brother, Frederick Augustus Conrad Muhlenberg, was pastor of Christ German Lutheran Church of New York, 1773 to 1776. He fled at the approach of the British in 1776 and was assistant to his father at New Hanover, 1777 to 1779. From 1779 to 1780 he was a member of Continental Congress; from 1780 to 1783, of the Pennsylvania General Assembly, and in 1789 of the state constitutional convention. He was president of the Pennsylvania Convention which ratified the federal consti-

[1] Perry, *Influence of the Clergy in the War of the Revolution,* p. 5.
[2] Muhlenberg, *Life of John Peter Gabriel Muhlenberg.*

tution, and from 1789 to 1797 he was a member of the national House of Representatives.

It is fortunate for Lutheranism in America that it possessed the Muhlenberg family to establish its reputation for loyal Americanism; many Lutherans were actively pro-British. When Frederick Augustus Conrad Muhlenberg was driven from his church in New York, but one Lutheran minister remained in the city, Hausihil, pastor of Trinity Church, an ardent loyalist, prominent in social circles and a trustee of King's College. His church had been burned in the conflagration of 1776. Upon the evacuation of the city by the British, he, with the larger part of his congregation, left for Nova Scotia, settling near Halifax. He received "orders" from the Church of England. In Georgia, the Reverend Triebner sympathized with the British and left with their troops for England at the close of the war.

President Washington could write to the Baptists in 1789:

"I recollect with satisfaction that the religious society of which you are members, have been throughout America, uniformly and almost unanimously the firm friends to civil liberty, and the persevering promoters of our glorious revolution." [1]

There is no disputing the zeal of this denomination for the cause of independence. By principle it was thoroughly democratic and endowed with the spirit of liberty. Heavily oppressed by the English law, as interpreted in America, it was almost to a man favorable to the political revolution, as a by-product of which they played for religious liberty. Armitage, the Baptist historian, claims, "that we have no record of so much as one thorough British Tory."[2] James proves[3] that the "Baptists were

[1] *Writings of Washington*, Spark's edition, vol. xii, p. 154.
[2] Armitage, *History of the Baptists*, p. 177.
[3] James, *Struggle of Religious Liberty in Virginia*, p. 197.

the first and only religious denomination that struck for independence from Great Britain, and the first and only one that made a move for religious liberty before independence was declared."

It is not surprising that the Baptists of Rhode Island favored the Revolution. Nor are we surprised that the British took possession of Newport and also landed at Warren, burning the meeting-house and parsonage, and carrying the Baptist minister away a prisoner. During this period the Americans made Providence a military post and occupied the college buildings as barracks. It may, however, seem strange that those of other New England states should have supported their Congregational oppressors rather than to have essayed to secure the support of England through disloyalty to the American cause.

In Massachusetts Backus informs us, "The Baptists were so generally united with their country in the defence of their privileges, that when the General Court at Boston passed an act, in October 1778, to debar all men from returning into their government, whom they judged to be their enemies, and named three hundred and eleven men as such, there was not one Baptist among them."[1]

This same Isaac Backus, agent and historian for the New England Baptists, gives us the following reasons why they joined the Revolutionary cause:

1. The Episcopalians, wherever they are in power, allow less liberty than the Baptists of New England enjoy. In England all are taxed and none admitted to civil office. "In Virginia they cruelly imprisoned Baptist ministers, only for preaching the gospel to perishing souls without license from their courts, until the war compelled them to desist."

2. The worst treatment received by the Baptists comes from the same principles and persons that the American war did.

[1] Backus, *Church History of New England*, edition of 1871, vol. ii, p. 247; abridged edition 1804, p. 213.

3. The first Baptist minister in America held to the compact theory.
4. The British claims are absolutely unjust.
5. The deliverance of America might return Baptist invaded rights.[1]

The Warren Association, met at Medfield September 13, 1774, agreed to send Mr. Backus, their agent, to present their grievances to Continental Congress at Philadelphia and they furnished him with the following certificate:

"To the Honorable Delegates of the several Colonies in North America, met in a General Congress in Philadelphia:

Honorable Gentlemen: As the Antipaedobaptist churches in New England are most heartily concerned for the preservation and defence of the rights and privileges of this country, and are deeply affected by the encroachments upon the same, which have lately been made by the British parliament, and are willing to unite with our dear countrymen, vigorously to pursue every prudent measure for relief, so we would beg leave to say that, as a distinct denomination of Protestants, we conceive that we have an equal claim to charter-rights with the rest of our fellow-subjects, and yet have long been denied the free and full enjoyment of those rights, as to the support of religious worship. Therefore, we, the elders and brethren of twenty Baptist churches, met in Association at Medfield, twenty miles from Boston, September 14, 1774, have unanimously chosen and sent unto you the reverend and beloved, Mr. Isaac Backus as our agent, to lay our case, in these respects, before you, or otherwise to use all the prudent means he can for our relief.

JOHN GANO, *Moderator*,
HEZEKIAH SMITH, *Clerk*."[2]

In a subsequent chapter[3] we shall note the methods whereby the New England leaders in Continental Congress prevented any recognition whatsoever of this matter by that body. Thwarted in Philadelphia, the Warren Association returned to the Massachusetts fight and memorialized the Provincial Assembly at Watertown,

[1] Backus, *op. cit.*, edition of 1871, ii, pp. 197-8; edition of 1784, vol. ii, pp. 299-300.

[2] Backus, *op. cit.*, edition 1784, vol. ii, pp. 302-303, edition of 1871, vol. ii, p. 200; Hovey, *op. cit.*, p. 202; Guild, *op. cit.*, p. 236.

[3] *Infra*, pp. 137-138.

September, 1775;[1] and addressed a letter to all the Baptist Churches on the Continent, "stating the true nature and importance of *religious liberty*" and proposing a general meeting of delegates from all the societies to consult upon the means by which this liberty might be secured.[2]

The Baptists were defeated in their endeavors to have religious freedom incorporated as a part of the Revolutionary constitution of Massachusetts. But they did secure a certain amount of recognition for their cause through their patriotic support of the more general cause of liberty. Samuel Stillman, pastor of the First Baptist Church in Boston, was selected to deliver the election sermon in 1779, May 26, and speaking before the Council and Representatives of the Commonwealth of Massachusetts Bay, he was enabled to place before the people of Massachusetts, an official statement of the Baptist principles of religious freedom. His text was, *Matthew*, xxii, 21, "Render, therefore, unto Caesar the things which are Caesar's; and unto God the things that are God's." He dealt first with the duties which the people owe to the civil magistrates and then with the duties which these same magistrates owe to the people. He endeavored to draw the line between the things that belong to Caesar and those things which belong to God. The foundation of civil society is "The consent of the governed." The authority of civil magistrates is, under God, derived from the people. The constitution is that by which, in all good governments, the authority of the magistrates and the rights of the people are determined with precision. Therein lies the indispensable necessity for a Bill of Rights, drawn up in the most explicit language,

[1] Backus, *op. cit.*, vol. ii, 203.
[2] Hovey, *Life and Times of Backus*, pp. 226-231 for text of the letter.

previously to the ratification of the constitution, which should contain its fundamental principles and which no person in the state, however dignified, should dare to violate except at his peril. Election ought to be free and frequent. Representation should be as equal as possible. Some of the natural rights of mankind are inalienable, and subject to no control but that of Diety. Such are the Sacred Rights of Conscience which in a state of nature, and of civil society are exactly the same. They can neither be parted with nor controlled by any human authority whatever. We should leave nothing to human virtue, that can be provided for by law or the constitution. The jurisdiction of the magistrate neither can nor ought in any manner to be extended to the salvation of souls. The very men who were appointed guardians and conservators of the rights of the people have dismembered the empire; and, by repeated acts of injustice and oppression, forced from the bosom of their parent country, millions of Americans. "Where is now the boasted freedom of the British government? Bribery and corruption seem nearly to have accomplished the prediction of the great Montesquieu. Nor is such an event to be wondered at, while we reflect on the inequality of their representation, and the base methods that are used in their elections of members of the house of commons, together with the length of time they are suffered to continue in their places." "The voice of the people is that the government should pay their first attention to the war."[1] Thus at the time when Jefferson was introducing his Bill for Religious Freedom into the Virginia Assembly, Stillman was placing the same principles before the Massachusetts Assembly.

[1] Stillman, *Election Sermon, preached . . . . . May 26, 1779,* Boston, 1779.

In Virginia "An Address from the Baptists in this colony" was presented to the Convention, August 16, 1775, and read, setting forth that however distinguished from the countrymen, by appellations and sentiments of a religious nature, they nevertheless considered themselves as members of the same community in respect to matters of a civic nature, and embarked in the same common cause; that, alarmed at the oppression which hangs over America, they had considered what part it would be proper for them to take in the unhappy contest, and had determined that in some cases it was lawful to go to war, and that they ought to make a military resistance against Great Britain, in her unjust invasion, tyrannical oppression, and repeated hostilities; that their brethren were left at discretion to enlist, without incurring the censure of their religious community; and, under these circumstances many of them had enlisted as soldiers, and many more were ready to do so.[1]

In October 1777, the House passed *An Act for Speedily recruiting the Virginia Regiments, etc.*, which contained the following provisions, "And whereas there are within this community some religious societies, particularly Baptists and Methodists, the members of which may be averse to serving in the same companies or regiments with others, and under officers of different principles, though they would willingly engage in the defence of their country under the command of officers of their own religion: Be it enacted, That such persons may raise companies, and if enough companies are raised, may form regiments having their own field officers, chaplains, and so on."[2] A preacher,

[1] *Journal of House,* August 16, 1775; James, *op. cit.*, pp. 51-53; 218-219; *Infra*. p. 373.
[2] Hening, *Statutes*, ix, p. 348.

Thomas McClanahan, raised a company of Baptists in Culpepper County, and took them into service. There is extant no more fascinating account of the war-record of a Revolutionary preacher than the *Biographical Memoirs of the Late Rev. John Gano.* When the war broke out, Gano had arrived at a very respectable situation for a Baptist minister, being in charge of the work in New York City. Driven from the city by the coming of the British, he entered the service of his country. He served throughout the war in various capacities, chaplain in Col. Charles Webb's regiment from Stamford, chaplain to the brigade of General Clinton, etc. For years he lived the camp life. In one instance he tells us, "General Washington moved his army (to Virginia). This movement was so sudden and unexpected to me, that I was totally unprepared for it. I had with me only one shift of linen of which I informed General Clinton, requesting leave of absence to get more; but to this he objected, and said I must go on with them, at all events. When we arrived at Newark, I found an old lady, who had been a member of my church in New York. I told her my situation, and she furnished me with what was needed for the campaign."[1]

Then came peace and "The Army was soon after disbanded, and we poor ruined Yorkers returned to our disfigured houses. My house needed some repairs and wanted some new furniture; for the enemy plundered a great many articles. We collected of our church, about thirty-seven members out of upwards of two hundred. Some were dead and others scattered into almost every part of the union."[2] In this situation, the Rev. John Gano himself decided to take up again the life of a pioneer

[1] *Memoirs of John Gano,* p. 104.
[2] *Ibid.,* p. 116.

missionary and removed to Kentucky where he spent the rest of his life.

Revolutionary Methodists have been branded, rather unjustly, as an unpatriotic body. Though many gave support to their country, their dependence upon Anglicanism and John Wesley and his assistants, mostly foreigners, rendered them, officially, incapable of appreciation of independence. Their foreign connection tarred them with Anti-Americanism.

Till well into the year 1775 John Wesley disapproved of the repressive measures of the British government. In 1768 he wrote *Free Thoughts on the Present State of Public Affairs*, in which he remarked, "I do not defend the measures which have been taken with regard to America; I doubt whether any man can defend them either on the foot of law, equity, or prudence."[1] And on receiving news of the Battle of Lexington, he felt that silence on his part would be a sin against God, against his country, and against his own soul, so waiting but one day, he wrote separately to Dartmouth and Lord North, June 15. Had the contents of this letter been known in America, it would have softened criticism of his followers for in it he says:

> "I cannot avoid thinking these, an oppressed people, asked for nothing more than their legal rights, and that in the most modest and inoffensive manner that the nature of the thing will allow . . . . .
>
> Is it common sense to use force towards America? They are as strong men; they are as valiant as you; they are one and all enthusiasts,—enthusiasts for liberty; they are calm, deliberate enthusiasts.
>
> They are terribly united; they think they are contending for their wives, children, and Liberty."[2]

[1] Buckley, *History of Methodists*, p. 158; McTyeire, *History of Methodism*, pp. 290-291.

[2] Stevens, *History of the Methodist Episcopal Church*, vol. i, pp. 283-284.

In 1775 Wesley read Dr. Samuel Johnson's *Taxation No Tyranny* and was convinced by its arguments. He abridged these and issued, in the Autumn of 1775, *A Calm Address to the American Colonies.*[1] This caused a sensation even in England, but in America, where it was printed by thousands, it created a rabid hostility towards Wesley's followers. In 1776, Wesley followed this up with a long pamphlet entitled *Some Observations on Liberty*, in which he compared John Hancock to a felon, contended against every proposition by which the Americans supported their cause, and called upon them to lay down their arms.[2]

In Virginia, the Methodists rushed to the defense of the established church. Nearly all of their missionaries were natives of Great Britain and in general they acted indiscreetly. Rodda distributed copies of the King's proclamation; Rankin talked too freely; while even that most liberal Francis Asbury refused to take the oath in Maryland and sought a retreat with Judge White in Delaware.[3] Two years after the Declaration of Independence, Asbury alone of all the clergy remained in America and he was in forced retirement. Thus Wesley and his missionaries were responsible for the un-American stigma which was attached to their faith.

A goodly part of the Methodists refused to follow the leadership of the Englishmen and rallied to the support of Liberty. The native ministers, Watters, Gatch, Garrettson, Morrell, Ware, and others, were true Americans and consistently loyal. But even their patriotism was not

[1] Buckley, *op. cit.*, pp. 158-168; McTyeire, *op. cit.*, p. 290; Tyerman, *Life and Times of John Wesley*, vol. iii, pp. 186-187.

[2] Wesley, *Works*, vol. vi, pp. 300-321.

[3] McTyeire, *op. cit.*, p. 289. In 1801 in reply to the taunt that he was an Englishman, Asbury replied that he was not ashamed of it for "Heaven was his Country".

sufficient to redeem the reputation of their society and Methodism suffered severe persecutions. Ministers were beaten, whipped, jailed, and tarred and feathered.

President Washington, in response to a letter of congratulation from the Roman Catholics, spoke thus of their part in the Revolution, "I presume your fellow-citizens will not forget the patriotic part which you took in the accomplishment of their revolution."[1]

Catholics were not numerous in America, except in the provinces of Maryland and Pennsylvania, nor were they well organized at the outbreak of the Revolution. Their influence grew as the contest advanced; and more especially after the recognition of the United States by the Catholic countries, France and Spain. They were of great aid in the campaigns along the Gulf and in the Ohio Valley.

Boucher wrote of them (1797):

"Catholics had not the fortitude to withstand a rebellion which was already begun; but, with all the bad principles respecting civil government so frequently imputed to them, they are clear of any suspicion of having begun that in America . . . . .

The Catholics of Maryland . . . . . seemed to hesitate and to be unresolved what part they should take in the great commotions of the country, which were then beginning. Their principles, no doubt, led them to side with government; whilst their inclinations, and . . . . . their interest, made it their policy to be neutral; but it soon became easy to foresee that neither they, nor any others, would long be permitted to enjoy neutrality . . . . . The persons in America who were the most opposed to Great Britain, had also, in general, distinguished themselves by being particularly hostile to Catholics; but then, though dissenters and republicans were their enemies, the friends of government could hardly be said to be their friends! In America, if they joined governent, all they had to look for was to be bitterly persecuted by one party, and to be deserted by the other. Hence, for some time, they appeared to be wavering and undetermined. This irresolution drew on them many suspicions, censures and threats.

[1] *Infra*, p. 504.

At length a Catholic gentleman, of good abilities, who was possessed of one of the first fortunes in that country (in short, the Duke of Norfolk of Maryland), actuated, as was generally thought, solely by his desire to become a public man, for which he was unquestionably well qualified, openly espoused the cause of Congress. Soon after, he became a member of that body. This seemed to settle the wavering disposition of the Catholics of Maryland: under so respectable a leader as Mr. Carroll, they all soon (at least in appearance) became good Whigs, and concurred with their fellow revolutionists in declaiming against the misgovernment of Great Britain; nay, they must have concurred in those very declarations which adduced the Quebec Act, by which the Papists in that province (almost the whole of its inhabitants) were tolerated, as a flagrant instance of her despotism and tyranny . . . . . Their leader, indeed, has been a member of Congress, and was once employed on an embassy: a relative of his, moreover, is now the Popish Bishop in the State."[1]

It is undoubtedly true, as Boucher states, that the Carroll influence was great in determining the course of Catholics with respect to the Revolution. They certainly personally furnished the cause with a whole-hearted support. Archbishop Carroll later wrote:

"Their (Catholic) blood flowed as freely, in proportion to their numbers, to cement the fabric of independence as that of any of their fellow-citizens. They concurred with perhaps greater unanimity than any other body of men in recommending and promoting that government from whose influence America anticipates all the blessings of justice, peace, plenty, good order, and civil and religious liberty (the Constitution). The Catholic regiment, 'Congress' Own', the Catholic Indians from St. John, Maine, under the chief Ambrose Var, the Catholic Penobscots under the chief Orono, fought side by side with their Protestant fellow colonists. Catholic Officers from Catholic lands, — Ireland, France and Poland, came to offer their services to the cause of liberty."[2]

The Reverend Francis Louis Chartier de Lotbinière of the Order of Malta was commissioned chaplain of "Congress' Own" regiment and served with his regiment in the

[1] Boucher, *op. cit.*, pp. 243-244.

[2] O'Gorman, *The Roman Catholics*, pp. 255-256; Shea, *op. cit.*, vol. ii, pp. 352-353.

advance on Canada.[1] Both Maryland and Pennsylvania furnished many men and officers to the American army.[2]

Shortly after assuming office as Commander-in-chief of the American forces, Washington was furnished with an occasion for showing his regard for the Catholics of America. On November 5, 1775, he issued official orders for the abolition of "Pope Day," the New England substitute for Guy Fawkes' Day, as follows:

"As the Commander-in-chief has been apprised of a design for the observance of that ridiculous and childish custom of burning the effigy of the Pope, he cannot help expressing his surprise that there should be officers and soldiers in this army so void of common sense as not to see the impropriety of such a step at this juncture; at a time when we are soliciting, and have really obtained the friendship and alliance of the people of Canada, whom we ought to consider as brethren embarked in the same cause — the defence of the liberty of America — At this juncture, and under such circumstances, to be insulted in their religion, is so monstrous as not to be suffered or excused; indeed instead of offering the most remote insult, it is our duty to address public thanks to these our brethren, as to them we are indebted for every late success over the common enemy."[3]

Catholic France and Spain were the first foreign nations to ally themselves with the American cause, — the one in 1778 and the other in 1779. The arrival of a French ambassador in Philadelphia was followed by a public Catholic recognition of American independence. Mr. Gerard, the ambassador, sent out the following invitation, July 2, 1779:

"You are invited by the Minister Plenipotentiary of France to attend the *Te Deum,* which will be chanted on Sunday the fourth of this month, at noon, in the new Catholic Chapel, to celebrate the Anniversary of the Independence of the United States of America."[4]

[1] Shea, *Life of Archbishop Carroll,* vol. ii, p. 144.
[2] *Ibid.,* vol. ii, p. 153; McSherry, *History of Maryland,* pp. 379 sqq.
[3] Shea, *Life and Times of Archbishop Carroll,* vol. ii, pp. 147-148.
[4] *Ibid.,* vol. ii, p. 175.

The President and Members of the Continental Congress were invited to this ceremony and a sermon was preached, which began as follows:

"We are assembled to celebrate the anniversary of that day which Providence had marked in his Eternal Decrees, to become the epocha of liberty and independence to thirteen United States of America."[1]

The Count d'Estaing, upon his arrival in America, published an address to the Canadians, exhorting them in the name of the King to join their fellow-countrymen in the fight against the English, urging them thereto in the name of their common blood, common language, common customs, laws and religion.[2] The effect of Catholic influence (propaganda) upon the Indians, the French and the Spanish, especially in the West and South, is well set forth by Shea in his *Life and Times of the Most Reverend John Carroll.*[3]

When the news of Cornwall's surrender at Yorktown reached Philadelphia, the French Ambassador, Mr. Gerard, invited Congress, and the Supreme Executive Council and Assembly of Pennsylvania to attend divine service and thanksgiving in the Roman Catholic Church. M. de Bandol again preached. His sermon was as follows:

"A numerous people assembled to render thanks to the Almighty for his mercies, is one of the most affecting objects, and worthy the attention of the Supreme Being. While camps resound with triumphal acclamations, while nations rejoice in victory and glory, the most honorable office a minister of the altars can fill is to be the organ by which public gratitude is conveyed to the Omnipotent.

[1] *Discours pronouncé le 4 Juillet, jour de l'Anniversaire de l'Independence, dans, l'Englise Catholique, par le Reverend Pere Seraphin Bandol, Recollet, Aumonier de son Excellence Mr. Gerard, Ministre Plenepotentiaire de France auprès de Etats Unis de l'Amerique Septentrinale.*

[2] D'Estaing, *A Declaration addressed in the Name of the King of France to all the ancient French in North America.* Boston, 1779.

[3] Shea, *op. cit.*, vol. ii, pp. 179-198.

Those miracles which He once wrought for his chosen people are renewed in our favor; and it would be equally ungrateful and impious not to acknowledge, that the event which lately confounded our enemies and frustrated their designs, was the wonderful work of that God who guards your liberties.

And who but He could so combine the circumstances which led to success? We have seen our enemies push forward amid perils almost innumerable, amid obstacles almost insurmountable, to the spot which was designed to witness their disgrace; yet they eagerly sought it as their theatre of triumph.

Blind as they were, they bore hunger, thirst, and inclement skies, poured their blood in battle against brave republicans, and crossed immense regions to confine themselves in another Jerico, whose walls were fated to fall before another Joshua. It is He, whose voice commands the winds, the seas and the seasons, who formed a junction on the same day in the same hour, between a formidable fleet from the South, and an army rushing from the North, like an impetuous torrent. Who but He in whose hands are the hearts of men could inspire the allied troops with the friendships, the confidence, the tenderness of brothers? How is it that two nations once divided, jealous, inimical, and nursed in reciprocal prejudices, are now become so closely united as to form but one? Worldlings would say, it is the wisdom, the virtue and moderation of their chiefs, it is a great national interest which has performed this prodigy. They will say that to the skill of the generals, to the courage of the troops, to the activity of the whole army, we must attribute this splendid success. Ah! they are ignorant, that the combining of so many fortunate circumstances is an emanation from the all perfect mind: that courage, that skill, that activity bear the sacred impression of Him who is divine.

For how many favors have we not to thank Him during the course of the present year? Your union, which was at first supported by justice alone, has been consolidated by your courage, and the knot which ties you together is become indissoluble by the accession of all the states, and the unanimous voice of all the confederates. You present to the universe the noble sight of a society, which, founded in equality and justice, secures to the individuals who compose it, the utmost happiness which can be derived from human institutions. This advantage, which so many other nations have been unable to procure, even after ages of efforts and misery, is granted by divine providence to the United States; and His adorable decrees have marked the present moment for the completion of that memorable happy revolution, which has taken place in this extensive continent. While your counsels were thus acquiring new energy, rapid multiplied successes have crowned your arms in the Southern states.

We have seen the unfortunate citizens of these states forced from their peaceful abodes; after a long and cruel captivity, old men, women and children, thrown without mercy into a foreign country. Master of their lands and their slaves, amid his temporary affluency, a superb victor rejoiced in their distresses. But Philadelphia has witnessed their patience and fortitude; they have found here another home, and though driven from their native soil they have blessed God, that He has delivered them from their presence, and conducted them to a country where every just and feeling man has stretched out the helping hand of benevolence. Heaven rewards their virtues. Three large states are at once wrested from their foe. The rapacious soldier has been compelled to take refuge behind his ramparts, and oppression has vanished like those phantoms which are dissipated by the morning ray.

On this solemn occasion, we might renew our thanks to the God of battles, for the success he has granted to the arms of your allies and your friends by land and by sea, through the other parts of the globe. But let us not recall those events which too clearly prove how much the hearts of our enemies have been obdurated. Let us prostrate ourselves at the altar, and implore the God of mercy to suspend His vengeance, to spare them in His wrath, to inspire them with sentiments of justice and moderation, to terminate their obstinacy and error, and to ordain that your victories be followed by peace and tranquillity. Let us beseech Him to continue to shed on the counsels of the King your ally, that spirit of wisdom, of justice and of courage, which has rendered his reign so glorious. Let us entreat Him to maintain in each of the states that intelligence by which the United States are inspired. Let us return Him thanks that a faction, whose rebellion He has corrected, now deprived of support, is annihilated. Let us offer Him pure hearts unsoiled by private hatred or public dissention, and let us, with one will and one voice, pour forth to the Lord that hymn of praise by which Christians celebrate their gratitude and His glory." [1]

[1] *Pennsylvania Packet*, November 27, 1781; *Pennsylvania Advertiser*, November 27, 1781.

CHAPTER VI

THE QUAKERS AND MORAVIANS IN THE REVOLUTION

The Quakers, that sect of "Conscientious Objectors," occupied the attention of governmental authorities — local, state and national, to a greater extent than did any other denomination; also, their line of conduct engaged an equal amount of solicitude from their own church officials.

Quakers had at times tried to follow the injunction of George Fox to keep clear of the "commotions" involved in government; but like Fox they had never succeeded in doing this. In Pennsylvania, their American stronghold, they had indulged in the dangerous game of politics until they were past masters in the art of governing. The state had been ruled by a Quaker oligarchy until about 1750.

Non-resistance was not a Quaker doctrine. They believed in a forceable preservation of their rights, up to the point where force might become criminal. Certain methods of resistance were contrary to their beliefs. They held that differences could generally be settled by common sense and forebearance; that moral resistance, to its fullest extent, was better than suffering iniquity to prevail; and that a citizen's duty was to oppose vigorously, and, if need be, suffer bravely, rather than to condone wrong in others, or to do it himself. They had achieved a memorable triumph in England the previous century and secured, with some completeness, their civil and religious rights, by methods demànding great endurance and strenuous resistance to persecution; they were convinced that similar methods would succeed in America. They stopped at war, because they considered it a crime which could not be justified by any results gained thereby.

Quakers supported the resistance policy of the early Revolution as it was championed by John Dickinson. They drew back as independence and aggressive military policies were espoused. They then officially assumed a policy resembling neutrality, a middle course position which was to prove absolutely untenable. The American cause involved such moral issues as to make non-participation in the struggle appear unrighteous, hence impossible to many Quakers; to governmental officials the Quaker position was treasonable.[1]

Backus thinks the Revolution weakened the Quakers greatly. He writes:

> "At the same time an event took place which weakened the society of Quakers more than anything had done before, since they first came into existence. With much art and labor, their church had become numerous in England and America, which they held to be but one church, and that all their children were born in it, and they did not allow them to hear any teachers but their own . . . . But after our war began, one of their most noted ministers published a pamphlet, to persuade them to pay what they were taxed for the war to defend America against Britain. Upon which they dealt with him as a transgressor of the rules of their church, and they expelled him from it in 1778. But this caused a division among them, and it reached Philadelphia, and it opened a door for their children to go to hear other teachers."[2]

The Revolution did split their church, but the question over which division came was one of religious principle and not one of pro-British or anti-American sympathies. In fact the more violent advocates of non-militarism considered themselves the better advocates of Americanism. Quakers resisted war but the majority were anti-British.

[1] Sharpless, *Quakerism and Politics*, p. 55.
[2] Backus, *op. cit.*, p. 55, abridged edition 1804, p. 213.

Some four hundred members of the church were disowned for participation in the war efforts of the colonies, while but a half dozen were disciplined for helping the British.[1] Many of the pro-American Friends followed the principles of James Logan, that military resistance to aggression was justifiable, and supported the war to their utmost. They broke with the orthodox and founded what was known as "Free Quakers" or "Fighting Quakers," pledged to perform all civil and military duties. For a time these schismatic Quakers were of considerable importance; Washington and Franklin subscribed to a fund for providing them with a meeting house. Of course with the end of the war they gradually disappeared; the last of the original members of the band of "Free Quakers" to die was Betsy Ross, maker of the first United States "Stars and Stripes."[2]

Brissot de Warville records the following impressions of the revolutionary Quakers, the results of his travels in America, 1788:

"It was at this epoch (Revolution) particularly that an animosity was excited against them (Quakers) which is not yet entirely allayed. Faithful to their religious principles, they declared they could take no part in the war, and disavowed or excommunicated every member of their Society who served with either the American or the British Army . . . . Notwithstanding my principles, I do not the less think that the violent persecution of the Quakers for their pacific neutrality was essentially wrong.

If their refusal had been the first of its kind; if it had been dictated solely by their attachment to the British cause; if it had only served them to conceal the secret proofs which they might have given of this attachment, certainly they had been culpable and perhaps persecution had been lawful. But this neutrality was enjoined upon them by the religious opinions which they profess, and which they have practiced from their origin. But exclusive of this, whatever prejudiced or ill-informed

[1] Sharpless, *Political Leaders in the Province of Pennsylvania*, p. 210.
[2] Wetherill, *History of the Free Quakers*.

writers may have asserted, the truth, which I have taken great pains to obtain, is that the majority of the Quakers did not incline more to one party than to the other; and that they did good indifferently to both, and in fact to all those who stood in need of assistance. If some of the Society of Quakers served in the British Army, there were some likewise who served in the American Army, and among others may be mentioned the names of General Greene, Mifflin and Lecy; but the Society excommunicated indifferently all those who took up arms . . . . .

I have heard no one speak more impartially of the Quakers than this celebrated man (Washington) whose spirit of justice is particularly remarkable. He acknowledged to me that in the course of the war he had entertained an unfavorable opinion of the Society; he, in fact, knew little of them because at that period there were few members of the sect in Virginia. He attributed to their political sentiments what was the effect of their religious principles. When he encamped in Chester County, principally inhabited by Quakers, he supposed himself to be in the enemy's country, as he could not induce a single Quaker to act for him in the character of a spy. But no one served as a spy against him in the employ of the British Army . . . . .

George Washington, having since better understood the spirit of the Society, concludes by esteeming them. He acknowledged to me that, on considering the simplicity of their manners, their fondness of economy, excellence of their morals, and the good example they afforded, joined to the attachment they showed for the Constitution, he regarded them as the best citizens of the new government, which required a great degree of obedience and the banishment of luxury."[1]

The call between religion and duty to country makes it difficult to tell where many of the Quaker community stood as regards the faith. John Dickinson, from 1764 to 1776, "the rising hope of the defenders of American rights," illustrates this. He was of Quaker stock, though it is not certain that he was ever an active member in good standing, yet his identification with Friends was so close, that he was usually considered one of them. His *Farmer's Letters*, published in 1768, gave the legal and historic basis for America's claims to liberty. Following each other in rapid succession (14 in all) and read by all classes,

[1] Brissot (de Warville), J. P., *Citoyen Francais, Noveau Voyage dans les Etats-Unis de l'Amerique Septentrional fait en 1788.*

they solidified and systematized the gathering opposition to Great Britain. They proved the justice of the American position and propounded a theory for unity of action. They proved by English law that constitutional resistance was legal and held out the hope that legal remedies might restore colonial rights. Boston voted, "that the thanks of the town be given to the ingenious author of a course of letters published at Philadelphia, and in this place, signed 'A Farmer' wherein the rights of American subjects are clearly and fully stated and fully vindicated." Princeton granted him an honorary LL.D.

As a member of Continental Congress Dickinson wrote nearly every important state paper during the preliminary stages of the Revolution; appeals to the King, and Parliament, to the British, Canadian, and American peoples, etc. He, however, would not follow the radical in forcing independence, and here for a time his popularity and influence waned. Later he entered the army. The family residence at Fair Hill was burned by the British during their occupation of Philadelphia in 1777. By 1782, Dickinson was returned to favor and became president of the supreme executive council. In 1787 he was a member of the Constitutional Convention from Delaware. He wrote a series of articles signed "Fabius" in explanation and support of the Constitution, and Delaware and Pennsylvania, Quaker strongholds, were the first states to ratify.[1]

One of the first Friends to be excommunicated for war activities was Thomas Mifflin of Philadelphia. Thomas Mifflin was a graduate of the College of Philadelphia (University of Pennsylvania) and his services to his country were distinguished; — member of the Pennsyl-

[1] Sharpless, *op. cit.*, essay on "John Dickinson;" *Dickinson, John, The Writings of*, Edited by Paul Leicester Ford.

vania House of Representatives, 1772-1775; member of the First Continental Congress, 1774; aide-de-camp to General Washington; Quartermaster General; Brigadier General; Major General; member of the Board of War; delegate to Continental Congress, 1782-1784; its president, 1783-1784; Speaker of the Pennsylvania General Assembly, 1785-1788; member of the Federal Constitutional Convention; Chief Executive of Pennsylvania, 1788-1790; president of the Pennsylvania Constitutional Convention, 1789-1790, and first governor of that state from 1790 to 1799.[1]

Of nearly equal rank was the excommunicated Nathaniel Greene of Rhode Island, member of the Rhode Island Legislature, 1770, 1771, 1772, 1775, member of a committee of the assembly to revise the militia laws, Brigadier General, Major General, Quartermaster General (succeeding Mifflin), and Commander-in-chief of the southern armies, and one of the early champions of independence. (He urges separation in his letters of October 1775, and January 1776, to Samuel Ward, the Rhode Island delegate to Continental Congress.)[2]

Quakers supported the pre-war stages of the Revolutionary struggle; some fifty of them, including the Pembertons and the Whartons, signed the non-importation agreement to defeat the Stamp Act in 1765;[3] and they wrote to the London Friends an explanation and defense of their position.

[1] Rawle, "Sketch of the Life of Thomas Mifflin" in *Memoirs of the Historical Society of Pennsylvania*, vol. ii, part 2; Merrill, *Memoranda relating to the Mifflin Family*.

[2] Greene, *Life of Nathaniel Greene*.

[3] Sharpless, op. cit., p. 209; Bowden, *The History of the Society of Friends in America*, vol. ii, p. 296; Thomas, *History of the Friends in America*, 5th Edition, 1919; Jones, *The Quakers in the American Colonies*, Chapter ix, "The Friends in the Revolution."

If Quakers as a whole inclined to the American cause at its inception, they soon were propelled in the opposite direction. The episode of *The Charming Polly* seems to have disclosed to them that the populace in the main "were incapable of judging prudently on a matter of so great importance" and that they might be called upon to exert force in the execution of their agreement. Accordingly the monthly Meeting for Sufferings for Philadelphia advised Friends to have nothing to do with non-importation measures.[1]

Some claim that the Friends turned from the patriotic cause less from religious principles than on account of economic interests. They quote a letter of Henry Drinker, a prominent Philadelphia Quaker merchant, December 9, 1769, which reads, "Interest all powerful interest, will bear down Patriotism . . . Romans we are not as they were formerly, when they despised Riches and Grandure, abode in extreme poverty and sacrificed every pleasant enjoyment for love and service of their country."[2]

The Quaker state of Pennsylvania was of vital importance to the Americans. It had grown more rapidly in wealth and material advantages than had any other colony; its internal affairs had been managed with greatest wisdom; its taxes were light; and Philadelphia was the largest, best lighted, best paved and best policed city in America. New England realized the value of Quaker support and sought it in its troubles of 1774. Paul Revere reached Philadelphia, May 19, with the Boston letter, and Thomas Mifflin, Charles Thomson, Joseph Reed, and John Dickinson immediately got together and

[1] Sharpless, *op. cit.*, pp. 77-80; Lincoln, *Revolutionary Movement in Pennsylvania*, p. 151.
[2] *Pennsylvania Magazine*, vol. xiv, p. 41.

devised a scheme for winning Quaker support. A meeting of several hundred citizens was assembled and such men as Thomas Wharton and Dr. Smith[1] helped to carry the pre-conceived motion "for an immediate declaration in favor of Boston." A committee of nineteen was named to answer the Boston letter. This committee called in for informal consultation six representatives from each of the religious societies in the city. This body, in turn, agreed upon a mass meeting, being careful, however, to pick its president and speakers in advance; also to supervise the manuscript for the speeches, to prepare the resolutions to be adopted, and finally, to adopt a slate for a new committee.[2] This new committee consisted of seventeen from the old committee together with twenty-seven added for the respective religious organizations; Dickinson was to be its chairman.

No congress of religions, of the character devised by the political leaders of Pennsylvania, was to arrange the war course of the Pennsylvania Quakers. By the time Continental Congress met, the Friends had decided to oppose the resumption of non-intercourse. On May 30, 1774, the day before the Boston Port Bill went into effect, the several meetings of the society in Philadelphia joined in declaring that, if any Quakers had countenanced or encouraged the proposal for suspending business on June 1, "they have manifested great inattention to our religious principles and professions, and acted contrary to the rules of Christian discipline established for the preservation of order and good government among us."[3]

[1] *Supra*, p. 138.
[2] Stillé, *Life of Dickinson*, p. 244 in Thomson's "Account"; Wharton's "Account" in *Pennsylvania Magazine*, vol. xxxiii, pp. 436-437; Dr. Smith's "Notes and Papers" in *Pennsylvania Historical Society's Manuscript*.
[3] *American Archives*, fourth series, vol. i, pp. 365-366.

At the June Meeting in 1774:

"A considerable time was spent in this meeting, in a weighty consideration of the fluctuating state of people's minds. In the situation of public affairs, it appeared to be the sense of the meeting, that it would be the safest, and most consistent for us, as a religious Society, to keep as much as possible from mixing with the people in their human policy and contrivances, and to forebear meeting in their public consultation. Snares and dangers may arise from meetings of that kind, however well disposed individuals may be to mitigate and soften the violent disposition too prevalent; it being a season in which it is abundantly needful to seek best Wisdom, to guide and preserve in safety and in consistency of conduct with our religious profession." [1]

The Yearly Meeting held in Philadelphia, while Continental Congress was in session there, issued a letter of advice to the Friends throughout the whole of North America. In part this ran:

"Our forefathers and predecessors, were raised to be a people in a time of great commotions, contests, and wars, begun and carried on for the vindication of religious and civil liberty, in which many of them were zealously engaged, when they received the knowledge of the truth; but through the influence of the love of Christ in their minds, they ceased from conferring with flesh and blood, and became obedient to the heavenly vision, in which they clearly saw that all wars and fighting proceeded from the spirit of this world, which is enmity with God, and that they must manifest themselves to be the followers of the Prince of Peace, by meekness, humility, and patient sufferings." [2]

Joseph Reed wrote, November 6, 1774, "They act their usual part. They have directed their members not to serve on the committee and mean to continue the same undecisive, neutral conduct until they see how the scale is like to preponderate . . . . . But American liberty in the meantime must take her chance with them."[3] December 15, the Meeting for Sufferings at Philadelphia

[1] Bowden, *History of the Society of Friends in America,* vol. ii, pp. 297-298.

[2] Bowden, *op. cit.,* vol. ii, p. 298.

[3] *American Archives,* fourth series, vol. i, 963-964.

appointed a committee to wait on the Quaker members of the Provincial Assembly and reprimand them for having given their votes to a resolution ratifying the doings of the Continental Congress five days earlier.[1]

When the Continental Congress met in Philadelphia in 1774 John Adams and his Congregational colleagues from New England were strangely upset by an encounter with Israel Pemberton and his fellow Quakers. The New England delegates had come to enlighten others on the question of political liberty; Backus came also and in conspiracy with Pemberton and other friends of religious freedom, they enticed the Congregationalists to a meeting at Carpenters' Hall. Pemberton very plainly affirmed that the "Friends had a concern about the condition of things in Massachusetts; that they had received complaints from some Anabaptists, and some Friends against certain laws of that Province restrictive of liberty of conscience.

The laws of New England and particularly of Massachusetts, were inconsistent with liberty of conscience, for they not only compelled men to pay for the building of churches and the support of ministers, but to go to some known religious assembly on First-days; and that his friends were desirous of engaging us to assure them that our state would repeal all the laws and place things as they were in Pennsylvania."[2] The quotation is from John Adams's diary. This turning of the tables was a sad blow to the complacency of the delegates of the "Sons of Liberty." They disclaimed the enforcement of such laws in recent years but insisted "that they might as well hope to turn the heavenly bodies out of their annual and diurnal course as the people of Massachusetts at the present

[1] Sharpless, *op. cit.*, p. 107.
[2] *Supra*, p. 118; Sharpless, *op. cit.*, pp. 212-213.

day from their Meeting House and Sunday laws." They also tried to explain how such laws were compatible with liberty of conscience, but Pemberton called out, "Don't urge liberty of conscience in favor of such laws." Unquestionably the Quaker had the better of the argument, and he was far too aggressive a pacifist not to carry the cause as far as his ammunition would reach.

Israel Pemberton had been styled by people in general, "King of the Quakers," and John Adams speaks of him as "the head of the Quaker interests." He was in many respects the most influential of three brothers, Israel, James, and John. We shall see later how he was persecuted for his sympathy towards the British cause.[1]

The Meeting for Sufferings of Pennsylvania and New Jersey, held at Philadelphia, January 5, 1775, disapproved the measures that were being prosecuted against Great Britain and members were requested to avoid joining in such measures as inconsistent with their religious principles.[2] The following exhortation was issued to those who might hold political offices:

> "As divers members of our religious Society, some of them without their consent or knowledge, have been lately nominated to attend on and engage in some public affairs, which they cannot undertake without deviating from these our religious principles; we therefore earnestly beseech and advise them, and all others to consider the end and purpose of every measure to which they are desired to become parties, and with great circumspection and care, to guard against joining in any for the assertion and maintaining of our rights and liberties, which, on mature deliberation, appear not to be dictated by that 'wisdom which is from above; which is pure, peaceable, gentle, full of mercy and good fruits'."[3]

[1] *Infra.*, pp. 146-151; Sharpless, *op. cit.*, p. 210.

[2] *American Archives*, fourth series, vol. i, pp. 1093-1094, 1176-1177; *New York Gazette*, January 30, 1775.

[3] Bowden, *op. cit.*, vol. ii, pp. 299-300.

Their public declaration of policy was as follows:

"The Testimony of the People Called Quakers, Given forth by a Meeting of the Representatives of said people, in Pennsylvania and New Jersey at Philadelphia, the 24th Day of the First Month, 1775.

Having considered, with real sorrow, the unhappy contest between the legislature of Great Britain and the people of these colonies, and the animosities consequent thereon; we have, by repeated public advices and private admonitions, used our endeavors to dissuade the members of our religious Society from joining with the public resolutions promoted and entered into by some of the people, which, as we apprehended, so as we now find, have increased contention, and produced great discord and confusion.

The Divine principle of grace and truth which we profess, leads all who attend to its dictates, to demean themselves as peaceable subjects, and to discountenance and avoid every measure tending to excite disaffection to the King, as supreme magistrate, or to the legal authority of his government; to which purpose many of the late political writings and addresses to the people appearing to be calculated, we are led by a sense of duty to declare our entire disapprobation of them — their spirit and temper being not only contrary to the nature and precepts of the gospel, but destructive of the peace and harmony of civil society, disqualify men in these times of difficulty, for the wise and judicious consideration and promoting of such measures as would be most effectual for reconciling differences, or obtaining the redress of grievances.

From our past experience of the clemency of the king and his royal ancestors, we have grounds to hope and believe, that decent and respectful addresses from those who are vested with legal authority, representing the prevailing dissatisfactions and the cause of them, would avail towards obtaining relief, ascertaining and establishing the just rights of the people, and restoring the public tranquillity; and we deeply lament that contrary modes of proceeding have been pursued, which have involved the colonies in confusion, appear likely to produce violence and bloodshed, and threaten the subversion of the constitutional government, and of that liberty of conscience, for the enjoyment of which, our ancestors were induced to encounter the manifold dangers and difficulties of crossing the seas, and of settling in the wilderness.

We are, therefore, incited by a sincere concern for the peace and welfare of our country, publicly to declare against every usurpation of power and authority, in opposition to the laws and government, and against all combinations, insurrections, conspiracies and illegal assemblies: and as we are restrained from them by the conscientious discharge of our duty to Almighty God, 'by whom kings reign, and princes decree justice,' we hope through His assistance and favor, to be enabled to maintain our testimony against any requisitions which may be made of us, inconsistent with our religious principles, and the fidelity we owe to the king and his government, as by law established; earnestly desiring the restoration of that harmony and concord which have heretofore united the people of these provinces, and been attended by the divine blessing on their labors.

Signed in and on behalf of the said meeting,

JOHN PEMBERTON, *Clerk at this time.*"[1]

On Friday, October 27, 1775, a committee from the Quakers waited on the Pennsylvania Assembly and presented "An Address" in behalf of that society, expressing deep concern and affliction over the state of the province but asserting that "for conscience sake" they "could not bear arms, nor be concerned in warlike preparations, either by personal service or by paying fines, penalties, or assessments imposed in consideration of . . . exemption from such service."[2] This called forth a remonstrance from "The Committee of the City of Philadelphia."[3]

Talk of independence caused the Friends to take a still more decided position. At their Meeting for Sufferings, January 20, 1776, it was resolved:

"That the benefits, advantages, and favors we have experienced by our dependence on and connection with the king and government . . . appear to demand from us the greatest circumspection, care, and constant endeavors to guard against every attempt to alter, or subvert, that dependence and connection." Accordingly they urge Friends to unite firmly "in the abhorrence of all such writings and measures as evidence a desire and design to break off the happy connection we have hitherto enjoyed with the Kingdom of Great Britain, and our just and necessary subordination to the king, and those who are lawfully placed in authority under him."[4]

[1] Bowden, *op. cit.*, vol. ii,, pp. 300-302; *American Archives*, fourth series, vol. i., pp. 1176-1177.

[2] *American Archives*, fourth series, vol. iii, pp. 1777-1779.

[3] *Ibid.*, vol. iii, pp. 1781-1783.

[4] *Ibid.*, vol. iv, pp. 785-787; Sharpless, *op. cit.*, pp. 125-128; *Philadelphia Ledger*, January 27, 1776; Bowden, *op. cit.*, vol. ii, pp. 306-307.

This reads as though it might have been written by the patriotic John Dickinson; it certainly represents the view of that leader of the early Congress. Such a decided stand on a vital current political question was hardly in conformity with the Fox advice, to keep clear of the commotions involved in government. Also it would be extremely difficult to convince the public that this expressed a pro-American attitude. Nor would Friends submit to the will of the majority when independence was finally voted, but soon thereafter, December 20, 1776, the Meeting for Sufferings issued the following proclamation:

"To our Friends and Brethren in Religious Profession, in these and Adjacent Provinces,

Dearly Beloved Friends and Brethren, — Our minds being renewedly impressed with a fervent religious concern for your spiritual welfare, and preservation in the love and fellowship of the Gospel of our Lord Jesus Christ, the Prince of Peace, by the constrainings of his love, we are engaged to salute you in this time of deep exercise, affliction, and difficulty; earnestly desiring that we may, by steady circumspection, and care, in every part of our conduct and conversation, evidence, that under the close trials which are and may be permitted to attend us, our faith and reliance is fixed on Him alone for protection and deliverance; remembering his gracious promise to his faithful followers, 'Lo, I am with you always, even unto the end of the world.' And as 'it became Him for whom are all things, and by whom are all things, in bringing many sons unto glory,' to make the Captain of their salvation perfect through suffering, 'let us not be dismayed, if we are led into the same path'. As we keep in the Lord's power and peaceable Truth, which is over all, and therein seek the good of all, neither sufferings, persecutions, nor any outward thing that is below, will hinder or break our heavenly fellowship in the light and spirit of Christ.

Thus we may, with Christian firmness and fortitude, withstand and refuse to submit to the arbitrary injunctions and ordinances of men, who assume to themselves the power of compelling others, either in person or by other assistance, to join in carrying on war and of prescribing modes of determining concerning our religious principles, by imposing tests not warranted by the precepts of Christ, or the laws of the happy constitution, under which we and others enjoyed tranquillity and peace.

We therefore, in the aboundings of that love which wisheth the spiritual and temporal prosperity of all men, exhort, admonish, and caution all who make religious profession with us, and especially our beloved youth, to stand fast in that liberty, wherewith, through the manifold sufferings of our predecessors, we have been favored, and steadily to bear our testimony against every attempt to deprive us of it.

And, dear Friends, you who have known the truth, and the powerful operations thereof in your minds, adhere faithfully thereto, and by your good example and stability, labor to strengthen the weak, confirm the wavering, and warn and caution the unwary against being beguiled by the snares of the adversaries of truth and righteousness. Let not the fear of suffering, either in person or in property, prevail on any to join with or promote any work in preparations for war.

Our profession and principles are founded on that spirit which is contrary, and will in time put an end to all wars and bring in everlasting righteousness; and by our constantly abiding under the direction and instruction of that spirit, we may be endued with that 'wisdom from above, which is first pure, then peaceable, gentle and easy to be entreated, full of mercy and good fruits, without partiality, and without hypocrisy.' That this may be our happy experience is our fervent desire and prayer. Signed in and on behalf of the Meeting for Sufferings held in Philadelphia, for Pennsylvania & New Jersey, the 20th day of the 12th. Month, 1776.

JOHN PEMBERTON, *Clerk*."[1]

Things went very badly for the Quakers in 1777. In that year Quaker affairs became a national scandal, and as such it occupied the attention of Congress. General Sullivan forwarded to Congress some "supposedly" seized Quaker letters and documents.[2] It is now quite certain that these were forgeries, "The Spanktown Forgeries,"[3] but that was not then apparent. A committee of Congress, consisting of John Adams, Mr. Drew, and Richard Henry Lee, reported; "That the several testimonies which have been published since the commencement of the present contest between Great Britain and America, and the uniform tenor of the conduct, and

[1] Bowden, *op. cit.*, vol. ii, pp. 309-310; *American Archives*, fifth series, vol. iii, p. 1309.

[2] *Journals of Congress*, viii, 688; Papers of the Continental Congress, No. 78 ii, Folio 233.

[3] "Spanktown," Rahway, New Jersey.

conversation of a number of persons of considerable wealth, who profess themselves to belong to the society of people commonly called Quakers, render it certain and notorious, that those persons are, with much rancor and bitterness, disaffected to the American cause; that, as these persons will have it in their power, so there is no doubt it will be their inclination, to communicate intelligence to the enemy, and, in various other ways, to injure the counsels and arms of America:

That, when the enemy, in the month of December, 1776, were bending their progress towards the city of Philadelphia, a certain seditious publication, addressed 'To our friends and brethren in religious profession in these and adjacent provinces, signed "John Pemberton, in and on behalf on the Meeting for Sufferings, held at Philadelphia, for Pennsylvania and New Jersey, the 20th of the 12th month, 1776",' was published, and, as your committee is credibly informed, circulated amongst many members of the society called Quakers, throughout the different states:

That, as the seditious paper aforesaid, originated in the City of Philadelphia, and as the persons whose names are under mentioned, have uniformly manifested by their general conduct and conversation, a disposition highly inimical to the cause of America, therefore, —

Resolved, That it be earnestly recommended to the Supreme Executive Council of the State of Pennsylvania, forthwith to apprehend and secure the persons of Joshua Fisher, Abel James, James Pemberton, Henry Drinker, Israel Pemberton, John Pemberton, John Jones, Samuel Pleasants, Thomas Wharton Senior, Thomas Fisher (son of Joshua), and Samuel Fisher, together with all such papers in their possession as may be of a political nature.

And whereas, there is strong reason to apprehend that these persons maintain a correspondence and connection highly prejudicial to the public safety, not only in this State, but in the several states of America.

Resolved, That it be recommended to the executive power of the respective States, forthwith to apprehend and secure all persons, as well among the people called Quakers as others, who have, in their general conduct and conversation, evidenced a disposition inimical to the cause of America: and that the persons so seized be confined in such places, and treated in such manner, as shall be consistent with their respective characters and security of their persons:

That the records and papers of the Meetings for Sufferings in the respective States, be forthwith secured and carefully examined, and that such parts of them as may be of a political nature, be forthwith transmitted to Congress."[1]

This report was agreed to and on motion it was "Ordered:

> That the Board of War remove, under guard, to a place of security out of the State of Pennsylvania, the honorable John Penn, Esq., and Benjamin Chew, Esq., and that they give orders for having them safely secured, and entertained agreeable to their rank and station." [2]

Minutes of the various Meetings for Sufferings were seized according to these resolutions but as they were found to contain nothing stronger than appeals to members to remain faithful to their principles, they were soon returned.

September 3, 1777, a letter from the Vice-President of

[1] Bowden, *op. cit.*, vol. ii, pp. 315-316.
[2] *Journals of Congress*, vol. iii, pp. 694-695.

the Supreme Executive Council of Pennsylvania informed Congress that:

> "In consequence of the recommendation of Congress, and their own persuasion of the propriety and necessity of the measure, the council have taken up several persons inimically disposed towards the American states (of the forty, only half were Friends, but among them were the three Pembertons); that few of the Quakers among these are willing to make any promise of any kind; and desiring the advice of Congress, particularly whether Augusta or Winchester in Virginia, would not be suitable places in which to secure these persons."

Whereupon it was resolved:

> "That Congress approve of the Quaker prisoners being sent to Virginia, and, in the opinion of Congress, that Staunton, in the county of Augusta, is the most proper place in the State of Virginia for their residence and security; and with regard to the other prisoners mentioned in their letter, Congress leave it to the Supreme Executive Council to do with them as their wisdom shall think best."[1]

It was also resolved, "That the Supreme Executive Council be informed that Congress has no objections to the enlargement of such persons now confined in the Lodge as will swear or affirm allegiance to this State."[2]

A remonstrance was received at this time from the Pembertons, Fishers, Drinker, Pleasants and Wharton and read. This was taken into consideration and it was resolved, September 6, "That it be recommended to the Supreme Executive Council of the State of Pennsylvania, to hear what the said remonstrants can allege, to remove the suspicion of their being disaffected or dangerous to the United States, and act therein as the said council judge most conducive to the public safety."[3] Congress was plainly already aware that it had acted precipitously, and was seeking to shift responsibility to the shoulders of

[1] *Journals of Congress*, vol. viii, p. 707.
[2] *Ibid.*, vol. viii. p. 713.
[3] *Ibid.*, vol. viii, pp. 714, 718.

the state of Pennsylvania. Yet it had to carry the matter farther. A letter from the Council of Pennsylvania with a list of the persons arrested in pursuance of the resolve of Congress was read, September 8, also a letter from Thomas Wharton, Junior, president of the Council of Pennsylvania. Whereupon it was:

"Resolved, That it would be improper for Congress to entertain any hearing of the remonstrants or the other prisoners in the Lodge, they being inhabitants of Pennsylvania; and, therefore, as the Council declines giving them a hearing, for the reasons assigned in their letter to Congress, that it be recommended to the said Council to order the immediate departure of such of the said prisoners as yet refuse to swear *or affirm* allegiance to the State of Pennsylvania, to Staunton in Virginia." [1]

It was thus, in accordance with orders from the national government that the Pennsylvania Quakers were persecuted. Without trial, despite urgent appeals and protests to the State Council, to Congress and to the People of Pennsylvania, and under conditions of great harshness, a large number of Quakers were imprisoned.

A *Protest*, signed by 113 Friends, and addressed "To the President and Council of Pennsylvania," September 9, 1777, stigmatized the whole proceedings against the Quakers as "an alarming violation of the civil and religious rights of the community" and set forth:

"The remonstrance and protest of the subscribers, herewith; That your resolve of this day was this afternoon delivered to us; which is the more unexpected, as last evening your secretary informed us, you had referred our business to Congress, to whom we are about to apply.

In this resolve, contrary to the inherent rights of mankind, you condemn us to banishment unheard.

You determine matters concerning us, which we could have disproved, had our rights to a hearing been granted.

The charge against us, of refusing 'to promise to refrain from corresponding with the enemy', insinuates that we have already held such correspondence, which we utterly and solemnly deny.

[1] *Journals of Congress,* vol. viii. p. 723.

The tests you proposed, we were by no law bound to subscribe, and notwithstanding our refusing them, we are still justly and lawfully entitled to all the rights of citizenship of which you are attempting to deprive us.

We have never been suffered to come before you to evince our innocence, and to remove suspicions, which you have labored to instill into the minds of others; and at the same time knew to be groundless; although Congress recommended you to give us a hearing,[1] and your President assured two of our friends this morning we should have it.

Upon the whole, your proceedings have been so arbitrary, that words are wanting to express our sense of them. We do therefore, as the last office we expect you will now suffer us to perform for the benefit of our country, in behalf of ourselves and those freemen of Pennsylvania who have any regard for liberty, solemnly remonstrate and protest against your whole conduct in this unreasonable excess of power exercised by you.

That the evil and destructive spirit of pride, ambition, and arbitrary power with which you have been actuated, may cease and be no more; and 'that peace on earth and good will to men', may happily take the place thereof, in your and all men's minds, is the sincere desire of your oppressed and injured fellow citizens."[2]

The prisoners had been sent off to Virginia on September 11. Congress could truthfully declare then, September 28, "They (Friends) are, with much rancor and bitterness, disaffected to the American cause."[3] But it was not proud of its part in the proceedings and soon essayed to cover its complicity in the matter. January 29, 1778, Congress passed a resolution for the discharge of the prisoners on their taking an affirmation of allegiance to the State of Pennsylvania, as a free and independent State.[4] This the Friends declined to do. Congress then resolved March 16, 1778, to place them at the disposal of the Council of Pennsylvania. The Council decided, April 8, 1778, to set them free, providing, "That the whole

[1] *Journals of Congress*, September 6, 1777; Bowden, *op. cit.*, vol. ii, pp. 317-318.

[2] Bowden, *op. cit.*, vol. ii, pp. 319-320.

[3] *Journals of Congress*, vol. x, p. 98.

[4] Bowden, *op. cit.*, vol. ii, p. 325.

expense of arresting and confining the prisoners sent to Virginia, the expenses of the journey, and all other incidental charges, be paid by the said prisoners."[1] According to this resolution the prisoners were brought North and discharged. Some, however, including the "King of the Quakers," Israel Pemberton, had died as a result of confinement.

Upon the return of the Americans to Philadelphia in 1778, after its evacuation by the British, two Quakers, Roberts and Carlisle, were hanged on the charge of treason.[2]

The whole matter had been a test and, as it were, a vindication of Quaker principles. The Meeting for Sufferings at Philadelphia, August 8, 1778, addressed to the Assembly of Pennsylvania a clear restatement of these principles:

"They respectfully represent that the government of the consciences of men is the prerogative of Almighty God, who will not give His glory to another; that every encroachment on this His prerogative, is offensive in His sight, and that He will not hold them guiltless who invade it, but will sooner or later manifest His displeasure to all who persist therein. These truths will, we doubt not, obtain the assent of every considerate mind. The immediate occasion of our applying to you is (that) we have received accounts from different places, that a number of our friends are and have been imprisoned, some for refusing to pay the fines imposed in lieu of personal services in the present war, and others for refusing to take the test prescribed by some laws lately made.

The ground of our refusal is a religious scruple in our minds against such compliance, not from obstinacy, or any other motive than a desire of keeping a conscience void of offence towards God, which we cannot, without a steady adherence to our peaceable principles and testimony against wars and fightings, founded on the precepts and example of our

[1] Bowden, *op. cit.*, vol. ii, p. 326; Thomas Gilpin, "Exiles in Virginia."

[2] Jones, Sharpless and Gummere, *The Quakers in the American Colonies*; Bowden, *op. cit.*, Chapter xii, "Difficulties of the Friends during the War of Independence." Windsor, vol. vi, pp. 393, 417; Hildreth, vol. iii, p. 195. Gordon, *Am. Rev.*, vol. iv, p. 377.

Lord Jesus Christ, the Prince of Peace; by conformity to which, we are bound to live a peaceable and quiet life, and restrained from making any declaration or entering into any engagements as parties in the present unsettled state of public affairs." [1]

They are seeking now redress from local persecution and express the desire that "the laws which have a tendency to oppress tender consciences may be repealed" and provision made for the release of those in "bonds for the testimony of a good conscience, and which may prevent others hereafter from suffering in like manner."[2] Records for five Quarterly Meetings show nine thousand five hundred pounds distraint.

The Quaker position was improving but it was by no means as yet entirely a happy one. A new law of the Pennsylvania Assembly had shut them out from teaching, so an appeal from Meeting for Sufferings, November 11, 1779, to the Assembly was carried:

"Our predecessors, on their early settlement in this part of America, being piously concerned for the prosperity of the colony, and the real welfare of their posterity, among other salutary institutions, promoted at their own expense the establishment of schools for the instruction of their youth in useful and necessary learning, and for their education in piety and virtue, the practice of which forms the most sure basis for perpetuating the enjoyment of Christian liberty and essential happiness. By the voluntary contributions of the members of our religious Society schools were set up, in which their children were taught; and careful attention hath been given to the instruction of the children of the poor, not of our Society only, but our liberality hath been extended to poor children of other religious denominations generally, great numbers of whom have partaken thereof; and these schools have been in like manner continued and maintained for a long course of years.

Duty to Almighty God made known in the consciences of men, and confirmed by the Holy Scriptures, is an invariable rule, which should govern their judgment and actions. He is the only Lord and sovereign of conscience, and to Him we are accountable for our conduct, as by Him all men are to be finally judged. — By conscience we mean, the appre-

[1] Bowden, *op. cit.*, vol. ii, pp. 330-331.
[2] *Ibid.*, *loc. cit.*

hension and persuasion a man has of his duty to God; and the liberty of conscience we plead for, is a free open profession and unmolested exercise of that duty — such a conscience, as under the influence of Divine Grace, keeps within the bounds of morality, in all the affairs of human life, and teacheth to live soberly, righteously, and godly in the world.

The matters we have now freely laid before you are serious and important, which we wish you to consider wisely as men, and religiously as Christians: manifesting yourselves friends to true liberty, and enemies to persecution, by repealing the several penal laws affecting tender consciences, and restoring to us our equitable rights, that the means of education and instruction of our youth, which we conceive to be our reasonable and religious duty, may not be obstructed, and that the oppressed may be relieved. In your consideration whereof we sincerely desire that you may seek for, and be directed by that supreme 'wisdom, which is pure, peaceable, gentle, and easy to be entreated, full of mercy and good fruits'."[1]

This was referred by the Assembly to the Committee on Grievance, who proposed March 4, 1780, a series of questions to the society, in writing. These related to the acknowledgment of the American Government, the validity of its laws, paper money, etc., and concluded, "As you are especially associated together, though not incorporated in Law, and issue public letters and recommendations, and promulgate opinions not only on religion, but political subjects, or at least uniting them together, you are requested to communicate the letters and testimonies which have been published from time to time for seven years past, and signed by the clerks of your General or Quarterly Meetings of this city, to be sent to other meetings, or to persons of your Society."[2]

The Society did not comply with this request of the Assembly but replied as follows:

"To the Committee of Grievances,

Your paper directed to Isaac Zane and others, propounding divers questions to our religious Society, hath been considered, and, agreeable to

[1] Bowden, *op. cit.*, vol. ii, pp. 332-333; Thomas, *op. cit.*, p. 117.
[2] Bowden, *op. cit.*, vol. ii, pp. 333-334.

the advice of an eminent Apostle to his Christian brethren, it become us 'to be always ready to give an answer to every man that asketh a reason of the hope that is in us with meekness and fear,' so also we think it necessary, according to their practice, after the example of their Lord and Master, to adapt the answer to the nature and tendency of the question proposed.

On reviewing the Memorial presented to the Assembly, and our address to you, they appear to us to contain matter of such importance, and so clearly point out the sentiments and practice of our religious Society, in the various changes and revolutions which have occurred in civil government since we were distinguished from other Christian professions, that a weighty, impartial attention to them, and a willingness to remove the cause of oppression complained of, would, we apprehend, sufficiently enable you, to represent to the House, the justice and expediency of relief, on the principles of Christianity and civil liberty.

Our religious meetings were instituted for the laudable intention of inculcating in our fellow-members, worship to Almighty God, benevolence to mankind, and to encourage one another in a steadfast, upright conduct, according to the pure principles of the Gospel; and have been continued for those Christian purposes for more than a century past; nor hath the original design of their institution been perverted to the purpose of political disquisitions, or anything prejudicial to the public safety: we therefore, conceive the queries you have proposed to us in a religious capacity, are improper, and a mode of redressing grievances new and unprecedented, and such an inquisition made on a religious Society, as we have not known nor heard of in America: nevertheless, we may briefly repeat what has been already declared on behalf of our religious Society, to revive the important subject of the Memorial in your view; which we think is still worthy of very serious and unbiased consideration.

Our Friends have always considered Government to be a divine ordinance, instituted for the suppressing of vice and immorality, the promotion of virtue, and protection of the innocent from oppression and tyranny. And they esteem those legislators and magistrates, who make the fear and honor of God the rule of their conduct, to be worthy of respect and obedience. And that it is our duty to live a godly, peaceable, and quiet life. It is also our firm belief that conscience ought not to be subject to the control of men, or the injunctions of human laws; and every attempt to restrain or enforce it, is an invasion of the prerogative of the Supreme Lord and Lawgiver . . . . .

As our Christian principle leads into a life of sobriety and peace, so it restrains us from taking active part in the present contest or joining with any measures which tend to create or promote disturbance or commotion in the government under which we are placed; and many of our brethren, from a conviction that war is so opposite to the nature and spirit of the Gospel, apprehend it their duty to refrain in any degree from voluntarily contributing to its support; some of whom, for a considerable number of years past on former occasions, have not actively complied with the payment of taxes raised for military services; and divers, from conscientious motives, have now avoided circulating the currency which hath been emitted for the immediate purpose of carrying on war; although on these accounts, they have been, and still are, subjected to great inconvenience, losses, and sufferings. It hath been the uniform practice of our religious Society, after the example of other Christian churches in every age, to issue epistles of counsel and admonition to their members as occasion required; those and the testimonies you allude to, contain seasonable exhortations to observe a godly conduct, consistent with the peaceable principles of our Christian profession; and the papers and records of some of our meetings were seized and detained in the Ninth Month, 1777, and after undergoing a scrutiny and examination, nothing seditious or prejudicial to the public good being found in them, they were returned.

In whatever mistaken or unfavorable light our religious Society may be held, by those who are unacquainted with us and our principles, or prejudiced against us, we hope to manifest by our conduct, that we are true friends to all men, and sincerely desirous to promote and inculcate such a temper of mind in our fellow-professors in general, as to enable us to forgive them who evilly entreat us, and pray for them who persecute us.

Signed on behalf of the Committee of the people called Quakers, who waited on the Assembly of Pennsylvania, with a memorial and address, in the Eleventh Month, 1779. ISAAC ZANE."[1]

There is little more to be recorded of the Revolutionary position of the American Quakers; the local Pennsylvnaia situation did not improve. In fact the Yearly Meeting of 1781 wrote to the London Yearly Meeting: "The sufferings of Friends in these parts have much increased, and continue increasing, in a manner which, to outward prospect, looks ruinous . . . . . Our two brethren who have been long imprisoned in Lancaster jail, are still under confinement there, although their innocence of any crime is acknowledged by those who detain them."[2] And the

[1] Bowden, *op. cit.*, vol. ii, pp. 334-336.
[2] *Ibid.*, vol. ii, p. 337.

Meeting for Sufferings in Philadelphia complained to the London Brethren in that same year, "Various are the trials and sufferings of Friends on this Continent, and in many instances very grievous: men actuated by the spirit of war, prejudiced and blinded by party fears and animosities, are unwilling to understand our peaceable Christian testimony, as anything more than a political enmity against them; and thus precluding themselves from the candid exercise of their own reason as men, they treat Friends in some cases with great rigor and inhumanity."[1]

Some of the rigors of 1781 were due to Friends refusing to celebrate the glorious victory of Yorktown. Outrages and violence were committed on their persons and property, by individuals and by companies of lawless people who paraded the streets of Philadelphia.[2]

The Meeting for Sufferings of Philadelphia in this year addressed another solemn appeal "To the President and Executive Council and General Assembly of Pennsylvania, and others whom it may concern:

> We are not incited by party views or vindictive motives in this representation, but to awaken your cool and dispassionate attention to our multiplied sufferings, and the abuses we have received; knowing that magistracy is intended for a terror to evil-doers, and an encouragement to the virtuous; but where the necessary care and exertions are not used for the prevention and suppression of profanity, tumults, and outrage, and a virtuous part of the community are oppressed and insulted, the true end of government is neglected, and anarchy, confusion, contempt of authority, and insecurity to persons and property will succeed; and although public fasts may be proclaimed, and days under the name of humiliation recommended and appointed, and confession of sin and transgression verbally made, yet unless these be a true and sincere fasting from ambition, strife, ill-will, animosities, infidelity, fraud, luxury, revelling, drunkenness, oppression, and all manner of evil, it cannot be

[2] Bowden, *op. cit.*, vol. ii, pp. 336-337.
[3] *Ibid.*, vol. ii, p. 341.

a fast, or acceptable day to the LORD, nor can we have a well-grounded hope, that the scourge with which the inhabitants have been visited will be removed, and days of peace and tranquillity restored.

The dispensation of war, bloodshed, and calamity, which hath been permitted to prevail on this continent, is very solemn and awful, demanding the most serious and heartfelt attention of all ranks and denominations among the people, individually to consider and examine how far we are each of us really and sincerely engaged to bring forth fruits of true repentance and amendment of life, agreeable to the spirit and doctrine of the Gospel. And although we have been exposed to great abuses and unchristian treatment, we wish to be enabled, through the assistance of Divine Grace, to cherish in ourselves, and inculcate in others with whom we have an influence, that disposition of forgiveness of injuries, enjoined by the precepts and example of Christ our holy lawgiver; *and to manifest our desires and endeavors to promote the real good of our country.*"[1]

Here at last we have an expression from the Quakers of their desire to assist in the work of establishing "Our Country." They came to be champions of the Constitution and Brissot de Warville asserts that Washington "regarded them as the best citizens of the new government."[2]

The attitude of the Moravian Brethren toward the Revolution was to be sadly misunderstood by both sides and their lot was to prove far more pitifully tragic than that of their fellow conscientious neutrals, the Quakers. Opposed as they were to an oath in any form, the first effect of hostilities was to terminate their evangelistic itinerancies. No one who refused to take the American test oath was allowed to proceed North or East of Easton, Pennsylvania. This in effect shut the body of their church off from their greatest field of activities, missions among the frontier Indians. Then too communication with the church authorities in Europe became very uncertain.

[1] Bowden, *op. cit.*, vol. ii, pp. 341-343.
[2] *Supra*, p. 134.

Though cheerfully responding to requisitions for supplies, their conscientious refusals to bear arms involved them in serious difficulties and brought financial penalties. They were notified that unless all males above sixteen years of age presented themselves for military duty on a certain day, they would be taxed three pounds and three shillings for each man under fifty. This tax they paid. As time wore on, however, some of the younger men accepted the new order.

Devoted hospital service tended to correct the bad impressions created by non-military service. The general hospital of the American Army was located at Bethlehem, Pennsylvania, their stronghold, from December 1776 to March 1777, and from September 1777 to June 1778. At another time their buildings at Lititz were requisitioned for a similar purpose.

At the Bethlehem hospital John Ettwein, one of their leaders, later created bishop, acted as army chaplain. Throughout the Revolution he received, in the name of the church, the many distinguished visitors that flocked to that town. His sturdy courage and strong good sense won for him the friendship of such men as Henry Laurens, Samuel Adams, John Hancock and General Washington; which friendships were in later trying times to prove of great value to the Brethren as a denomination. Though a Tory in his earlier sympathies, Ettwein was induced by his co-religionist, Von Schweinitz, to accept the independence of the colonies as an act of providence. Upon becoming Bishop in 1784, he was to find his Americanism of great service in fitting his church to the new nation. In 1787 he founded the "Society for the Propagation of the Gospels among the Heathen," which society speedily secured incorporation from the Pennsylvania

Assembly, and large endowments from the national government.[1]

It was chiefly in their Indian missions that the Moravians influenced the course of the Revolution, and paradoxically it was there that they most seriously suffered from the effects of the Revolutionary war-hysteria. In 1772 Ettwein had led the Christian Indians from the valley of the Susquehanna to the Tuscarawas in Ohio. There three prosperous civilized villages had been founded, the centres of the missionary activities of six Moravian missionaries, chief of whom was David Zeisberger. It was his influence in the councils of the Iroquois and Delawares that restrained these nations from war activities in those gloomy years of war, when their power might have proven a serious menace to the American cause.

Three Indian departments had been organized by Congress in July 1775, and through Chief White Eyes, Congress immediately approached the Delaware tribes.[2] The Delawares, in council, decided to abide by the Moravian church, and the leadership of Zeisberger. Zeisberger becomes a far more powerful figure in Revolutionary Delaware annals than their Chief White Eyes.

It has been computed that the Indians of New York, Ohio, and the Lake regions could muster, at the beginning of the Revolution, not less than ten thousand warriors. If the British had succeeded in establishing, as they tried, an offensive confederation among these Indian tribes the results would have been fearful. While Samuel Kirkland secured the neutrality of the Oneidas and Tuscaroras, so that the Iroquois were divided, Zeisberger prevented

[1] *Transactions of the Moravian Historical Society*, Series II, pp. 247-263; Hamilton, J. T., A *History of the Unitas Fratrum, or Moravian Church in the United States of America*, p. 472.

[2] *Infra*, pp. 421-422.

the Delawares from taking up the hatchet, in the earlier years of the war. If the greater part of the Delawares eventually went over to the enemy, it was when the State had gained a decisive victory over the forces of Burgoyne and when French aid made their cause more hopeful. It was in the gloomy years of the war that Zeisberger kept back the Western hordes. In his Manuscript *History of the Indians*, Zeisberger says, "If the Delawares had taken part against the Americans in the present war, America would have had terrible experiences; for the neutrality of the Delawares kept all the many nations that are their grandchildren neutral too, except the Shawenese."[1] The importance of this service was acknowledged by such men as Generals Butler, Hand, Brodhead, Gibson, Irvine, and Neville. The following is the testimony of General Butler, "Had the chiefs of the Delaware nation, together with the Christian Indians, pursued a different course than that which they adopted, all joined the enemy, and taken up the hatchet against the Americans, it would have cost the United States much blood and treasure to have withstood and checked their progress besides weakening our already feeble armies on the sea-board, by draining them of troops for the Western service, and this might have proved fatal to the cause."[2]

The Christian Indians were placed between the two frontier centres of influence, Pittsburgh for the Americans and Detroit for the British. Their neutrality exposed them to hostilities from both sides. And yet the Pittsburgh forces were enabled to secure an attitude of benevolent

[1] De Schweinitz, *Life and Times of David Zeisberger*, p. 444.

[2] Note 2, p. 444, De Schweinitz, *Life and Times of David Zeisberger* quoting from Heckewelder's *Report of the Mission to the Society for Propagating the Gospel* in the archives of the Moravian Society at Bethlehem.

neutrality. By an Indian Treaty entered into at Pittsburgh, September 17, 1778, it was stipulated that, 1, The Americans should at any time be allowed to march troops through the Delaware country, and erect a fort within their territory, in return for which, 2, The Delawares should be admitted to a perpetual alliance and confederation with the United States.[1] This treaty was to prove a blunder for it gave the Indians nothing tangible and raised false hopes on both sides.

The non-militant Christian Indians frequently were able to persuade war-parties to turn back and by request of the Delaware council they wrote letters to the commandant at Pittsburgh informing him of projected raids. These acts were not performed as American spies, nor in the interest of the American cause politically considered, they were in the name of humanity. But unfortunately a position such as this, was incomprehensible to the British authorities; the Moravian missionaries became to them, not the upholders of humanitarian principles, but the abettors of the American rebellion, on a par with its frontier scouts.[2]

In August 1781, a force of a hundred and fifty Whites and Indians, under British officers, soon augmented to over three hundred by the Indians, appeared and, after plundering their homes, forced the Missionaries and their Christian Indians to enter the British lines at Sandusky. They were deserted in October practically without food. Their leaders, including Zeisberger, were summoned to Detroit for trial as American spies. This trial resulted in complete acquittal, but the disaster to the mission could not be remedied with a word. A dreadful winter was

[1] De Schweinitz, *op. cit.*, pp. 468-469.
[2] *Ibid.*, pp. 488-489.

spent on the Sandusky, a pint of corn becoming the allowance for each member of the mission family. At length about a hundred and fifty of the converts obtained permission to return to the Tuscarawa Valley to secure whatever of the unharvested corn might remain. But here they were to experience a calamity of misplaced American indignation.

Although the Christian Indians had repeatedly shown their consistent adherence to non-combatant principles, they were mistakenly identified with the perpetrators of border raids and massacres that had horrified the border settlements during the preceding winter. To avenge these wrongs about ninety men under Colonel Williamson had set out from Monongahela. These militiamen arrived among the Christian Indians on the evening before they were to have commenced their return journey, and were hospitably received because the Indians felt that the Americans had come to deliver them from the trouble that had originated at Detroit. The next morning Williamson's force herded the Indians into two buildings, wantonly named the "slaughter-houses" and there, in cold blood, butchered ninety Christian Indians and six heathen visitors; included in the number were five assistant missionaries. Only two lads escaped to tell the tale. A part of the original band located some distance away escaped to the Sandusky, only to find upon their arrival there, that Zeisberger and his associates had again been summoned to Detroit on a renewal of the old charge.[1]

At Detroit Zeisberger was again successful in establishing his innocence and finally was able to conduct the

[1] Zeisberger, *Diary*, March 1782, pp. 78-82; De Schweinitz, *op. cit.*, pp. 530-557; Taylor, *History of Ohio*; Heckewelder, *English Narrative of the Massacre* (Bethlehem Archives); Heckewelder, *History of the Mission; Pennsylvania Archives*, vol. ix; Howell, *Atlantic Monthly*, vol. 22, p. 95.

remnant of his flock by way of Lake St. Clair and the Huron River to the Chippewa country in Michigan, where he founded New Gnadenhutten. After peace had been concluded, and Ettwein had secured from Congress the grant of land in the Tuscarawas Valley, a party of one hundred and seventeen converts set out for their old homes. But they halted at Pilgerruh, on the Cuyahoga, on account of the inveterate hostility of border American public sentiment. At length, after various wanderings caused by Indian wars, Goshen, Ohio, was settled in 1798 and Zeisberger ministered here.

PART TWO

NATIONALIZATION OF THE AMERICAN CHURCHES

CHAPTER VII

THE METHODIST EPISCOPAL CHURCH IN AMERICA

The first church in the United States to work out an independent, national form of ecclesiastical organization and discipline was the Methodist Episcopal Church. Moreover, the change which it thereby effected was more revolutionary in character than was that accomplished by any other denomination. As soon as the colonies became free from the mother country, the Methodist societies broke with their parent in England. With them separation and reorganization were the work of but a few months. The year 1784, following the signing of the Peace of Paris, saw the New Methodist Episcopal Church fully organized, though not in its final form; complete separation from dependence on the Church of England, revision of the founder's conception of complete dependence upon his authority, and an adoption of the American ideal of a republican commonwealth government through a general conference. That the Methodist Episcopalians thus anticipated other sects in the work of constitution-making, resulted from several peculiarities of their situation.

Colonial Methodism was in every sense of the word a part of Anglicanism. Its congregations were not a church; its missionaries and preachers were not a clergy. It was but a series of clubs for the promotion of holiness; places of assembly were but "Meeting Houses" or "Chapels." Its places of worship were always open to the regular Anglican clergy for preaching or the administration of the sacraments.[1] Preachers were simply unordained lay missionaries, dependent upon the Anglican clergy for the administration of the sacraments and strictly warned against the sacrilege of administering the ordinances of baptism and the holy supper. So vital was this independence that in Virginia, where their greatest colonial strength lay, we find them fighting shoulder to shoulder with the Church of England, for the preservation of the established church.[2]

The war temporarily disrupted the Church of England in the colonies; establishments were abolished, the clergy fled, and the church itself was looked upon as a part of the government with which the United States was at war.[3] This left the Methodists destitute of the ordinary Christian ceremonials. Mr. Wesley complains of this situation in a letter of September 10, 1784, as follows: "In America there are none (bishops with a legal jurisdiction), and but few parish ministers; so that for some hundred miles together there is none either to baptize or to administer the Lord's Supper."[4]

The Methodist missionaries themselves were largely Englishmen. All ten of the preachers who composed the first American conference in 1773 had been of English or Irish origin, not one of them was a native American. And within two years of the signing of the Declaration of Independence, Francis Asbury was the only one of English preachers remaining in America. Connection between English and American Methodism had been shattered.

[1] *Minutes of the Annual Conferences of the Methodist Church for the Years 1773-1823*, edition of 1840, pp. 11-13.

[2] *Journal of the House of Delegates*, October 28, 1776.

[3] *Supra*, chapter ii.

[4] *British Minutes of 1785*, ed. 1812, pp. 179-181.

A yearly conference for the colonial Methodists had existed since 1773. This had accustomed the preachers to governmental procedure even previous to the Declaration of Independence and the flight of the English assistants.[1] The stress of the situation in 1778 caused this body to assume temporary governmental powers and at the close of the War it had gained a very definite conception of the part which a representative assembly might and, as they thought, should play in any form of government.

American Methodism throve throughout the period of the war and reconstruction. The First Conference of 1773 had reported ten preachers and 1166 members of the denomination; the Conference of 1784 revealed 83 preachers and 14,998 members.[2] The old order was entirely inadequate to the needs of such expansion.

The ministers were all young and enthusiastic. Coke says of the Conference of 1784, "They were indeed a body of devoted, disinterested men, but most of them young."[3] William Watters was but twenty-seven years of age, when he presided over the Conference of 1778; Francis Asbury was thirty-three at that time; Thomas Coke was thirty-one. They were filled with the spirit of youth; they were out to conquer a continent. They were progressives wishing to construct American Christianity in terms of the future rather than to follow blindly those Anglican traditions which all realized to be historically weak in spots.

The vision of John Wesley was a vital element in the working out of definite plans to meet the American situation. No one was more conscious of the dilemma

[1] Tipple, *Francis Asbury*, p. 117, "This was the first steps towards separation."
[2] *Minutes*, 1773 and 1784.
[3] Coke, *Journal*.

of the American branch of Methodist Episcopalianism than was its founder. He seems to have been the first to realize the effects of independence on the old order. The new church was built solidly upon a foundation proscribed by Wesley himself. It is true that he seems never to have realized fully the new spirit of the younger men. The church used his foundations but the superstructure was to belong to the younger generation. Not all the vision was his.

Few people in England knew the intricacies of ecclesiastical politics better than did John Wesley. It is clear that he realized that other plans were afoot in Great Britain for the reorganization of American Episcopacy. Samuel Seabury had arrived in England in 1783 seeking consecration as Bishop of Connecticut. There is no doubt but that Mr. Wesley hoped to and did forestall all others by the organization of his American Methodist Episcopalian Church. Wesley's first "Superintendent" or "Bishop" had been set apart to his task by the laying on of hands and had reached America, and was already performing his Episcopal functions when at last, on November 14, 1784, Samuel Seabury was consecrated by the Scottish bishops at Aberdeen.

And why shouldn't Methodist Episcopalianism become the American form of Episcopalianism? Wesley considered Anglicanism as distinctly a national religion, to be sure the very best form;[1] but why not a new form more in keeping with primitive Christianity and nearer to the needs of primitive American surroundings. It seemed more than doubtful whether the United States would ever consent to the presence of any church dependent upon a foreign authority. Episcopalianism of the sort that

[1] *British Minutes* of 1785, pp. 179-181.

had existed in the colonies had been civil as well as ecclesiastical. Now Wesley's Methodist Episcopalianism was to be Episcopalian both as to form and tradition. Prompt action might install it as American Episcopalianism. John Wesley was not the man to let opportunity pass him by. He acted quickly;[1] and for a brief period American Methodists may have felt that they were actually the complete Episcopal Church of America.

That Wesley's church failed to become the national church of the United States resulted primarily from the American spirit of abhorrence of any establishment. The American religious spirit was one of "religious liberty"; and the converse of King James' dictum, "No Bishop, No King," seemed to hold, — "No King, No Bishop." It is not surprising then that the "Methodist" part of Wesley's institution has been emphasized to the neglect of its Episcopalian character. Then too there was the fatal question about the orthodoxy of Wesley's power to institute "Superintendents" or "Bishops." In addition free America resented the conception of the "prerogative" of the traditional bishop. And the politicians in the Virginia General Assembly persisted in regarding the Protestant Episcopal Church as the legal successor to the Established Church.

John Wesley's plans contemplated an American Church dependent upon his authority during his life and after that upon the authority of his lawfully designated successor; the spirit of America was repelled by the plans which Mr. Wesley handed to them in 1784, and erected thereon a church in which these plans and traditions were interpreted in terms of the future of American Christianity.

[1] McConnell, *American Episcopal Church* speaks of this as "secession" begun in 1784 from the Protestant Episcopal Church.

They read into them a great deal that Wesley could not approve; they transformed his plans for an Episcopacy exercising a very limited degree of autonomy, delegated from his plethora of autocracy, into a democratic republican institution, governed by its own general conference and electing its own bishops. Those same forces which caused Methodism to effect reorganization in advance of its rivals in America, also, as we shall see, stamped upon it a most distinctly American character. They created a church marked by independence, liberality, progressiveness, self-reliance, and representative democracy.

At the outbreak of the Revolution the Methodists in the English colonies were for strictest adherence to Anglican traditions. Mr. Wesley instructed them in a letter dated March 1, 1775, to observe strictest neutrality:

> "My dear Brethren: You were never in your lives in so critical a situation as you are at his time. It is your part to be peace makers; . . . to addict yourself to no party. In spite of all solicitations . . . . . say not one word against one or the other side." [1]

These instructions the Conference of 1775 resolved to follow implicitly; as Rankin, Wesley's first-assistant, says, "We came unanimously to this conclusion, to follow the advice that Mr. Wesley and his brother had given us, and leave the event to God."[2] Strict neutrality did not prevent their agreeing to "A general fast for the prosperity of the work, and for the Peace of America, on Tuesday, the 18th of July."[3] It did, however, prevent their taking any notice of American Independence when that came. The term "United States" does not appear in the minutes of their meetings until the Baltimore Conference of 1783."[4]

[1] Wesley, *Works*, American edition, vii, 7, 8.
[2] *Ibid.*, vii, p. footnote.
[3] *Minutes*, edition of 1795, pp. 13-15, edition of 1840, pp. 6-7.
[4] *Ibid.*, edition of 1840, pp. 17-19.

The very complexion of American Methodism made its attitude of neutrality impossible. All of Wesley's assistants were native Englishmen; so were a majority of the preachers. We have already noted,[1] that in Virginia where nearly two-thirds of the Methodists were located,[2] they in 1776 officially:

"Beg leave to declare they are a religious society in communion with the Church of England, and do all in their power to strengthen and support the said church, and . . . . . pray that the Church of England, as it ever hath been, may still continue to be the established church."[3]

Events in America moved so rapidly that not even a religious organization was to be allowed the attitude of neutrality. The people could not overlook that Methodist preachers were mostly Englishmen with British sympathies; that they were all communicants of the Church of England. Methodists as a body were subject to the not unreasonable suspicion of being disaffected to the cause of American Independence. They were subjected to annoyance, mob violence, and military arrests. Times were too strenuous for a continuance of Methodist neutrality. It became apparent that the Britishers must be sent home and that an American control should replace British.

The Conference of 1777 realized this necessity and took action. William Watters, who as an American participant was deeply interested in the outcome, has left us an account of the proceedings. He says:

"There appearing no probability of the contest between Great Britain and this country ending shortly, several of our European preachers thought that if an opportunity should offer, they would return to their

[1] *Supra*, p. 124
[2] Stevens, *History of the Methodist Episcopal Church*, vol. ii, p. 42.
[3] *Journal of the House of Burgesses*, October 28, 1776.

homes in the course of the year. To provide against such an event five of us, Gatch, Dromgoole, Ruff, Glendenning, and myself, were appointed a committee to act in the place of the general assembly in case they should all go before the next conference. It was also submitted to the consideration of this Conference whether in our present situation, of having but few ministers left in many of our parishes to administer the ordinances of baptism and the Lord's supper, we should not administer them ourselves . . . . . In fact we considered ourselves, at this time, as belonging to the Church of England, it being before the separation and our becoming a regularly formed Church. After much conversation of the subject, it was unanimously agreed to lay it over for the determination of the next Conference, to be held in Leesburg, the 19th of May." [1]

Asbury was very blue over the outlook. His Journal informs us that, "When the time of parting came, many wept as if they had lost their first-born sons. They appeared to be in the deepest distress, thinking, as I suppose, they should not see the faces of the English preachers any more.[2] The lot of the Englishmen was to be as was feared. Rankin, Wesley's general-assistant, who had presided over the conference of 1777, returned to England in March 1778; Asbury himself having refused to take the Maryland State oath was for two years a refugee, in Delaware; for a time he seriously considered leaving the country. Interest in the controversy of 1779-1780 caused him to stay on and he alone of all "The Britishers" remained throughout the Revolution.

Watters, an American, — in fact the "first native itinerant," had been placed at the head of "the committee" by the Conference of 1777. As the first American chief of administration he exercised, in fact if not in name, the superintendency during this period of the Revolution. The Conference had designated its own leader. As Tigert says,

[1] Watters, *Christian Experiences and Ministerial Labours*, 1806, pp. 56-57.

[2] Asbury, *Journal*, p. 186.

"Thus closed the first period of close connection with England and of the occupancy of the Conference Chair by Mr. Wesley's appointed delegate and representative. The War effectually cut off communication with the home office; and with the Conference of 1778, William Watters, the American in the Chair, begins a new era, which continues till 1784, when Mr. Wesley's hand again appears and his control asserts itself." [1]

"Having no old preachers with us, we were as orphans bereft of our spiritual parents; but though young and inexperienced in business, the Lord looked graciously upon us,"[2] says William Watters, who at twenty-seven years of age presided over the Leesburgh Conference of 1778. Bereft of English guidance, the members of this Conference were to learn in a way that they would never forget, the potentialities of the conference as a governing body. Wesley's temporal control having vanished, American Methodism learned how to rely solely upon its own powers of self-government as a means of interpreting and administering the spiritual inheritance which it had received from Wesley. Never again, as in 1776,[3] shall we find it working for a temporal establishment.

The years of 1779 and 1780 disclosed a schism in the ranks of American Methodists. A Conservative North faced a Progressive South. The North represented the orthodox English system; the South undertook a programme of radical reorganization. The North could claim regularity from the point of view that it held the Wesleyan authority through the person of Asbury. From his place of retirement, Asbury led the North. The South possessed the regularly constituted organization of American Methodism, led by William Watters. The North in their Conference of 1779 in Delaware, dominated by

[1] Tigert, J. J., *Constitutional History of American Episcopal Methodism*, p. 93.
[2] Watters, *op. cit.*, p. 68.
[3] *Supra*, p. 173.

Asbury, decided to follow Episcopalian traditions; the South, assembled in Virginia, deliberately erected themselves into a self-governing presbyterial organization.

The Delaware Quasi Conference (Northern) was in the nature of a "Snap Convention"; irregularly called and composed of merely a few of Asbury's immediate disciples. In as much as Asbury couldn't go to the regular conference, an irregular conference came to him. Southerners were not even invited to attend. To be sure, Watters did hear of the projected meeting and appeared thereat in person. As the champion of orthodoxy, this conference took several steps of vast consequences for American Methodism. It designated Asbury as General Assistant in America:

"Question 12. Ought not brother Asbury to act as General Assistant in America? Answer. He ought: 1st, on account of his age; 2nd, because originally appointed by Mr. Wesley: 3rd, being joined with Messrs. Rankin and Shadford, by express orders from Mr. Wesley."[1]

Having provided for a General Assistant the Conference then vested him with power. "No helper," reads the *Minutes*, "is to make any alteration in the circuit, or appoint preaching in any new place, without consulting the Assistant: every exhorter and local preacher to go by the directions of the Assistant where, and only where they shall appoint." This assumption of authority on the part of Asbury is not a pleasing act for an American of today to contemplate.[2]

Such were the decisions of this highly irregular meeting of a very small minority of the Methodist preachers in America. Yet the sixteen present, because they stood for orthodox traditions and had with them the only person

[1] *Minutes*, ed. 1795, pp. 27-29.
[2] Faulkner, *The Methodists*, pp. 67-69.

in America who could claim to represent Wesley, styled themselves a conference and assumed absolute legislative functions. Without waiting to consult the sentiments of the majority of the ministers, or the opinion of the regular conference, they decided the sacramental question absolutely and finally, — Methodist preachers must not administer the sacraments; they designated "Brother Asbury" General Assistant for America and conferred on him "the right of determination for and against what is in debate." It is small wonder that Asbury again took interest in America, and decided to remain on this side of the water. This conference hoped to forestall and counteract action which they anticipated from the regular Southern Conference. It did, and furnished doctrinal controversies which lasted until the American Methodist Episcopalian constitution was finally completed.

The regular Conference of 1779 met at Fluvanna in Virginia. It was presided over by a member of the committee of control, Philip Gatch; it represented the majority of the circuits, preachers and members of the American Methodists. It took no notice of the Northern Conference or of the election of Asbury. It appointed a new Committee of Control. The following illustrations taken from the questions and answers show the radical steps taken by the Southerners:

"Question 14. What are our reasons for taking up the administration of the ordinances among us? Answer. Because the Episcopal establishment is now dissolved, and, therefore, in almost all our circuits the members are without the ordinances, — we believe it to be our duty.
Question 19. What form of ordination shall be observed, to authorize any Preacher to administer? Answer. By that of a Presbytery.
Question 20. How shall the Presbytery be appointed? Answer. By a majority of the Preachers.
Question 22. What power is vested in the Presbytery by this choice? Answer. 1. To administer the ordinances themselves. 2. To authorize

any other Preacher or Preachers, approved by them, by the form of laying on of hands." [1]

Philip Gatch, Reuben Ellis, and James Foster were appointed a presbytery: "First to administer the ordinances themselves, second to authorize any other preacher or preachers, approved of by them, by the form of laying on of hands."

Both conferences had acted boldly; and both extra-legally. A schism seemed imminent. The North had constructed an essentially Episcopalian form of government and discipline, but without proper Episcopalian authorization. The South had departed far from the recognized principles of Episcopalianism and had adopted a presbyterial system. But if either body ceased to be Episcopalians in a little more than five years, John Wesley himself, was to follow them therein. How much their actions influenced the measures of Wesley in his plan for reorganization of American Methodism cannot be estimated. Both sections did anticipate points in his new system.

The Conference of 1781 shows that an agreement had been reached between North and South. Asbury wrote, "Tuesday (April) 24 . . . . . All but one (preachers from Virginia and North Carolina) agreed to return to the old plan, and give up the administration of the ordinances: our troubles now seem over from that quarter."[2]

The first question of this Conference was:

"What preachers are now determined, after mature consideration, close observation, and earnest prayer, to preach the old Methodist doctrine, and strictly enforce the discipline as contained in the Notes, Sermons,

[1] "Philip Gatch's Manuscript Journal" as quoted by Dr. L. M. Lee, *Life and Times of Jesse Lee*, pp. 79-81; McTyeire, *op. cit.*, pp. 316-317.

[2] Asbury, *Journal*, i, p. 328.

and Minutes, published by Mr. Wesley, so far as they respect both preachers and people, according to the knowledge we have of them, and the ability God shall give and are firmly resolved to discountenance a separation among either preachers or people?[1]

Tradition and authority appear to have triumphed. The Conference of 1782 decided who was to enforce both: "the brethren in Conference unanimously choose brother Asbury to act to Mr. Wesley's original appointment, and preside over the American Conference and the whole work."[2] But new American principles had been asserted by both sections of the Society and the mere assertion had established tradition which was to win Asbury to a more democratic point of view. It was only through Republican principles that Asbury could hope to rule in America and "beyond a shadow of a doubt . . . . Asbury during those months of study and reflection (in seclusion) . . . . . had arrived at the conclusion that separation from Mr. Wesley was inevitable, and that a new organization of the societies in America must be effected."[3]

The war closed in 1783 and Mr. Wesley immediately turned his attention to the problems of his American followers. His first act was to reassert control. This he did by recognizing as General Assistant, Mr. Asbury[4] who had been elected to that office by the Conference. At the same time he formally recognized the Conference itself. His letter of October third, 1783, enjoined:

"1. Let all of you be determined to abide by the Methodist doctrine and discipline, published in the four volumes of Sermons, and the Notes upon the New Testament together with the Large Minutes of the Conference.

[1] *Minutes*, edition 1795, p. 41.
[2] *Ibid.*, edition of 1840, pp. 15-17.
[3] Tipple, *Francis Asbury*, p. 132.
[4] Asbury, *Journal*, p. 367.

3. Neither should you receive any preachers, however recommended, who will not subject to the American Conference and cheerfully conform to the Minutes of the English and American Conferences.

4. I do not wish our American brethren to receive any who make any difficulty of receiving Francis Asbury as the General Assistant." [1]

American Methodism being again under his care, he proceeded to constitute for it an organization suitable to independent America. Almost every incident in the process by which the constitution of the Methodist Episcopal Church for the United States was evolved, — from the ordination of Coke to the adjournment of the Christmas Conference,— has been the subject for vigorous and bitter partisan controversy. The certainty of the following fundamental point seems established: 1. That an Episcopal Church was planned and established; 2. That through the laying on of hands the leaders were made as near "regular" bishop as was considered necessary for the establishment of a "moderate episcopacy"; 3. That a ministry in three grades, "superintendendents" or bishops, elders and deacons were permanently provided for; 4. That the Christmas Conference and Mr. Wesley were in agreement; 5. That Mr. Wesley was not imposed upon by the "ambition" of either Coke or Asbury; 6. That the Christmas Conference did not foist a "spurious episcopacy," never designed by the founder or intelligently accepted by the church, upon American Methodism; 7. That Mr. Wesley approved what Dr. Coke, his envoy and representative, had done.[2]

It was an important day in the history of the American church that second day of September, 1784, when Wesley,

[1] Lee, Jesse, *History of Methodists*, p. 85-86; Bangs, *History of The Methodist Episcopal Church*, vol. i, pp. 148-149.

[2] Tigert, *Constitutional History of American Episcopal Methodism*, pp. 204-205.

assisted by other Presbyters of the Church of England, laid hands upon the head of Thomas Coke and commended to him the superintendency of the Methodist work in America as colleague with Francis Asbury.

In the previous February, Wesley had called Coke into his private chamber in London, and there introduced the subject of providing for American Methodists. The substance of his remarks was: that as the revolution had separated the United States from the mother country, and the Episcopal establishment was utterly abolished, the societies had been represented to him as being in a most deplorable condition; that an appeal had been made to him by Mr. Asbury, in which he was requested to provide for them some form of church government suited to their exigencies; and having long and seriously revolved the subject in his thoughts, he intended to adopt the plan which he was about to unfold; that, as he had invariably endeavored, in every step he had taken, to keep as closely to the Bible as possible, so, on the present occasion, he hoped he was not about to deviate therefrom; that, keeping his eye on the conduct of the primitive church in the age of unadulterated Christianity, he had much admired the mode of ordaining bishops, which the church of Alexandria had practiced; that, to preserve its purity, that Church would never suffer the interference of a foreign bishop in any of its ordinations, but the Presbyters of that venerable apostolic church, on the death of a bishop, exercised the right of ordaining another for their own body, by the laying on of their hands; that this practice continued among them for two hundred years, till the days of Dionysius; and finally, that, being himself a Presbyter, he wished Dr. Coke to accept ordination from his hands and to proceed in that character to the continent of America, there to superintend the societies in the United States.[1]

Dr. Coke consented and "on September first, 1784, at Bristol, England, the Rev. John Wesley, Thomas Coke, and James Creighton, Presbyters of the Church of England, formed a Presbytery and ordained Richard Whatcoat and Thomas Vasey deacons. On September second, by the same hands Richard Whatcoat and Thomas Vasey were ordained elders and Thomas Coke, D.D., was ordained Superintendent for the Church of God under our care in North America."[2] Wesley's own statement is, "On Wednesday, September first, being now clear in my own mind, I took a step which I had long weighed, and appointed Mr. Whatcoat and Mr. Vasey to go and serve the desolate sheep in America. Thursday, the second, I added to them three more."[3] Or as Coke later (April 24, 1791) wrote to Bishop White, "He did, indeed, solemnly invest me, as far as he had the right so to do, with Episcopal authority.[4]

Upon this occasion Mr. Wesley presented Dr. Coke with the following credentials:

"To All to whom these present shall come, John Wesley, late Fellow of Lincoln College in Oxford, Presbyter of the Church of England, sendeth greetings.

Whereas many of the people in the southern provinces of North America, who desire to continue under my care, and still adhere to the doctrines and discipline of the Church of Engand, are greatly distressed for want of ministers to administer the sacraments of baptism and the Lord's Supper, according to the usage of the said Church; and whereas

[1] Drew, *Life of Coke*, pp. 71-72, quoted Tigert, *op. cit.*, p. 167; McTyeire, *op. cit.*, p. 341.

[2] Whatcoat, *Journal*, quoted Tigert, *op. cit.*, pp. 172-173.

[3] *Minutes*, edition of 1812, vol. i, p. 173, Tigert, *op. cit.*, p. 173.

[4] White, *Memoirs*, 1820, p. 424.

there does not appear to be any other way of supplying them with ministers:

Know all men, that I, John Wesley, think myself to be providentially called, at this time, to set apart some persons for the work of the ministry in America. And, therefore, under the protection of Almighty God, and with a single eye to His glory, I have this day set apart as Superintendent, by the imposition of my hands, and prayer (being assisted by other ordained ministers), Thomas Coke, doctor of civil law, a Presbyter of the Church of England, and a man whom I judge to be well qualified for that great work. And I do hereby recommend him to all whom it may concern, as a fit person to preside over the flock of Christ.

John Wesley."[1]

Having thus constituted his ministry in three orders, Wesley thereupon abridged the thirty-nine Articles, — omitting the third, eighth, thirteenth, seventeenth, eighteenth, twentieth, twenty-first, twenty-third, thirty-fifth, thirty-sixth, and thirty-seventh; also parts of the sixth, ninth, and nineteenth; and introducing verbal changes in others, — to constitute a doctrinal basis for the new organization, and from the Book of Common Prayer he framed a liturgy for public worship. These he embodied in a work, which he entrusted to Coke's custody, entitled, *The Sunday Service of the Methodists in North America, With Occasional Services*, London 1784. This contained the forms of prayer, the form and manner of making and ordaining Superintendents, Elders, and Deacons, and the Articles of Religion. Backus writes:

"He (Wesley) and his followers reduced the Thirty-nine Articles of the Church of England to twenty-four, with new forms of worship and order, and published them in London, in 1784, and called them 'The Sunday service in North America'; thus they undertook to be law givers for all North America, and to form a church therein that never had any existence until the year 1784."[2]

[1] Tigert, *Constitutional History of American Episcopal Methodism*, p. 174; Drew, *op. cit.*, p. 66; McTyeire, *op. cit.*, p. 342.

[2] Backus, *op. cit.*, edition of 1796, vol. iii, pp. 24-25.

Wesley's part in the establishment of American Methodist Episcopalianism is well stated by Abel Stevens:

"Whatever view we take of the subject we are compelled to one conclusion: that Wesley did create and establish the American Methodist Episcopacy . . . . . the organization on scriptural principles of the first (and therefore at that time *the one*) Episcopal Church on the American continent. Hitherto the American Methodists had received the sacraments from the English clergy resident in the colonies, and regarded themselves as members of that Church. In 1784, when the Methodist Episcopal Church in America was organized, neither the English nor the Protestant Episcopal Church existed here in legal complete form. The American Methodists, by the help of Mr. Wesley, therefore, organized themselves into an American Episcopal Church, taking the name and style already indicated. They regarded themselves as the successors of the old Church, then defunct, and entered upon their work accordingly. The Methodist Episcopalians still adhered to the doctrines and discipline of the Church of England . . . . . The Methodist bishops were the first Protestant bishops, and Methodism was the first Protestant Episcopal Church of the New World; and as Mr. Wesley had given it the Anglican articles of religion (omitting the seventeenth, on predestination), and the liturgy wisely abridged, it became, both by its precedent organization and its subsequent numerical importance the real successor to the Anglican Church in America. As for schism or separation, the thought never so much as entered the heads of such conscientious Episcopalians as Asbury: the thing itself was impossible, as there then existed in America no organized Episcopal Church from which to separate." [1]

Fortified with Wesley's certificate of ordination and equipped with his form of service and ritual, — a commissioner with extraordinary powers,— Coke, accompanied by Whatcoat and Vasey, landed in New York, November 3, 1784. That night he preached in the John Street Chapel. On Sunday, the seventh, he filled the pulpit of St. Paul's in Philadelphia. Drs. McGraw and White (later the first Bishop of the Protestant Episcopal Church

[1] Stevens, *History of Methodism*, ii, p. 215; Tigert, *Constitutional History of American Episcopal Methodism*, p. 207; Tigert, *The Making of Methodism: Studies in the Genesis of Institutions.*

in Pennsylvania) called on him on Monday and Dr. White offered the use of his church for the next Sunday's service. On Sunday, the fourteenth of November, he went from the house of Judge Bassett to that famous meeting with Asbury at Barratt's Chapel in Delaware. On this same Sunday, Samuel Seabury was consecrated Bishop of Connecticut at Aberdeen, Scotland. Mr. Wesley had succeeded in establishing his organization in America before a rival could secure episcopal orders.

At that memorable first interview between Coke and Asbury at Barratt's Chapel, Asbury, cordially supported by the American preachers present, proposed the calling of an American Conference to accept the constitution sent over by Wesley. Coke accepted the proposal. Now Mr. Wesley had never included in his plans the assembling of the American preachers to pass judgment upon his proposals. Herein American Methodism was destined to work a form of government not contemplated by its founder. It had, during the period of separation,[1] tasted the sweets of Independence and Self-Government: it demanded its General Conference. And Francis Asbury championed the American Method. "He had witnessed the stirring struggle for American Independence; he had imbibed the spirit of democracy, ... he could not consent to the proposals of Mr. Wesley, until they had been considered by the preachers in Conference."[2]

It was the germ of Conference authority, manifesting itself in the Annual Conferences, that gradually separated the American Methodists from the English Methodists, that declined to elect the nominee of Wesley himself to

[1] *Supra*, pp. 173-178.

[2] Tipple, *Francis Asbury*, pp. 142-143; Coke, *Journal*, p. 16; Asbury, *Journal*, vol. i, p. 484.

the American episcopate, that omitted Wesley's name from the minutes, that dropped the title of "Superintendent" and took that of "Bishop." The unexpected organization of the Christmas Conference opposed itself as a barrier to any autocracy on the part of Wesley and ultimately gave the American Church independence from the English Conference. The Conference was to become the most American part of Methodism.

The Conference was not, however, responsible for the separation of the Methodist Episcopalians of America from the authority of the Church of England; any bonds between these two bodies that had survived the revolution had been severed by Wesley himself.

Dr. Coke was always uneasy about the part which he played in the establishment of the conference; he seems to have regretted yielding to American ideals, though he never questioned his own ordination. The conference had never entered into Wesley's consideration; Dr. Coke in a letter to Bishop White, 1791, admits that he probably went further in the organization of the American Church than Mr. Wesley had intended.[1]

As originator of the United Societies, Wesley had been the fountain of authority, both legislative and executive, for England and, up to this time, for America as well. He doubtlessly intended that Coke and Asbury, as general superintendents, should exercise in America his delegated powers; — to make regulations and to enforce them; to distribute preachers according to their own judgments, — subject to his final authority. He held himself to be head of the whole Methodist connection, a scriptural bishop and, by appointment of Divine Providence, its patriarch and

[1] White, *Memoirs*, pp. 424-429; McTyeire, *op. cit.*, p. 348; *Southern Quarterly Review*, July 1885, p. 377.

apostle. If Asbury had known and accepted the Wesley conception there would have been no independent American conference, ever. It was due to the sagacity and far-sightedness of Francis Asbury that a General Conference was subsequently incorporated into the fundamental organism of American Methodism.

Very great indeed is the debt that American Christianity owes to Francis Asbury, certainly as great as to any man of his generation. It may reasonably be doubted whether any one clergyman, from the foundation of the Methodist society in America till now, has achieved more from his works. It is very certain that Wesley himself, with his despotic temper and his High-Church and Tory principles, could not have guided the Methodist movement in the New World through the perils of its infancy to so eminent a success as that which was reaped by Asbury. Questions of the utmost difficulty and of vital importance arose in the first years of its organization. They would not have been decided so wisely for the country and the church if Asbury had not been governed by the ministry and the members of the society. Perhaps unwillingly at first, but of a fixed purpose later, Francis Asbury, more than any other person worked to make the Methodist Societies of the United States an American Church. In spite of the sturdy dictum of Wesley, "We are not republicans, and do not intend to be," the changes necessary to accommodate the forms and practices of the church to the habits and temper of a free people were initiated by Asbury. This he was consciously striving to do, even at this, the first meeting under the new Wesleyan plan of organization. The Methodist Church owes constitutional government to Francis Asbury.[1]

[1] Tipple, *Francis Asbury, The Prophet of the Long Road.* New York, 1916. Strickland, *The Pioneer Bishop*; Janes, E. L., *The Character and*

Coke had agreed to Asbury's plan for a conference and American Methodism met accordingly in Philadelphia, December 24th, 1784. This was a meeting of epochal significance; "the most important conference of Methodist Preachers ever held in America."[1] It ratified Wesley's Magna Charta of religious rights; it fixed the form of government and discipline, and the order of worship for the new American Church. That the members of the Conference were fully conscious of the importance of their labors is evidenced by the writings of one of their number, William Phoebus, who wrote, "We assembled at the city of Baltimore, in the State of Maryland, and received Thomas Coke, LLD., with his testimonials from the greatest man in the world. He proceeded to form the first church that ever was organized under a pure republican government, and the first that was ever formed in this happy part of the world."[2]

The minutes as published for 1785 contain this preliminary notice, "As it was unanimously agreed at this Conference that circumstances made it expedient for us to become a separate body, under the denomination of the Methodist Episcopal Church, it is necessary that we here assign some reasons for so doing.

The following extract of a letter from Rev. John Wesley well affords as good an explanation as can be given on this subject."[3] They may well be styled the Magna Charta of American Methodism.

Career of Francis Asbury; Briggs, *Bishop Asbury;* Smith, *Life and Labors of Francis Asbury.*

[1] Tipple, *Francis Asbury*, p. 145.

[2] Myles, *Chron. History of Methodists*, p. 202.

[3] Watters, *op. cit.*, "We became, instead of a religious society, a separate Church." British *Minutes* of 1785, edition of 1812, vol. i, pp. 179-181.

"Bristol, September 10, 1784.

To Dr. Coke, Mr. Asbury, and our brethren in North America: —

1. By a very uncommon train of Providences, many of the provinces of North America are totally disjoined from the British Empire, and erected into independent states. The British government has no authority over them, either civil or ecclesiastical, any more than over the states of Holland. A civil authority is exercised over them, partly by congress, partly by the state assemblies. But no one either exercises or claims any ecclesiastical authority at all. In this peculiar situation, some thousands of inhabitants of these states desire my advice; and in compliance with their desire I have drawn up a little sketch.

2. Lord King's account of the primitive church convinced me, many years ago, that bishops and presbyters are the same order, and, consequently, have the same right to ordain. For many years I have been importuned, from time to time, to exercise this right, by ordaining part of our travelling preachers. But I still refused, not only for peace's sake, but because I was determined as little as possible to violate the established order of the national church, to which I belonged.

3. But the case is widely different between England and North America. Here are bishops who have a legal jurisdiction. In America there are none, and but a few parish ministers; so that for some hundreds of miles together there is none either to baptise or to administer the Lord's supper. Here, therefore, my scruples are at an end; and I conceive myself at full liberty, as I violate no order, and invade no man's right by appointing and sending laborers into the harvest.

4. I have, accordingly, appointed Dr. Coke and Mr. Francis Asbury to be joint superintendents over our brethren in North America; as also Richard Whatcoat and Thomas Vasey to act as elders among them by baptising and administering the Lord's Supper. And I have prepared a liturgy, little differing from that of the Church of England (I think the best constituted national church in the world), which I advise all the travelling preachers to use on Lord's Day in all congregations, reading the litany only on Wednesday and Friday, and praying extempore on all other days. I also advise the elders to administer the Supper of the Lord on every Lord's Day.

5. If any one will point out a more rational and scriptural way of feeding and guiding those poor sheep in the wilderness, I will gladly embrace it. At present I cannot see any better method than that I have taken.

6. It has indeed been proposed to desire the English Bishops to ordain part of our preachers for America. But to this I object. 1. I desired the Bishop of London to ordain one only, but could not prevail. 2. If they consented, we know the slowness of their proceedings but the

matter admits of no delay. 3. If they would ordain them now, they would likewise expect to govern them. And how grievously would this entangle us! 4. As our American brethren are now totally disentangled, both from state and from the English hierarchy, we dare not entangle them again either with the one or the other. They are now at full liberty to follow the Scriptures and the primitive church. And we judge it best that they should stand fast in that liberty wherewith God has so strangely made them free.

John Wesley." [1]

The Conference Minutes notes:

"Therefore at this Conference, we formed ourselves into an independent church; and following the counsel of Mr. John Wesley, who recommended the episcopal mode of church government, we thought it best to become an episcopal church, making the episcopal office elective, and the elected superintendents, or bishops, amenable to the body of ministers and preachers." [2]

Francis Asbury declined ordination to the superintendency, unless in addition to the appointment by Wesley, his brethren should formally elect him to that office, which they did. He has left us the following concise statement of what was done:

"It was agreed to form ourselves into an Episcopal Church, and to have superintendents, elders, and deacons. When the Conference was seated, Dr. Coke and myself were unanimously elected to the superintendence of the church and my ordination followed, after being previously ordained deacon and elder . . . . .

Twelve elders were elected and solemnly set apart." [2]

The Conference adopted the first Discipline of the Methodist Episcopal Church under the title, "Minutes of several conversations between the Rev. Thomas Coke, LLD., the Rev. Francis Asbury, and others, at a Conference begun in Baltimore in the State of Maryland on Monday the 24th of December, in the year 1784. Compos-

[1] Wesley, *Works*, vol. vii, pp. 311-312.

[2] British *Minutes* of 1785, edition of 1812, vol. i, pp. 179-181; McTyeire, *op. cit.*, pp. 343-344.

[3] Asbury, *Journal*, vol. i, pp. 377-378.

ing a Form of Discipline for the Ministers, Preachers, and other Members of the Methodist Episcopal Church in America."[1]

The Answer returned to Question Three of this discipline was, "We will form ourselves into an Episcopal Church, under the direction of superintendents, elders, deacons, and helpers, according to the forms of ordination annexed to our Liturgy, and the Form of Discipline set forth in these minutes."[2]

But in assuming this power of self-government, the Conference voluntarily limited its exercise by what is known as the "Engagement Clause," Question Two and Answer:

"During the life of Rev. Mr. Wesley, we acknowledge ourselves his sons in the gospel, ready, in matters belonging to church government, to obey his commands. And we do engage, after his death, to do everything we judge consistent with the cause of religion in America, and the political interests of these States to preserve and promote our union with the Methodists in Europe."[3]

And to make sure that this question of the "political interests" was properly noticed, to the twenty-four Articles (so reduced from thirty-nine by Wesley) the Conference added this,

"The President, the Congress, the General Assemblies, the Governors, and the Councils of State, *as the Delegates of the People*, are the Rulers of the United States of America, according to the division of power made to them by the Constitution of the United States, and by the Constitutions of their respective States. And the said States are a sovereign and independent Nation, and ought not to be subject to any foreign jurisdiction."[4]

[1] Emory, *History of Discipline*, p. 25.
[2] *Ibid.*, p. 27.
[3] *Ibid.*, p. 3; Schaff, *Creeds*, vol. iii, pp. 807 sqq.
[4] Buckley, *History of Methodism*, vol. i, p. 297.

The ten days' work of this Christmas Conference has been before the world for more than a century and as a constitution for Methodist Episcopalianism it may well challenge comparison with the results of the Philadelphia Federal Constitutional Convention, which three years later framed a political government for the United States of America, both from the point of view of independent nationalism and republican self-government.

The "Engagement Clause," just mentioned, proved too binding and the Conference of 1787 annulled it. At this time they asserted a surprising degree of disregard for their founder. They refused his nominee, Freeborn Garrettson, a superintendency for the British Dominion in America; and they substituted the title of "Bishop" for Wesley's "Superintendent."[1]

Wesley's nominal authority lasted till his death in 1791. A General Conference, properly so-styled, met the following year, — the first of those Quadrennial General Conferences, which were thereupon instituted as the supreme legislative tribunal of American Methodism. The Christmas Conference was as we have noted, not properly speaking a General Conference, but rather a General Convention, embodying those principles which were to characterize the formal constitutional conventions of the America of this period. A formal constitution for American Methodist Episcopalianism was not adopted till 1808.

The year 1784, however, had seen the organization by Methodists of the first national church society in America, with modes of thought suited to independent American opportunity. Upon leaving the convention, Asbury immediately took up the work of his superintendency. His first tour, starting from Baltimore took him as far South as

[1] McTyeire, *op. cit.*, chapter xxviii.

Charleston, and back to Mount Vernon, where he called on General Washington. Soon thereafter, we find him in Delaware with his friend, Richard Bassett, who was to represent American Methodism in the Federal Constitutional Convention. Asbury's tireless itineracy did much to unify the church. He travelled an average of six thousand miles a year, usually on horseback; and visited every state in the union many times.[1]

Methodism was organized to win a continent. Missionary work was begun in Connecticut in 1787 and their first society there was founded at Stratford in 1789.[2] "The Book Concern" was established in 1789 to publish the necessary devotional books of the church, such as hymnal, discipline, theological works, religious experience, and magazines and papers.

[1] Tipple, E. S., *Francis Asbury, The Prophet of the Long Road*, N. Y., 1916.

[2] Stevens, Abel, *Memorials of the Introduction of Methodism into the Eastern States*, Boston, 1852 pp. 45 sqq.

CHAPTER VIII

THE PROTESTANT EPISCOPAL CHURCH IN THE UNITED STATES OF AMERICA

The Protestant Episcopal Church in the United States of America is a product of the American Revolution and the Reconstruction period which followed. As a colonial institution of all the churches in America the Church of England was nearly, if not quite, the most powerful. The Revolution had divided it seriously in relation to political loyalty, yet, independence secured, loyalty to the church remained. Hence the pressing problem of Americanization by which the Anglican Church was transformed into the Protestant Episcopal Church in the United States of America. The change was speedily effected, in fact so expeditiously that the national constitution of the church antedates that of the state government; Episcopalianism became a pioneer in the movement for unity in America, and thereby gained a prestige of leadership which extended far beyond religious matters.

It was only after a bitter partisan struggle, involving nearly all the issues which were later to play parts in state politics that Dr. William White put through his plan for a church constitution. But so thoroughly suited was this to the spirit of America in reconciling liberty with authority through constitutional government under a bicameral legislative body and an executive with carefully prescribed delegated powers, that it harmonized conflicting interests and effected true unity. This opened the way for similar action on the part of the state authorities. And the influence of the former on the latter was not merely one of abstract spiritual leadership; the actual personnel of the two conventions which framed church and state constitutions show that a remarkable number of federal statesmen were trained in earlier Episcopalian politics.

Numerous elements of the situation urged immediate unification. Foremost was the absence of church government and church support. Even previous to the Revolution the authority of the Bishop of London in America had faded to such a pale tradition, that, in spite of laws establishing the Church of England, which still remained on the statute-books of some of the colonies, a contemporary historian was justified in stating broadly that there was really no provincial church government.[1] Bishop White has left us a summary of some of the reasons for reorganization, in a sermon,

"*The Past and the Future: A Charge on Events Connected with the Organization of the Protestant Episcopal Church in the United States of America and the Lessons they Inculcate, delivered before the Fiftieth Convention of the Diocese of Pennsylvania.* Philadelphia, 1834.

During our colonial state, the tie which connected our congregations was the superintendence of the Bishops of London, under delegation from the Crown. That being withdrawn, every congregation was independent of all exterior control, either in England or in America. There remained, however, the principles inherited by them from the mother church, in doctrine, in worship, and in ecclesiastical constitution. These were materials, giving reason to hope that there might be raised from them a religious communion, resembling that from which we were descended, as nearly as local circumstances could permit.

What aggravated the exigency, was the very small number to which our ministry was reduced; partly by death, and partly by the migration of some to Great Britain, and of others to the colonies on this continent. It will probably be new to the greater number present, to be informed that, for a short time, he who addresses you was the only Episcopalian clergyman in the commonwealth of Pennsylvania; and that when he was

[1] Douglas, *Summary*, vol. i, p. 230; Cross, *The Anglican Episcopate*, p. 247.

elected to the Episcopacy there were only three of his brethren present and voting.[1]

In addition to the privation, there was the withdrawal of much of the pecuniary supply for ministerial support. In all the colonies to the north of Maryland, with the exception of the larger cities, the clergy were missionaries, in the service of the Society for the Propagation of the Gospel in Foreign Parts. Their salaries ceased with the acknowledgment of our independence, and an addition to the migration of our clergy was the consequence. The withdrawing of the stipends ought not to attach blame to the Venerable Society, whose charter limited their operations to the dependencies of the British Crown: so that there remains the debt of gratitude for the fostering care extended to us in our infancy.[2]

In the midst of the discouragements, measures were put into operation, for the organizing of our church, in the states individually and in the United States. Some, with the best intentions as to the object, did not approve of this as an incipient step; but after a while the general opinion was in its favor; especially as it appeared, by information relied on from the quarter to which we looked for the completing of the orders of our ministry, that there was nothing to be expected in virtue of an application from our clergy in their individual characters, and without its carrying with it evidence of the concurrence of our Episcopal population, who, as well as the clergy, possessed an interest in the favor to be solicited. The information received, gave great encouragement to the endeavors which had been begun . . . . . .

The prejudices gradually declined, under the weight of more correct statements, and especially under the irresistible conviction, that the obtaining of the episcopal order was essential to the keeping of us together as a branch of the christian church; that a great proportion of our population would have adhered to a constitution which they knew to have been from the beginning, had prevailed universally during fifteen hundred years, and had been transmitted to them by a church, considered in the character of a parent, although now severed from them by a revolution, which had turned on questions of civil polity and duties.

[1] Tiffany, *op. cit.*, pp. 288-289; White, *op. cit.*, p. 81, "there were (1783) very few Episcopalian pulpits in the United States"; Hawks, *op. cit.*, vol. i, pp. 153-154., "(in Virginia) 23 of 95 parishes had become extinct and 34 were vacant; and only 28 of her 91 clergy remained in the Colony."

[2] Perry, *Journals*, vol. iii, p. 10, Letter of Rev. Abraham Beach to Wm. White, Mar. 22, 1784. "To Save the church of which we are members from utter Decay and consequently to promote the real Happiness and Prosperity of the Country."

The privilege of acting for themselves in this matter, was secured by the liberal constitution of these states; and if there should be any organized opposition to the design, there was no other alternative, than either conformity to the views of their more consistent brethren, or of their relinquishment of communion with them. It was easy to perceive that, in the latter event, the dissentients must have become merged in the many societies marked by discrepant principles, and abounding within our civil union."[1]

Then too competition was keen in the new religious atmosphere in America; the Episcopalians must take steps to maintain their prestige, or,— so critical was the situation,—to regain a fast vanishing leadership. In this scramble for converts the Roman Catholic Church immediately exhibited such powers that it furnished cause for Episcopalian concern. Dr. White wrote to Charles Miller, December 3, 1785:

"Let me Sir, entreat you to recollect how much more serviceable it will be to the common cause of Christianity, if we can accomplish a great and liberal plan for connecting in one system the members of our widely extended communion: rather than for every congregation to be in all respects selfgoverning: or, if this cannot be, that we may at least continue one in each state. I am amazed that the importance of this is not more seen, in relation to guarding against the progress of a church as yet scarcely known in your country. When the church of Rome claims the subjection of all Christendom to St. Peter's chair, the rise of her power is too well known for the pretention to have weight; but when she shall talk of the unity of the members of the church in the same neighborhood or district, and of their being linked together under one common head, antiquity will be so much on her side, that I am afraid it will make many take the less exception to her erroneous doctrines. Of all the members of the Protestant body, the Church of England has been thought the strongest bulwark against her, from the circumstance of retaining more than others of those ancient institutions which were prior to her corruption. I cannot bear the thought of our communion's losing in the new world what has been our glory in the old."[2]

[1] White, *The Past and the Future: A Charge on Events Connected with the Organization of the Protestant Episcopal Church in the United States of America and the Lessons they Inculcate.* Philadelphia, 1834.

[2] Wilson, *Memoir of the Life of the Right Reverent William White,* pp. 326-327.

Nor was the Roman Catholic Church the only denomination to be feared. The Reverend Jeremiah Leaming wrote to Bishop White, June 16, 1788:

"He (Dr. P——— Priestly) has contrived it to make this country all Unitarians; for, to accomplish that, he must demolish the Church in these states.

Perhaps you will say, you cannot think there is any such scheme on foot. It will not be long before you will find that what I have told you is fact. The Presbyterians are employed by ——— to fill all the Southern States with their sort of Ministers, before the Church is supplied with Episcopal Clergymen. Where people have no principles about the nature of a Christian Church, a man ordained by the Laity is as good as any. And a man who professes to believe no creed, but only this, that he believes not in any creed, is as good a Christian as any man can be. By this scheme the Unitarian doctrine is to take place . . . . . If true Christianity is not preserved by the Episcopal Church, it will soon take its flight from these States, for Unitarians will be the whole." [1]

It was also evident that some sort of supervision and control was necessary in order to effect that moral uplift of which the Episcopal clergy was so sadly in need. James Madison wrote to Robert Walsh, "On the subject of the negro slavery, of moral character, of religion, and of education in Virginia, as affected by the Revolution, and our public institutions"; in which he remarked on

"the indolence of most and the irregular lives of many of the established clergy, consisting, in a very large proportion, of foreigners, and these in no inconsiderable proportion, of men willing to leave their homes in the parent country where their demerit was an obstacle to a provision for them, and whose degeneracy here was promoted by their distance from the controlling eyes of their kindred and friends, by the want of ecclesiastical superiors in the colony, or efficient ones in Great Britain who might maintain a salutary discipline among them, and finally by their independence both of their congregations and of the civil authority for their stipends." [2]

[1] Perry, *op. cit.*, vol. iii, pp. 367-368; Wilson, *op. cit.*, pp. 103-105.
[2] *Writings of James Madison*, vol. viii, pp. 425-433.

There is abundant evidence for the charges against the colonial clergy. The Bishop of London said of the colonial clergy in a letter to Dr. Doddridge, 1743, "Of those who are sent hence, a great part are of the Scotch or Irish, who can get no employment at home, and enter into the service more out of necessity than choice. Some others are willing to go abroad to retrieve either lost fortune or lost character."[1] Bishop Meade said of them, "Many of them had been addicted to the race-field, the card-table, the theatre—nay, more to drunken revel."[2] Dr. Hawks writes, they "could babble in a pulpit, roar in a tavern, exact from their parishioners, and rather by their dissoluteness destroy than feed the flock."[3] And one of the first acts of the Virginia Assembly in 1776 was, "Be it further enacted by this Grand Assembly, and by the authority thereof, that such ministers as shall become notoriously scandalous by drunkenness, swearing, fornication, or other heinous and crying sins, and shall thereof be lawfully convicted, shall, for every such their heinous crimes and wickedness, etc."[4]

Unbecoming conduct on the part of the clergy did not cease with American independence; it had to be eradicated. One of the earliest acts of the semi-organized national Episcopalian Church had to do with this matter. The Convention of 1786 refused to give a testimonial to Bishop-elect William Smith of Maryland on moral grounds; it was alleged that he had been intoxicated at the New York Convention.[5] This action by the national body prevented his confirmation and illustrates the value of supervision by higher authority as a factor in determining the morals of the clergy, one of the first fruits of nationalization.

[1] Quoted, James, *op. cit.*, p. 28.
[2] Meade, *Old Parishes and Families of Virginia*, vol. i, pp. 118, 385.
[3] Hawks, *op. cit.*, p. 64-65.
[4] Hening, *Statutes*, vol. ii, p. 384.
[5] *Infra*, p. 225

Deprived of state control the church must organize its own direction and control. Religious freedom in the United States was giving to each denomination the full power to form its own ecclesiastical government, discipline and worship; also the means of promoting its own welfare. The Episcopalian church had been deprived of, or released from, its old world canon law, a system complicated, dilatory, expensive and corrupt; it was necessary to develop a new set of canons. If the church was to have a well regulated, orderly existence in America it must constitute a legislature and proceed to formulate canons.

The forces opposed to unification were numerous and powerful; in fact the struggle for nationalism within the church seems to have brought to light a great many of those issues which were to play so important a part in party politics within the new nation.

First and foremost came the spirit of sectionalism, that ever present menace to a unified America. In the Episcopalian struggle we find it in The East *vs.* The West or The North *vs.* The South. Revolutionary Episcopalianism had been found most patriotic where it was strongest, namely in the Southern and Middle colonies; in the North the church had been too weak, too dependent upon England for support, to feel that it could join the American cause. Dr. William White represented the Southern element. "East" *vs.* "West" is but another way of speaking of "North" *vs.* "South."[1]

The "States-rights" issue, personal animosities, liberalism *vs.* conservatism, and even crooked politics, were other points at isssue.[2]

[1] Perry, *op. cit.*, vol. iii, pp. 319-320; White, *Memoirs*, p. 79.

[2] *Ibid.*, vol. iii, pp. 370-371, where the Rev. Dr. Purcell challenges the legality of the Wilmington Convention, charging that the meeting was

A doctrinal basis was found in the question of relative powers of clergy and laity. The North seemed to emphasize the episcopal power; the South inclined to magnify the power of the laity. South Carolina seems to have gone farthest in opposition to the clergy and was inclined to oppose the introduction of any bishop at all. Of course the patriotic question comes in here, for so many of the clergy had been Tory that even in post-Revolution days, they seemed still to carry the odium of submission to a foreign jurisdiction. Fear of foreign influences certainly played an important part in the opposition to unification under any kind of bishops, Scotch or English, in their ordination.

The Reverend Samuel Seabury, the younger, in the memorial sermon for Bishop White which he delivered at St. Luke's Church, in New York, 1836, *A Brief View of the Origin and Results of Episcopacy in the Protestant Episcopal Church in the United States of America*, has left us an excellent near view of the conflicting interests:

"The extraordinary man whose death has now spread a universal gloom through our communion, was the chief instrument, under God, in effecting our deliverance. So peculiarly, indeed, was he qualified for the task, that he seems to have been specially raised up by Providence for the purpose. In his political views and feelings he had been, during the Revolutionary struggle, on the American side, and was thus calculated to inspire confidence where doubt and suspicion existed. As Chaplain of Congress, he had had intercourse with leading men, from different sections of the country, who were engaged in political life, and was thus enabled to prepossess them favorably in regard to the Church, and on some occasions to enlist their kind offices in her favor. (John Adams, the one time arch-enemy of Episcopacy, even stood sponsor for White and Provoost at their consecration at Lambeth Palace.) [1] To illustrate this crisis of our affairs, and to reconcile what might else seem incongruous in the statement, it should be observed that a difference of opinion pre-

held by Dr. White, after an adjournment *sine die*. A majority of the States being unrepresented, while a minor and an unbaptized layman were called on to act as delegates.

[1] *Infra*, pp. 219-220.

vailed, on some important points, between Episcopalians at the North and at the South. In the North, Episcopalians, almost without exception, believed in what are termed the distinctive principles of our church. In the South, on the contrary, many of them, clergy as well as laity, discarded these principles, and deemed a presbyter, in all the essentials of his office, the same as a bishop: and in the conflict for independence, the former class had generally sided with the mother country, while the latter had espoused the American cause. Thus it happened, that when the former made a movement towards obtaining the episcopacy, it was thought to be an indication of their monarchical preferences; it was loosely argued that the Church might take an independent ground, and appoint bishops for herself. Such a step would manifestly have been fatal to our ecclesiastical existence;[1] for if the presbyters had a right to appoint bishops, the people had an equal right to appoint presbyters; so that the operation of this principle would have been for every body of men to make ministers according to their fancy, and thus we would have had the seeds of dissension and schism sown throughout the church. (Reverend Samuel Provoost of New York in his violent opposition to the Reverend Samuel Seabury on the grounds of his disloyalty to America illustrates this.) But when such a man as William White, whose attachment to the American cause had been thoroughly proved, went to England to receive episcopal consecration, less prejudice or hostility was excited; and the same episcopacy which in one individual was thought to exhibit the odious features of monarchical deformity, appeared in another to be invested with the charms of republican beauty.

But if the influence of Bishop White was felt in procuring a favorable introduction for the episcopacy into the American Church, it was much more felt in organizing the Church after the episcopacy was obtained." (Note here that our author reverses the historical order of events; he has the Northern bias. Actually White advocated an American organization first, then bishops with proper English consecration, if they could be obtained.) "All that is essential to the unity of a Church which is sound in faith is, that it have duly authorized bishops. It might have happened therefore, after bishops were obtained, that churches would exist, in the several states, bound together by the general ties of Catholic unity, without being compacted, as they are now, in one organized body. Our Catholic unity, by which we are members of the Universal Church of Christ, is one thing: our constitution, by which we are rendered one consolidated body, known as the Protestant Episcopal Church of the United States, is another. We might have had the former blessing, and lost the latter, and it was in the procurement of the latter blessing, that

[1] This was just the step that the Methodist branch of the Church of England did adopt. *Supra*, p. 186.

the services of Bishop White were chiefly conspicuous. And this was indeed a work of delicacy and magnitude, the difficulties and dangers of which it is almost impossible to estimate. *Here was to be laid the foundation of that influence which, as a United Church, we were to exert for the salvation of our country and of mankind.* In this work a mistake would have been fatal: for *in it were to be combined either the elements of future discord and dissolution, or of harmony and prosperity. And here it was that the genius of Bishop White shone forth.* He brought to the task an accurate knowledge of the principles of civil and ecclesiastical legislation, habits of cool deliberation, and sound judgment, great foresight and discretion, promptitude and perseverance in action, blended with bland and conciliatory manners, learning that was ever respected, and a singleness and dis-interestedness of purpose that were never impeached . . . . .

At that time civil and religious matters were so intermingled that it was impossible to separate them, they (Clergy) sorely differed also in their political sentiments. The clergy at the North carried their views of episcopal prerogative so far as to contend that the Church was to be governed by bishops alone: while those at the South, ... inclined to the other extreme, and advocated the episcopal office simply as a prescriptive usage, or on grounds of human expediency. This difference alone made it difficult to adjust many points of the Prayer-book, such as the office of ordination, and the administration of the communion, to the mutual satisfaction of both sides. It led also to collision in regard to the rights and influence of the laity, whom a portion of the clergy were for excluding from all legislation in the councils of the Church, while the laity in other instances, showed themselves in turn apprehensive of the clerical ascendancy. Now it was the peculiar feature of Bishop White's agency that he was admirably qualified to become the bond of union to dissentient brethren. His own views were understood, both on political and religious questions, to coincide generally with those of the Southern clergy; but his mind was capacious and liberal, and his temper conciliatory, while his simplicity and integrity of character procured for him the confidence of all. Thus while he took that prominent part in the work of legislation, which his singular discretion and learning so well qualified him to act, his influence was even more felt in smoothing asperities as they arose, and in harmonizing discordant materials. To him, therefore, under God, are we mainly indebted for that ecclesiastical constitution by which we are exhibited to the world in the attitude of one undivided church."[1]

[1] Seabury, Samuel, *A Brief View of the Origin and Results of Episcopacy in the Protestant Episcopal Church in the United States of America*, pp. 14-20.

Bishop White himself gives us some of the points at issue in his sermon, *The Past and the Future*, delivered in Philadelphia, 1834. He says:

"It may be thought, that after the establishment of American independence, and, of course, the ceasing of the dangers supposed to result from an episcopacy subject to the English hierarchy, the dread of encroachments on the liberties of our citizens had ceased. It is true, that the grounds of the former fear of evils, whether real or imaginary, was done away: so that to have opposed exterior hindrances to what we were contemplating, would have been an avowed persecution, not likely to be countenanced by popular opinion. If this laid a restraint on any, we may hope that, among our fellow citizens generally, it was a Christian spirit which caused them to refrain from all agency in our concerns. Notwithstanding this advantage, however, it happened that in the heat of the foregoing controversies, Episcopacy, even in its general character, and independently of what might have rendered it unacceptable by incidental associations, had been exhibited as exceedingly adapted to alarm. It had been described as in itself hostile to civil liberty, as nourishing pride and arrogancy in those elevated to the station, as the means of acquiring more wealth than was salutary to the church, and as indulgent to idleness and expensive living. All these charges were contended to be verified in the persons of the English bishops; and it was often in vain to plead, in addition to the absence of proof, that in every age from that of the reformation, records had been left by many of them, not only of distinguished piety and of unblemished lives and conversation, but of prominence in every branch of learning, especially of the theological. Had the allegations been true, as certainly was not the case, they were evidently irrelative to the merits of the subject, and imputable to an indiscreet or else corrupt organization.

The prejudices gradually declined, under the weight of more correct statements, and especially under the irresistible conviction, that the obtaining of the episcopal order was essential to the keeping of us together, as a branch of the Christian church; that a great proportion of our population would have adhered to a constitution which they knew to have been from the beginning, had prevailed universally during the fifteen hundred years, and had been transmitted to them by a church, considered in the character of a parent, although now severed from them by a revolution, which had turned on questions of civil policy and duties. The privilege of acting for themselves in this matter, was secured by the liberal constitution of these states; and if there should be any organized opposition to the design, there was no other alternative, than either conformity to the views of their more consistent brethren, or of their relinquishing of communion with them. It was easy to perceive that, in the latter event, the dissentients must have become merged in the many societies marked by discrepant principles, and abounding within our civil union.

While the hindrances within ourselves were decreasing, under the force of argument and of expediency, we were not insensible of the uncertainty of success in the contemplated application to the English prelacy. We had knowledge of the restraint to which they were subjected by the civil enactments of their kingdom. In the endeavors for an American Episcopacy made before the war, it had been held, that nothing more than the royal consent was required for the accomplishment of the object. This opinion had been decidedly expressed by the excellent Archbishop Secker, who, of all the English prelates, was the most prominent in exertions for the supply of the wants of what was called 'The Church of England in America.' Under such a sanction he certainly would not have hesitated to proceed in the good work. But the case had become materially altered by the transfer of the allegiance of the former colonies. The laws of England did not then, and do not now, except conformably to the act provided for our case, warrant her bishops to extend their powers of office beyond the limits of the laws of the land. This matter had been remarkably visible in the instances of portions of the episcopal chapels in Scotland, in which the worshippers, not uniting with the bishops of that country, because of their disallowance of a right to the crown in the reigning dynasty, presented an anomaly similar to that, which, for a few years, characterized our communion on a much larger scale, of bodies of professed episcopalians severed from all Episcopal superintendence. The inconsistency has been since done away, by their joining themselves to the bishops of that land, on the ceasing of the ground of the non-juring scruples, in which they had persevered through so long a tract of time. That the three estates of Great Britain, having cautiously avoided what might have proved an interference offensive to the Scottish establishment, for the remedy of a privation so near, and cause by adherence to the existing government, would be less scrupulous in regard to another so distant, and under governments which might take umbrage at the measure, was at best uncertain. What added to the danger of a refusal was, that the power to be applied to, having but lately made a peace with their former colonies, with the irritations remaining of a protracted war, might be the more apprehensive of offence to the new authorities which had been established by them. This hesitation had been foreseen, and was therefore met by written assurances from the individuals who had been elected to the chief magistracies, in the states in which were designated the men intended for the Episcopacy, that compliance with the request of our church would not be inconsistent with the constitution or the laws of the said several states, or with those of the United States . . . . . The enlargement of the narrative has been owing to the pretence, not only sedulously propagated at the time, but to this day affirmed and believed in some districts of our country, that our American bishops are in subjection to the hierarchy of England, and of course to its head, in the sovereignty of that country.

After determination on the measure of applying to the English bishops for consecration, there occurred a point of difficulty and delicacy in the consequent procedure. We were rendered uneasy by an opinion, confidently maintained and propagated, that the Right Reverend persons whom we had addressed could not but be offended, by its not merely being implied through the whole tenor of the application, but expressed in plain although in respectful language in the beginning of it, that we were a church competent in the point of right to government of ourselves being now separated from that by which we had been fostered, and of which we had been so long a part. This may be classed as another difficulty; for although we were aware that it was founded on error, yet the tendency of it was to weaken our hands in the work before us. Accordingly, it was a great relief, when we found in the first letter from our former superiors, that they not only noticed as 'Christian' and 'brotherly' the address which had been pronounced by some among ourselves to be contumacious, but avoided whatever might have seemed to dictate; or rather, they so expressed themselves as might be considered to admit our claim of independence in its extent.

There was another source of embarrassment generated among ourselves. It was the question of including the laity in our ecclesiastical legislature. The first movements to the point were made in this state. Although the example was soon followed in several of the other states, yet there was strong repugnancy against it in certain respectable members of our ministry. This must have been owing to their not having duly considered the constitution of the church from which we are descended. In construing the canons of that church, a distinction is always taken in the courts of law between those which are binding '*proprio vigore*' as being the ancient canon-law of the realm, and so applying, like common law, on the footing of immemorial usage, and other canons, enacted by the convocation only. The latter are held to be binding on the clergy, but no further; not having had the sanction of the laity in parliament. It is not so, in regard to the liturgy and its rubrics. Those possesss the concurrence of the said authority, and it is held that the same is necessary to any alterations which may be thought expedient in future. This point is ably handled by the Reverend Richard Hooker, in his immortal work on Ecclesiastical Polity, in which he defends the sanction given by the parliament, as the only form in which the laity can consent to laws by which they are to be governed: a circumstance which the sagacious man contends for, as what ought to be attached to every provision intended to have the force of law. Certain it is that the English bishops never found fault with our lay representation, which met their eyes in our proceedings. It was probably owing to this, added to more mature consideration, that the prejudice gradually died away, until now it no longer shows its head, except as at present, in notice taken of it in the light of an historic fact.

There was the danger of a more important hindrance to our expectations in the right which we claimed, and which we exercised in the form of a 'Proposed Book,' recommended to our American churches; of the making of alterations in the articles and in the liturgy; not only accommodated to the change of our civil relations, but further, as in our judgments expediency had rendered eligible; there being still an adherence to the doctrines of the Gospel as held by the mother church. So far as the subject, either of the articles or of the liturgy was a matter of human judgment and discretion, the English bishops did not manifest any disposition to interfere. But they were jealous for the integrity of their faith, our invasion of which had been affirmed to them by persons whom they could not but respect, but whose political attachments had betrayed them into unfounded suspicions and reports. The bishops, on receiving the details of our transactions, were satisfied of our orthodoxy; and although a few points were thought to require reconsideration, yet their suggestions to this effect were complied with, consistently with the not surrendering of any right on our side, and the not relaxing of Christian vigilance on theirs." [1]

The process by which a national American ideal was worked into the constitution of the Protestant Episcopal Church in the United States is outlined in the minutes of the various conferences and conventions by which this was effected.

Dr. White inaugurated the movement although the Reverend Abraham Beach of Brunswick, New Jersey, was the first to propose to the several states the advisability of a joint meeting to consider the matter.

[1] White, *The Past and the Future: A Charge on Events Connected with the Organization of the Protestant Episcopal Church in the United States of America, and the Lessons they Inculcate. Delivered before the Fiftieth Convention of the Diocese of Pennsylvania.* Philadelphia, 1834.

We have noted the patriotic activities of Dr. White.[1] In line with his political activities, before he had heard of the prospects of peace, he began to advocate the Americanization of his church. "Despairing," as he says in a letter to Bishop Hobart, "of a speedy acknowledgment of our independence . . . . . and perceiving our ministry gradually approaching to annihilation," he published, anonymously, in 1782, a pamphlet which was republished in 1783, *The case of the Episcopal Churches in the United States Considered. 'To make new articles of faith and doctrine, no man thinketh it lawful: new laws of government, what commonwealth or church is there which maketh not at one time or another'*. In this he proposed: 1. A church free from spiritual jurisdiction connected with the temporal authority of any foreign state; 2. A provisional government "to[2] procure the union of all the Episcopal Churches in the United States in one body" under a "superintendent" or "Overseer"; 3. An organization consisting of the following units, — nation, province, and diocese; 4. A triennial national convention; 5. Clerical and lay representation; 6. An immediate organization, not awaiting the presence of regularly ordained bishops.[3] Such was the earliest proposal for the organization of the American Protestant Episcopalian Church, fathered by Dr. White.[4] In 1783 he proposed such a plan at a meeting of his church as a means of effecting a state organization in Pennsylvania.

[1] *Supra*, pp. 43-44.

[2] White, *The Case of the Episcopal Church in the United States Considered*. Philadelphia, 1783; Wilson, *op. cit.*, p. 81.

[3] Perry, *op. cit.*, vol. iii, p. 11; Wilson, *op. cit.*, p. 81.

[4] On March 25th, 1783, ten of the fourteen remaining priests in Connecticut met at Woodbury in a "Voluntary Convention" and chose for their bishop Dr. Samuel Seabury. Perry, *History of the American Episcopal Church*, vol. ii, p. 49. This meeting was not in that series which developed the church constitution.

The Reverend Abraham Beach in a letter to Dr. White, dated January 26, 1784, suggested the first inter-state conference, advocating a preliminary meeting for the purpose of reviving the Society for the Support of Widows and Children of Deceased Clergymen.[1] He added, "If anything should occur to you as necessary to be done, in order to put us upon an equal footing with other denominations of Christians, and cement us together in the Bonds of Love, I shall be happy in an opportunity of assisting in it." The Philadelphia churches resolved in response to this proposal, March 29, 1784, "that the subject ought to be taken up with the general concurrence of the Episcopalians of 'The United States'." The Reverend Beach approached Provoost and Moore of New York. They approved, though James Duane wished the meeting to take place in New York.

Beach also took up with White the questions of publicity, lay representation and the necessity for receding from ancient usages. In a letter of April 23, 1784, he writes:

> "I wish you would be so good as to advertise it (the Brunswick Meeting) in one of your News Papers, with an invitation to all clergymen of the Episcopal Church, and perhaps you may think it proper to invite respectable characters of the laity, as matters of general concern to the Church may probably be discussed . . . . .
>
> "I had the pleasure of reading it (White's pamphlet) . . . . and am happy to agree with you in every particular, *excepting the necessity of receding from ancient usages.* If this necessity existed in time of war, I cannot think that it does at present."[2]

The first argument to be used against White's plan was that of the conservative. White's was no radical program. He tells us that his "expedient (an ecclesiastical representatve body . . . . . to make a declaration

[1] Perry, *Journals,* vol. iii, pp. 8-9.
[2] *Ibid.,* vol. iii, p. 11.

approving of episcopacy, and professing a determination to possess the succession when it could be obtained, but . . to carry the plan into immediate act) was sustained by the plea of necessity and by opinions of various authors of the Church of England, acknowledging a valid ministry under circumstances similar to those of the existing case, although less imperious."[1]

The Preliminary Conference was held in New Brunswick, May 11, 1784. Ten clergymen from New Jersey, New York, and Pennsylvania, members of the Corporation for the Relief of Widows and Orphans of the Clergy,[2] were present and "there happened to be in town, on civil business, some lay-gentlemen, who being represented by the clergy from New York and New Jersey as taking an interest in the welfare of the church, were requested to attend."[3] Pennsylvania communicated resolutions from a meeting of the clergy and laity "tending to the organization of the church throughout the union." This called for Committees of Correspondence; "it is expedient to appoint a standing committee of the Episcopal Church in this state, consisting of clergy and laity; that the said committee be empowered to correspond and confer with representatives from the Episcopal Church in the other states, or any of them; and assist in framing an ecclesiastical government; that a constitution of ecclesiastical government, when framed, be reported to the several congregations." The first resolution of instruction, — on fundamental principles for the guidance of the delegates,— was "the Episcopal Church in these states, is, and ought to be independent of all foreign authority, ecclesiastical

[1] Wilson, *op. cit.*, p. 81-85.

[2] This corporation, founded by Dr. Smith, was the only general institution of the colonial Episcopal Church.

[3] Perry, *Journals*, vol. iii, p. 11; White, *Memoirs*, p. 78.

or civil." This last was going too fast for the Northerners. White was taken aside by Moore of New York, "who expressed the wish of himself and others, that nothing should be urged on the subject, as they had joined the clergy of Connecticut in their application for the consecration of a bishop. The clergy from Philadelphia had up to this point been in ignorance of the fact that Dr. Seabury had sailed for England just before the evacuation of New York by the British, carrying with him a petition to the English bishops for his consecration."[1]

A committee was named to canvass the three states and it was instructed to propose "a proper substitute for the State Prayers in the Liturgy" to be adopted for temporary use. We have no evidence that they ever complied with the latter injunction. A delegation was appointed to seek co-operation from Connecticut, "in such measures as may be deemed conducive to the union and prosperity of the Episcopal Churches in the States of America."[2] Committees of Correspondence were chosen to interest the clergymen and members of the scattered churches in a proposed meeting in New York. Also it was recommended that a committee of Clerical Examiners be appointed in each State to consider the applications of persons desirous of officiating as lay readers, and the congregations were advised not to suffer any layman to officiate in their churches without the certificates of these Examiners.

This New Brunswick Conference showed clearly that union would not be effected without a struggle. Dr. White observed that,

"notwithstanding the good humor which prevailed . . . . . the more Northern clergymen were under apprehension of there being a

[1] White, *op. cit.*, p. 78; Perry, *op. cit.*, vol. iii, pp. 6-12.
[2] Perry, *op. cit.*, vol. iii, p. 7.

disposition on the part of the more Southern, to make material deviation from the ecclesiastical system of England, in the Articles of Church Government." At the same time he wondered, "that any sensible and well informed persons should overlook the propriety of accommodating that system, in some respects, to the prevailing sentiments and habits of the people of this country; now become an independent and combined commonwealth . . . . . When the crisis presented a subject of deliberation entirely new, it was difficult to detach it in the minds of many, from a past habitual train of thinking. Some were startled at the very circumstance, of taking the stand of an independent Church. There was a much more common prejudice, against the embracing of the laity in a scheme of ecclesiastical legislation. Besides these things the confessed necessity of accommodating the service to the newly established civil constitution of the country, naturally awakened apprehensions of unlimited license."[1]

The Preliminary Conference of New York, October 6-7, 1784, was a body of men notable in Episcopalian circles: White and Griffith of Virginia: Provoost, Moore, and Duane of New York; Smith of Maryland; Parker for Massachusetts and Rhode Island; Ogden from New Jersey; and White and Peters of Pennsylvania. White, Moore, Parker, and Provoost later became bishops; Ogden, Smith and Griffith were elected though never consecrated to that office.

As the delegates had been variously and irregularly chosen and as they possessed no delegated authority, the meeting could only act in a recommendatory capacity. Dr. White presided and a committee of four clergymen: Parker, Provoost, Smith, and White; and four laymen: Clay, Clarkson, Dr. Hart, and Duane, "to essay the fundamental principles of a general constitution," reported the following program:

"The body now assembled recommend to the Clergy and the Congregations of their Communion, in the States represented as above, and propose to the States not represented, That as soon as they shall have

[1] White, *op. cit.*, pp. 79, 81-82; Perry, *op. cit.*, vol. iii, p. 12.

organized or associated themselves in the States to which they respectively belong, agreeably to such Rules as they think proper, they unite in a general ecclesiastical Constitution, on the following fundamental Principles.

I. That there shall be a General Convention of the Episcopal Church in the United States of America.

II. That the Episcopal Church in each State send Deputies to the Convention, consisting of Clergy and Laity.

III. That associated Congregations in two or more States may send Deputies jointly.

IV. That the said Church shall maintain the Doctrines of the Gospel, as now held by the Church of England; and shall adhere to the Liturgy of the said Church as far as shall be consistent with the American Revolution and the Constitution of the respective states.

V. That in every State where there shall be a Bishop duly consecrated and settled, he shall be considered as a member of the Convention, *ex officio*.

VI. That the Clergy and Laity assembled in Convention shall deliberate in one Body, but shall vote separately; and the concurrence of both shall be necessary to give validity to every measure.

VII. That the first Meeting of the Convention shall be at Philadelphia the Tuesday before the Feast of St. Michael next; to which it is hoped and earnestly desired, That the Episcopal Churches in the respective States, will send their Clerical and Lay Deputies, duly instructed and authorized to proceed on the necessary business, herein proposed for their deliberation."[1]

This New York Preliminary Conference of 1784 in proposing a constitutional convention, closely parallels in points of purpose and procedure the Annapolis Convention which met preliminary to the Federal Constitutional Convention at Philadelphia. It is noteworthy though, that the Church worked out its method two years in advance of the national body, — October 1784 as against October 1786.

In the meantime state churches were organizing. Maryland inaugurated this movement in 1783, when her clergy drew up the first declaration of rights of any of the

[1] Perry, *op. cit.*, vol. i, pp. 12-13; vol. iii, pp. 62-66; White, *op. cit.*, pp. 79-81.

American churches, "A Declaration of Certain Fundamental Rights and Liberties." In this they took the name, "Protestant Episcopal Church,"— the first public assumption of that title by a representative body of the Church;— they asserted "ecclesiastical and spiritual independence"; and they announced that the "Church when duly organized, constituted, and represented in a Synod or Convention of her ministers and people" was "competent to revise her Liturgy, Forms of Prayer, and Public Worship in order to adapt the same to the late revolution and other local circumstances of America." Here we have an authoritative recognition of the right of the laity to admission to the councils of the Church.[1]

Pennsylvania organized, May 1785, providing for an annual convention of clergy and laity wherein each congregation should have one vote, the clergy and laity deliberating as one and voting as two bodies, — a concurrence being necessary for action. They appointed delegates to the Philadelphia General Convention.

The Constitutional Convention of the Protestant Episcopal Church of the United States of America, their first General Conference, met in Christ Church in Philadelphia from September 27 to October 7, 1785,[2] — the Federal Constitutional Convention was to meet in the same city two years later, 1787. Sixteen clergy and twenty-six laymen were present. New York, New Jersey, Delaware, Pennsylvania, Maryland, Virginia, and South Carolina were represented. Prominent among the delegates were the following:

William White, unanimously chosen president of the Convention.
David Griffith, of Virginia, elected Vice-President.

[1] White, *op. cit.*, pp. 92-96.

[2] Perry, *Journals*, vol. i, pp. 14-29, iii, pp. 69-212; *Handbook of the General Convention*, pp. 8-42; White, *Memoirs*, pp. 22-24; 96-111.

Samuel Provoost, of New York, a King's College man, and at the time Chaplain of Continental Congress.

James Duane, mayor of New York 1783-1789, one of the most influential members of the Convention in New York to ratify the Federal Constitution.[1]

Richard Peters, of Pennsylvania, a Philadelphia College man, member of Continental Congress, secretary of the Pennsylvania War Board, 1776-1781; later District Judge, 1792-1828.

Edward Shippen, of Pennsylvania, later Chief Justice of the Supreme Court of that state.

John Page, of Virginia, a framer of the Virginia Constitution, 1776; member of the Virginia Committee of Public Safety; Congressman from Virginia, 1789-1797; and Governor, 1802-1805.

Charles Pinckney, of South Carolina, prominent in the Federal Constitutional Convention, 1787.[2]

The New England States were unrepresented. The Reverend John Bowden could write, "It is much to be feared, that there will be a separation of the Eastern and Western Churches. The former, steadfast in Episcopal Principles, would send no delegates to the grand Convention at Philadelphia last September, because, the year preceding, the Convention held at New York, departed from the Principles of the Church, in regard to government."[3] Moreover, Bishop Seabury, having been duly consecrated, their church was already fully organized.

The work of the Convention was preformed largely through a committee composed of two members from each state, one lay and one cleric, appointed to draft "an Ecclesiastical Constitution for the Protestant Episcopal Church in the United States of America" and "to alter the Liturgy as shall render it consistent with the American Revolution and the Constitutions of the respective states; with such further alterations in the Liturgy as it

[1] *Infra.*, p. 453.
[2] *Infra.*, p. 454.
[3] Perry, *op. cit.*, vol. iii, pp. 319-320.

may be advisable for this Convention to recommend to the consideration of the Church here represented;[1] while later this committee was charged with reporting a plan for obtaining the consecration of bishops, together with an address to the Most Reverend the Archbishops, and the Right Reverend the Bishops of the Church of England for that purpose."[2]

The committee began its work on Tuesday; on Saturday, October 1, they reported on the Constitution and Liturgy. This report was considered article by article and on the next Tuesday it was adopted; on Wednesday, the new Prayer-book was ordered printed. On Friday, the convention adjourned after a session of ten days. Few legislative bodies have accomplished so much in so short a time. A general constitution had been produced which the church as a whole proceeded to act under immediately though it was not finally ratified until another session of the Convention, in 1789.

This constitution was but the acceptance of Dr. White's principles. The more important provisions of this *General Constitution of the Protestant Episcopal Church in the United States of America* are as follows:

"Whereas, in the course of Divine Providence, the Protestant Episcopal Church in the United States of America is become independent of all foreign authority, civil and ecclesiastical: . . . . .

And whereas, ... Clerical and Lay Deputies have been duly appointed from the said Church in the States of New York, New Jersey, Pennsylvania, Delaware, Maryland, Virginia, and South Carolina:

The said Deputies being now assembled, and taking into consideration the importance of maintaining uniformity in doctrine, discipline, and worship in the said Church, do hereby determine, and declare,

1. That there shall be a General Convention of the Protestant Episcopal Church in the United States of America, which shall be held

[1] Perry, *op. cit.*, vol. i, pp. 18-19.
[2] *Ibid.*, vol. i, p. 23.

in the city of Philadelphia on the third Tuesday in June, in the year of our Lord 1786, and for ever after once in three years, on the third Tuesday of June, in such place as shall be determined by the Convention; and special meetings may be held at such other times and in such place as shall be hereafter provided for; and this Church, in a majority of the States aforesaid, shall be represented before they proceed to business; except that the representation of this Church from two States shall be sufficient to adjourn; and in all business of the Convention freedom of debate shall be allowed.

2. There shall be a representation of both Clergy and Laity of the Church in each State, which shall consist of one or more Deputies, not exceeding four, of each Order; and in all questions, the said Church in each State shall have one vote, and a majority of suffrages shall be conclusive.

3. In the said Church in every State represented in this Convention, there shall be a Convention consisting of the Clergy and Lay Deputies of the Congregation.

4. "The Book of Common Prayer, and Administration of the Sacraments, and other Rites and Ceremonies of the Church, according to the use of the Church of England," shall be continued to be used by this Church, as the same is altered by this Convention, in a certain instrument of writing passed by their authority, entitled, "Alterations of the Liturgy of the Protestant Episcopal Church in the United States of America, in order to render the same conformable to the American Revolution and the Constitutions of the respective States."

5. In every State where there shall be a Bishop duly consecrated and settled, and who shall have acceded to the articles of this General Ecclesiastical Constitution, he shall be considered as a member of the Convention *ex officio*.

6. The Bishop or Bishops in every State shall be chosen agreeably to such rules as shall be fixed by the respective Conventions; and every Bishop of this Church shall confine the exercise of his Episcopal office to his proper jurisdiction, unless requested to ordain or confirm by any church destitute of a Bishop.

7. A Protestant Episcopal Church in any of the United States not now represented, may at any time hereafter be admitted, on acceding to the articles of this union.

8. Every clergyman, whether bishop, or presbyter, or deacon, shall be amenable to the authority of the Convention in the State to which he belongs, so far as relates to suspension or removal from office; and the Convention in each State shall institute rules for their conduct, and an equitable mode of trial.

9. And whereas it is represented to this Convention to be the desire

of the Protestant Episcopal Church in these States, that there may be further alterations of the Liturgy than such as are made necessary by the American Revolution; therefore the *Book of Common Prayer and Administration of the Sacraments and other Rites and Ceremonies of the Church, according to the use of the Church of England,* as altered by an instrument of writing passed under the authority of this Convention, entitled, *Alterations in the Book of Common Prayer and Administration of the Sacraments and other Rites and Ceremonies of the Church, according to the use of the Church of England, proposed and recommended to the Protestant Episcopal Church in the United States of America,* shall be used in this Church when the same shall have been ratified by the Conventions which have respectively sent Deputies to this General Convention.

10. No person shall be ordained or permitted to officiate as a minster in this Church, until he shall have subscribed the following declaration: 'I do believe the Holy Scriptures of the Old and New Testament to be the word of God, and to contain all things necessary to salvation; and I do solemnly engage to conform to the doctrines and worship of the Protestant Episcopal Church, as settled and determined in the Book of Common Prayer, and Administration of the Sacraments, set forth by the General Convention of the Protestant Episcopal Church in these United States.'

11. This General Ecclesiastical Constitution, when ratified by the Church in the different States, shall be considered as fundamental, and shall be unalterable by the Convention of the Church in any State." [1]

Dr. White was chairman of the committee which drafted this constitution. James Duane was on the committee on revision.[2]

The above mentioned *Alterations in the Book of Common Prayer,* contained startlingly radical proposals and was destined to threaten trouble for the Church, so much so that very little of the revision was retained. Dr. Smith was chairman of the committee that produced this revision. Among other alterations were the reduction of the thirty-nine articles to twenty (afterwards to seventeen) and the omission of the "descended into Hell" clause from

[1] Perry, *op. cit.*, vol. i, pp. 21-23; vol. iii, pp. 69-212; White, *op. cit.*, pp. 12-24, 96-111; Perry, *Handbook of the General Convention*, pp. 8-42.

[2] Sprague, *Annals of the American Pulpit*, vol. v, p. 160.

the Apostles' Creed, and the total suppression of the Nicene and the Athanasian Creeds. Of course it was necessary to legislate on the subject of prayers for the American Holidays; two services were accordingly added, one for the Fourth of July and one for Thanksgiving. It was resolved, "That the Fourth of July shall be observed by this Church forever, as a day of thanksgiving to Almighty God for the inestimable blessings of religious and civil liberty vouchsafed to the United States."[1] And further, "that the first Tuesday in November in every year forever shall be observed by this church as a day of general Thanksgiving to Almighty God for the fruits of the earth, and for all the other blessings of His merciful providence."[2] The forms of Prayer were accordingly prepared for these days.

It was moreover resolved; "that a committee be appointed to publish the Book of Common Prayer and that the Committee be authorized to publish . . . . . such of the reading and singing Psalms and such a Calendar of proper lessons for the different Sundays and Holy Days . . . . . as they may think proper."[3]

This same committee was also charged with reporting "a plan for obtaining the consecration of Bishops, together with an address to the Most Reverend the Archbishops, and the Right Reverend the Bishops of the Church of England for that purpose."[4]

Immediately, without awaiting ratification by the various state churches, the address of the Convention as prepared by this committee was presented to the Archbishop of Canterbury through John Adams, the American

[1] Perry, *Journals*, vol. i, p. 23.
[2] *Ibid.*, vol. i, p. 24.
[3] *Ibid.*, vol. i, p. 28.
[4] *Ibid.*, vol. i, p. 19.

Minister to the Court of St. James. In connection with this matter, Adams later wrote to Bishop White, October 29, 1814, "There is no part of my life on which I look with more satisfaction, than the part I took . . . . . in the introduction of Episcopacy into America."

The proceedings of the Episcopalian movement in America was of more than local import. Our Minister to the French Court, Thomas Jefferson, was kept informed relative to the actions of the various meetings. His letter to Edmund Randolph, July 26, 1785, thanks him for a copy "of the ecclesiastical journal," possibly a reference to the minutes of the Virginia state convention of 1785. John Page forwarded him a copy of the journal of the national convention of 1786.

A second session of the Constitutional Convention was held in Philadelphia, June 20-26, 1786 and at Wilmington, Delaware, October 10-11.[1] It read the proposed constitution a second time and effected some alteration therein: Bishops were always to preside at a General Convention if present; and the requirement for ratification was changed so that the Constitution was to go into effect when accepted "by the Church in a majority of the states assembled in general convention with sufficient power for the purpose of ratification."

The Wilmington session was chiefly concerned with the question of bishops. Strong political opposition had become manifest to the recognition of the validity of the consecration of Samuel Seabury of Connecticut (November 14, 1784), partly on the grounds that it had been performed by Scottish bishops at Aberdeen, which proceedings might place American bishops under canonical subjection to Scotland, partly because of Seabury's Tory

[1] Perry, *Handbook*, pp. 43-62; *Journals*, vol. i, pp. 31-62.

war record, and partly because there seemed to be excellent prospects that American bishops might regularly and speedily be consecrated from England itself.[1] And of course the Seabury question was made to involve all the other points of difference that were to be found in Episcopalian circles.

Letters which had been received from the Archbishops of England were spread upon the minutes. They showed that the mother church was eager to recognize the new national church and to accommodate the situation to the interests of the daughter in America. They desired, however, assurance that the American church would continue the doctrine, discipline, and worship of the parent church. The following is indeed a sort of *Concordat* between the two churches:

"Letter from the Archbishops to the Committee of the General Convention at Philadelphia.

It was impossible not to observe with concern, that if the essential doctrines of our common faith were retained, less respect, however, was paid to our Liturgy than its own excellence, and your declared attachment to it, had led us to expect. Not to mention a variety of verbal alterations, of the necessity or propriety of which we are by no means satisfied, we saw with grief that two of the Confessions of our Christian faith, respectable for their antiquity, have been entirely laid aside; and that even in that called the Apostles' Creed, an article is omitted, which was thought necessary to be inserted, with a view to a particular heresy, in a very early age of the Church, and has ever since had the venerable sanction of universal reception. Nevertheless, as a proof of the sincere desire which we feel to continue in spiritual communion with the members of your Church in America, and to complete the Orders of your Ministry, and trusting that the communications which we shall make to you, on the subject of these and some other alterations, will have their desired effect, we have, even under these circumstances, prepared a Bill for conveying to us the powers necessary for this purpose. It will in a few days be presented to Parliament, and we have the best reasons to hope that it will receive the assent of the Legislature. This Bill will

[1] Perry, *Bishop Seabury and Bishop Provoost.*

enable the Archbishops and Bishops to give Episcopal consecration to the persons who shall be recommended, without requiring from them any oaths or subscriptions inconsistent with the situation in which the late Revolution has placed them; upon condition that the full satisfaction of the sufficiency of the persons recommended, which you offer to us in your address, be given to the Archbishops and Bishops. You will doubtless receive it as a mark both of our friendly disposition toward you, and of our desire to avoid all delay on this occasion, that we have taken this earliest opportunity of conveying to you this intelligence, and that we proceed (as supposing ourselves invested with that power which for your sakes we have requested) to state to you particularly the several heads upon which that satisfaction which you offer will be accepted, and the mode in which it may be given. The anxiety which is shown by the Church of England to prevent the intrusion of unqualified persons into even the inferior offices of our Ministry, confirms our own sentiments, and points it out to be our duty, very earnestly to require the most decisive proofs of the qualifications of those who may be offered for admission to that Order to which the superintendence of those offices is committed. At our several Ordinations of a Deacon and a Priest, the candidate submits himself to the examination of the Bishop as to his proficiency in learning; he gives the proper security of his soundness in the Faith by the subscriptions which are made previously necessary; he is required to bring testimonials of his virtuous conversation during the three preceeding years; and that no node of inquiry may be omitted, public notice of his offering himself to be ordained is given in the Parish Church where he resides or ministers, and the people are solemnly called upon to declare if they know any impediment, for the which he ought not to be admitted. At the times of Ordination, too, the same solemn call is made on the congregation then present.

Examination, subscription, and testimonials are not indeed repeated at the consecration of an English bishop, because the person to be consecrated has added to the securities given at his former ordinations, that sanction which arises from his having constantly lived and exercised his ministry under the eyes and observation of his country. But the objects of our present consideration are very differently circumstanced; their sufficiency in learning, the soundness of their faith, and the purity of their manners, are not matters of notoriety here. Means, therefore, must be found to satisfy the Archbishop who consecrates, and the Bishops who present them, that, in the words of our Church, 'They be apt and meet for their learning and godly conversation, to exercise their ministry duly to the honor of God and the edification of His Church, and to be wholesome examples and patterns to the flock of Christ.'

With regard to the first qualification, sufficiency in good learning, we apprehend that the subjecting a person, who is to be admitted to the office of a Bishop in the Church, to that examination which is required previous to the ordination of Priests and Deacons, might lessen that reverend estimation which ought never to be separated from the Episcopal character: we therefore do not require any further satisfaction on this point, than will be given to us by the forms of testimonials in the annexed paper, fully trusting that those who sign them will be well aware, how greatly incompetence in this respect must lessen the weight and authority of the Bishops and affect the credit of the Episcopal Church. (The forms of testimonials were spread on the minutes of the Convention.)

Under the second head, that of subscription, our desire is to require that subscription only to be repeated which you have already been called upon to make by the Tenth Article of your Ecclesiastical Constitution: but we should forget the duty which we owe to our own Church, and act inconsistently with that sincere regard which we bear to yours, if we were not explicit in declaring, that, after the disposition we have shown to comply with the prayer of your address, we think it now incumbent upon you to use your utmost exertions also for the removal of any stumbling block of offence which may possibly prove an obstacle to the success of it. We, therefore, most earnestly exhort you, that previously to the time of your making such subscription, you restore to its integrity the Apostles' Creed, in which you have omitted an article, merely, as it seems, from misapprehension of the sense in which it is understood by our Church; nor can we help adding, that we hope you will think it but a decent proof of the attachment which you profess for the services of your Liturgy, to give the other two Creeds a place in your Book of Common Prayer, even though the use of them should be left discretional. We should be inexcusable, too, if, at the time when you are requesting the establishment of Bishops in your Church, we did not strongly represent to you that the Eighth Article of your Ecclesiastical Constitution, appears to us to be a degradation of the Clerical, and still more of the Episcopal character. We persuade ourselves, that in your ensuing Convention, some alteration will be thought necessary in this article, before this reaches you; or, if not, that due attention will be given to it in consequence of our representation.

On the third and last head, which respects purity of manners, the reputation of the Church, both in England and America, and the interest of our common Christianity, is so deeply concerned in it, that we feel it our indispensable duty to provide, on this subject, the most effectual securities. It is presumed, that the same previous public notice of the intention of the person to be consecrated, will be given in the Church where he resides in America, for the same reasons, and therefore, nearly in the same form with that used in England before our ordinations. The call upon the persons present at the time of consecration, must be deemed of little use before a congregation composed of those to whom the person to be consecrated is unknown. The testimonials signed by persons living in England, admit of reference and examination, and the characters of those who give them are subject to scrutiny, and in cases of criminal deceit to punishment. In proportion as these circumstances are less applicable to testimonials from America, those testimonials must be more explicit, and supported by a greater number of signatures. We therefore think it necessary that the several persons, candidates for Episcopal consecration, should bring to us, both a testimonial from the General Convention of the Protestant Episcopal Church, with as many signatures, as can be obtained, and a more particular one, from the respective Conventions in those States which recommend them. It will appear from the tenor of the letters testimonial used in England, a form of which is annexed, that the ministers who sign them bear testimony to the qualifications of the candidates of their own personal knowledge. Such a testimony is not to be expected from the members of the General Convention of the Episcopal Church in America on this occasion. We think it sufficient, therefore, that they declare they know no impediment, but believe the person to be consecrated is of a virtuous life and sound faith. We have sent you such a form as appears to us proper to be used for that purpose. More specific declarations must be made by the members of the Convention in each State from which the persons offered for Consecration are respectively recommended; their personal knowledge of them there can be no doubt of; we trust, therefore, they will have no objection to the adoption of the form of a testimonial which is annexed, and drawn upon the same principles, and containing the same attestations of personal knowledge with that above mentioned, as required previously to our Ordinations. We trust we shall receive these testimonials signed by such a majority in each Convention that recommend, as to leave no doubt of the fitness of the candidates upon the minds of those whose consciences are concerned in the consecration of them.

Thus much we have thought it right to communicate to you, without reserve, at present, intending to give you farther information as soon as we are able. In the meantime, we pray God to direct your counsels in this very weighty matter, and are

Mr. President and gentlemen
Your affectionate Brethren
J. Cantuar.
W. Ebor."[1]

[1] White, *Memoirs*, pp. 303-307; Perry, *Journals*, vol. i, pp. 51-54.

The spirit of the English clergy was appreciated by the Americans. The words "He descended into Hell" were restored to the Apostles' Creed and the Nicene Creed was re-inserted in the Book of Common Prayer. The Anthanasian Creed was rejected by the following vote; nays, New York, Pennsylvania, and South Carolina; New Jersey and Delaware divided. In accordance with the actions of their respective state conventions, Drs. White, Griffith, and Provoost were certified as Bishops-elect from the states of Pennsylvania, Virginia, and New York respectively. It does not so appear on the Journals but the application of the Reverend William Smith, Bishop-elect for Maryland, was refused certification on the grounds of conduct.[1] New York, through Dr. Provoost, tried to pledge the Convention "not to consent to any act that may imply the validity of Dr. Seabury's ordinations."[2] Dr. White tells us, "The question of the Scottish Episcopacy gave occasion to some warmth . . . . . The convention did not enter into the opposition to the Scottish succession. A motion, as may be seen on the Journals, was made to the effect, by the Reverend Mr. Provoost, seconded by the Rev. Robert Smith of South Carolina; who only, of the clergy were of that mind. But the subject was suppressed as the Journal shows . . . . . by the previous question; moved by the Rev. Dr. Smith and seconded by the author."[3] A resolution was carried unanimously . . .

"recommending this church in the States here represented, not to receive to the pastoral charge within their respective limits, clergymen professing canonical subjection to any Bishop in any State or Country, other than those Bishops who may be duly settled in the States repre-

[1] Perry, *Journals*, vol. iii, pp. 334-341.
[2] *Ibid.*, vol. i, p. 37.
[3] White *op. cit.*, pp. 115-116; Perry *op. cit.*, vol. i, p. 37, vol. iii, p. 312.

sented in this Convention." This resolution was offered to meet the allegation made on the floor of the Convention that Bishop Seabury required a pledge of canonical obedience from those who receive Holy Orders at his hands, wherever they might reside. But the charge was denied by a deputy who had been ordained by the Bishop of Connecticut, and since, as Bishop White expressly states, there was never "any ground" for this apprehension, the resolution was carried without opposition.[1]

Embarrassment had arisen from the rejection of the proposed Book of Common Prayer published by the committee in 1786, in some of the states, and its use in others, so the expedient was adopted of "letting matters remain for a time in the present state."[2]

Before adjournment the Committee of Correspondence was appointed as follows: David Griffith, William White, William Smith, Samuel Provoost, James Duane, Samuel Powell, Francis Hopkinson, and John Jay.[3] John Jay was one of the most influential lay men of the State of New York. Later as one of the authors of *The Federalist* he was to exert great influence in securing the ratification of the Federal Constitution. Francis Hopkinson of New Jersey, was a signer of the Declaration of Independence, a delegate to Continental Congress and one of the drafters of the Articles of Confederation.

No one can deny that this Convention did great work for the unity of the Protestant Episcopal Church. Its spirit and influence must have reacted upon the country at large. Dr. White tells us that it "assembled under circumstances, which bore strong appearances of a dissolution

[1] White, *op. cit.*, p. 116; Wilson, *op. cit.*, pp. 112-113; Perry, *op. cit.*, vol. i, pp. 37-38; vol. iii, pp. 312-313. *Connecticut Church Documents*, vol. ii, p. 300.

[2] White, *op. cit.*, p. 115.

[3] Perry, *op. cit.*, vol. i, p. 43.

of the union, in this early stage of it."[1] Certainly the issues within the church were no less conducive of disunion than those with the nation, "interfering instructions from . . . . . different states,. embarrassment over the proposed Book, the Scottish Episcopacy and the demur of the English Bishops." That they were solved so successfully was due to the prevalence of a firm conciliatory spirit of independence. Not one iota of American independence was thus sacrificed. In fact Dr. White tells us of a letter to the English clergy which Dr. Smith had drafted but which was "considerably altered on a motion of the Hon. John Jay, Esq., who thought the draft too submissive."[2] The alterations in the constitution were made "before the receiving of the objections made against it, on the part of the English bishops,"[3] and "without even an opposition."[3] "The silence of it (the *Concordat*) in regard to the including of the laity, gave a great advantage over those of the clergy, who were representing the introduction of that order as in opposition to correct principles of ecclesiastical government."[4] "The moderation which governed in this convention, must be conspicuous. One principal reason, was the moderation of the English prelates. They who were thought the least devoted to the Episcopal Regime, acknowledged the great forebearance in there being no such high notions of the subject, as had been avowed by some of the clergy on our side of the Atlantic. Added to this, there was noticed the absence of the most distant intimation of offence taken at the presumed independency of the American church. For although the bishops could not

[1] White, *op. cit.*, p. 115.
[2] *Ibid.*, p. 116.
[3] *Ibid.*, p. 117.
[4] *Ibid.*, p. 119.

have denied this, consistently with the known principles of their own church; yet it had been reckoned on, as a source of difficulty."[1] The spirit of accommodation which was manifested in this Convention was to solve the various and vexation problems which still disrupted the American Episcopacy.

Bishops-elect White and Provoost, upon adjournment of the convention, proceeded to England for consecration; Bishop-elect Griffith was unable to go at this time. On reaching London they were introduced "to his Grace the Archbishop of Canterbury, by his Excellency Mr. Adams, who, in this particular, and in every instance in which his personal attention could be either of use or an evidence of his respect and kindness, continued to manifest his concern for the interests of a church, of which he was not a member."[2] Drs. White and Provoost were ordained and consecrated bishop at the Archiepiscopal Palace of Lambeth by the Archbishop of Canterbury, Dr. John Moore, February 4, 1787, in the presence of the Archbishop of York, and the Bishop of Bath and Wells and the Bishop of Peterborough.

The first Triennial Convention of the Protestant Episcopal Church assembled July 28, 1789. It completed the episcopacy, it ratified the constitution of 1785, and it formulated certain canons for the American Church. The session for the ratification of the constitution of the church was held in the State House, in the very same room in which the Federal Constitution had previously been signed.[3]

The first question of importance was the perpetuation of

[1] White, *op. cit.*, p. 119.
[2] *Ibid*, *op. cit.*, p. 27.
[3] *Ibid.*, pp. 28-30, 140-171; Perry, *op. cit.*, vol. i, pp. 63-144; vol. iii, pp. 392-416.

the succession. This matter presented considerable difficulty. Dr. Griffith had not been ordained; his resignation and death left but two bishops in America of English consecration. The clergy in Massachusetts and New Hampshire had elected the Rev. Edward Bass their bishop, and had addressed a letter to the bishops of Connecticut, New York, and Pennsylvania, praying them to unite in consecrating him. White laid the letter addressed to him before the convention, "intimating his sincere wish to join in such measures as they might adopt, for the forming of a permanent union with the churches in the Eastern states, but at the same time, expressing his doubt of its being consistent with the faith impliedly pledged to the English prelates, to proceed to any consecration, without first obtaining from them the number held in their Church to be canonically necessary to such an act."[1] The convention concurred in this sentiment but voted their opinion in favor of the validity of Bishop Seabury's consecration. In order to carry the sentiments of the convention into effect, they signified their request to the two bishops consecrated in England, that they would unite with Bishop Seabury in the consecration of Mr. Bass; and they framed an address to the archbishops and bishops of England, requesting their approbation of the measure, for the removing of any difficulty or delicacy which might remain on the minds of the bishops whom they had already consecrated. The difficulty, however, was to be removed in another way; the Virginia convention elected the Rev. Dr. James Madison, President of William and Mary College, their bishop and he was consecrated in England.

An invitation was extended to Bishop Seabury and their

[1] White, *op. cit.*, pp. 28, 29.

brethren in the eastern states to meet with them on the twenty-ninth of September, which was accepted.

At the July session the constitution was remodeled so as to provide for two houses, the house of bishops, and the house of cleric and lay deputies, who must vote, when required by either cleric or lay representation from any state by orders. Also the time of the stated meetings was to be the second Tuesday in September every third year.

The Constitution provided that as soon as three bishops should belong to the convention, that body should arrange itself into two houses. This accordingly was effected at the September session, the bishops forming a "House of Revision." All measures passing the Convention were to receive the sanction of this House of Revision before becoming effective. A veto of the House of Revision might be overruled by a majority of three-fifths (later four-fifths) of the General Convention. But the House of Revision must approve or disapprove in writing within two days (later three days) of the passage of an act, — failing which the act became a law.

An amending clause finally agreed upon read,

"This Constitution shall be unalterable, unless in General Convention by the church of a majority of the states which may have adopted the same; and all alterations shall be first proposed in General Convention, and made known to the several state conventions, before they shall be finally agreed to or ratified in the ensuing General Convention." [1]

The national constitution for the Protestant Episcopal Church of the United States of America, having been duly ratified by the Convention of 1789, it was then engrossed and signed. Thereupon the delegates proceeded to their work as the legislature of the federated episcopalian body by adopting ten canons. The two houses entered on a

[1] Perry *op. cit.*, vol. i, p. 100.

review of the Liturgy, both houses proposing alterations. The result was the Book of Common Prayer, which has ever since been used.[1]

Bacon thus describes the form of Constitution effected:

"The extreme feebleness of Episcopalianism in the several states conspired with the tendencies of the time in civil affairs to induce upon the new organization a character not at all conformed to the ideal of episcopal government. Instead of establishing as the unit of organization the bishop in every principal town, governing his diocese at the head of his clergy with some measure of authority, it was almost a necessity of the time to constitute dioceses as big as kingdoms, and then to take security against excess of power in the diocesan by overslaughing his authority through exorbitant powers conferred upon a periodical mixed synod, legislating for a whole continent, even in matters confessedly variable and unessential. In the later evolution of the system, this superior limitation of the bishop's powers is supplemented from below by magnifying the authority of representative bodies, diocesan and parochial, until the work of the bishop is reduced as nearly as possible to the merely 'ministerial' performance of certain assigned functions according to prescribed directions. Concerning this frame of government it is to be remarked: 1. That it was quite consciously and confessedly devised for the government of a sect, with the full and fraternal understanding that other 'religious denominations of Christians' (to use the favorite American euphemism) 'were left at full and equal liberty to model and organize their respective churches' to suit themselves. 2. That judged according to its professed purpose, it has proved itself a particularly good and effective government. 3. That it is in no proper sense of the word an episcopal government, but rather a classical and synodical government, according to the common type of the American church constitutions of the period."[2]

Dean George Hodges, of the Episcopal Theological School at Cambridge, Massachusetts, gives us the following analogy between the constitutions of the new national, federal constitution and the new, national, Episcopalian, church constitution:

[1] Schaff, *Creeds,* vol. iii, pp. 487-516 gives Anglican and American Articles in parallel Columns. Preface to the *American Book of Common Prayer,* 1789.

[2] Bacon, *American Christianity,* pp. 210-211.

"Each was founded on a written constitution. By adopting this constitution, thirteen independent ecclesiastical provinces became the dioceses of one church, as thirteen independent colonies had become the states of one nation. Diocesan conventions answered to State convention, and the General Convention to the Congress of the United States. The House of Clerical and Lay Deputies was like the House of Representatives; and the House of Bishops was like the Senate except in the matter of tenure of office. The principles of representative government controlled the Church as they controlled the State. The congregation elected the vestry; the vestry, sometimes with the formal approval of the congregation, selected the rector. The rector and certain elected deputies from the congregation represented the parish in the diocesan convention. These representatives jointly chose the bishop. The bishop and certain elected deputies, clerical and lay, from the diocesan conventions represented the diocese in the General Convention. In that convention no change could be made in the constitution or in the Prayer-book unless it were first enacted by one General Convention, then reported back to all the dioceses, and then at the next General Convention reenacted. In one respect, the Church was more democratic than the State; it gave no man executive authority. There was a presiding bishop, but no president. This likeness of the administration of the Church and the State came naturally from the fact that the same men were engaged in the two transactions."[1]

The Reverend Samuel Seabury, the younger, gave the following estimation of the value of the constitution effected:

"The value of this constitution the experience of nearly fifty years has served to illustrate and confirm. For a long time its effects were not obvious. But, when the generation which had been educated under a different régime had passed away, and a new generation arose, whose views and character were formed upon its model, then its fruits were manifested. The union of clerical and lay influence in our councils has been attended with the happiest effects. Representation has been so wisely ordered, and ecclesiastical power so happily balanced as to lead to most harmonious results. The excellence of our laws in discouraging the spirit of caprice and innovation without repressing a prudent zeal — in investing executive officers with well-defined powers, and thus preventing the abuses of arbitrary and irresponsible authority, in guarding the sacred

[1] Hodges, *Three Hundred Years of the Episcopal Church in America*, pp. 95-97.

rights of private judgment from invasion by the ministry, and at the same time checking its licentious operation by the silent influence of collective wisdom embodied in a primitive and catholic Liturgy, is becoming more and more a theme of eulogy . . . . . Our constitution is acknowledged to have worked well where other systems have failed. Had legislation been more minute, it would probably have led to disruption. As it is, it is certain that the spirit which once charged us with want of piety has itself launched out into the wildest extravagances, and that the wholesome restraints of our discipline, far from checking the flow of piety, have served rather to guide it in channels of peace and order. Under this system our church has become the asylum in which a calm and unobtrusive piety has sought a refuge from the excesses of fanaticism; our members have been multiplied, and our energies evolved, till, at the present time, our missionaries, bishops as well as presbyters, are found in the distant extremes of both hemispheres, and our theological seminaries send out every three years a larger number of clergy than, at the distance of thirty years since, our whole church contained. These blessings, it is true, are primarily owing to the possession of the word of God and the Church of God, in the union in which they were first instituted, and to the prevailing conviction that the existing order, in its great outlines, is a divine appointment, and as such is universally, imperatively and perpetually obligatory: a conviction which goes far to settle the mind of our Communion, and to arrest the tendency to innovation, and check the love of experiment so characteristic of our age and country. In a secondary sense, however, they may be ascribed to that judicious organization which the illustrious prelate (Bishop White), was mainly instrumental in effecting."[1]

[1] Seabury, *A Brief View of the Origin and Results of Episcopacy in the Protestant Episcopal Church in the United States of America*, pp. 20-23.

CHAPTER IX

THE ROMAN CATHOLIC CHURCH IN THE UNITED STATES

Dr. William White in 1785 had wished for a strongly organized Protestant Episcopal Church in America as a means of "guarding against the progress of a church (Roman Catholic) as yet scarcely known" in America. Their numbers at that time surely were not large enough to cause any concern; the official *Relation on the State of Religion in the United States*, presented to the Holy See by the Prefect Apostolic, John Carroll, shows that there were in 1785 only about 18,200 Catholics in the United States, exclusive of an unascertainable number destitute of priests in the Mississippi Valley, and that their clergy totalled twenty-four, mostly former members of the Society of Jesus. It was not numbers but organizing ability that Dr. White feared. The few Catholics of America had been quick to note the possibilities of the American ideal that "All men are created equal." They were early at work to Americanize their institutions so as to meet the requirements of the new nation.

The Catholics of the colonies had long fought for religious toleration in America. Their own fight for the right to exist had thoroughly imbued them with the American ideal of separation of church and state as a political theory. Herein they were distinctly in advance of the Episcopalians, since in many colonies the later church had, till 1776, enjoyed considerable prestige as an established religion. Maryland and Pennsylvania, where

Catholicism was strongest, had been the first of the English speaking colonies in the New World to permit the legal existence of Catholicism. The Roman Catholics had but to transfer their efforts for colonial toleration to a fight for federal recognition of religious liberty. This effort was one of the major forces in effecting a speedy nationalization of American Catholicism.

But if the Roman Catholics possessed and championed an American ideal in the separation of church and state, they were at the same time working for a distinctly most un-American and undemocratic church organization. Republican government was to be the most distinctive feature of the United States. Thomas Hooker phrased one of its leading principles in a sermon before the Connecticut General Court in 1638, when he declared that "the choice of public magistrates belongs unto the people by God's own allowance" and that "they who have the power to appoint officers and magistrates, it is in their power, also, to set the bounds and limitations of the power and place unto which they call them." Roman Catholic government in America was not to originate in the governed; it was secured by petition from a foreign supreme authority. Dr. White was able to convince the Episcopalians that to be American their government must be derived from a popularly representative body, an assembly of delegates, composed of laymen and clergy. The Catholics did secure an American church capable of electing its own bishops but the authority for the system was the Supreme See in Rome.

But though the organism of Roman Catholicism in America was to correspond less closely than does that of the Episcopal Church to the ideals of political democracy in America, it was not to follow that foreign authority was to weaken the Catholic spirit for American unity. The Americanized Roman Catholic Church became one of the strongest of the politico-religious forces of the critical constitution-making period of our history, and its power was consistently used to strengthen American national unity.

American independence found a very weak Roman Catholic Church. We have noted[1] how few were their numbers. Even the vaunted organism of the Roman Catholic hierarchy was gone. By the bull, *Dominus ac Redemptor*, Clement XIV had suppressed the Society of Jesus in July, 1773. This act deprived the colonies of all their Jesuit missionaries by transforming them into dioscesan priests. When John Carroll, a former member of the suppressed order, returned to Maryland in 1774, he found there "no public Catholic Church." To add to the disorder resulting from the suppression of the Jesuits, with the recognition of American independence, the Vicar-Apostolic of London disclaimed further jurisdiction over the United States. Left to themselves the nineteen American fathers formed a legal corporation for the purpose of securing the property of the former Society of Jesus, but they made no attempt to restore their dependence on the Vicar-Apostolic of London, lest this might excite prejudice among their fellow colonists. Rather they began negotiations to secure a local superior chosen from themselves and directly subject to the Holy See. The Carroll family led this movement.

The Carroll family had performed great deeds for America during the struggle for independence. The Reverend John Carroll had acted as one of the commissioners sent by Congress to Canada in 1776.[2] His

[1] *Supra.*, p. 234.
[2] Shea, J. G., *Life and Times of the Most Reverend John Carroll.*

brother Daniel Carroll, was a member of the Maryland Assembly, president of the Maryland Senate, and a member of Continental Congress. Later this Daniel Carroll was to help frame the Federal Constitution. Their cousin, Charles Carroll, was perhaps Washington's most ardent supporter; another of the committee sent to Canada in 1776, member of the Maryland Assembly, member of the Maryland Constitutional Convention, member of three different provisional committees, member of Continental Congress, and a member of the War Board charged with the conduct of the war, he had been the first man to sign the Declaration of Independence, also, he was the richest man to sign it, and the last of the signers to die.[1] The present national capitol, Washington, is located upon what was the estate of the Carrolls.

The religious views of this family were as well known as was their Americanism. They had long fought the fight for religious freedom in Maryland, and their views were influential in determining the final character of American religious liberty.

The treatment of Roman Catholics is an unsavory subject in Maryland history. During the French and Indian Wars every possible pretext for infringement of their liberties was used by the Legislature. Protests were made against their appointment to responsible positions as "favors shown to Catholics"; charges were made in the House that they were in collusion with the French. In 1756, when the vote of 40,000 pounds was passed, a double tax was placed upon the lands of the Roman Catholics; their petition to Governor Sharpe to veto the bill and their threats to appeal to the King in Council had

[1] Leonard, Lewis A., *Life of Charles Carroll of Carrolton*, New York, 1918.

no effect. In the same year it was even proposed in the Assembly to disarm all Roman Catholics in the province and the opposition to this prevailed only by a slender majority of one.[1]

During a period of religious persecution in 1773, just on the eve of the Revolution, Charles Carroll thus expressed himself in an open letter which appeared in the Maryland *Gazette*:

"I am as averse to having a religion crammed down people's throats, as a proclamation. These are my political principles, in which I glory; principles not hastily taken up to serve a turn, but which I have always avowed since I became capable of reflection. I bear not the least dislike to the Church of England, though I am not within her pale, nor indeed to any other church; knaves and bigots, of all sects and denominations, I hate and despise.

'For modes of faith let zealous bigots fight,
His can't be wrong, whose life is in the right.' — *Pope.*

Papists are distrusted by the laws, and laid under disabilities. They cannot, I know (ignorant as I am), enjoy any place of profit or trust while they continue Papists; but do these disabilities extend so far as to preclude them from thinking and writing on matters merely of a political nature? Antillon would make a most excellent inquisitor, he has given some striking specimens of an arbitrary temper; the first requisite — He will not allow me freedom of thought or speech . . . . . To what purpose was this threat thrown out, of enforcing the penal statutes by proclamation? Why am I told that my conduct is very inconsistent with the situation of one, who 'owes even the toleration he enjoys to the favor of the government?' If, by instilling prejudices into the governor, and . . . you can rouse the popular resentment against certain religionists, and thus bring on a persecution, it will then be known whether the toleration I enjoy be due to the favor of the government or not. That you have talents admirably well adapted . . . to stoop to the basest, is too true."

The Carrolls had been contending for religious freedom in Maryland for years before the Revolution; the gaining of independence imposed on them the greater task of securing

[1] *Proceedings* of the Maryland Assembly, Sept., 1756; Black, *Maryland's Attitude in the Struggle for Canada*, vol. vii, of the tenth series of *Johns Hopkins University Studies*, pp. 370-371.

from the new federal government a continuance of the war policy of Continental Congress. They were to be largely instrumental in reading into the Federal Constitution a principle of religious freedom drawn from that phrase of the Declaration of Independence that "All men are created equal and endowed by their Creator with certain inalienable rights."

But before they could work effectively for a recognition of their rights under the new government, it was necessary that they create for themselves centralized national ecclesiastical institutions. The Reverend John Carroll led the movement for an organized American Roman Catholic Church, and it was extremely fortunate both for the church and for the young republic that he did, for he was a man not only versed in the theology and the polity of the church, but also imbued with American principles and feelings.

Six Roman Catholic priests met at Whitemarsh, Maryland, June 27, 1783, and there drew up a plan of government which they submitted to the priests of Maryland and Pennsylvania. In the same year a meeting of seven clergymen of the Southern District met at Newton, September 23, and suggested ammendments. Priests of the Middle States, November 6, revised this Plan and Rules but deferred adoption thereof to a future meeting. A committee was appointed to petition the Pope to constitute Reverend John Lewis as "Superior" with power to administer confirmation, bless chalices and impart faculties to the priests in the mission. The petition read:

"We . . . . . missionary priests, residing in the Thirteen United States of North America, assembled together from the neighboring stations to take counsel for the good of the missions, our fellow-priests residing in the more remote parts of this mission agreeing herein and approving by letter, in our name and in the common name of our brethren, with all respect represent to your Holiness, that we, placed under the recent supreme dominion of United America, can no longer have recourse, as formerly, for necessary spiritual jurisdiction to the Bishops and Vicars-Apostolic residing in different and foreign states (for this has very frequently been intimated to us in very positive terms by the rulers of this Republic), nor recognize any one of them as our ecclesiastical Superior, without open offense to this supreme civil magistracy and political government. Wherefore we, placed in this difficult position, have recourse to your Holiness, humbly beseeching you to vouchsafe to confirm anew the ecclesiastical superior whom we now have, namely John Lewis, a priest already approved and confirmed by the Vicar-Apostolic of London, to whom this whole mission was subject before the change of political government, and to delegate to him the power of granting the necessary faculties to priests coming into these missions, as it shall seem expedient; that said superior may delegate this power to at least one or more of the most suitable missionaries as the necessity and distance of time and place may require.

Moreover, as there is no Bishop in these regions, who can bless the holy oils, of which we were deprived for several years during the confusion of the war, no one to bless the chalices and altar stones needed, no one to administer the sacrament of confirmation, we humbly beseech your Holiness to empower the said John Lewis, priest, Superior, to perform these things in the present necessity, and until otherwise provided for this mission by your Holiness, that our faithful, living in many dangers, may be no longer deprived of the Sacrament of Confirmation nor die without Extreme Unction according to the rite of the Church.

Moreover, we also pray your Holiness to bestow on this mission the indulgences of the Jubilee, and to extend to the missionaries the ample faculties which may seem seasonable in these vast and remote regions racked by a long bitter war, where on account of the constant military movements, neither the Jubilee on the exaltation of your Holiness to the See of Peter, nor the Jubilee of the year 1775, could be promulgated, much less celebrated or enjoyed.

This, Most Holy Father, is what we the aforesaid petitioners, missionary priests in these regions of the United North America, humbly solicit from your Holiness' supreme wisdom and providence for the good of the Catholic religion." [1]

John Carroll was commissioned to transmit this petition to the Holy See and in doing so he accompanied it with

[1] Shea, *Life and Times of Archbishop Carroll*, vol. ii, pp. 209-210.

the following letter, explanatory of the American situation:

"You are not ignorant that in these United States our religious system has undergone a revolution, if possible, more extraordinary than our political one. In all of them free toleration is allowed to Christians of every denomination; and particularly in the States of Pennsylvania, Delaware, Maryland, and Virginia, a communication of all civil rights, without distinction or diminution, is extended to those of our religion. This is a blessing and advantage which it is our duty to preserve and improve, with the utmost prudence, by demeaning ourselves on all occasions as subjects zealously attached to our government and avoiding to give any jealousies on account of any dependence on foreign jurisdictions more than that which is essential to our religion, an acknowledgment of the Pope's spiritual supremacy over the whole Christian world. You know that we of the clergy have heretofore resorted to the Vicar-Apostolic of the London District for the exercise of spiritual powers, but being well acquainted with the temper of Congress, of our assemblies and the people at large, we are firmly of opinion that we shall not be suffered to continue under such a jurisdiction whenever it becomes known to the public. You may be assured of this from the following fact. The clergy of the Church of England were heretofore subject to the Bishop of London, but the umbrage taken at this dependence was so great, that notwithstanding the power and prevalence of that sect they could find no other method to allay jealousies, than by withdrawing themselves as they have lately done, from all obedience to him.

Being therefore thus circumstanced, we think it not only advisable in us, but in a manner obligatory, to solicit the Holy See to place the episcopal powers, at least, such as are most essential, in the hands of one amongst us, whose virtue, knowledge, and integrity of faith, shall be certified by ourselves. We shall annex to this letter such powers as we judge it absolutely necessary he should be invested with. We might add many very cogent reasons for having amongst them, a person thus empowered, and for want of whom it is impossible to conceive the inconvenience happening every day. If it be possible to obtain a grant from Rome vesting these powers in our superior *pro tempore*, it would be most desirable. We shall endeavor to have you aided in this application by a recommendation, if possible, from our own country and the minister of France. You will know how to avail yourself of so favorable a Russian minister at Rome; and if Mr. Thorpe will be pleased to undertake the management of the business there, we will with cheerfulness and gratitude answer all expenses which he may incur in the prosecution of it. He will be the judge, how and whether the annexed petition ought in prudence to be presented to His Holiness, but at all events the powers therein contained are those which we wish our Superior to be invested with." [1]

The Memorial of the American Clergy having been referred to the *Congregation de Propaganda Fide*, the Cardinal Prefect sought more light relative to the American situation. The Apostolic Nuncio wrote John Carroll, May 12, 1784:

"The interests of religion, Sir, requiring new arrangements relative to the missions in the United States of North America, the Congregation of the Propaganda direct me to request from you a full statement of the actual condition of those missions. In the meantime, I beg you will inform me what number of missionaries may be necessary to serve them, and furnish spiritual aid to Catholic Christians in the United States; in what provinces there are Catholics, and where there is the greatest number of them; and lastly, if there are among the natives of the country, fit subjects to receive holy orders, and exercise the functions of missionaries. You will greatly oblige me personally by the attention and industry which you will exercise in procuring for me this information." [2]

Accompanying this was the following:

"Extract of a Memorandum.

1. To have exact statements of the conduct and capacity of the ecclesiastics and missionaries who are in the different states of North America; who among them might be the most worthy, and at the same time, agreeable to the members of the assembly of those provinces to be invested with the character of bishop in partibus, and the quality of Vicar-Apostolic. It is thought that it will be convenient for him to fix his residence where there is the greatest number of Catholics.

2. If among these ecclesiastics there is a native of the country, and he should be among the most worthy, he should be preferred to all others of equal merit. If otherwise, choice should be made of one from some other nation. In default of a missionary actually residing in those provinces, a Frenchman will be nominated, who will go to establish himself in America, in the state above designated.

3. To know the probable number of the ecclesiastics and missionaries, as well as how many that of the Catholics in the different states, and their

[1] Shea, *op. cit.*, vol. ii, pp. 211-212.
[2] *Ibid.*, vol. ii, p. 221.

standing would render necessary; we think that it is in Pennsylvania and Maryland there is the greatest number — it would be to the purpose to know if there are also any in the other states.

4. To know whether there are schools in these states where Latin is taught; such that the young men of the country who might wish to prepare for the ecclesiastical state could study their humanities, before passing to France or Rome, there to enter at once on their philosophical and theological studies."[1]

Without waiting for a reply from John Carroll, the Secretary of the Congregation of the Propaganda presented to the Pope, Pius VI, a report on the Church in the United States and the Sovereign Pontiff ratified the appointment of Reverend John Carroll as Superior of the Mission in the Thirteen United States of North America and conferred upon him the power to administer the sacrament of confirmation during his Superiorship. This decree was issued June 9, 1784 and read:

"The Sacred Congregation on the report of the Rev. Stephen Borgia, its Secretary, declared Superior of the missions in the thirteen United States of North America, the Rev. John Carroll, secular priest, with authority to exercise the functions which regard the government of the missions, according to the tenor of the decrees of the Sacred Congregation, and of the faculties granted to him, and not otherwise, nor in a different manner."

"Audience of the Most Holy Father, held June 6, 1784. Our Most Holy Father, by divine Providence, Pope Pius VI, on the report of the undersigned, secretary of the Sacred Congregation de Propaganda Fide, granted to the Rev. John Carroll, Superior of the Mission in the thirteen United States of North America, the faculty of administering the sacrament of Confirmation, in the said provinces during his superiorship — the said faculty to be executed in accordance with the rules prescribed in the instruction published by order of the Congregation on the 4th of May, 1784.

STEPHEN BORGIA, Secretary of the Sacred Congregation de prop. fide."[2]

[1] Shea, *op. cit.*, vol. ii, pp. 221-222; Campbell, *Life and Times of Archbishop Carroll; United States Catholic Magazine*, vol. iii, p. 378.

[2] *Ibid.*, vol. ii, p. 224.

British jurisdiction was thus officially terminated for the Roman Catholic Church in the United States and a native American officially appointed to undertake its direction. The formal announcement of his appointment which reached John Carroll, through Dr. Franklin, November 26, 1784, contained the statement that he had been appointed, among other reasons, "to please and gratify many members of the Republic and especially Mr. Franklin, the eminent individual who represents the same Republic at the Court of the Most Christian King."[2]

This appointment had been made without any consideration of the wishes of the American priests. When the Chapter opened its first session, October 11, 1784, John Carroll attended as a simple delegate; no official notice of his promotion was taken. The important action of this Chapter was the adoption of "The Form of Government" and the "Rules for the particular Government of Members belonging to the Body of the Clergy," thus completing the work inaugurated at the Whitemarsh gathering. This new government was declared to be "binding on all persons, at present composing the Body of the Clergy in Maryland and Pennsylvania." The Rev. John Aston was elected Procurator General of the Chapter.

Under the new system, the priests in Maryland and Pennsylvania were to form a body corporate to hold, until the restoration of the Society of Jesus, the property formerly held in the names of individual members of that order. The affairs of the corporation were to be managed by a chapter composed of two deputies from each of the three districts, to be chosen by the priests belonging to the corporation stationed therein.

The Chapter was to meet every three years, and was to

[1] Shea, *op. cit.*, vol. ii, p. 244.

appoint a Procurator-General, who was to take general charge of the property. It was empowered to make rules, which were to take effect only when approved by the districts or at a subsequent meeting of the Chapter. It could hear and determine complaints and appeals. At the triennial meeting the Procurator-General was to report on the condition of each estate, so that the Chapter might examine into the general state of its temporal affairs.

The self-governing character of the Chapter is shown in the following articles:

"XIII. When any person not before incorporated into the Body of the Clergy desires to be admitted therein, the Superior in Spiritualibus on being well certified of his doctrine, morals and sufficient learning, shall propose him to the members of Chapter of the district where his services are wanted, and in case of his being accepted by them, some member of Chapter in that district shall lay before him the general regulations of the Body of Clergy, and require him to sign his submission thereunto: direct him to repair to the place allotted for his residence. But if the members of Chapter do not agree to receive him into their district, then the said Superior is to propose him to any other where there is need, and proceed in the same manner as above. If no district will admit him, he is to be informed, that he does not belong to the Body of Clergy, that he owes no services to, and consequently is not entitled to any provision from them; and when any member of the Body of Clergy through discontent leaves his former place of residence without the approbation of lawful authority and applies for another place he is not to be imposed on any district without their consent expressed by the members of Chapter."

Priests seeking admission into the Body of the Clergy were required to subscribe to the following formula:

"I promise to conform myself to the forms and regulations established for the government of the clergy residing in Maryland and Pennsylvania so long as I expect maintenance and support from them."

XIV. With respect to members actually forming part of the Body of the Clergy there shall be no arbitrary power of removing them at will, or for greater convenience; but when a vacancy happens which the good of religion requires to be supplied, the members of Chapter of the district in which the vacancy lies, shall endeavor to prevail upon the person they judge fittest to accept of the vacant charge, application having been first made to the Superior in Spiritualibus.

XVI. When the Superior in Spiritualibus has withdrawn his faculties from any clergyman, on account of his misconduct or irregularity of life, the Procurator-General shall have power to deprive him of any maintenance from the estates of the clergy.

XIX. The person invested with spiritual jurisdiction in the country shall not in that quality have any power over or in the temporal property of the clergy."[1]

The Superior in Spirituals was, however, to receive from the Chapter an annual salary of one hundred pounds, with a servant, a chaise, and a horse.

It was decided and a committee was appointed to draw up a petition to the Pope that a "bishop is at present unnecessary," but that a superior with power to give confirmation, bless oils, grant faculties and dispensations, was sufficient; and they resolved:

"That if one (bishop) be sent it is decided by the majority of the Chapter, that he shall not be entitled to any support from the present estates of the clergy."[2]

It is clear that the American clergy aimed at an independent control of their own membership and finances. One of the bitterest controversies of the early American church was to arise over this issue.[3]

Though the Rev. John Carroll accepted his appointment when it reached him, November 26, 1784, it was not until after he had carefully weighed the important points at issue.

Accompanying the appointment was the following letter from Cardinal Antonelli, dated June 9, 1784:

"In order to preserve and defend Catholicity in the Thirteen United States of North America, the Supreme Pontiff of the Church, Pius VI., and his Sacred Congregation, have thought it extremely proper to desig-

[1] Shea, *op. cit.*, vol. ii, pp. 239-241.
[2] *Ibid.*, vol. ii, p. 242.
[3] *Infra.*, pp. 253-254.

nate a pastor who should, permanently and independently of any ecclesiastical power, except the same Sacred Congregation, attend to the spiritual necessities of the Catholic flock. In the appointment of such a pastor, the Sacred Congregation would have readily cast its eyes on the Rev. John Lewis if his advanced age and the labors he has already undergone in the vineyard of the Lord, had not deterred it from imposing on him, a new and very heavy burden; for he seems to require repose rather than arduous labor. As then, Rev. Sir, you have given conspicuous proofs of piety and zeal, and it is known that your appointment will please and gratify many members of that Republic, and especially Mr. Franklin, the eminent individual who represents the same Republic at the court of the Most Christian King, the Sacred Congregation, with the approbation of his Holiness, has appointed you Superior of the Mission in the Thirteen United States of North America, and has communicated to you the faculties, which are necessary to the discharge of that office; faculties which are also communicated to the other priests of the same States, except the administration of confirmation which is reserved for you alone, as the enclosed documents will show.

These arrangements are meant to be only temporary. For it is the intention of his Holiness soon to charge a Vicar-Apostolic, invested with the title and character of bishop, with the care of those states, that he may attend to ordination and other episcopal functions. But, to accomplish this design, it is of great importance that we should be made acquainted with the state of the orthodox religion in those thirteen states. Therefore we request you to forward to us, as soon as possible, a correct report, stating carefully the number of Catholics in each state; what is their condition, their piety and what abuses exist; also how many missionary priests labor now in this vineyard of the Lord; what are their qualifications, their zeal, their mode of support. For though the Sacred Congregation wish not to meddle with temporal things, it is important for the establishment of laborers, that we should know what are the ecclesiastical revenues, if any there are, and it is believed there are some. In the meantime for fear the want of missionaries should deprive the Catholics of spiritual assistance, it has been resolved to invite hither two youths from the states of Maryland and Pennsylvania, to educate them at the expense of the Sacred Congregation in the Urban College; they will afterwards, on returning to their country, be substitutes in the mission. We leave to your solicitude the care of selecting and sending them . . . Such are the things I had to signify to you; and whilst I am confident you will discharge the office committed to you with all zeal, solicitude and fidelity, and more than answer the high opinion we have formed of you, I pray God that He may grant you all peace and happiness."[1]

[1] Shea, *op. cit.*, vol. ii, pp. 243-245.

American Catholics were very much disturbed over the character of this appointment. They disliked the temporary nature of the arrangement, the absolute dependence on the Society of the Propagation of the Faith, and the extremely limited powers granted to the Superior. The American way called for complete independence from any foreign jurisdiction, even dependence on the Sacred Congregation might give offence to ultra-Americans.

John Carroll expressed his disquietude over these matters in a circular letter, the first which he prepared for the priests of America. He discusses at length the dependence on the Propaganda:

"I consider powers issued from the Propaganda, not only as improper, but dangerous here. The jealousy in our governments of the interference of any foreign jurisdiction is known to be such, that we cannot expect, and in my opinion, ought not to wish that they would tolerate any other than that which being purely spiritual, is essential to our Religion, to wit, an acknowledgment of the Pope's spiritual supremacy, and of the See of St. Peter being the centre of the Ecclesiastical Unity. The appointment, therefore, by the Propaganda of a Superior for this country, appears to be a dangerous step, and by exciting the jealousy of the government here, may tend much to the prejudice of Religion, and perhaps expose it to the reproach of encouraging a dependence on a foreign power, and giving them an undue internal influence by leaving with them a prerogative to nominate to places of trust and real importance, and that '*ad suum beneplacitum*'.

The Congregation of the Propaganda, if I understand its institution, was formed only for the government and superintendence of missions, etc.; and I observe, that they affect in their commission to me and other acts, to call our ecclesiastical state here a mission; and the laborers therein missioners. Perhaps this denomination was heretofore proper enough; but it cannot now be so deemed. By the constitution, our religion has acquired equal rights and privileges with that of other Christians; we form not a fluctuating body of laborers in Christ's vineyard, sent hither and removable at the will of a Superior, but a permanent body of national clergy, with sufficient powers to form our own system of internal government, and I think, to choose our own superior and a very just claim to have all necessary spiritual authority communicated to him, on his being presented as regularly and canonically chosen by us. We have further a reasonable prospect, which I soon hope to see realized, of forming an establishment for educating and perpetuating a succession of clergy among ourselves; and as soon as that measure is in a promising forwardness, we shall have a right to a diocesan Bishop of our own choice. (Steps were taken for the organization of Georgetown University in 1786.) 'Ought not the immense territory possessed by the United States to have an Ecclesiastical Superior as independent as the Bishop of Quebec?' says one of our zealous friends in England.

I am, moreover, advised by Cardinal Antonelli, that his Holiness intends to appoint hereafter (but no term mentioned or even insinuated) a Vicar-Apostolic with Episcopal character, and with such powers as may exempt this country from every other ecclesiastical dependence, beside that on the aforesaid Congregation. But not the slightest intimation is given of the person designed for that preferment.

We shall in a few years stand in absolute need of a Bishop, but that of a Bishop Vicar-Apostolic would give great umbrage, on account of his entire dependence, both for his station and conduct, on a foreign jurisdiction; he must be a diocesan Bishop, and his appointment must come neither from his Holiness, for that would create more jealousy in our government, than even in France, Germany or Spain, nor from the Assemblies or different Executives . . . . . but he should be chosen by the Catholic clergy themselves." [1]

Urged to do so by his fellow-Catholics in America, Rev. John Carroll decided to accept the appointment but in so doing he was not one to conceal from his superiors the views which he held and which he had already expressed to his subordinates. February 27, 1785, he wrote a long personal letter to Cardinal Antonelli, explaining why "no Vicar Apostolic dependent on the pleasure of the Sacred Congregation (should) ever be appointed for Republican America." Accompanying this letter was the *Relation on the State of Religion in the United States* which the Cardinal had requested.

In his letter he was careful to point out that nothing should be done for the Church in the United States until the actual conditions were clearly understood. The

[1] Carroll, Very Rev. J., *Draught of a Circular Letter Announcing his Appointment as Prefect*; Shea, *op. cit.*, vol. ii, pp. 249-251.

Revolution had emancipated the Catholics of America. "In most places, however," he wrote, "they are not admitted to any office in the State unless they renounce all foreign jurisdiction, civil or ecclesiastical." Then he continues:

"But how long we are to enjoy the benefits of this toleration or equal rights, I would not dare to assert. Many of our people especially in Maryland, fear that we shall be absolutely excluded from holding office; for my own part, I have deemed it wiser not to anticipate evils, but to bear them when they come. I cherish the hope that so great a wrong will not be done us; nay more I trust that the foundations of religion will be so firmly laid in the United States, that a most flourishing part of the Church will in time be developed here, to the great consolation of the Holy See.

The Church of England had been the dominant body, directed by ministers dependent on the Bishop of London, but after the war they were not allowed to depend on an English or any foreign bishop. They were free to appoint and elect bishops of their own, as they had in fact done, although none had yet been consecrated according to their rites. They have adopted a form of government for their church, and desire it to be called and to be national, in that it admits no foreign Superior, that they may be freed from such fear for the future as many Catholics felt. . . . . . . The Catholic body . . . . . think that some favor should be granted to them by the Holy Father, necessary for their permanent enjoyment of the civil rights which they now enjoy, and to avert dangers which they fear. From what I have said, and from the framework of public affairs here, your Eminence must see how objectionable all foreign jurisdiction will be to them. The Catholics therefore desire that no pretext be given to the enemies of our religion to accuse us of depending unnecessarily on a foreign authority; and that some plan may be adopted by which hereafter an ecclesiastical Superior may be appointed for this country, in such a way as to retain absolutely the spiritual jurisdiction of the Holy See, and at the same time remove all ground of objecting to us, as though we held anything hostile to the national independence. Many of the leading Catholics thought of laying this before his Holiness in a general Memorial, especially those who have been either in the Continental Congress or the legislature of Pennsylvania and Maryland: but I induced them to refrain from any such step at least for the present. The Holy Father will perhaps see more clearly what is to be done in this matter, if he considers the Sixth of the Articles of perpetual Confederation between the States, which enacts that no one who holds any office under the United States, shall be allowed to receive any gift, office or title of any kind whatsoever from any king, prince or foreign government, and though this prohibition seems to extend only to those who are appointed to offices in the republic, it will perhaps be wrested by our opponents to apply also to ecclesiastical offices.

We desire therefore, Most Eminent Cardinal, to provide in every way, that the faith in its integrity, due obedience towards the Apostolic See and perfect union should flourish, and at the same time that whatever can with safety to religion be granted, shall be conceded to American Catholics in ecclesiastical government; in this way we hope that the distrust of Protestants now full of suspicion will be diminished, and that thus our affairs can be solidly established.

You have indicated, Most Eminent Cardinal, that it was the intention and design of His Holiness to appoint a Vicar-Apostolic for these States, invested with the episcopal character and title. While this paternal solicitude for us has filled us with great joy, it also at first inspired some fear; for we knew that heretofore American Protestants never could be induced to allow even a Bishop of their own sect, when the attempt was made during the subjection of these provinces to the King of England; hence a fear arose that we would not be permitted to have one. But some months since in a convention of Protestant ministers of the Anglican, or, as it is here called, the Episcopal Church, they decreed, that as by authority of law they enjoyed the full exercise of their religion, they therefore had the right of appointing for themselves, such ministers of holy things, as the system and discipline of this sect required; namely bishops, priests, and deacons; this decision on their part was not censured by the Congress appointed to frame our laws. As the same liberty in the exercise of religion is granted to us, it necessarily follows that we enjoy the same right in regard to adopting laws for our government.

While the matter stands thus, the Holy Father will decide, and you, Most Eminent Cardinal, will consider whether the time is now opportune for appointing a bishop, what his qualifications should be, and how he should be nominated. On all these points, not as if seeking to obtain my own judgment, but to make this relation more ample, I shall note a few facts.

First, as regards the seasonableness of the step, it may be noted, that there will be no excitement in the public mind, if a bishop be appointed, as Protestants think of appointing one for themselves; nay, they even hope to acquire some importance for their sect among the people from the episcopal dignity; so too we trust that we shall not only acquire the same, but that great advantages will follow; inasmuch as this church will then be governed in that manner which Christ our Lord instituted. On the other hand, however, it occurs that as the Most Holy Father has already deigned to provide otherwise for conferring the sacrament of confirmation, there is no actual need for the appointment of a bishop, until some candidates are found fitted to receive holy orders; this we hope will be the case in a few years, as you will understand, Most Eminent Cardinal, from a special relation which I purpose writing. When the time comes, we shall perhaps be better able to make a suitable provision for a bishop, than from our slender resources we can now do.

In the next place, if it shall seem best to his Holiness to assign a bishop to this country, will it be best to appoint a Vicar-Apostolic or an ordinary with a see of his own? Which will conduce more to the progress of Catholicity, which will contribute most to remove Protestant jealousy of foreign jurisdiction? I know with certainty that this fear will increase if they know that an ecclesiastical superior is so appointed as to be removable from office at the pleasure of the Sacred Congregation 'de Propaganda Fide', or any other tribunal out of the country, or that he has no power to admit any priest to exercise the sacred function, unless that Congregation has approved and sent him to us.

As to the method of nominating a bishop, I will say no more, at present, than this, that we are imploring God in his wisdom and mercy to guide the judgment of the Holy See, that if it does not seem proper to allow the priests who have labored for so many years in this vineyard of the Lord to propose to the Holy See, the one whom they deem most fit, that some method will be adopted by which a bad feeling may not be excited among the people of this country, Catholic and Protestant."[1]

In the *Relation on the State of Religion in the United States*, which accompanied this letter, John Carroll reported that there were 15,800 Catholics in Maryland, 1,500 in New York, 7,000 in Pennsylvania, and 200 in Virginia. The number in the Mississippi territory was unascertainable. Formerly they had been under the jurisdiction of the Bishop of Quebec. "I do not know," writes Carroll, "whether he wishes to exercise any authority there now that all these parts are subject to the United States. The small number of priests is cause why the Catholics here cannot attend worship, receive the sacraments, hear the Word of God, as frequently as they should, or as is customary in Europe.

[1] Shea, *op. cit.*, vol. ii, pp. 251-256.

There are nineteen priests in Maryland and five in Pennsylvania. They are maintained chiefly from the proceeds of the estates held by the clerical corporation. There is no ecclesiastical property held by the church as such."[1]

Thus John Carroll accepted his "very delicate" and "very laborious" position. So fearful was he that trouble would arise if its nature were public property that he did not publish the documents relative thereto but communicated them to the priests in each district.

In reply to Dr. Carroll's communications, Cardinal Antonelli informed him in a letter dated July 23, 1785, that it had been the intention of the Pope to appoint him as the first bishop. The erection of a Vicariate or See was, however, in accordance with the wishes of the American clergy, deferred, and they were to be permitted to nominate their candidate.[2]

The Very Rev. John Carroll went about his visitation. The General Chapter at its meeting at Whitemarsh, November 13, 1786, adopted resolution concerning the institution of a school, the first step toward the foundation of Georgetown College.[3] This meeting also decided that a diocesan Bishop, depending directly on the Holy See, was alone suited to the American Church and that the selection ought to be made by the clergy on the mission.

In 1787 a conflict arose in New York to vex the domestic calm of the American Catholic Church. The Catholics of New York City, then the capital of the United States, including the Catholics of the Spanish and French legation, had been incorporated in 1785 as the "Trustees of the Roman Catholic Church in the City of New York,"

[1] Shea, *op. cit.*, vol. ii, pp. 257-261.
[2] *Ibid.*, vol. ii, p. 273.
[3] *Ibid.*, vol. ii, pp. 301-303.

and had erected a church in Barclay Street. Then they placed in charge thereof a priest of their own selection. They held that the congregation had the right not only to choose its pastor but to dismiss him at pleasure, and that the ecclesiastical superior had not the right to interfere. In taking this stand, they lost sight of the contervailing principle, that if they had a right to do as they would with their building, the bishop, as representative of the supreme authority in the church, had a like right to do as he would with his clergy. The building was theirs, but the superior controlled the clergy and communion; these had not been brought under local authority. Superior Carroll wrote to the trustees of the New York church:

"If ever such principles (as yours) should become predominant, the unity and catholicity of our church would be at an end; and it would be formed into distinct and independent societies, nearly in the same manner as the Congregational Presbyterians. Your misconception is that the officiating clergyman at New York is a parish priest, whereas there is yet no such office in the United States. I cannot tell what assistance the laws might give you; but allow me to say that you can take no step so fatal to that responsibility in which as a religious society you wish to stand, or more prejudicial to the Catholic cause."

Accordingly Dr. Carroll removed the offending priest and restored order in the New York congregation. When he laid the matter before the Body of the Clergy it became evident that it was now time to solicit a bishop and the erection of a see in America. The following petition was prepared, addressed to the Most Holy Father:

"We, the undersigned, petitioners approaching the Apostolic See with all due veneration, and prostrate at the feet of your Holiness, humbly set forth the following: That we are priests who have been specially deputed by our fellow priests, exercising with us the religious ministry in the United States of America, in order that we may, in the first place, return unbounded thanks to your Holiness for the truly paternal care, which you have deigned to extend to this remote part of the Lord's vineyard;

and in the next place, to mainifest that we all had been stimulated by this great care, to continue and increase our labors to preserve and extend the faith of Christ our Lord, in these States, which are filled with the errors of all the sects. In doing so, we are convinced that we not only render meet service to God, but also render a pleasing and acceptable homage to common Father of the faithful . . . . .

. . . . . Inasmuch as his Eminence Cardinal Antonelli intimated to one of your petitioners, in a letter dated July 23, 1785, that it was the design of the Sacred Congregation de Propaganda Fide to appoint a Bishop, Vicar-Apostolic, for these States as soon as possible, whenever the said Sacred Congregation understood that this would be seasonable, and desired to be informed as to the suitable time for that appointment, by the priest to whom the said letter was addressed, we declare, not he only but we in the common name of all the priests laboring here, Most Holy Father, that in our opinion the time has now come when the Episcopal dignity and authority are very greatly desired. To omit other very grave reasons, we experience more and more in the constitution of this very free republic, that if there are even among the ministers of the sanctuary, any men of indocile mind, and chafing under ecclesiastical discipline, they allege as an excuse for their license and disobedience, that they are bound to obey bishops exercising their own authority and not a mere priest exercising any vicarious jurisdiction. This was the boast of the men who recently at New York sought to throw off the yoke of authority, and alleged this pretext, which seemed most likely to catch the favor of Protestants, in that more than in any other State, contending forsooth that the authority of the ecclesiastical superior whom the Sacred Congregation has appointed for us, was forbidden by law, because it not only emanates from a foreign tribunal, but is also dependent on it for its duration and exercise. We refrain from setting out all this more at length to your Holiness, inasmuch as we have learned that certain original documents have been transmitted to Rome, from which it can be more clearly seen, with what powers the person should be invested, to whom the ecclesiastical government of those States is confided.

With this view, we represent to the Supreme Pastor of the faithful on earth, that all the grounds on which the authority of the Superior as now constituted may be rendered odious, will have equal weight against a bishop to whom the powers of a vicar and not of an ordinary, are granted.

Therefore, Most Holy Father, we express in the name and by the wish of all, our opinion that the political and religious condition of these states requires that form of ecclesiastical government, by which provision may be most efficaciously made in the first place for the integrity of faith and morals, and consequently for perpetual union with the Apostolic See, and due respect and obedience towards the same, and in the next place, that if any bishop is assigned to us, his appointment and authority may be rendered as free as possible from suspicion and odium to those among whom we live. Two points, it seems to us, will contribute greatly to this end; first, that the Most Holy Father, by his authority in the Church of Christ, erect a new episcopal see in these United States, immediately subject to the Holy See; in the next place, that the election of the bishop, at least for the first time, be permitted to the priests, who now duly exercise the religious ministry here and have the cure of souls. This being established, your most vigilant wisdom, Most Holy Father, after hearing the opinions of our priests of approved life and experience, and considering the character of our government, will adopt some course by which future elections may be permanently conducted."[1]

This petition was promptly acted upon and Dr. Carroll could write to his friend, Rev. Charles Plowden:

"Communicating freely with you as I do, you would not forgive me, were I to omit informing you, that a grant had been made to allow our officiating clergy to choose one of their body, as bishop; and it is left to our determination whether he shall be an ordinary taking title from some town of our appointment, or a titular bishop, by which I understand, a bishop constituted over a country without the designation of any particular See."[2]

Cardinal Antonelli's letter was as follows, July 12, 1788:

"Inasmuch as all the laborers in this vineyard of the Lord agree in this, that the appointment of one bishop seems absolutely necessary to retain priests in duty and to propagate more widely piety and religion — a bishop who can preside over the flock of Christians scattered through these States of Confederate America, and rule and govern them with the authority of an ordinary, Our Most Holy Lord Pope Pius VI, with the advice of this holy congregation, has most benignly decided that a favorable consent should be given to your vows and petitions. By you therefore, it is first to be examined in what city this episcopal see ought to be erected, and whether the title of the bishopric is to be taken from the place of the see, or whether a titular bishop only should be established. This having been done, his Holiness as a special favor and for this first time, permits the priests who at the present time duly exercise the ministry of the Catholic religion and have care of souls to elect as bishop a person eminent in piety, prudence, and zeal for the faith, from the said clergy, and present him to the Apostolic See to obtain confirmation. And the Sacred Congregation does not doubt but that you will discharge this

[1] Shea, vol. ii, pp. 326-329.
[2] *Ibid.*, *op. cit.*, vol. ii, p. 333.

matter with becoming circumspection, and it hopes that this whole flock will derive not only great benefit but also great consolation from this episcopate. It will then be for you to decide both the proper designation of a see, and the election of a bishop, that the matter may be further proceeded with." [1]

A meeting of the Body of the Clergy at Whitemarsh, New Jersey, cast twenty-four of its twenty-six votes for John Carroll as first bishop in the United States. It decided on Baltimore as the See. On September 14, 1789, the Cardinals constituting the Sacred Congregation, after reading the letter of the American clergy selecting Baltimore as the See, and the Very Rev. John Carroll as their choice for Bishop, approved the nomination. They so formally reported to the Pope on the seventeenth. Pope Pius VI issued a Bull to this effect, November 6, 1789:

"We . . . . . having nothing more at heart than to ensure success to whatever tends to the propagation of true religion, and to the honor and increase of the Catholic Church, by the plenitude of our apostolic power, and by the tenor of these presents, do establish and erect the . . . town of Baltimore into an Episcopal See forever, for one Bishop to be chosen by us in all future vacancies; and we, therefore, by the apostolic authority aforesaid, do allow, grant and permit to the Bishop of the said city and to his successors in all future times, to exercise episcopal power and jurisdiction, and every other episcopal function which Bishops constituted in other places are empowered to hold and enjoy in their respective churches, cities and dioceses, by right, custom, or by other means, by general privileges, graces, indults and apostolical dispensations, together with all preeminences, honors, immunities, graces and favors, which other Cathedral Churches, by right or custom, or in any other sort, have, hold and enjoy. We moreover decree and declare the said Episcopal See thus erected to be subject or suffragan to no Metropolitan right or jurisdiction, but to be forever subject, immediately to us and to our successors the Roman Pontiffs, and to this Apostolic See. And till another opportunity shall be presented to us of establishing other Catholic Bishops in the United States of America, and till other dispositions shall be made by this Apostolic See, We declare, by our apostolic authority, all the faithful of Christ, living in Catholic communion, as well ecclesiastics as seculars, and all the clergy and people

[1] Shea, *op. cit.*, vol. ii, pp. 333-334.

dwelling in the aforesaid United States of America, though hitherto they may have been subject to other Bishops of other dioceses, to be henceforward subject to the Bishop of Baltimore in all future times; And whereas by special grant, and for this first time only, we have allowed the priests to elect a person to be appointed Bishop by us, and almost all their votes have been given to our beloved son, John Carroll, Priest; We being otherwise certified of his faith, prudence, piety and zeal, for as much as by our mandate he hath during the late years directed the spiritual government of souls, do therefore by the plenitude of our authority, declare, create, appoint and constitute the said John Carroll, Bishop and Pastor of the said Church of Baltimore, granting to him the faculty of receiving the rite of consecration from any Catholic bishop holding communion with the Apostolic See, assisted by two ecclesiastics, vested with some dignity, in case that two bishops cannot be had, first having taken the usual oath according to the Roman Pontifical.

And we commission the said Bishop elect to erect a church in the said city of Baltimore, in form of a Cathedral Church, inasmuch as the times and circumstances may allow, to institute a body of clergy deputed to divine worship, and to the service of said church, and moreover to establish an episcopal seminary, either in the same city or elsewhere, as he shall judge most expedient, to administer ecclesiastical incomes, and to execute all other things which he shall think in the Lord to be expedient for the increase of Catholic faith and the augmentation of the worship and splendor of the new erected church. We moreover enjoin the said Bishop to obey the injunctions of our venerable brethren, the Cardinals Directors of the Sacred Congregation *de Propaganda Fide*, to transmit to them at proper times a relation of his visitation of his church, and to inform them of all things which he shall judge to be useful to the spiritual good and salvation of the flock trusted to his charge. We therefore decree that these our letters are and ever shall be firm, valid and efficacious, and shall obtain their full and entire effect; and be observed inviolable by all persons whom it now doth or hereafter may concern; and that all judges ordinary and delegated, even auditors of causes of the sacred apostolical palace, and Cardinals of the holy Roman Church, must thus judge and define, depriving all and each of them of all power and authority to judge or interpret in any other manner, and declaring all to be null and void, if any one, by any authority should presume, either knowingly or unknowingly, to attempt anything contrary thereunto. Notwithstanding all apostolical, general or special constitutions and ordinances, published in universal, provincial and synodical councils, and all things contrary whatsoever."[1]

[1] Shea, *op. cit.*, vol. ii, pp. 337-343; *A Short Account of the Establishment of the new See of Baltimore, in Maryland, and of consecrating the Right Rev. Dr. John Carroll, etc.* London, 1790.

Dr. Carroll accepted the new responsibilities of the appointment and proceeded to England where he was consecrated in the chapel of Lulworth Castle, August 15, 1790. The Rev. Charles Plowden preached the sermon of the day wherein he sat forth that "the earliest and most precious fruit" of the American Revolution, "had been the extension of the kingdom of Christ, the propagation of the Catholic religion, which, heretofore fettered by restraining laws, is now enlarged from bondage, and is left at liberty to exert the full energy of divine truth."[1] Certainly the Catholics of the United States were now in a more favorable position than were their fellow-Catholics in England, where they still remained under the direction of Vicars-Apostolic.

On September 27, 1791, Bishop Carroll officially summoned the priests of his diocese to a convocation, and November 7, 1791, he opened the first Synod. Here statutes were adopted relative to baptism, confirmation, holy eucharist, collections, charity, instruction, penance, matrimony and extreme unction. Regulations were also drawn up for divine offices, and for the life and support of the clergy. The acts of this Synod form the first body of laws adopted for the government of the Roman Catholic Church in this country.

[1] Shea, *op. cit.*, vol. ii, p. 361.

CHAPTER X

THE PRESBYTERIAN CHURCH IN THE UNITED STATES

The making of a constitution for the Presbyterian Church in the United States of America, was less the work of a single individual than was the case with most of the other denominations; rather, it was effected through the agency of certain powerful committees composed of the leaders of American Presbyterianism. The church was possessed of many well-educated and prominent leaders such as: President John Witherspoon of the College of New Jersey; John Rodgers of New York, probably the most popular minister in the American church; Dr. Ewing of Philadelphia, Provost of the University of Pennsylvania; Dr. George Duffield of Philadelphia, a Chaplain of Continental Congress; Dr. Patrick Alison of Baltimore; Dr. Alexander McWhorter of Newark; Latta, Smith, Blair, Wilson, Balch, and others. Dr. Witherspoon was the most prominent of the group because of the combination of ancestry, education and position. Breed says of him, "He saw the Presbyterian church organized on a national basis."[1] Committee responsibility is one of the striking features of constitution-making with American Presbyterianism.

Because of the unanimity with which this denomination had supported the American cause of independence its movement for ecclesiastical nationalism was much simpler than that of most sects. There was enthusiasm for an

[1] Breed, *Witherspoon*, p. 78.

independent American church, though there developed strenuous objection to unification through centralization. This arose largely because the proposed General Assembly was an innovation: and even the former synodical government had tended to override its strictly delegated powers. The demand for nationalization was so strong that it triumphed. All that the opponents of a strongly centralized church organization could do was to strive to modify the demands of the federalist through pleas for the preservation of some of the traditional local autonomy.

An American ministry had grown up, largely educated in American Colleges, and filled with the distinctive spirit of America. In fact the union of the various national elements in the American ministry even tended to a distinctly new American type. DeWitt finds that:

> "The formation of a national General Assembly under the constitution of the Church was the product of the very spirit that governed the Constitutional Convention of the Colonies, which met in the same city during the same period. The Presbyterian ministers of 1789, brought this national spirit into the councils of the church. It dominated and even depressed . . . . . local and ancestral pride."[1]

This American spirit stood for the widest ecclesiastical liberty. When they came to change the political sections of the Westminister Confession, they recognized the civil magistrates only as protectors of the church and they expunged that phrase from the catechism which asserted that "to tolerate a false religion" was a sin forbidden in the second commandment. This was adding a new spirit to Presbyterianism, and the problem of the various conventions was to maintain that this was in the interest of the true faith.

[1] DeWitt, *The First General Assembly of the Presbyterian Church in the United States of America*, p. 20.

To survive in the midst of independent, competitive denominations organization was essential. A minute of the Synod of 1787, May 18, gives strength and unity against other sects, as the cause for reorganization:

"We are all members one of another; there should be no schism in the body, but we should comfort, encourage and strengthen one another by the firmest union in our common Lord. We are Presbyterians, and we firmly believe the Presbyterian system of doctrine, discipline and church government, to be nearer to the word of God, than that of any other sect or denomination of Christians. Shall all other sects and parties be united among themselves *for their support and increase*, and Presbyterians divided and sub-divided, so as to be the scorn of some and the prey of others?"[1]

Great increase in the size of the church added to the inconvenience consequent on the obligation of each minister to attend each yearly synod and made the adoption of some form of representative (Republican) government imperative.

The ministry was progressive: it realized that it was working in a critical and formative period, that it had to think in terms of the future. It was out to conquer a continent, to rescue it from the wilderness and the foe of Christianity.

We have noted that Joseph Galloway asserted before a parliamentary committee that the Presbyterians of America caused the Revolution.[2] Politically this is really disapproved; religiously or spiritually there are grounds for the charge. Officially the church had not interfered in the political controversy yet, independence was the keynote of Presbyterianism and the American church had gone far in exhibiting that spirit even with regard to their fellow Presbyterians in Great Britain and Ireland. An

[1] *Records*, p. 533.
[2] *Supra*, pp. 66-71.

overture of the Synod of New York and Philadelphia, May 24, 1773, illustrates this:

"Whereas there have been repeated complaints from serious persons of the degeneracy of many of the Presbyterian denomination in Great Britain and Ireland, and their falling off from the great doctrines of the Reformation, so that it is very possible there may be Presbyteries the majority of which would not be unwilling to license, ordain or recommend ministers unsound in the faith; it seems to be of moment to guard against the admission of strangers into this body, before their principles and character are thoroughly ascertained: Therefore, it is overtured, that no Presbytery be permitted to receive any stranger under the character of minister or candidate, or to give him appointments in the congregation under our care, until the Synod that shall meet next after their arrival, that the whole testimonials and credentials offered by such persons be laid before the Synod, to be by them considered and judged of, in order to their admission or rejection."[1]

The overture was voted but thereafter vigorous opposition caused first its suspension and then its modification. Two main objections to the act appeared: first, it tended to break with the British and Irish Churches, and second it was a high-handed usurpation of power on the part of the Synod, — so much so as to be unconstitutional. Dissent was entered upon the minutes as follows:

"Because . . . . . this overture evidently tends to stigmatize and throw scandal on the British and Irish Churches, to the breaking the bonds of peace, union, charity and mutual love between them and us.

Because it takes away from the Presbyteries some of their essential rights, restraining them from performing the duties of ordaining and admitting ministers agreeably to the scriptures and the constitution, and practice of the Presbyterian Church."

Because the precedent hereby established is not only wrong in itself, as it divests our Presbyteries of their inherent rights, but extremely pernicious in its consequences. If the Synod is allowed this power with respect to ministers or probationers from Europe, why may it not at any time be pleaded with respect to those from every other part of the world? Why may not the Synod, claiming thus far, extend their authority to the ordination of all our American probationers under some plausible

[1] *Records*, pp. 442-443.

pretences, such as, that the Synod is more faithful, or more learned, or fitter to judge of the piety of those who are to be received?

A Synod . . . . . is only a voluntary association of different Presbyteries, or a council to give advice in difficult matters, and to secure peace, orthodoxy, edification and mutual confidence, and has not power to make any arbitrary decisions.

If the Synod will assume these high, unscriptural powers, it may be expected that some Presbyteries will resign their connection with a power they esteem tyrannical, and returning to their original state claim the enjoyment of their own inherent privileges." [1]

The constitutional objection is seen far to outweigh any fear of the break with Great Britain and Ireland. Because of the feeling which had developed in opposition to the overture, it was modified. First an explanation was adopted that "it should be put on record that the word strangers . . . . . should not be extended to any persons from any part of the continent of America."[2] Then it was agreed "that the Presbytery to which any such gentlemen may offer themselves, may be allowed, if they see their way clear, to employ them in their vacancies, but that they be not admitted to full membership until the next Synod, when their testimonials and recommendations shall be laid before the Synod."[3] The constitutional objection had been met, that of independence seems to have been affirmed.

At the Synod of 1774, May 20, it was moved to reconsider the foregoing action. Dr. Witherspoon, Dr. Duffield, and others opposed reconsideration but it was voted. Whereupon Dr. Rodgers, and the Rev. Messrs. Treat and McWhorter, brought in the following overture which was unanimously accepted:

"Whereas, it is of the highest importance to the interest of the Redeemer's Kingdom, that the greatest care be observed by church judicatures to

[1] *Records*, pp. 443-445.
[2] *Ibid.*, p. 445. [3] *Ibid.*, p. 448.

maintain orthodoxy in doctrine, and purity in practice, in all their members, this Synod do earnestly recommend it to all their Presbyteries to be very strict . . . . . in examining the certificates and testimonials of ministers and probationers who come from foreign churches; and that they be very cautious about receiving them, unless the authenticity of their certificates and testimonials be supported by private letters, or other credible and sufficient evidence; and in order more effectually to preserve this Synod, our Presbyteries, and congregations from imposition and abuse, every year when any Presbytery may report that they have received any ministers or probationers from foreign churches, that Presbytery shall lay before the Synod the testimonials, and all other certificates upon which they received such ministers or probationers, for the satisfaction of the Synod, before such foreign ministers or probationers shall be enrolled as members of our body; and if the Synod shall find the said testimonials false or insufficient the whole proceedings had by the Presbytery in the admission shall be held to be void; and the Presbytery shall not from that time receive or acknowledge him as a member of this body, or in ministerial communion with us. And, on the other hand, whensoever any gentlemen from abroad shall come duly recommended, as above, we will gladly receive them as brethren, and give them every encouragement in our power." [1]

The controversy was thus settled, but not to the complete satisfaction of everybody. Direct offense to Great Britain and Ireland, had been avoided, but the serious constitutional question of the relative authority of local and central government had been raised and not settled, — merely postponed. Accordingly, another overture was brought in, May 23, 1774, "Respecting the power by which the Synod makes such acts to restrain Presbyteries from acting to the best of their judgment in things, that before these acts were allowed to be lawful, and not forbidden by the word of God."[2] Action upon this was deferred until the next Synod. Meanwhile on May 26, 1774, the Reverend Matthew Wilson proposed "a method to secure the lasting union and credit of the Presbyterian body," and the Synod recommended it to its members to

[1] *Records*, p. 455.
[2] *Ibid.*, pp. 456-457.

make themselves well acquainted with the fundamental principles of the Presbyterian Constitution.[1] The outbreak of the Revolution further postponed the work of constitution-making which events seem otherwise to have forecast as inevitable for the Synod of 1775, even before the outbreak of the Revolution.

During the Revolution Synods were sparsely attended; yet they kept in close touch with the spiritual direction of American affairs, and took full advantage of their opportunities. We have seen how they supported the American cause and assumed guidance in civil matters.[2] The church was growing rapidly; new presbyteries were being formed: Orange, 1770; Redstone, 1781; South Carolina, 1784; Abingon, 1785; Transylvania, Lexington, and Carlisle, 1786. Two hundred and thirty new ministers were ordained between the years 1758 and 1789. Missionary work and education were attended to. Missionaries were appointed and supported; collections of books were sent out; and legacies were accepted for the support of missions. A minute of 1779, May 21, records the attitude of the church:

"An application by a member of Hanover Presbytery praying that some missionaries might be sent into the state of Virginia to preach the gospel, and especially that a few ministers of genius, prudence, and address might spend some considerable time in attempting to form that people into regular congregations, under the discipline and government of the Presbyterian Church, and to settle among them, and undertake the education of their youth, representing that there appears at present in many parts of that state, a very favorable disposition towards religion in general, and towards the Presbyterian church in particular; that it is greatly for the interest of the church to pay particular attention to the Southern and Western parts of this continent; that congregations which may be formed there will be permanent and fixed, whereas the continued migration of the inhabitants of our interior congregations, diminish their

[1] *Records*, p. 460.
[2] *Supra*, Ch. IV.

importance and threaten their dissolution; that it is not desirable, nor to be expected that that most extensive country should continue long without some form of religion; that this Synod has now an opportunity of promoting the interest of religion extensively, which in a few years may be utterly lost by the prevalency and preoccupying of many ignorant and irreligious sectaries; the Synod do, therefore, earnestly recommend it to all their Presbyteries to turn their attention to this object, as peculiarly interesting and important; and if it is by any means possible, to furnish some missions to the state of Virginia, and such especially as shall endeavor to form congregations, and to effect a settlement among them, having respect to the popular talents as well as piety of such missionaries, and to their capacity for directing the education of youth." [1]

Expansion was bound up with the question of procuring a suitable ministry for the work. Of the 250 new ministers (mentioned above) admitted between the years 1758 and 1789, one hundred and twenty came from the College of New Jersey; Yale furnished about two score; others came from the University of Pennsylvania, Newark Academy, Hampden Sydney College, Washington Academy and elsewhere. And still there was a dearth of educated men to fill vacancies. The Synod of 1783, May 23, answered in the negative a query from the Presbytery of Philadelphia as to "whether a person without a liberal education may be taken on trials, or be licensed to preach the gospels."[2] The Synod of 1785, May 21, by a large majority, again reaffirmed their opposition on a question as to

"whether in the present state of the church in America and the scarcity of ministers to fill our numerous congregations, the Synod or Presbyteries, ought to relax, in any degree, the literary qualifications required of intrants into the ministry." [3]

In fact a counter-proposal was made to raise the requirements and to add a two-year divinity course to the liberal arts standard; but this was laid over for the year and was rejected in 1786.

[1] *Records*, pp. 484-485.
[2] *Ibid.*, p. 499. [3] *Ibid.*, p. 511.

The Synod of 1785, May 23, adopted the following minute relative to education:

"The Synod considering the education of youth, and their being early instructed in just principles of religion, as one of the most useful means of promoting the influence of the gospels in our churches . . . . . Resolved . . . . . that it be enjoined on all congregations to pay a special regard to the good education of children, as being intimately connected with the interests of morality and religion; and that, as schools under bad masters and a careless management, are seminaries of vice rather than of virtue, the session, corporation or committee of every congregation, be required to endeavor to establish one or more schools in such place, or places, as shall be most convenient for the people, that they be particularly careful to procure able and virtuous teachers; that they make the erection and care of schools a part of their congregational business, and endeavor to induce the people to support them by contribution, being not only the most effectual, but eventually, the cheapest way of supporting them; that the Presbyteries appoint particular members, or if possible committees, to go into vacant congregations to promote similar institutions; that the corporation, session, or committee of the congregation, visit the school, or schools, at least once in three months, to inquire into the conduct of the master, and the improvement of the children, and to observe particularly his care to instruct them, at least one day in the week, in the principles of religion; that the Presbyteries, in appointing ministers to supply vacant congregations, require it as an indispensable part of their duty, to visit at the same time the schools; and require at the next meeting of the Presbytery, an account of their fidelity in this respect, and of the state of the schools; and that, in these schools effectual provision be made for the education of the children of the poor; and that, at the visitations of the schools, one or two of the most ingenious and virtuous of the poor children be annually selected, in order to give them a more perfect education, and thereby qualify these ingenious charity scholars, to become afterwards useful instructors in our congregational schools."[1]

The nation recognized the importance of Presbyterianism in assigning one of the Chaplaincies of Continental Congress to Dr. George Duffield. Elder Robert Aitken of Philadelphia was appointed to issue the first American edition of the Bible and Congress officially commended his

[1] *Records*, p. 513.

work to the public. In 1782, May 18, the Synod appointed "a committee to prepare an address to the minister of France, congratulating him on the birth of a dauphin, son and heir to the crown of his royal master, expressing the pleasure the Synod feel on this happy event."[1]

The Synod of 1783, May 21, announced its American principle in reference to the numerous other sects within the country:

"It having been represented to Synod, that the Presbyterian Church suffers greatly in the opinion of other denominations, from an apprehension that they hold intolerant principles, the Synod do solemnly and publicly declare, that they ever have, and still do renounce and abhor the principles of intolerance; and we do believe that every peaceable member of civil society ought to be protected in the full and free exercise of their religion."[2]

Active constitution-making was begun for America by the Synod of 1785. On motion, it was ordered, May 23:

"That Dr. Witherspoon, Dr. Rodgers, Mr. Robert Smith, Dr. Alison, Dr. Smith, Messrs. Woodhull, Cooper, Latta, and Duffield, with the moderator, Mr. Wilson, be a committee to take into consideration the constitution of the Church of Scotland, and other Presbyterian Churches and agreeably to the general principles of the Presbyterian government, compile a system of general rules for the government of the Synod, and the several Presbyteries under their inspection, and the people in their communion, and to make report of their proceeding herein at the next Synod."[3]

But views were already at hand for the organization of the administration and without waiting for the report of the committee, an overture was immediately brought in:

"That for the better management of the churches under our care, this Synod be divided into three Synods, and that a General Synod, or Assembly, be constituted out of the whole. The Synod agreed to enter on the consideration of this overture, on the first Friday after their next

[1] *Records*, p. 495.
[2] *Ibid.*, p. 499.
[3] *Ibid.*, p. 512.

meeting, and appoint Dr. Smith to transmit a copy of this overture to such of the Presbyteries as are not at present represented in Synod, and earnestly urge their attendance at our next meeting."[1]

Also it was thought wise to consider the form of services to be used in the churches; the following motion was affirmed, on that same day.

"Whereas the nearest uniformity that is practicable in the external modes of Divine worship is to be desired, and the using different books of psalmody is matter of offence, not only to Presbyterians of different denominations, but also to many congregations under our care; it is queried, if the Synod might not choose out, and order some of their members to take the assistance of all the versions in our power, and compose for us a version more suitable to our circumstances and tastes than any we yet have."[2]

Dr. Alison, Dr. Davidson, Dr. Ewing, Mr. Blair, and Mr. Jones were appointed to report at the next Synod.

The question of publicity and the extent to which the church in general should be informed of acts of the Synod was involved in the following motion of the same date:

"It was moved and seconded, that the Synodical clerk be required to transmit annually to each Presbytery belonging to the Synod, an attested copy of all general regulations of Synod, as well as of those that more immediately regard any Presbytery in particular, and that each Presbytery be required to enjoin on their clerk to furnish each member of the Presbytery with an authentic copy of the same, that by a general intelligence of the acts of the supreme judicature being thus communicated to all, the whole body may be brought to operate with concert and vigor, and that none may have ingorance as a plea for neglect of duty."[3]

Consideration of this matter was deferred to the next meeting. It is not surprising that a feeling of reserve was thus exhibited by the Synod; the Federal Constitution of the same period shunned "pitiless publicity" and was made in complete secrecy, nor were the various state constitutions of popular origin or approval.

[1] *Records*, p. 513.
[2] *Ibid.*, pp. 513-514.
[3] *Ibid.*, p. 512.

Constitution-making was complicated by an effort that was being made to join together the various presbyterial sects of America. At the 1785 Synod, May 19, it was recorded,

"The committee appointed by the Synod last year, to meet with the committee of the Low Dutch Reformed Synod of New York and New Jersey, report, that they were disappointed of meeting by a mistake, and one of the members of the committee informing the Synod that some of the brethren of the Dutch Synod, and one of the members of the Associate Reformed Synod, had expressed a desire of some measures being taken for promoting a friendly intercourse between the three Synods, or laying a plan for some kind of union among them, whereby they might be enabled to unite their interests, and combine their efforts, for promoting the great cause of truth and vital religion; and at the same time giving it as their judgment, that such plan was practicable: The Synod were happy in finding such a disposition in the brethren of the above Synods and cheerfully concur with them in thinking that such a measure is both desirable and practicable, and therefore appoint Drs. Witherspoon, Jones, Rodgers, McWhorter, Smith, Messers. Martin, Duffield, Miller, Read, Woodhull and Kerr, a committee to meet with such committees as may be appointed by the Low Dutch Synod now sitting in New York, and by the Associate Synod, to meet in that city next week, at such time and place as may be agreed upon, to confer with the brethren of said Synods on this important subject, and to concert such measures with them for the accomplishment of these great ends as they shall judge expedient, and report the same to the next meeting of this Synod." [1]

Consideration of the action of this joint convention for church unity occupied a large part of the thought of the Synod of 1786. Of great note is the "representation" as to the formulae of doctrine and worship which their committee had made to the New York meeting and which was reported back to the Synod; which were:

"Article 1; The Synod of New York and Philadelphia adopt, according to the known and established meaning of the terms, the Westminister Confession of Faith as the confession of their faith, save as every candidate for the gospel ministry is permitted to except against so much of the twenty-third chapter as gives authority to the civil magistrates in matters

[1] *Records*, p. 508.

of religion. The Presbyterian Church in America considers the Church of Christ as a spiritual society, entirely distinct from the civil government, having a right to regulate their own ecclesiastical policy, independently of the interposition of the magistrate.

The Synod also receives the directory for public worship and the form of church government recommended by the Westminster Assembly as in substance agreeable to the institutions of the New Testament. This mode of adoption we use, because we believe the general platform of our government to be agreeable to the sacred Scriptures; but we do not believe that God has been pleased so to reveal and enjoin every minute circumstance of ecclesiastical government and discipline as not to leave room for orthodox churches of Christ, in these minutiae, to differ with charity from one another.

Article 5; The rules of our discipline and the form of process in our church judicatures, are contained in Pardovan's (alias Stewart's), collections in conjunction with the acts of our own Synod, the power of which, in matters purely ecclesiastical, we consider as equal to the power of any Synod or General Assembly in the world. Our church judicatures, like those in the church of Scotland, from which we derive our origin, are Church Session, Presbyteries and Synods, to which it is now in contemplation to add a National and General Assembly." [1]

A committee appointed to draw up instructions to govern the conduct of the delegates, to meet with the Dutch Reformed and Associate Reformed delegates in October, laid them before the Synod and, as amended, they contained the following, May 23:

"The delegates on the part of this Synod are to inform the convention that this body is about to divide itself into four Synods, subordinate to a General Assembly. That they have now under consideration a plan of church government and discipline, which it is hoped will, when completed be sufficient to answer every query of the convention upon that head; and that the mutual assurances mentioned in minutes of the last convention, may, as far as they respect this Synod, be made with much more propriety after the intended system is finished than at present." [2]

Thereupon to advance their own constitution-making, the Synod resolved, May 23, that:

"the book of discipline and government be recommended to a committee to meet in the city of Philadelphia on the second Tuesday of

[1] *Records*, pp. 518-519. [2] *Ibid.*, pp. 524-525.

September next, who shall have powers to digest such a system as they shall think to be accommodated to the state of the Presbyterian Church in America, that they shall procure three hundred copies to be printed and distributed to the several Presbyteries in proportion to the number of their members under the engagement of this Synod, to have the expense of printing and distribution reimbursed to the committee at their next meeting; and every Presbytery is hereby required to report, in writing, to the Synod at their next meeting, their observations on the said book and discipline.

The committee appointed to attend to the above business, were Drs. Witherspoon, McWhorter, Rodgers, Sproat, Duffield, Alison, Ewing, and Smith and Messrs. Wilson, Snowden, Taggert, and Pinkerton, elders."[1]

The committee that had been appointed to prepare a selection from the different versions of the psalms reported May 20, that it had not yet completed its work and was continued.[2] It was decided to proceed with the matter of division of the Synod and it was so overtured, May 19:

"The Synod, considering the number and extent of the churches under their care, and the inconvenience of the present mode of government by one Synod, resolved, that this Synod, will establish out of its own body, three or more subordinate Synods, out of which shall be composed a General Assembly, Synod, or Council, agreeably to a system hereafter adopted."[3]

For this matter the following committee was named: Drs. Rodgers, Smith, Duffield and Alison, and Messrs. Latta, Martin, Wilson, Graham, Houston, Finley, and Hall. Their report, May 22, decided to increase the number of the Presbyteries from twelve to sixteen and to group them into four Synods, with a provision as to the number of ministers and of ruling elders each Presbytery should elect annually to a General Assemble of the Presbyterian Church in the United States of America.[4] The Synod adopted the report of its committee "so far as respects the

[1] *Records*, pp. 524-525.
[2] *Ibid.*, p. 522.
[3] *Ibid.*, p. 517.
[4] *Ibid.*, pp. 522-524; *infra.*, p. 279.

arranging of Presbyteries . . . . . The consideration of the remaining part of the report was deferred till our next stated meeting, at which time the several Presbyteries are desired to attend prepared to determine respecting it."[1]

The special committee appointed to digest a church government met as directed in September, 1786, and prepared and published *A Draught of a Plan of Government and Discipline for the Presbyterian Church in North America, Proposed by a committee Appointed for that Purpose.* This outlined a government to consist of congregations, presbyteries, synodical assemblies and a general council, but enjoying no civil jurisdiction and incapable of inflicting civil penalties. It was to function through Church Sessions, Presbyterial Assemblies, Synodical Assemblies and a General Council; the former bodies were so well known as to require little mention, the latter were carefully outlined as to jurisdiction. The entirely new body, the General Council, was described. The report outlined modes of ordination, election, licensing, installation, translation, resignation, etc., as well as forms of processes in Presbyterial judicatures.

Synodical Assemblies were to judge appeals from Presbyteries, review the presbytery books, redress orders of the presbytery contrary to their rights, see that presbyteries observed the constitution of the church and propose measures to the General Council.

The General Council was to review the minutes of every Synod, — to approve or censure; give advice and instruction in all cases submitted to them, — determine in cases of conscience, consult, reason and judge in controversies of doctrine and discipline, reprove, warn and bear testimony against errors in doctrine or immorality of

[1] *Records*, p. 526.

practices in any church or presbytery; correspond with foreign churches; put a stop to schismatical contentions or disputations; recommend reformation of manners; promote charity, truth and holiness; and erect new Synods when they judge necessary.

It was to be composed of an equal delegation of ministers and elders from each presbytery, called commissioners to the general assembly, according to the following apportionment; one minister and one elder for six ministers in a presbytery; two of each for from six to twelve ministers; three each for from twelve to eighteen. Fourteen commissioners of whom one half were ministers was to constitute a quorum.[1]

The Synod of 1787 held in Philadelphia, was busy debating and amending the reports of its various committees at the very same time that the Federal Constitutional Convention was in session in the same city. It made considerable progress in matters of faith and discipline; governmental organization, however, was still uncompleted.

The Synod allowed that Dr. Watts's imitation of David's Psalms, as revised by Mr. Barlow, be sung in the churches and families under their care.[2]

The Synod took into consideration the last paragraph of the twentieth chapter of the Westminister Confession of Faith; the third paragraph of the twenty-third chapter; and the first paragraph of the thirty-first chapter; and having made some alterations, agreed that the said paragraphs, as now altered, be printed for consideration,

[1] *A Draught of a Plan of Government and Discipline for the Presbyterian Church in North America, Proposed by a Committee Appointed for that Purpose.* Philadelphia, 1786.

[2] *Records*, p. 535.

together with the draft of a plan of government and discipline.[1] The alterations suggested were finally adopted by the Synod of 1788; they aimed to eliminate the principle of established church and religious persecution and to proclaim the religious liberty and legal equality of all Christian denominations. In chapter xx, section 4, the last sentence, "and by the power of the civil magistrates" was omitted, so as to read, "they (offenders) may lawfully be called to account, and proceeded against by the censures of the Church." The original text of chapter xxiii, section 3 (1647 A.D.), "Of the Civil Magistrates" had read:

"The civil magistrate may not assume to himself the administration of the Word and Sacraments, or the power of the keys of the kingdom of heaven; yet he hath authority, and it is his duty to take order, that unity and peace be preserved in the Church, that the truth of God be kept pure and entire, that all blasphemies and heresies be suppressed, all corruption and abuses in worship and discipline prevented or reformed, and all the ordinances of God duly settled, administered, and observed. For the better effecting whereof he hath power to call Synods, to be present at them, and to provide that whatsoever is transacted in them be according to the mind of God."

As revised by the American Church this reads:

"Civil Magistrates may not assume to themselves the administration of the Word and Sacraments, or the power of the keys of the kingdom of heaven; or, in the least, interfere in matters of Faith. Yet, as nursing fathers, it is the duty of civil magistrates to protect the church of our Common Lord, without giving the preference to any denomination of Christians above the rest, in such a manner that all ecclesiastical persons whatever shall enjoy the full, free and unquestioned liberty of discharging every part of their several functions without violence or danger. And, as Jesus Christ has appointed a regular government and discipline in his church, no law of any commonwealth should interfere with, let or hinder the due exercise thereof, among the voluntary members of any denomination of Christians, according to their own profession and belief. It is the duty of civil magistrates to protect the person and good name of

[3] *Records*, p. 539.

all their people, in such an effectual manner as that no person be suffered, either upon pretence of religion or infidelity, to offer any indignity, violence, abuse or injury to any other person whatsoever, and to take order that all religious and ecclesiastical assemblies be held without molestation or disturbance."

The original text of chapter xxxi, 1647, "Of Synods and Councils," was as follows:

"1. For the better government and further edification of the church, there ought to be such assemblies as are commonly called Synods or Councils.

2. As magistrates may lawfully call a Synod of ministers and other fit persons to consult and advise with about matters of religion; so, if magistrates be open enemies to the church, the ministers of Christ, of themselves, by virtue of their office, or they with other fit persons, upon delegation from their churches, may meet together in such assemblies."

The American text for the same chapter xxxi, reads:

"1. For the better government and further edification of the church, there ought to be such assemblies as are commonly called Synods or Councils.

And it belongeth to the overseers and other rulers of the particular churches, by virtue of their office, and the power which Christ hath given them for edification, and not for destruction, to appoint such assemblies; and to convene together in them, as often as they shall judge it expedient for the good of the Church."[1]

The Synod, having gone through the consideration of the draft of a plan of government and discipline, appointed, May 28, 1787, Drs. Rodgers and McWhorter and Messrs. Miller and Wilson, Jr., a committee to have a thousand copies thereof printed as now amended, and to distribute them among the Presbyteries for their consideration, and the consideration of the churches under their care.[2] This committee was also instructed to revise the Westminister Directory for public worship and to have it when thus revised, printed together with the draft for considera-

[1] Schaff, *Church and State in the United States*, p. 49.

[2] *Records*, p. 539.

tion. It was agreed that when the above proposed alterations in the Confession of Faith should have been finally determined on by the body, and the Directory should have been revised as above directed, and adopted by the Synod, the said Confession, thus altered, and the Directory thus revised and adopted would be styled, "The Confession of Faith, and Directory for Public Worship, of the Presbyterian Church in the United States of America."[1]

The Synod of 1788, marks an epoch in the history of American Presbyterianism. It completed the process of constitution-making; it organized the General Assembly; it promulgated the constitution of the church; it ratified and adopted the Confession of Faith, the Larger Catechism and the Shorter Catechism; and it divided and distributed the Presbyteries into Synods. Organization of the church was completed with this meeting.

On May 28, 1788, the Synod, having fully considered the draft of the form of government and discipline, did, on a review of the whole, ratify and adopt the same, as altered and amended, as the Constitution of the Presbyterian Church in America, and did order that the same be considered and strictly observed as the rule of their proceedings, by all the inferior judicatures belonging to the body. They also ordered that a correct copy be printed, and that the Westminister Confession of Faith, as altered, be printed in full along with it, as making a part of the constitution.[2] Furthermore it was resolved, that the true intent and meaning of the above ratification by the Synod was, that the Form of Government and Discipline and the Confession of Faith, as ratified, was to continue to be the Constitution and the Confession of Faith and

[1] *Records*, pp. 539-540.
[2] *Supra.*, pp. 276-277; Thomson, *op. cit.*, p. 348.

Practice, unalterable, unless two-thirds of the Presbyteries under the care of the General Assembly should propose alterations or amendments, and such alterations or amendments should be agreed to and enacted by the General Assembly.[1]

On May 29, it was resolved unanimously:

"That this Synod be divided and it is hereby divided into four Synods, agreeably to an act made and provided for that purpose in the sessions of Synod in the year 1786; and that this division shall commence on the dissolution of the present Synod."[2]

The act of 1786 which is affirmed by the above overtures read:

"Your committee beg leave . . . . . to report, that they conceive it will be most conducive to the interests of religion that this Synod be divided into four Synods, and therefore submit to the Synods the following plan for dividing the Synod of New York and Philadelphia into four Synods, subordinate to a General Assembly to be constituted out of the whole."

Here followed the details by which the Presbyteries, sixteen in all, were distributed among the four Synods;

1. The Synod of New York and New Jersey.
2. The Synod of Philadelphia.
3. The Synod of Virginia.
4. The Synod of Carolinas.

"Out of body of these Synods a General Assembly shall be constituted in the following manner, viz: That every Presbytery shall, at their last stated meeting preceding the meeting of the General Assembly, depute to the General Assembly commissioners in the following proportion; each Presbytery consisting of not more than six ministers shall send one minister and one elder; each Presbytery consisting of more than six ministers and not more than twelve, shall send two ministers and two elders, and so in the same proportion for every six ministers. And these commissioners or any fourteen of them whereof seven to be ministers, being met on the day and at the place appointed, shall be competent to

[1] *Records*, pp. 546-547.
[2] *Ibid.*, p. 547.

enter upon business. And the judicatory thus constituted, shall bear the style and title of the General Assembly of the Presbyterian Church in the United States of America." [1]

The Synod took into consideration the draft of a directory for the worship of God, as reported by the committee appointed for that purpose in 1787. Drs. Witherspoon and Smith, together with the moderator, were appointed, May 29, a committee to revise the chapter of the draft respecting the mode of inflicting church censures, and to lay this, as then revised, before the General Assembly at their first meeting, to be by them considered and finally enacted.[2] The same three were appointed to revise that part of the draft which respected public prayer, and prayers to be used on other occasions, and to prepare it for printing with the constitution. May 29, the Synod, having revised and corrected the draft of a directory for worship, did approve and ratify the same, and appoint the said directory to be the directory for the worship of God in the Presbyterian Church in the United States of America.[3]

The Synod also took into consideration the Westminister Larger and Shorter Catechisms, and having made a small amendment to the larger, approved and ratified the said Catechisms as the Catechisms of the Presbyterian Church in the United States. In Question 109 of the Larger Catechism, they struck out the words, "tolerating a false religion" among the sins forbidden in the second Commandment.

The Synod ordered that the said Directory and Catechism be printed and bound up in the same volume with the Confession of Faith and Form of Government and

[1] *Records*, p. 522-524.
[2] *Ibid.*, p. 547.
[3] *Ibid.*, p. 547, Thompson, *op. cit.*, pp. 348-349

Discipline, and that the whole be considered the standard of Presbyterian doctrine, government, discipline, and worship in the United States, agreeably to the resolutions of the Synod in this session. It was ordered that Dr. Duffield and Messrs. Armstrong and Green be a committee to superintend the printing and publishing of the abovesaid Confession of Faith and Catechism with the Form of Government and Discipline and the Directory for the Worship of God, adopted and ratified by the Synod as *The Constitution of the Presbyterian Church in the United States of America*, and that they divide the several parts into chapters and sections properly numbered.[1]

We have noted that the constitution-making period for the Presbyterian Church extended from 1785 to 1788. The slowness of the procedure was due in part to a desire to conserve Presbyterian principles, but mostly to a realization that local opposition was to be successfully overcome only through a cautious advance. The case of the Presbytery of Suffolk illustrates the method by which the Synod won the good-will of rebellious elements. This presbytery in May, 1787, prayed the Synod on its part for a dissolution of its union with the Synod. To which the Synod replied:

"You say 'that concurrence with the draft of the form of government and discipline for the Presbyterian Church in North America is impracticable.' That is only a draft or overture for consideration and amendment, and we should have rejoiced much to have your company and aid in pointing out those impracticabilities in altering, correcting and completing the said draft. We apprehend there are no principles in it different from the Westminister Directory, only *the same rendered more expedient in some things and more conformable to the state and circumstances of the Presbyterian Church in America* . . . . .

We are fully of opinion that the general principles in said draft contain

[1] *Records*, p. 547; Drake, *Acts and Proceedings of the Synod of New York and Philadelphia, A. D. 1787 and 1788.* Philadelphia, 1788.

the plan of church discipline and government revealed in the New Testament, and are conformable (allowance being made for the differences in the states of civil society and local circumstances), to the practices and usages of the best reformed churches.

You well know that it is not a small thing to rend the seamless coat of Christ, or to be disjoined parts of one body his Church. We are all members one of another; there should be no schism in the body, but we should comfort, encourage, and strengthen one another by the firmest union in our common Lord. We are Presbyterians, and we firmly believe the Presbyterian system of doctrine, discipline and church government, to be nearer to the word of God than that of any other sect or denomination of Christians. Shall all other sects and parties be united among themselves for their support and increase and Presbyterians divided and subdivided, so as to be the scorn of some and the prey of others?"[1]

The Presbytery of Suffolk withdrew its request in 1788.[2]

As a final step in surrendering its jurisdiction over the Presbyterians of America, the Synod of New York and Philadelphia fixed upon Philadelphia and the third Thursday of May, 1789, as the time and place for the meeting of its successor, the first General Assembly; also they selected Dr. Witherspoon, or in his absence, Dr. Rodgers, to open this General Assembly with a sermon, and to preside till a moderator be chosen. They arranged similar meetings for the four Synods at New York, Philadelphia, New Providence (Virginia), and Center Church (Roan County, North Carolina). Their Constitution had been established.[3]

[1] *Records*, p. 532-533.
[2] *Ibid.*, p. 544.
[3] *Ibid.*, p. 548.

CHAPTER XI

THE DUTCH REFORMED, GERMAN REFORMED, LUTHERAN, MORAVIAN, QUAKER, AND UNITARIAN CHURCHES OF AMERICA

The tasks of unification and Americanization in the Dutch Reformed Church in the United States fell largely to one man, the Reverend John H. Livingston. Dr. Livingston was especially well qualified for his work. Of an old American family, he had been graduated from Yale in 1762. To qualify himself for the ministry, he went to Holland for theological studies. He was the last of the American youth to take this orthodox method of qualifying through a Dutch education and ordination. He spent the four years, 1766 to 1770 in Holland. Two great problems confronted him upon his return to America as pastor of the Fulton Street Church in New York in 1770; first, the healing of a schism which had rent the church for sixteen years, and secondly the problem of constitution-making which so speedily developed as a result of the new Americanism.[1]

A sad division had existed in the Dutch Reformed Church in America, since 1755. It is known as the Coetus and Conferentie controversy, and involved a variety of issues. The American Church had labored under crippling conditions because of its subjection to the Classis of Amsterdam. Under a constantly increasing sense of this disadvantage, — ministers had to resort to Holland for

[1] Gunn, Alexander, *Memoir of Rev. John H. Livingston*, 1829, second edition, 1856.

ordination and no colonial ecclesiastical officials possessed authority to call to account delinquent ministers, etc.,—efforts were made to secure a delegation of powers from the Classis. After long pleading the Conferentie was partially successful. Meanwhile the Coetus or American Classis continued to exercise independent powers, although it continued in constant correspondence with the Classis of Amsterdam. It examined and ordained young men as opportunity permitted. A pamphlet controversy developed between the two parties led by Ritzema of New York and Leydt of New Brunswick, centering mainly around the question of the right to organize independently to meet spiritual conditions in new surroundings. Contests and suspensions took place. A strong argument for independence was found in the oath of allegiance to Great Britain which was considered as inconsistent with subordination to the foreign state church of Holland. The matter was complicated by the introduction in 1763, of preaching in the English language. There arose a triangular issue of independence, dependence on the mother church in Holland, and political allegiance to Great Britain. The Classis of Amsterdam vacillated, and threatened to abandon both parties.

Dr. John Witherspoon had visited Holland in 1768 and a Plan of Union was drawn up similar to the one finally adopted but providing that the American Dutch youth studying for the ministry should be educated at the College of New Jersey. When the scheme was brought back to America, the Coetus opposed the union with the College of New Jersey and the Conferentie rejected the whole scheme. Education was a prominent issue. Previous to this efforts had been made to make an arrangement with King's College in New York.

The Coetus obtained a charter for Queen's (now Rutgers) College in 1770. The repressive and expensive routine of the educational policy of the Conferentie had paralyzed extension, and had left vacant about two-thirds of the pulpits in the church. The preamble to the charter of Queen's College stated that the people of the Reformed Faith and Discipline, were very numerous, and were desirous of a learned and well-qualified ministry, and therefore desired a college not only for the usual reasons, but especially that young men might prepare for the ministry; that the inconveniences were many and the expenses heavy in procuring ministers from Europe, or sending young men thither for education; that there was a great necessity for an increased number of ministers, and that a charter was necessary for the preservation of collegiate funds. The institution was designed "to promote learning for the benefit of the community, and the advancement of the Protestant religion of all denominations; and more especially to remove, as much as possible, the necessity our said loving subjects have hitherto been under of sending their youth intended for the ministry to a foreign country for education, and of being subordinate to a foreign ecclesiastical jurisdiction."[1]

Efforts to heal the schism seemed hopeless; churches and even families were divided and religion was in disgrace.[2] To find a remedy for this condition was to be the first labor of Dr. Livingston. Through his efforts the ecclesiastical authorities in Holland were induced to act. When he returned to America in 1770 he brought with him a plan. He had obtained from the Synod of North Holland

[1] Corwin, *Manual*, p. 38.
[2] Corwin, *The Reformed Church, Dutch*, pp. 157-158; Corwin, *Manual of the Reformed Church.*

the reference of the whole subject of union of the contending factions in America to the Classis of Amsterdam with power. This Classis had endorsed the plan which he had brought with him. It was discussed privately and by correspondence for a year, and then proposed to a general convention of the churches, summoned by the New York Consistory for October 1771.

The Union Convention met in New York, October 15, 1771. Twenty-two ministers were present. Of these eight were Europeans, nine had been ordained in America, and five had gone to Holland for ordination; seven were classed as Conferentie ministers; ten favored the Coetus, and five were neutral. The church at the time was composed of thirty-four ministers for over a hundred churches. Action was accomplished through a committee of twelve, three from each faction, with an equal number of ministers and elders represented. Livingston, Westerlo, Roosevelt, and Gansevoort were neutrals on the committee.

A plan, brought from Holland but undoubtedly the work of Livingston, was presented and with slight amendment unanimously adopted. The preamble acknowledged a bond of union with the church in Holland, but stated that certain misunderstandings had grown up respecting it. To prevent future misunderstandings and in accordance with the advice of the Classis, they now united and pledged themselves to regulate their ecclesiastical government and union with the mother-church in Holland in the following manner. They would abide by the doctrines of the Netherland Reformed Church and its constitution as established in the Synod of Dort. One General Meeting and five Particular Bodies, three for New York and two for New Jersey, were to be organized which were to meet annually. The General Meeting was to assume the long-desired privilege of licensing and ordaining men to the ministry; but the names of all such, together with the names of all newly called ministers, and of such as changed their vocations, were to be transmitted to Holland for registration, together with a copy of their acts from year to year. Appeals concerning doctrines, depositions, etc., might be carried to Holland. One or more professors were to come from the Netherlands with the advice of the Classis, but they were to have no connection with any English academies.[1]

A second convention of 1772 received a letter of approval from the Classis of Amsterdam for this plan.[2] Thus ended the sixteen-year feud during which the Coetus had ordained but nine men and the Conferentie but one. The church in America was reunited but it still remained a dependent organization. The Articles of Union asserted, "We organize . . . . . such ecclesiastical bodies as are consistent with the Government and Constitution of the Church of the Netherlands and our relation to the same."[3] It was to take twenty-one years before the Dutch Reformed Church was to achieve a thoroughly American constitution, a result of the American Revolution.

At the close of the Revolution, Dr. Livingston wrote the Reverend Dr. Westerlo, October 22, 1784:

> "The revolution in our political interests has made a change in the general fact of our American world, and as it has removed some difficulties which were taken into consideration in our former plan, so it has introduced others which deserve a very weighty and impartial discussion. The common enemy to our religious liberties is now removed;

[1] *Acts and Proceedings,* vol. i, pp. 1-20; Gunn, *Memoirs of the Reverend J. H. Livingston,* pp. 225-237; *Ecclesiastical Records,* vol. vi, pp. 4210-4227.

[2] Gunn, *op. cit.,* p. 238.

[3] *Acts and Proceedings,* vol. i, p. 9.

and we have nothing to fear from the pride and domination of the Episcopal Hierarchy . . . . .

Our correspondence with our mother churches in Holland, and the possibility of being increased by emigrations from thence, should at least incline us to remain as pure and unsuspected of any mixture as possible — unless some generous and proper plan, formed by a genius equal to the task, should be drawn for uniting all the Reformed Churches in America into one national church — which, notwithstanding the seeming difficulties in the way, I humbly apprehend will be practicable and, consistent with the outlines drawn by Professor Witsius for King William the Third, I yet hope to see accomplished."[1]

The task of fitting the Dutch Reformed Church to an independent United States of America was commenced in 1784, at the first meeting after the close of the War. The Reverend Body determined to leave to the notice of the civil magistrates the conduct of the Tory Rubel and to consider only "that during the war, he was frequently carried away by unchristian passions, and often from the pulpit and other places cursed the inhabitants of this land who were opposed to him, declaring with foul, irreligious and unbecoming expressions, that he would show that they would all go to everlasting destruction."[2] It elected Dr. Livingston as its Professor of Theology. But most important, at the Fall Meeting it was decided to nationalize the organization, a step which was to bring it into difficulties with the parent Holland church. This was effected by merely altering the status of its governing bodies, by giving them national titles. The Meeting adopted the following article (xxiii):

"Since the names of the respective Bodies have associated with them many difficulties and inconveniences in the use of them, especially in the Minutes, and are also to an extent unintelligible to other persuasions, and have thus tended to the discredit of our otherwise respectable Church, the Reverend Body . . . . . have seen fit to change the

[1] Gunn, *op. cit.*, pp. 257-264.

[2] *Acts and Proceedings*, vol. i, pp 108-110.

same in accordance with the provision made in the Article of the Plan of Union, and henceforth to apply to the *General Body* the name of *Synod*, and to the *Particular Bodies* the name of *Classis*; under this restriction, however, that this change shall in no measure be prejudicial to the Articles of Union, which this Reverend Body solemnly declare shall remain inviolable."[1]

They were rendered distinctly conscious of the peculiar position which an American church held in the new state by a controversy which had arisen respecting ownership of church properties. Objections were raised at the Meeting of 1784 to an Act of the Legislature of the State of New York "to enable all the religious denominations in this State to appoint Trustees, who shall be a body corporate for the purpose of taking care of the temporalities of their respective congregations, and for other purposes."[2] The Reverend Body advised the respective churches not to be hasty in accepting the said act but to abide a more particular consideration of the subject at its next meeting of the Synod.[3]

The Synod of 1785, — the first to use the title of "Synod," resolved, Article xv:

"Since it has become further apparent to the Reverend Body that there are highly objectionable features in the Act of Ecclesiastical Incorporation, passed by the Legislature of the State of New York, the Reverend Body determine to appoint a committee both from the congregations in the State of New York and those in New Jersey, to solicit of the Supreme Magistrates of the respective states the right and privilege by means of an Act, or change of Act or Acts already passed, to incorporate the Ecclesiastical Societies of the same according to the State and Constitution of the Reformed Dutch Churches, and agreeably to the manner and mode in which some of the same, as those of New York and Albany, Hackensack, New Millstone and others, have already been long actually incorporated."[4]

[1] *Acts and Proceedings*, vol. i, p. 128.
[2] Gunn, *op. cit.*, p. 284.
[3] *Acts and Proceedings*, vol. i, p. 129.
[4] *Ibid.*, vol. i, pp. 141-142.

The committee was appointed, and prepared a petition to their Excellencies, the authorities, together with a plan which would make each Consistory, for the time being, a legal Board of Trustees. This recommendation was approved by the Synod at its October meeting in 1786.[1]

Doctor Livingston was quite concerned about the character of the control over churches which the new government was seeking to assume, — it was much too Republican to suit his Dutch tradition. He wrote Dr. Romeyn, March 1786:

"The business of our incorporations, I found was not properly understood by some, and very warmly opposed by others. The ideas adopted by the authors of the incorporation act, were to keep the temporalities of all churches perfectly distinct from spirituals. For this reason, without adverting to the customs or discipline of any religious denomination, the body corporate in one and all of them was to be formed in a new mode, and this mode be adopted by every congregation. In this plan, there are many of our great folks so established, that I despaired of any opening for redress in our case. I applied, however, constantly to some leading members in both houses, and at last obtained their consent to a bill . . . But, even as to this bill, it is suggested to me, that it will be insisted upon, and probably a clause for that purpose added to the bill, that our Elders and Deacons shall be chosen at large by the people, and not by the Consistories, as at present, being, as they say, more republican. Should this last be urged, I would rather drop the whole application, as that remedy would be worse than the present disease, and would infallibly bring confusion into our Churches."[2]

Not having been able to achieve their ends by the time of the May meeting of 1787, it was decided to try political pressure from the church at large, — petitions, Article xiii:

"The Reverend Synod, having learned from the Reverend Professor J. H. Livingston, that there has already been presented to the supreme authority of the State of New York a petition for the incorporation of

[1] *Acts and Proceedings*, vol. i, pp. 150.
[2] Gunn, *op. cit.*, pp. 285-286.

Consistories as Trustees of the property of the churches, in accordance with the Constitution of the Netherland Church, but that the same has not yet been answered, judge that, for the further promoting and effecting the object of said petition, there shall also be received a request from the respective members of the various congregations, to be presented at the next session, in accordance with the form on the subject drawn and approved by the present Synodical Meeting; of which a copy shall be taken and presented to the respective Classes, that the same may be subscribed by all the congregations in a uniform manner, before the coming session of the honorable Assembly of the State of New York, in such a way as the respective Consistories shall judge most suitable." [1]

Political pressure from the influential Dutch Reformed members was finally partially effective and a law was obtained,

"that the Minister or Ministers, and Elders and Deacons, and, if during any time, there be no Minister, then the Elders and Deacons, during such time, of every Reformed Protestant Dutch Church, or congregation, now or hereafter to be established in this State, and elected according to the rules and usages of such Churches within this State, shall be the Trustees for every such Church or Congregation." [2]

Internally the Reverend Body and the church at large was experiencing increasing difficulties in trying to run according to the old order. The Meeting of 1786 raised the question of the use of an English Psalmody. The matter was referred to the next meeting but before it was finally settled it was to involve a reconstruction of the whole constitution of the church.[3]

The Synod of 1787 decided to act in the matter, Article xxi:

"The Reverend Body, convinced of the necessity for another and better version of the Psalms of David, than the congregations as yet possess in the English language, which is continually increasing in our churches, to be used for their benefit in public worship (no congrega-

[1] *Acts and Proceedings*, vol. i, pp. 156-157.

[2] Gunn, *op. cit.*, p. 287; *Revised and Session Laws of the State of New York*, edition of 1802, section 2, chapter 79.

[3] *Acts and Proceedings*, vol. i, p. 151.

tion, however, to be obliged thereto, where that of the New York Consistory is in use), have determined as speedily as possible to form such a new versification out of other collections of English Psalms in repute and received in the Reformed Churches. As a committee for this purpose are appointed . . . . . Livingston, Westerlo, Linn, Hardenbergh, Romeyn, Froelich, and Blauvelt who are requested to engage in the work with all practicable speed, and lay it before this Synod for ecclesiastical approval."[1]

Dr. Livingston soon came to a realization that a much larger problem than that of securing a suitable English version of the psalms was involved. In March 1788, he wrote:

"I have digested only from the first psalm to the fiftieth inclusive . . . I suppose it will be proper, when we get the new Psalms printed, to have the Catechism, Articles of Faith, and Liturgy, printed and bound up with some of the books, and leave it to the purchasers to get the Psalm-book either with or without those additions . . . . . But a fair opportunity will now be offered to publish with our articles and liturgy, the form of our discipline and government. The Churches in America are all assuming a new complexion. From being the appendages of national churches in Europe, they now become national Churches themselves in this new Empire. All denominations of any importance in America, have considered themselves in this new light, and have made regulations accordingly: and it deserves our attention to see what ought to be done with respect to ourselves in this particular and how far we may proceed consistent with the relation we yet claim to our mother church in Holland. We are not represented, and we cannot have representation in the Churches in Holland, — as such, we have already formed ourselves into an independent Synod, and we have sufficient proof that some of our brethren in Amsterdam would rather we had not done this, but their views are contracted and cannot be our rule. It is necessary we should revise some articles in our fundamental agreement respecting our church government of 1771, and see whether some of those articles do not militate against our independent state."[2]

The Synod of 1788 resolved, Article xxi, relative to the work of arranging the psalms:

"The Reverend Body, learning from some of the gentlemen appointed a committee *ad hanc rem*, that this work is not yet sufficiently executed to

[1] *Acts and Proceedings*, vol. i, p. 167. [2] Gunn, *op. cit.*, pp. 298-299.

enable the committee to make a full report, but that progress has been made, ordain, upon mature deliberation:

1. That the same committee be continued.

2. That in the performance of this work, the committee limit themselves to the known Psalm-books of the New York congregation, of Tate and Bracy, and of Watts; from which three books a complete Psalm-book shall be drawn, as nearly approaching and agreeable to the original Psalms as is possible, consistently with the rules of English poetry.

3. That inasmuch as there may, in the judgment of the committee, be found in said books some Psalms which are not expressed in accurate agreement with the Confession of Faith in our churches, the committee shall have liberty to supply this lack from some other authors of acknowledged orthodoxy.

4. That the committee (by reason of the urgent necessity of the churches, which cannot suffer long delay without great danger of confusion) are hereby also empowered, as soon as the majority agree in relation to this compilation, to forward said Psalm-book to the press, that the Reverend Synod may, if practicable, be able at their next meeting to present it in the most discreet and suitable manner to the congregations.

5. And since it is regarded necessary that some well-composed spiritual hymns be connected as a supplement with this new Psalm-book, it is ordained that the committee also have a care over this matter, and print such hymns in connection with the Psalms.

6. And lastly, it is deemed necessary that the Heidelberg Catechism, Confession of Faith, and Forms of our Church as translated into the English language and printed in the present New York Psalm-book, be reprinted and inserted in the new edition."[1]

Dr. Livingston announced the completion of this work, March, 1789.

"I have received answers from all the gentlemen of the commitee, and am authorized and requested by them to proceed with the printing. . . . As to the translations, and what respects our Church discipline and government, these, I suppose, may be brought in such readiness as to enable us to make some report in the Synod of May, and take such further steps, as to lay the whole before the Synod of October."[2]

[1] *Acts and Proceedings*, vol. i, p. 182.

[2] Gunn, *op. cit.*, p. 299.

At the October meeting in 1789, Article xix:

"The Reverend Committee upon this subject report, that said book is already committed to the press, and they expect ere long the satisfaction of beholding its issue."[1]

And at the October meeting in 1790, Article xxxi:

"The Reverend Synod perceive with much satisfaction that the English Psalms, together with the selection of Hymns formerly approved by Synodical decrees, have been happily committed to the press, and are printed and already in use in many congregations; and the present Synod cannot on this occasion omit publicly to render thanks in the name of the Church to the gentlemen composing the committee on this subject, and especially to the Reverend Professor Livingston, who particularly has lent his hand and help. They observe, likewise, in addition, that the Dutch churches are not restricted to the versification by Petrus Dathenus, as recently a new translation and versification of the Psalms has been introduced into the Netherland Churches; and that, according to the intention of the Synod of Dordrecht, hymns which have been approved by a Synod should not be excluded from the churches."[2]

The October Meeting of 1792 again referred to Dr. Livingston's work, Article xvii:

"The Reverend Body direct that Professor Livingston be thanked for his services in compiling and editing, as well as procuring a copy-right of the English versification of the Psalms; and said Professor is hereby appointed, in the name of this Reverend Body, to do whatever further pertains to this subject."[3]

By 1788 it had become evident that the whole church order must be overhauled in order to fit American conditions. It was accordingly resolved, Article xxvii:

"Since the circumstances of our churches, especially in relation to the general protection of the civil authorities in freedom of worship, necessarily demand that not only the Confession of Faith, but also the order of our Church and its Form of Church Government, should be made known to our countrymen in the English language, by the press, as has

[1] *Acts and Proceedings*, vol. i, p. 199.
[2] *Ibid.*, vol. i, p. 212.
[3] *Ibid.*, vol. i, p. 239.

already been done by all the chief persuasions in our American States: and since the English language is our national tongue, and is making progress, and has already been adopted wholly or in part in worship in the most of our congregations, and the rising generation seem to be little acquainted with the Dutch tongue: the Synod therefore feel themselves bound, both as regards our fellow-citizens and the civil government in general, and also for the preservation of our Dutch Church and the instruction of its adherents, and of the children in particular, to attend to this subject. Whereupon, it is resolved to appoint a committee to translate into the English language the Articles of Church Government of the National Synod, held at Dordrecht, 1618 and 1619, which being accompanied by such articles taken from the proceedings of this Reverend Body as have particular reference to the circumstance of the Church in this country will exhibit the true nature and form of government of our Dutch Churches in America. And it is further resolved, that the Reverend Committee endeavor to have this collection and translation in readiness to lay before this Reverend Synod at its next ordinary convening, in order that the same, with our standards may as speedily as practicable, consistently with all prudence, be given to the public by the press. Messrs. Livingston, Westerlo, Linn, Meyer, Romeyn, Hardenbergh, Rysdyk, and Peter Low were appointed the committee."[1]

Theirs was to be a work of no mean magnitude and it was not until the Synod of 1790 that the report of the committee was presented. It was thereupon resolved, Article xx:

"1. That the distinct translations of the Articles of Church Order of the Reverend Synod of Dordrecht in the years 1618 and 1619, and of the Plan of Union adopted 1772, both made in English by Drs. Dirck Romeyn and Eil. Westerlo, be referred to a committee, who shall carefully compare the same with the original Dutch, and alter and amend all such English words and phrases as either are not pure, or do not actually and appropriately express the true and literal meaning.

2. That the same committee likewise prepare some observations upon the articles of Church Order, to be incorporated among them, in which the proper sense and meaning of them, if necessary, shall be briefly declared, or sufficient reasons be assigned why some articles are not inserted, or cannot be carried out in our American churches.

3. That the Reverend Ministers of the congregation of New York, as residing in close proximity to each other, and most conveniently situated

[1] *Acts and Proceedings*, vol. i, pp. 184-185.

readily to confer together, be appointed a committee on the subject by this Synod.

4. That in the coming Spring, an extra Synod be convoked in order to revise said Plan of Union, and with common consent enlarge it, by inserting or adding some further rules, made in subsequent General Convenings or Synods, and thus, upon previous investigations, approving *Synodaliter* the aforesaid translation and observations.

5. That if necessary, the following Autumn, a General Ecclesiastical Meeting be solicited, calmly to weigh the whole subject, and determine *finaliter*, whether the same shall be issued in full or in part, and in what language, or whether both in Dutch and English, for the special benefit of our congregations." [1]

In March 1791 Dr. Livingston wrote:

"I have not been able, until within a few days, to take up the subject of our constitution and discipline. Upon considering the design of the publication, I am fully of your opinion, that there is no necessity of adhering strictly to a translation *totidem verbis*, of the Synod of Dort: nor even of giving every article, as many of them are local and only applicable to the Netherlands. It is not a history of the Dutch Church as it is in Europe, which we are to compile, but a true and regular detail of the constitution of the Reformed Dutch Church in America. As our charters and our discipline refer us to the Synod of Dort, we must show that we build upon that basis, with such deviations as time and circumstances have rendered unavoidable. We have two sources from whence we draw our present constitution, — one, the Synod of Dort; — and the other, the resolutions and fundamental articles agreed upon by our Churches, and ratified by the Classis of Amsterdam, in the name of the Synod of North Holland. From these and some subsequent acts of our own Synod, our discipline is formed. . . . . . To this end, suppose a title like this was made. *The Constitution and Form of Government of the Reformed Dutch Church in America, as established in the Synod Nat: of Dort, 1618-19; and agreed upon in the Assembly held at New York, 1771-1972, by and with the approbation of the Classis of Amsterdam, and finally ratified in Synod, held at New York, October 1791.* This, or some shorter, which may comprehend these ideas, will justify us in making such extracts from each of these sources as shall, altogether, bring forward one complete system. This will show to the world what our present constitution is, and sufficiently prove our connection and adherence to the Synod of Dort." [2]

[1] *Acts and Proceedings*, vol. i, pp. 210-211.
[2] Gunn, *op. cit.*, pp. 313-315.

Considerable progress had been made by the time of the May meeting of 1791. Their resolutions show, Article ix:

"The gentlemen appointed a committee to specify the subjects to be included in the Constitution of the Reformed Dutch Churches of America, to be issued in accordance with the intentions of Synod report, that after mature deliberation, it appears to them that such publication should be entirely restricted to what constitutes the Doctrine, Liturgy, and Government of said churches, that it may not only not form an unnecessarily large volume, but also not perplex the English reader, by the introduction of anything that does not essentially pertain to our ecclesiastical regulations; that therefore, all that relates to the Church in the Netherlands, and especially to the agency of the magistrate in ecclesiastical matters in that country, is not properly included in the regulations which are the basis of the government of our churches in America. The committee further remark, that the Proceedings of the National Synod, held at Dordrecht, are the basis of the government of all Reformed churches throughout the world, and that all charters which have been given to the Dutch churches in the States of New York and New Jersey, are also founded thereon; that yet, since in these proceedings many things occur which have particular reference to the Netherlands, the Dutch churches in other portions of the world have been necessitated to adapt them to their particular circumstance, as was also done by our churches in America in the general meetings held in New York in the years 1771 and 1772, when a Plan of Church Government was formed and adopted, which was also approved by the Reverend Classis of Amsterdam, as appointed for that purpose, by the Supreme Synod of North Holland, and this plan has been enlarged and amended by subsequent Synodical Acts. The committee, therefore, judge it advisable that the Reverend Synod further direct and authorize their committee upon this subject to frame out of said proceedings a suitable plan which shall constitute the whole ecclesiastical discipline and government of the Dutch Reformed churches in America, as now situated, and which shall be the only rule by which such churches are directed to abide, and by which they shall be known and distinguished as Dutch churches. This, in our estimation, will answer the expectations of the public, satisfy the desires of the civil government, and serve for the direction of all the members of our Church; since it will likewise appear from this plan, that the proceedings of the National Synod of Dordrecht are the basis of the government of the Dutch churches in America, cordially received and carefully adapted to its particular circumstances in this country; and that thus, the different charters may be ratified, and the attachment of the members of said churches to the Reformed Dutch churches in the Netherlands may be fully confirmed.

The Reverend Synod, having deliberated upon this report, resolved, that the committee be requested to frame a draft of Church Government and Discipline, agreeably to the principles stated in the report, and lay an accurate copy if practicable, before the Reverend Synod, at their next meeting. In order, however, also to secure the counsel and assistance of all their members in this weighty matter, it is likewise ordained, that the President of this Synod communicate to each of the respective Classes the request of this Synod, that each and every minister, with an elder (besides those who are appointed by the Reverend Classes as delegates to Synod), please to appear at the meeting in New York, on the first Wednesday in the ensuing October, so that the Synod may be able to avail themselves of the presence and counsel of the whole body of ministers and elders in issuing their Ecclesiastical Constitution, as also in relation to the Professorship and other weighty matters." [1]

At the October meeting of 1791, Article xxiii:

"Professor Livingston, as one of the committee on the subject, reported to this Reverend Body that he had adapted, as was deemed necessary, the English translation of the rules for the regulation of Dutch churches ordained in the Synod of Dort, to local and other circumstances, and now presented it for approval at the table of the Reverend Body; whereupon the Reverend Body proceeded to revise the same, article by article, which being done, it seemed fit to them to appoint a committee to revise them anew, and present them at the Extra Meeting of Synod in the next Spring. The Reverend Professor Livingston and Drs. Linn and Kuypers, each with one of their Elders were appointed the committee." [2]

At the May Meeting, Article v, 1792:

"Professor Livingston reports, in the name of the committee, that upon mature consideration of this subject, it appears to them that, besides a translation of the articles Synod Dort, it will be necessary to add some articles in explanation of the way and manner in which said Church Order of Dort is put into practice, agreeably to the Articles of Union ordained 1771, to the end that thus from one or the other the people in general may be able to form a correct conception of our mode of Church Government. He further informed the Reverend Body, that not only was the translation of said articles Synod National completed, but in part, also, the draft of the explanatory articles; and *Deo volente,* they

[1] *Acts and Proceedings,* vol. i, pp. 217-219.
[2] *Ibid.,* vol. i, pp. 226-227.

would be ready to be presented for approval at the next Synod in October. Resolved, That the Reverend Body in the highest manner approve of such mode of exhibiting their form of Church Government, and will expect that all the papers pertaining thereto will be carefully presented at the Synod which is to be held at New York the coming October."[1]

In October, 1792, Article vii:

"Professor Livingston reported, that he had completed the work intrusted to him at the Extra Synod on Church Order, and brought to the table a draft of explanatory articles for Synodical approval; whereupon, Synod were pleased to appoint a committee carefully to examine said draft, and report thereon, *stante Synodo*. Professor Livingston, Linn, Romeyn, Froelich, Basset, Studiford, Smith, Duryee, Schuyler, Van Veghten, Bunn and Wortmen, Elders, were appointed.

The Reverend Committee brought in the following report, which was made a Synodical decree:

The Reverend Body, taking up this Lemma, find that it originated in the year 1778 (Article xxiii), since which time it has been continued, and has been made a subject of action from time to time, until the present session, when we have the happiness of seeing all the branches pertaining to this weighty subject completed and brought to the table.

The Reverend Body having inspected the same, and read it article by article, and approved both the translation of the ecclesiastical regulations of the Synod of Dort, in the years 1618 and 1619, and the explanatory articles relative to the same, showing how they are applied to the Reformed Church in this country, agreeably to the Articles of Union, of the years 1771 and 1772, all the Reverend Brethren formally and solemnly recognized said articles as a just exposition of the nature and mode of the government and discipline received and established in said churches; and the same are to that end in the most earnest manner commended to all the members of their widely extended congregations, as the ecclesiastical rule of the Dutch Reformed Church in North America; and Professor Livingston and Dr. William Linn, and the Elder, Mr. Peter Wilson, are appointed a committee to issue said work, who shall exercise care over its phraseology, without assuming to attempt the least change in its sense and meaning."[2]

The October meeting of 1793 finally enacted, Article vi:

"The issuing of the Constitution of the Reformed Dutch Churches in America having been regarded as a matter of great importance, and

[2] *Acts and Proceedings*, vol. i, p. 229.
[1] *Ibid.*, vol. i, pp. 235-236.

measures having been taken by many successive Synods to carry the same into execution; and the proposal of Professor Livingston, made in the Extra Synod of May 1792, to embrace, in certain explanatory articles, a general account of the government and discipline of the Dutch churches, as well as the particular manner in which the regulations adopted in the last National Synod, held in Dordrecht, are to be followed, and applied to local circumstance in America, having been likewise received, and said explanatory articles placed upon the table of the General Synod, held in New York, in October 1792; the translation also of the Ecclesiastical Rules of said Synod of Dordrecht having been unanimously, approved, and orders given that the whole should be committed to the press: Professor Livingston, in the name of the committee, reported to this Body, that the same had been happily completed, and exhibited the book containing the Liturgy and Government of the Church, embraced in the Ecclesiastical Rules, and Explanatory Articles of the Reformed Churches in America. Agreeably to the foregoing resolutions of the Synod, Synod received the same full approbation, and with thanksgiving to the Lord Jesus Christ, on whose shoulders is the government of the Church, and who has hitherto preserved and blessed the Reformed Church, and enabled its members to present their Constitution in a manner which they regard acceptable to Him, and not without expectation that the same will be contemplated with satisfaction by other persuasions, being convinced that it will subserve the promotion of piety and good order in the respective congregations. The Reverend Synod, therefore, with all earnestness, recommend this publication to all their congregations, and cannot, at the same time, refrain from testiy!ng their thankfulness to the members of the committee appointed to carry forward this work." [1]

In 1789 the title of the church was altered. Article xxv ordered:

"By reason of the happy extension of our church far beyond its former limits, it is seen fit by the Reverend Synod that henceforth, in all their Ecclesiastical Acts, North America shall be substituted for New York and New Jersey; and that in all *translations of our proceedings* into the English language, which by reason of circumstance must frequently occur, in place of '*De Hoog Eerw*' (The Highly Reverend), 'The Most Reverend' shall be employed." [2]

[2] *Acts and Proceedings,* vol. i, pp. 245-246.
[1] *Ibid.,* vol. i, p. 201.

This whole proceedings had resulted in the preserving of the eighty-four Articles of Dort on Church Order, with an addition of seventy-three Explanatory Articles, showing how the former were to be applied to the American Dutch Church.

The Explanatory Articles particularly enlarged on the subject of candidates, their qualification, the manner of their entering the ministry, and the privileges which belonged to them as such: a formula to which licentiates must subscribe was also incorporated, as well as a formula for the subscriptions of ministers before ordination. The present form of call was prepared and inserted. The particular powers and duties of the Classes were more fully defined. The power of examining students was given to the Classes, although a student or licentiate could yet be examined by the Particular Synod if he so preferred. The deputies of the Synod were always to be present at examinations by the Classes, and to report to the Synod (Article xxxvii). Article xli of Dort, directed the president of the Classis to inquire of the respective members "whether church discipline be exercised; whether the poor and the schools be properly taken care of; and whether they stand in need of the advice and assistance of the Classis in anything respecting the regulations of their churches"; and Article xliv directed each Classis to appoint visitors, "whose business it shall be to enquire whether the ministers, Consistories, and schoolmasters do faithfully discharge their offices; whether they adhere to sound doctrines; whether they observe in all things the received discipline, etc." Explanatory Article xliv expounded these, "Once every year the Classis shall direct what shall be deemed necessary and practicable with regard to the visitation of the churches within their respective jurisdiction, and report the same to the Synod. For the more uniform and proper execution of this important duty, such particular questions and inquiries as shall be agreed upon in any General Synod, for that purpose shall be inserted in the book of records of every Classis, and by the visitors be faithfully proposed to the ministers, elders, and deacons of every Congregation in their respective visitations."

The particular powers and duties of the General Synod and of Particular Synods were more fully defined. The latter were to be representative bodies, consisting of two ministers and two elders from each Classis. They might yet examine and license students. They were "to exchange every year a copy of their acts with the Synod of North Holland, and express in their letters the desire of the Reformed Church in America to preserve a connection and cultivate a correspondence which they esteem and have found to be beneficial (Explanatory Article 1).

It had been found impracticable in Holland to hold a triennial General Synod (notwithstanding Article 1 of Dort so directed), owing chiefly to certain civil complications. Hence the several Particular Synods in Holland exercised each the power of a General Synod within their respective local jurisdictions, and adopted a mutual correspondence. The General Synod in Holland, according to the above article, was to consist of two ministers and two elders from every Particular Synod both of the Dutch and Walloon Churches. But in America it was determined that the General Synod should be conventional, consisting of all the ministers in the church and an elder from each congregation. It was to meet triennially. The General Synod, however, was given the privilege of changing its conventional character to a representative one by resolution.

The First General Synod was organized, June 3, 1794, and the old Synod became a Particular Synod. An American organization had been achieved.

In the meantime relations with Holland were anything but satisfactory. Though the customary relations were supposed to have survived the Revolution, yet the Church in Holland completely ignored the alterations which, beginning in 1784, actual conditions forced on the American Church. This placed the self-constituted "Synod" in an embarrassing position and led to many attempts to secure some sort of recognition from abroad. In 1786 the Synod records, Article vi:

"There was delivered at the table of this Body, by the *Deputatus*, J. H. Livingston, a letter from the Reverend Classis of Amsterdam, of the 10th January of this year, with the Acts of the Synod of North Holland, of the years 1784 and 1785. The Reverend Body rejoice in the highest degree in this new token of unbroken union and edifying fellowship, and return thanks to the Reverend Classis of Amsterdam for their continued fraternal care in transmitting the above mentioned Synodical Acts."[1]

The Synod of 1787 also noted the receipts of a letter from the Reverend Classis of Amsterdam together with the Acts of the Synod of North Holland.[2] But these communications were not to the satisfaction of the American branch of the church. Dr. Livingston thus expressed his disapproval of them:

"The letter accompanying the acts of Synod, I have not opened, but have only taken notice of the address, in which I find they implicitly deny our being a Synod, by giving us the same title we had before our present organization; and this is one thing I wish to know your sentiments upon; whether it would not be proper for us by some article in our minutes, or by some clause in our letter, to express our sensibility upon their silence respecting our present judicatories; for, if we correspond,

[1] *Acts and Proceedings*, vol. i, p. 145.
[2] *Ibid.*, vol. i, pp. 160-161.

it ought to be continued upon the footing of mutual respect, or it may, in its consequences, soon be productive of some disagreeable events. Perhaps we have been too remiss in not taking notice of this before, or it is possible that silence may be the most prudent and eligible." [1]

Matters grew steadily worse. The Synod of 1788 had received no word[2] and that of 1789 noted:

"No letter of the Reverend Classis of Amsterdam nor Acts of the Reverend Synod of North Holland, which would be to the Reverend Synod like good news from a far country, and, in the midst of all the pressing evils under which the churches of this land continue to sigh, like cold water to a thirsty soul, have been received. The Reverend Synod long, and pant ere long to be gladdened with those agreeable tokens of paternal remembrance on the part of the highly honored churches of the Netherlands." [3]

The Synod of 1790 is beginning to wonder at the long silence, Article vi:

"No letter from the Reverend Classis of Amsterdam nor Acts of the Reverend Synod of North Holland have been received. The Reverend Synod are greatly surprised at this long delay, not comprehending what can be the reason thereof, except that our letters and acts have not been received. The Synod, not being inclined to break off the correspondence, desire the Deputati to prepare a letter of inquiry to the Reverend Classis of Amsterdam, and lay it before this Synod for approval." [4]

The Synod of 1791 records, Article vi:

"The Deputatus reports that agreeably to the resolution of the last Ordinary Meeting, a letter was sent to the Reverend Classis of Amsterdam, to which no answer has yet been received. The Reverend Body therefore continue to entertain expectation of a favorable reply." [5]

But such was not received. The Synods of 1792[6] and the First General Synod which met in 1793 still continue to lament the silence of the parent church.[7]

[1] Gunn, *op. cit.*, pp. 296-297.
[2] *Acts and Proceedings*, vol. i, p. 176.
[3] *Ibid.*, vol. i, p. 196.
[4] *Ibid.*, vol. i, pp. 204-205.
[5] *Ibid.*, vol. i, pp. 221-222.
[6] *Ibid.*, vol. i, p. 236.
[7] *Ibid.*, vol. i, p. 248.

The General Synod of 1793 signalized the completion of the Constitution of the American Dutch Reformed Church in America. This had been accomplished without the least advice or assistance from abroad.[1]

Nationalization of the German Reformed Church in America progressed much more slowly and less independently than was the case with the Dutch Reformed Church. The years immediately succeeding the Revolution are historically unimportant for the German Reformed sect. It is true that the members of the Coetus occupied a position which for local dignity and influence has seldom been equaled in the Reformed Church. There were, however, few signs of growth or advancement. Apparently they were incapable of adapting themselves to the spirit of independent America. Every year the minister received his proportion of a Holland stipend, amounting to a couple hundred of dollars; and as this fact was well known the people did not interest themselves greatly in the support of their religion. The condition of the church was peaceful but there was no consciousness of a special mission. The connection with Holland was a burden and there was no Livingston in the German Reformed Church to loose them from their load.

As early as 1771, when the Dutch Reformed Churches were about to assume a somewhat American form of government, they invited the German Reformed Churches to unite with them but the German Coetus declined on the ground of their affection for the fathers in Holland. Their love for the Dutch in Holland was much greater apparently than for American Dutch; they were much more inclined to mingle with other German sects in America than with

[1] *Constitution of the Reformed Dutch Church in the United States*, New York, 1793.

Dutch Reformed congregations. Arrangements with German Lutherans for the use of union churches became numerous; and in some instances where both congregations were weak and poor a single pastor was called, and the congregations thus united were known as "Evangelical" or "Protestant."

In 1787 an attempt was made in South Carolina to establish an ecclesiastical body, which was officially known as *Corpus Evangelicum* or *Unio Ecclesiastica.* It consisted of five Lutheran and two Reformed ministers, together with delegates from fifteen churches. This union, however, was short lived.[1]

Out of the association of the two German denominations grew the desire to found a German college; it is impossible to say which first suggested the idea. The honor may be divided between four ministers: Helmuth and Muhlenberg, Lutherans; and Weyberg and Hendel, German Reformed. The new institution was opened in June 1787, and named Franklin College in honor of Benjamin Franklin, the largest individual contributor to its endowment. Its first president was Dr. Muhlenberg, and Dr. Hendel was vice-president.

In the Coetal letter of 1789 the German Reformed Church announced to its parent in Holland that it realized that steps must be taken to meet the new American situation:

"Since the new Constitution and established government of the country bring changes with them, we notice, among other things, that the several denominations throughout the States unite, form Classes, and then Synods. This will also become necessary for us, the German Reformed, and then the name, Coetus of Pennsylvania, would be too limited. In this matter we await the opinion of the Reverend Fathers. As the establishment, growth, and reputation of the Reformed religion

[1] Bernheim, *History of the Lutheran Church in the Carolinas.*

was always the chief aim of your noble exertions, we hope that the information concerning the union of the High German Reformed Churches throughout the extensive American States will be most agreeable and desirable to the Most Reverend Fathers."[1]

The Reverend Fathers in Holland ignored this appeal as they had in the case of the Dutch Reformed church; the American church could not wait, so in 1791, adopted their declaration of independence, Article iii:

"Resolved, That the Coetus has the right at all times, to examine and ordain those who offer themselves as candidates for the ministry, without asking or waiting for permission to do so from the Fathers in Holland."[2]

And it was further resolved, Article iv, to send to Holland, "report of their proceedings, accompanied by suitable explanations, when it is necessary."[3] It is noteworthy that these proceedings were sent merely as a matter of explanation or courtesy and not as formerly for revision, and that Articles iii and iv were not sent at all.

Having taken the first step the Coetus of 1792 went forward with the business of organization. At Philadelphia in May, Article ii:

"It was moved that a committee be chosen to prepare such fundamental rules as would make closer the bond of union in the Reverend Coetus, each member of the Committe to draw up his ideas in writing, in order to compare them later on. The following were appointed on this committee: Drs. Hendel, Pomp, and Blumer."[4]

No answer came from Holland. In 1793 the Synod held its first meeting at Lancaster, where, by the adoption of the *Synodalordnung*, it became an independent body consisting of about 178 congregations and 15,000 communicants.[5] In the preamble to the *Synodalordnung*, it is said

[1] *Minutes and Letters of the Coetus of the German Reformed Congregations in Pennsylvania*, p. 431-432.

[2] *Ibid.*, p. 446; Dubbs, *op. cit.*, p. 323.

[3] *Ibid.*, p. 446.

[4] *Ibid.*, p. 449.

[5] Dubbs, *op. cit.*, p. 323.

to have been established by "all the Evangelical Reformed churches of Pennsylvania and certain neighboring States"; but in the first article it is declared that the body which has hitherto been known as the Coetus of Pennsylvania shall hereafter be entitled the "Synod of the Reformed German Church in the United States." Ministers who had been sent to America by the Synods of Holland, or who might hereafter be sent, were entitled to membership, those who came from other parts of Europe were required to present certificates of ordination and testimonials of good conduct. For one year all ministers received from a foreign country remained honorary members, without a seat or vote. Candidates for the ministry were required to be well grounded in the ancient languages, except in special cases when the applicant was more than twenty-five years of age and was otherwise well qualified for the office. Delegated elders were entitled to a seat and vote in Synod, except that elders representing vacant charges had no vote. The powers of the president were carefully guarded, but he seems to have been an influential personage. It was not only made his duty to reprimand delinquents, but under certain circumstances to suspend them from office until the next meeting of Synod. Pastors were required to present annual reports of their ministry, which were read in open Synod; and the elders were then questioned, not only formally, but minutely. At every session of the Synod a private meeting was to be held, at which orthodoxy of the sermons which had been preached during the convention was discussed, and private difficulties between the members considered and settled.

In 1800 additional series of rules were adopted, by which the Synod was made to consist of ordained ministers, licentiates, and catechists. Catechists were not to administer the sacraments, in fact they were merely candidates for the ministry. Licentiates were authorized to administer the sacraments and could serve congregations, but licensures were annually renewed.

As for a hymn-book, the Coetus had used the Marburg which contained the Heidelberg Catechism, Psalms and Hymns, Morning and Evening Prayers, Gospel and Epistle Lessons, and an account of the destruction of Jerusalem. In 1793 the Synod adopted the following resolution:

"Resolved, That a hymn-book be prepared, of which the psalms shall be taken from Lobwasser and Spreng's improved version, and that the Palatinate hymn-book shall form the basis of the hymns, with this difference only: that some unintelligible hymns be exchanged for better ones."

The committee on the hymn-book was: Hendel, Hellfrich, Blumer, Wagner, Pauli, and Mann. The resultant work is often called Hendel's Hymn-book. The preface says:

"We have chosen the most edifying and best known hymns in the Marburg and Palatinate hymn-books, composed by Joachim Neander, Frederich Adolph Lampe, Casper Zollikofer and other godly men among the Protestants. To these we have added a number of edifying spiritual songs taken from hymn-books recently published in various parts of Germany. The meters are arranged throughout according to the Palatinate hymn-book."

The Heidelberg catechism was not reissued until 1795; the first edition published in Pennsylvania in English was in 1810.

The Synod of 1793 suggested that whenever a number of ministers — not less than three — resided at so great a distance from the center of the church as to render it inconvenient to attend the meetings of Synod, it was competent for them to organize a Classis, to be represented in Synod by one or more delegates. In 1819 the Synod divided itself into eight districts or Classes. With the establishment of the Classis, the organization of the German Reformed Church in America was completed.

It was unfortunate for the Lutheran Church in America that its membership in general, and indeed even its leaders, did not seem to equal Henry Melchoir Muhlenberg in their grasp of the problem presented to their church by this period. We have previously quoted Dr. Helmuth's supremely disinterested view of the early course of the Revolution.[1] Contrast with this the words and actions of the Muhlenberg family[2] and you have an excellent picture of the two extremes of the church. Muhlenberg would Americanize immediately; other leaders would remember their German nationality.

Henry Melchoir Muhlenberg wrote in 1783:

> "It would be a most desirable and advantageous thing if all the Evangelical Lutheran congregations in the North American States were united with one another, if they all used the same order of service, the same hymn-book, and, in good and evil days, would show an active sympathy and fraternal correspondence with one another."[3]

This was but an aspiration on the part of Muhlenberg, at that time in the last years of his life, looking upon a church divided into "five or six different, distinct and unconnected synods,"[4] which were to remain independent until 1820.

Muhlenberg had spent a large part of his time in America working for an organized church. His favorite motto was *Ecclesia plantanda.* He would transform the congregational organism, which he found upon his arrival in America

[1] *Supra.*, p. 19.
[2] *Supra.*, pp. 114-116.
[3] Mann, *Life of Henry Melchoir Muhlenberg*, p. 501.
[4] Schmucker, S. S., *Retrospect of Lutheranism in the United States*, p. 16.

in 1742, into a church. He did during the period of his ministry (1742-1786) effect the beginnings of a synodical organization.

The first stage in the completion of an organized church was reached when Muhlenberg effected the *Ministerium* of Pennsylvania in 1761, with the title of The Annual Preachers' Assembly of the United Swedish and German Ministerium. Earlier synods had been attempted but with varying degrees of success.

In 1760 Muhlenberg sent out the call for a convention to deliberate concerning a future plan. Among the topics which he proposed for discussion were the following: 1. Whether it be necessary and useful to continue an annual convention of the ministers and elders in the United German congregations? 2. What are the impediments to such fraternal convention and union? 3. At what place should the annual conventions be held? 8. Whether a president should be elected annually and such provision should be made that he should make a visitation in all the United Congregations, and should attend the meeting of the Swedish Synod as a delegate? Twelve pastors and catechists responded to his call; laymen were also present from Philadelphia, New York, and Lancaster.

In 1761 the convention assumed the title mentioned above. In 1763 it was decided to ask pastors for annual reports of baptisms, confirmations and deaths. A synodical constitution gradually grew up which was transcribed into the minute-book begun in 1781 as a definite constitution.

The main features of this Constitution were as follows: The name was "The Evangelical Lutheran Ministerium in North America." The president "is to be respected and honored as having the oversight, both during the meeting of the synod and at other times (ii, 1)." Only "the fittest and most learned" were eligible to the office of secretary (iii, 2). Pastors were pledged not to declare themselves independent of the synod as long as they served in North America (iv, 6. 2). Lay delegates were to be heard at the beginning of the sessions and then dismissed to their homes (v, 14 sq.). The ministers, thereupon, proceeded to the consideration of congregational affairs and questions of conscience, committees of the elder pastors being appointed to recommend action (v, 21). This finished, they conferred concerning the blessings and difficulties of their labors, reported concerning baptisms, confirmations, funerals and communicants, and listened to the reading of the diaries of the licensed candidates (v, 25). Ordinations at special conferences were forbidden, unless so directed by the synod (v, 31). Every pastor pledged himself to endeavor to introduce into his congregation constitutions corresponding as nearly as possible to those then in use and harmonizing with that of the ministerium (vi, 1). Every minister was required to use the liturgy introduced (vi, 3), and to pledge himself in writing to that effect (vi, 6. 2). Any one absenting himself for three years without excuse was to be expelled (v, 4).[1] From the synod of 1760 on there was no break in the meetings of the Pennsylvania Ministerium; Henry Melchoir Muhlenberg had effected a church organism for that state.

His son Frederick Augustus Muhlenberg was to project the Evangelical Ministry for New York State in 1774 according to the constitution of the Pennsylvania Ministerium. But, due to the war, and other causes, it was

[1] Translation of this constitution in *Lutheran Church Review*, vol. ix, pp. 225-269; Jacobs, *op. cit.*, pp. 261-262.

left to Dr. Kunze to effect a permanent organization of that body in 1786.

As organized in 1786 the New York ministerium comprised three pastors and the congregations of New York and Albany. At least eight regular Lutheran pastors within its territory, with their congregations, stood aloof. Such was the strength of the congregational tradition among Lutherans. During the first ten years of its existence it comprised but thirteen pastors, four of whom came from the Ministerium of Pennsylvania.

Muhlenberg early complained of the variety of hymn-books is use among the congregations. Of these, though, the Marburg gained precedence and an American edition was published in 1762. This contained, in addition to more than six hundred hymns, the litany, a number of prayers, the Small Catechism, the gospels and epistles, with a collect for each Sunday and festivals, and the history of the destruction of Jerusalem.

This hymn-book was supplanted generally by one prepared for the Ministerium of Pennsylvania in 1786, by a committee composed of Drs. H. M. Muhlenberg, Helmuth, Kunze, and H. E. Muhlenberg. They were instructed to follow the order of the Halle Hymn-book, to omit none of the standard hymns of Luther and Paul Gerhardt, but to omit the gospels and epistles for the apostles' days and other festivals, also the history of the destruction of Jerusalem, the prayer-book and the catechism. A new prayer-book was prepared for the appendix by Dr. Helmuth. Muhlenberg's contribution to this work was merely the preface and a participation in the selection of the hymns.[1]

The liturgy of 1786 was essentially the same as that of

[1] Jacobs, *op. cit.*, pp. 336-337.

1748, with certain striking alterations. These were chiefly the work of Dr. Helmuth, president of the Ministerium after Muhlenberg had ceased to attend its sessions. Dr. B. M. Smucker, remarks that these changes were "all of a piece." "Every one of them," according to Dr. Smucker, "is an injury to the pure Lutheran type of the old service."[1] A new general prayer was substituted for the one of 1748, one article of which throws a clear light on the question of the relation which Dr. Helmuth and his disciples were to maintain with regard to "nationalism." The prayer read:

"And since it has pleased Thee chiefly, by means of the Germans to transform this State into a blooming garden, and the desert into a pleasant pasturage, help us not to deny our nation, but to endeavor that our youth may be so educated that German schools and churches may not only be sustained but may attain a still more flourishing condition."[2]

It was with this spirit that Dr. Helmuth, assisted by Dr. Kunze, revised the Synodical Constitution of the Pennsylvania Ministerium in 1792. The corporation of Zion's and St. Michael's in Philadelphia had petitioned the Ministerium for lay representation in the synod. Drs. Helmuth and Kunze were appointed a committee to prepare a plan whereby this could be effected. The result was a thorough revision of the constitution. The synod became The Evangelical Lutheran Ministerium in Pennsylvania and Adjacent States. An office of "senior" was instituted as distinct from that of "president." Three orders of ministers were established; ordained ministers, licensed candidates and catechists. All confessional tests were eliminated and all reference to the Augsburg Confession or to the other symbolic books vanished. But

[1] *Lutheran Church Review*, vol. i, p. 22.
[2] Jacobs, *op. cit.*, p. 338.

most important for the solution of the question which we are seeking, the reconstructed Ministerium was to be officially "German."

The eighteenth General Synod of the Moravian Brethren held at Marienborn, 1769, had confirmed the principle that the British and American provinces of the Unity were to be regarded merely as outlying subordinate branches, semi-missionary in Charter. They were to be managed by boards known as Provincial Helpers, appointed by and responsible to the Unity's Elders Conference and not to the congregations whose general interests they superintended. The representative principle was hardly recognized. For a period of about eighty years from this time no American Provincial Synod was empowered to convene—this in a land where the national life was becoming dominated by the spirit of independence and self-government, a disastrous state of affairs. A complicated financial arrangement was suffered to link the several congregations and the provinces as such with the Unity as a whole. Rules demanded, possibly, by the vexatious alliance of church and state in Europe were made binding in the land of religious liberty, and became shackles on the church. An excessive application of the use of the lot, consequent upon an exaggerated conception of the headship of Christ over the church, and the ascetic regulations of the choir system intensified a spirit of aloofness and exclusiveness; the abnormal dread of incurring the charge of proselytism led to a refusal to follow natural and lawful methods of church extension. Early in the seventies a commission from the general board had solved the most difficult problems involved in the Unity's former ownership of the real estate in America. This seemed at the time the greatest difficulty of the church. With a foothold in no less than nine of the colonies, the church should have risen to its opportunities and become a valuable factor in the national life. It did not, and hardly held its own.[1]

Bishop John Frederick Reichel, a member of the Unity's Elders Conference, officially visited the American Congregations in the spring of 1779. A most important transaction of a conference of ministers over which he presided in April 1781, previous to his return to Europe, was the adoption of the Brotherly Agreement, as the basis of the statutes of the various congregations.

By the General Synod of 1782, at which no American delegates were present, the connection of the American congregations with the governing board in Germany was strengthened and the dominance of European, especially German, Moravian conceptions confirmed.

With the abrogation of the Test Act and the assured separation of church and state in the United States, there was no reason why the Brethren in America, after recovery from the financial distress of the war, should not have entered upon a period of new life and extension. But operations were cramped by unwise retention of regulations out of keeping with the national life. Painfully minute attention was given to the development of subjective phases of piety in the exclusive settlements, to the cramping of the church's energies in other directions. The financial demands of the church's work were met by the proceeds of business enterprises carried on for its benefit, rather than by the voluntary gifts of the people. The use of the German language in worship was perpetuated, to the loss of members in the cities and the keeping of strangers at a distance. Persons who lived away from the settlements, but sought the fellowship of the church, were formed into societies sustaining only quasi-

[1] Hamilton, *op. cit.*, pp. 468-469.

connection with it, and not into regular congregations — a usage that had little meaning or purpose in a land free from governmental ecclesiasticism. The laymen had practically no voice in the general management. There was a deficiency of well-qualified ministers. Men of mature years, who were sent from Europe, however scholarly, could not readily adjust themselves to the conditions and spirit of American institutions or appreciate the opportunities which were offered here. Administrative affairs of highest importance had to be referred to a foreign executive board. The whole conduct of Moravian affairs for this period illustrates the folly of opposition to Americanization. This church is perhaps the most striking example of the self-destructive policy which opposed nationalization in ecclesiastical affairs.

There was, however, a slight national movement even amongst the Moravians. In 1787 their missionary society was revived under the title of the "Society of the United Brethren for Propagating the Gospel among the Heathen." Its headquarters were at Bethlehem; Ettwein was its president, Von Schweinitz its treasurer, and Van-Vleck its secretary. A charter was obtained from the Assembly of Pennsylvania in February, 1788. Ettwein communicated to General Washington an account of the organization of the society, and received in reply the following appreciation.

"So far as I am able of judging, the principles upon which the Society is founded, and the rules laid down for its government, appear to be well calculated to promote so laudable and arduous an undertaking; and you will permit me to add that if an event so long and so ardently desired as that of converting the Indians to Christianity and consequently to civilization can be effected, the Society at Bethlehem bids fair to bear a very considerable part of it." [1]

[1] Mss. letter in Bethlehem Archives, quoted in Hamilton, *op. cit.*, p. 476.

The spirit of independence which caused and accompanied the War for Independence resulted in the establishment of the Unitarian Church in America. Long before the war Arianism had showed itself in numerous separate localities in America, but it had not been organized into any definite set of ecclesiastical institutions or beliefs.

By the middle of the eighteenth century many Congregational ministers in New England were tainted with Unitarian beliefs and their thought was reflected in the teachings of Harvard University. Dr. Sprague in his *Annals of the American Pulpit,* records the lives of forty-nine ministers of known Unitarian beliefs settled in Congregational churches during this century. The most prominent of them was Jonathan Mayhew, of the West Church in Boston, 1747-1766.[1] Dr. Mayhew preached the strict unity of God, the subordinate nature of Christ, and salvation by character. Charles Chauncy of the First Church of Boston, 1727-1787, as the chief opponent of Jonathan Edwards exhibits both Unitarian and Universalist beliefs.[2] Others classed as Unitarians by Dr. Sprague were: Ebenezer Gay of Hingham, styled "The Father of American Unitarianism"; Samuel West of New Bedford; Thomas Barnard of Newbury; John Prince and William Bentley of Salem; and Aaron Bancroft of Worcester. The Reverend William Hazlitt visited the United States in 1783-1785 and published the fact that there were Unitarians in Philadelphia, Boston, Charleston, Pittsburgh, Hallowell, on Cape Cod and elsewhere.

The first official organization of Unitarianism in America resulted from the Revolution. Mr. James Freeman, a graduate of Harvard, was called to fill the vacancy in

[1] *Supra.,* pp. 50-52.
[2] *Supra.,* pp. 52-53.

King's Chapel (Episcopalian) in Boston, caused by the flight of the loyalist rector. At first he officiated as lay-reader but later the question of his ordination arose. In 1782 the congregation decided to settle him in his ministry. In 1785 they proceeded to revise their Prayer Book into a mild Unitarian Liturgy. By a vote of twenty to seven it was decided to strike out from the order of service whatever taught or implied the Doctrine of the Trinity. Freeman himself published a *Scripture Confutation of the Thirty-nine Articles.* It is not, then, surprising that both Bishops Seabury and Provoost should refuse to ordain Mr. Freeman. Thereupon on November 18, 1787, representatives of King's Chapel Congregation proceeded "to set Freeman apart to his office." Thus the first Episcopalian Church in New England as a result of the American Revolution was turned into the First Unitarian Church in America.

On the whole very little change was effected in the organization of American Quakerism by the independence of the United States. It still continued to hold its Yearly Meetings and to maintain the same close connections with the Mother Church in England. We find ten Quakers from America present at the London Yearly Meeting which followed the establishment of Peace, 1784.

CHAPTER XII

THE BAPTIST AND CONGREGATIONAL CHURCHES IN AMERICA

It may seem strange to speak of the nationalization of the Baptists, those apostles of "local independence." This of itself stamps the Baptists with a most distinctive American character, which they have preserved through most trying circumstances. There was a time, during this "Critical Period" of the organization of American institutions, when it looked as though the Baptist organization might take the form of an efficient, centralized republic. The difficulties of the struggle for their American principles forced upon the Baptists in Virginia and in New England centralized state organisms. For a very short time it seemed as though these State organisms might be welded into a national unity, as it became necessary to carry their fight for religious freedom to a national issue. But there the victory was so speedily won that a national form of government for Baptists did not have time to mature. Then even in state affairs, the instant that victory was achieved the cry that the organization was violating fundamental principles of Baptist polity, resulted in partial discarding of the centralized machinery.

The Baptist fight from 1774 to 1789 was, however, long enough and strenuous enough to develop a national spirit, a national Baptist tradition and a national Baptist College, even if the organization which had been utilized was largely transient. The Baptists were chiefly instrumental in establishing the American principle of the non-interference of the state with religion, Religious Liberty.

Other sects, notably the Presbyterians, were energetic and effective in demanding their own liberties; the Quakers and the Baptists agreed in demanding liberty of conscience and worship, and religious equality before the law, for all alike. But the active labor in this cause was mainly done by the Baptists. It is to their consistency and constancy in the warfare against the privileges of the powerful "standing Orders" of New England and of the moribund establishments of the South, that we are chiefly indebted for the final triumph, of the principle of separation of church and state, — one of the largest contributions of the New World to the cause of civilization and Christianity.[1]

The period of 1774 to 1789 was a great period for American Baptists, a period of organization and growth. Organization took the form of Associations. Of these, three chief regional sets were formed, those of New England, those of the Middle States, and those of Virginia and the South. It has been pointed out that in the history of American Baptists their rapid growth is exactly conterminous with the development of associations in their churches. Certainly associations became powerful implements for the advancement in evangelizing the new regions opened up for settlement in the first years of peace.

It has sometimes also been conjectured that Baptists borrowed their idea of association from the Yearly Meetings of the Quakers. Some of these clearly antedate the Baptists Associations of this country. Yet the Quaker meeting more nearly resembles a Presbyterian Synod.

The oldest of the associations was that of Philadelphia, organized in 1707. This was the parent association and to it, American Baptists, to a large degree, owe the form

[1] *Supra.*, p. 6.

of their faith as well as the principles upon which later Associations grew. The earliest known copy of its minutes is that for 1769 which show that it then consisted of 34 churches and 34 pastors, situated in Pennsylvania, New Jersey and New York.[1]

In 1742 the Philadelphia Association had adopted the Articles of Faith, since known as the Philadelphia Confession. These were little more than a revision of the Westminister Confession, consisting of thirty-four articles and an appendix. The distinctive article was, "We believe that laying on of hands with prayer, upon baptized believers, as such, is an ordinance of Christ, and ought to be submitted unto by all persons that are admitted to partake of the Lord's Supper."[2] This confession of faith has served as the basis of probably the majority of the Baptist churches of this country; and it is still, with the omission of the article on the laying on of hands and revisions here and there, in no wise affecting its substance, the confession that generally obtains in the Baptist Churches of the Southern and South-Western States.[3] The adoption of this strongly Calvinistic Confession was the turning point in the early history of American Baptists, and fixed the character of the denomination for all time.

From 1742 the influence of the Philadelphia Association in matters of Dogma was paramount. Its missionary zeal was great; men closely connected with this body, and fully believing its confession, became preachers in New England, New York, and the Carolinas. By the close of the century the Calvinistic party was in the

[1] *Minutes of the Philadelphia Association.*
[2] *Ibid.*, p. 46.
[3] Vedder, *History of the Baptists in the Middle States*, pp. 92-100.

ascendency everywhere; it had completed its triumph by capturing the stronghold of Arminianism, the First Baptist Church of Providence, through the establishment of the Warren Association and the Rhode Island College under President Manning.[1]

Another debt must be added by American Baptists to this Parent Philadelphia Association, — for the definite settlement by this body of the associational form of constitution. In 1767 it was called upon to decide, "Whether an appeal from any member of the associated churches, or from one excommunicated from any said churches, may be made to the Association?" It was ruled "That the word appeal was not quite proper, as the Association claims no jurisdiction, nor power to repeal anything settled by any church; but if, before settlement, parties agree to refer matters to the association, then to give their advice."[2]

In 1751 the Charleston Association (S. C.) was formed, consisting of four churches. This organization is directly traceable to the Philadelphia body. Mr. Hart, the pastor of the Charleston church, had seen in the Philadelphia Association, the happy consequences of union and regular intercourse among churches maintaining the same faith and organization. He turned for aid to the Philadelphia Association in 1755 when his association had authorized him to engage a suitable person for missionary work; he visited the parent association and prevailed upon the Reverend John Gano to undertake the task.

Associations spread rapidly in the Southern, Middle, and

[1] Guild, *op. cit.* pp. 43-62; Backus, *op. cit.*, vol. ii, chapt. 13; Hovey, *op. cit.*, pp. 151-156.

[2] Gillette, *Minutes*, pp. 90, 101, 105; Edwards, *Materials*, vol. i, pp. 123-124.

Northern States. The following list indicates the spontaneity of the movement:

1751 Charleston Association, S. C.
1758 Sandy Creek Association, N. C.
1765 Kehukee Association, N. C.
1766 Ketocton Association, Va.
1767 Warren Association, R. I. and Mass.
1770 Rapidan or the General Association of Separate Baptists, Va.
1771 Congaree Association, S. C. (Bethel Association after 1789).
1772 Stonington Association, Conn. and R. I.
1776 Strawberry Association, Vt.
1776 Redstone Association, Pa.
1776 Brentwood Association, Me. and N. H.
1780 Shaftsbury Association, Vt., Mass. and N. Y.
1781 Holston Association, Tenn.
1782 Salisbury Association, Md.
1783 Woodstock Association, N. H.
1783 Dover Association, Va.
1783 Middle District Association, Va.
1784 Georgia Association.
1784 New Hampshire Association.
1785 Vermont Association.
1785 Groton Union Conference, Conn., R. I. and Mass.
1785 Elkham Association, Ky.
1785 Salem Association, Ky.
1786 Shaftsbury Association, Vt.
1787 Bowdoinham Association, Me.
1788 Roanoke Association, Va.
1789 Meredith Association, N. H. and Vt.
1790 Portsmouth Association, Va.
1790 Danbury Association, Conn. and Mass.
1790 Yadkin Association, S. C.
1791 Warwick Association, N. Y.
1792 Goshen Association, Va.
1792 Baltimore Association, Md.
1792 Shilo Association, Va.
1793 Lyden Association, Mass., N. H. and Vt. (New Windham).
1793 New River Association, Va.
1793 Tates Creek Association, Ky.
1794 Hepziba Association, Ga.
1794 Neuse Association, N. C.
1795 Richmond Conference, Vt. (Fairfield).
1795 Ostego Association, N. Y.

1796 Rensselaerville Association, N. Y.
1796 New District Association, Tenn.
1796 Chemung Association, Penn.
1796 Fairfield Association, Vt.
1797 Miami Association, O.
1798 Mayo Association, N. C.
1798 Sparta Association, Ga.
1799 Cumberland River Association, Ky.

By 1800 the Baptists had established nearly fifty associations, active in the work of evangelization and powerful in promoting the unity, piety and mutual communion among their churches, systematizing their efforts and provoking others to good works.[1] They had proceeded from a single parent, center, the Philadelphia Association, mother of them all. They were based on common principles, possessed a common form of organization and similar aims. Their mutual relations were friendly, and a bond of unity had been provided for the American Baptist Churches. All that was now necessary for the creation of a national church was a common danger or a common paramount interest. This was furnished by the questions of education, missionary activities and the struggle for religious liberty in America.

Their national educational endeavor centered around the College of Rhode Island (Brown University).[2] This, the first Baptist College in the world, was conceived by James Manning, a graduate of the College of New Jersey and a member of the Philadelphia Association. Backus gives us the following account of its origin:

"On a voyage to Halifax, in July 1763, he (Manning) called in at Newport, and proposed the affair (to a number of Baptist gentlemen),

[1] Vedder, *op. cit.*, pp. 95-100; Burrage, H. S., *History of the Baptists in New England*, pp. 80-103; Nippold, *Handbuch der neusten Kirchengeschichte*, vol. iv, p. 51.

[2] Guild, *Life, Times and Correspondence of James Manning and the Early History of Brown University.*

> who liked it well; and though they met with some opposition, yet they obtained a charter for a college, in February 1764, from their legislature, in which the president was always to be a Baptist, and so were the majority of the corporation, though some of the Episcopal, Quaker, and Congregational denominations were to be of it. No religious test was ever to be imposed upon the scholars, though great care was taken about their morals.
>
> And no government on earth ever gave anything towards said building, or for the college fund; though vast sums had been given by the governments of Massachusetts and Connecticut to their colleges. But the buildings, library, and funds of this college were all produced voluntarily, and chiefly from the inhabitants of Providence, many of whom sprung from the planters of the first Baptist Church in America." [1]

From the first this college was considered a national affair by all sections, and we find that the Philadelphia Association in 1774 approved the plan already adopted by the Charleston and Warren Associations to request every Baptist to pay six pence annually for three successive years to their elders or some suitable person, the money to be paid to the treasurer of Rhode Island College.[2]

Possessed of Dr. Manning and Rhode Island College, together with Isaac Backus, the Warren Association assumes very great importance in the nationalization movement of this the constitution-making epoch of the church. As Backus, their historian, phrased it, they did "much to defend their privileges, as well as to unite and quicken each other in religion."[3]

This association was formed in 1767 by Dr. Manning with the assistance of the Rev. John Gano, from the Philadelphia Association, his brother-in-law,[4] who was made moderator, and the Rev. Isaac Backus who was made clerk. Four churches joined the association at

[1] Backus, *op. cit.*, pp. 183-184.
[2] Vedder, *op. cit.*, p. 212.
[3] Backus, *op. cit.*, p. 192.
[4] *Supra.*, pp. 122-123.

that time. In 1769 a plan of organization, drawn up by Dr. Manning, was adopted.

The aims and advantages of association were stated to be:

"1. That such a combination of churches is not only prudent, but useful, as has appeared even in America by the experience of upwards of sixty years. Some of the uses of it are: union and communion among ourselves; maintaining more effectually the order and faith once delivered to the saints; having advice in cases of doubt, and help in distress; being more able to promote the good of the cause, and becoming important in the eyes of the civil powers, as has already appeared in many instances on this Continent.

2. That such an Association is consistent with the independency and power of particular churches, because it pretends to be no other than an advisory council, utterly disclaiming superiority, jurisdiction, coercive right, and infallibility."[1]

The form of organization was as follows:

"1. The association to consist only of messengers chosen and sent by the churches. These messengers to be their ministers . . . . . together with some judicious brethren. Their expenses to be borne by the churches which send them.

2. With the messengers the churches send letters addressed to the Association. In those letters mention is made of the messengers, and their authority to act for their churches; also of the state of the churches touching their peace; their increase by baptism, and by letters dismissive and commendatory from other churches; touching their diminution by death, excommunication and dismission to other churches, and the present number of members. If any questions are to be put to the Association, any advice to ask, or business to propose, these are expressed in the said letters.

3. All matters to be determined in this Association by the suffrage of the messengers, except what are determinable by Scripture; such matters are never put to the decision of votes. All that speak are to address the moderator, who is to take care that none be interrupted while speaking, and that no other indecorum take place.

4. Churches are to be received into this Association by petitions setting forth their desire to be admitted, their faith, order and willingness to be conformable to the rules of the associated body. When a petition is read, and the matter ripened for a vote, the moderator states the question. Suffrage being given in favor of the petition, the said moderator

[1] Guild, *op. cit.*, p. 78.

declares that such a church is received into the Association, in token of which he gives the messengers the right hand of fellowship, and bids them take their seats.

5. The Association to meet annually, at Warren, on Tuesday next after the first Wednesday in September, at two o'clock in the afternoon, and to continue till business be finished. It is to be opened with divine service; after which a moderator and clerk are chosen; the letters from the churches are read; the names of the messengers are written, that they may be called over at after meetings; then business is attended to, and minutes thereof made; a circular letter to the churches is prepared and signed, and a copy of it sent to every church, containing the minutes of the Association, the state of the churches, when and by whom vacancies are to be supplied, who is to preach the next Association sermon, and whatever else is needful for the churches to know.

6. A connection to be formed and maintained between this Association and that of Philadelphia, by annual letter and messenger from us to them and from them to us.

7. The faith and order of this Association are expressed in confession put forth by upwards of a hundred congregations in Great Britain, in the year 1689, and adopted by the Association of Philadelphia, 1742. Some of the principles in said confession are: The imputation of Adam's sin to his posterity; the inability of man to recover himself; effectual calling by sovereign grace; justification by imputed righteousness; immersion for baptism, and that on profession of faith and repentance; congregational churches and their independency; reception into them upon evidence of sound conversion." [1]

At this meeting of 1769 three brethren from Philadelphia were present. Petitions to the General Courts of Massachusetts and Connecticut were prepared and a committee chosen to present them. "Many of the letters from the churches," says Backus, "mentioned grievous oppressions and persecutions from the 'standing order', especially the one from Ashfield, where religious tyranny has been carried to great lengths."[2] Accordingly the following plan to collect grievances was read and approved:

"Whereas, complaints of oppressions, occasioned by a non-conformity to the religious establishment in New England have been brought to

[1] Guild, *op. cit.*, 79-80.

[2] Backus, *op. cit.*, edition of 1784, vol. ii, p. 253; Guild, *op. cit.*, p. 80.

this Association; and whereas the laws obtained for preventing and redressing such oppressions have, upon trial, been found insufficient (either through defect in the laws themselves or iniquity in the execution thereof) and whereas humble remonstrances and petitions have not been duly regarded, but the same oppressive measures continue: This is to inform all the oppressed Baptists in New England that the Association of Warren (in conjunction with the Western or Philadelphia Association) is determined to seek remedy for their brethren where a speedy and effectual one may be had. In order to pursue this resolution by petition and memorial, the following gentlemen are appointed to receive well-attested grievances, to be by them transmitted to the Rev. Samuel Stillman of Boston; namely, Rev. Hezekiah Smith of Haverhill, Rev. Isaac Backus of Middleborough, Mr. Richard Montague of Sunderland, Rev. Joseph Meacham of Enfield, and Rev. Thomas Whitman of Groton in Connecticut." [1]

Guild observes:

"Gradually the Association won the confidence of the denomination, until in a few years it had extended over New England. By its means mutual acquaintance and harmony were promoted; the weak and the oppressed were relieved; errors in doctrine and in practice were exposed and guarded against; warnings against false teachers in religion were published; feeble and destitute flocks were provided with preachers; the college was materially aided and strengthened; students were encouraged to study for the ministry, and the gospel was preached in the wilderness. During the period of the Revolution it presented able addresses in behalf of civil and religious freedom to the Governments of Massachusetts and Connecticut and to the Continental Congress." [2]

A collection was made at the annual meeting for the widows and children of poor ministers. A society was incorporated to collect money to assist pious youths in obtaining learning, with a view to the ministry. A missionary society was founded to collect money to support travelling ministers and to instruct them and to direct them. Its benefits soon became visible to everybody.

Such activity led to rapid expansion. At the outbreak of the Revolution it extended well over Massachusetts and

[1] Guild, *op. cit.*, p. 81.
[2] *Ibid.*, pp. 81-82.

Rhode Island and into neighboring states. It included 27 churches with 393 members. Its activities throughout the Revolution were such as to encourage its growth and by 1783, it possessed 44 churches and 570 members.

The outstanding feature of its work and the one which caused the rapid growth of all Baptist communities in America was its championship of the cause of religious Freedom for America. To this end it collected grievances, appointed committees to compile them, addressed agents, committees, memorials, and petitions to the various political agents who either were responsible for the persecution or from whom redress and justice might be obtained. Isaac Backus was chairman of the committee on grievances from 1772 to 1782 and, in addition, he was agent for the Warren Association and various others before the courts and other governmental bodies. In him the Baptists developed a very efficient and, for them, a surprisingly autocratic official.

New England Baptists felt that the Revolution furnished them with their great opportunity for religious freedom. At the College Commencement in 1774, Dr. Manning, Hezekiah Smith, John Gano, and others proposed to Mr. Backus that he officially represent their church before Continental Congress. We have already[1] cited the official credential with which the Warren Association delegated Mr. Backus to present their position with respect to the Revolution.

Upon his arrival in Philadelphia, Mr. Backus immediately conferred with President Manning, with leading Quakers, and with the Philadelphia Association, then in session in that city, and a course of action was maped out. On the evening of October 14th, says Backus,

[1] *Supra.*, p. 118.

"there met at Carpenter's Hall, Thomas Cushing, Samuel Adams, John Adams and Robert Treat Paine, Esqrs., delegates from Massachusetts; and there were also present James Kinzie of New Jersey, Stephen Hopkins and Samuel Ward of Rhode Island, Joseph Galloway and Thomas Miflin, Esqrs., of Pennsylvania, and other members of Congress. Mr. Rhodes, Mayor of the city of Philadelphia, Israel and James Pemberton, and Joseph Fox, Esqrs., of the Quakers, and other gentlemen; also Elders Manning, Gano, Jones, Rogers, Edwards, etc., were present. The conference was opened by Mr. Manning, who made a short speech, and then read the memorial which we have drawn up."[1]

The Baptist memorial, copies of which were afterwards delivered to every member of Congress, together with Mr. Backus's *Appeal to the Public*,[2] which had been printed the year previous, was as follows:

"It has been said by a celebrated writer in politics, that but two things were worth contending for, — Religion and Liberty. For the latter we are at present nobly exerting ourselves through all this extensive continent; and surely no one whose bosom feels the patriotic glow in behalf of civil liberty, can remain torpid to the more ennobling flame of Religious Freedom.

The free exercises of private judgment, and the unalienable rights of conscience, are of too high a rank and dignity to be submitted to the decrees of councils, or the imperfect laws of fallible legislator. The merciful Father of mankind is the alone Lord of conscience. Establishments may be enabled to confer worldly distinctions and secular importance. They may make hypocrites, but cannot create Christians. They have been reared by craft or power, but liberty never flourished perfectly under their control. That liberty, virtue, and public happiness can be supported without them, this flourishing province (Pennsylvania) is a glorious testimony; and a view of it would be sufficient to invalidate all the most elaborate arguments ever adduced in support of them. Happy in the enjoyment of these undoubted rights, and conscious of their high import, every lover of mankind must be desirous, as far as opportunity offers, of extending and securing the enjoyment of these inestimable blessings.

[1] Backus, *op. cit.*, edition of 1871, vol. ii, pp. 200-202; Hovey, *op. cit.* pp. 200-214; 349-351.

[2] Backus, Isaac, *An Appeal to the Public for Religious Liberty, against the oppressors of the present day. "Brethren, ye have been called unto liberty; only use not liberty for an occasion to the flesh, but by love serve one another."* *Gal.* v. 13. Boston, 1773.

These reflections have arisen from considering the unhappy situation of our brethren, the Baptists, in the province of Massachusetts Bay, for whom we now appear as advocates; and from the important light, in which liberty in general is now beheld, we trust our representation will be effectual. The province of Massachusetts Bay, being settled by persons who fled from civil and religious oppression, it would be natural to imagine them deeply impressed with the value of liberty and nobly scorning a domination over conscience. But such was the complexion of the times, they fell from the unhappy state of being oppressed, to the more deplorable and ignoble one of becoming oppressors.

But these things being passed over, we intend to begin with the charter obtained at the happy restoration. This charter grants, 'that there shall be liberty of conscience allowed in the worship of God, to all Christians except Papists, inhabiting or which shall inhabit or be resident within this province or territory'."

Hereupon follows a history of the struggle of dissenters for liberty in Massachusetts and in conclusion the memorial sets forth:

"Men unite in society, according to the great Mr. Locke, with an intention in every one the better to preserve himself, his liberty and property. The power of the society, or Legislature constituted by them, can never be supposed to extend any further than the common good, but is obliged to secure every one's property. To give laws, to receive obedience, to compel with the word, belong to none but the civil magistrate; and on this ground we affirm that the magistrate's power extends not to the establishing any articles of faith or forms of worship, by force of laws; for laws are of no force without penalties. The care of souls cannot belong to the civil magistrate, because his power consists only in outward force; but pure and saving religion consists in the inward persuasion of the mind, without which nothing can be acceptable to God.

It is a just position, and cannot be too firmly established, that we can have no property in that which another may take, when he pleases, to himself; neither can we have the proper enjoyment of our religious liberties, (which must be acknowledged to be of greater value), if held by the same unjust and capricious tenure; and this must appear to be the case when temporary laws pretend to grant relief so very inadequate.

It may now be asked — What is the liberty desired? The answer is; as the kingdom of Christ is not of this world, and religion is a concern between God and the soul with which no human authority can intermeddle; consistently with the principles of Christianity, and according to the dictates of Protestantism, we claim and expect the liberty of worshipping God according to our consciences, not being obliged to support a ministry we cannot attend, while we demean ourselves as faithful subjects. These we have an undoubted right to, as men, as Christians and by charter as inhabitants of Massachusetts Bay." [1]

The outcome of the conference was unsatisfactory, for, as John Adams expressed it, "they might as well turn the heavenly bodies out of their annual and diurnal courses, as the people of Massachusetts at the present day from their meeting-houses and Sunday laws."[2] Samuel Adams intimated that "the complaint came from enthusiasts who made it a merit to suffer persecution."[3]

The meeting had not succeeded in establishing the Baptist cause as a national political grievance, and Backus and his supporters were obliged to carry the matter back to Massachusetts. But here they had at least upset the equipoise of the Bostonians and their Connecticut allies. Dr. Manning, in a letter dated December 2, 1774, quotes the Rev. Ezra Stiles as saying:

"That the Baptists had made an application to the Congress against the Massachusetts Bay; that the delegates of that province expected only a private interview with some of the Baptists; but instead of that, when they came they found a house full, etc.; that they were attacked and treated in the most rude and abusive manner; that the Baptists pretended they were oppressed, but, after all their endeavors, they could only complain of a poor fourpence; that they were ashamed of their errand, and gave up their point, except one or two impudent fellows, who, with Israel Pemberton, abused them in a most scandalous manner; that all the delegates present were surprised at and ashamed of them, and thought they complained without the least foundation." [4]

When the General Court of Massachusetts met a few weeks latter Backus was there with a memorial, November 22, 1774, in which the wrongs of his people were rehearsed

[1] Hovey, *op. cit.*, pp. 204-210.
[2] *Works of John Adams*, vol. ii, pp. 397-399.
[3] Burrage, *op. cit.*, p. 112.
[4] Hovey, *op. cit.*, p. 215.

and their demands for religious liberty fully insisted on.[1] The Provincial Congress, through its president, John Hancock, notified Mr. Backus, December 9, 1774, of their Resolution:

"That the establishment of civil and religious liberty to each denomination in the province, is the sincere wish of this Congress. But being by no means vested with powers of civil government, whereby they can redress the grievances of any person whatever, they therefore recommend to the Baptist churches, that when a General Assembly shall be convened in this colony, they lay the real grievances of said churches before the same, when and where this petition will most certainly meet with all that attention due to the memorial of a denomination of Christians so well disposed to the public weal of their country." [2]

Following this advice another memorial was presented to the Assembly at Watertown in 1775. This was referred to a committee of seven, three of whom were Baptists. The report of the committee being favorable, it was ordered that Dr. Asaph Fletcher, — a Baptist member of the committee, have liberty to bring in a bill for the redress of such grievances as he apprehended the Baptists to be under. The bill was reported and read once, but no action resulted.[3] Puritanism was too strongly entrenched in New England to yield to assault, even in the rear; the Baptists must win their fight elsewhere.

Meeting with no success before Continental Congress or the Massachusetts Assembly, the Warren Association next turn to a united Baptist Church of America, for relief. The Meeting of 1775,

"Agree that our agent and committee be desired to draw up a letter to all the Baptist societies on this continent, stating the true nature and importance of religious liberty, and signifying that we think that a

[1] *Hovey, op. cit.*, pp. 215-221.
[2] *Ibid.*, pp. 222-223.
[3] *Ibid.*, pp. 226-228.

general meeting of delegates from our societies in every colony is expedient, as soon as may be to consult upon the best means and methods of obtaining deliverance from various encroachments which have been made upon that liberty, and to promote the general welfare of our churches, and of all God's people throughout the land; and to desire that our friends in each Colony would communicate their sentiments concerning the design, and time and place of meeting, with all convenient speed."[1]

In accordance with this direction an address was prepared:

"To all Christian people in the American Colonies, and especially to those who are of the Baptist denomination."[2]

But a national convention of American Baptists did not result from this plea of the Massachusetts Baptists; the Virginia Baptists were to meet with success in their state struggle and a national organization was too gigantic a movement for Baptists as a whole to follow.

Missionary zeal was the third great force which tended to nationalize American Baptists. Here again we find the New Englanders in the van. In 1778 the Warren Association requested three of its members to visit "the Northern parts of our country." In 1779 a report of their labors was made, when "very agreeable accounts were received of their free reception in many places, and some instances of very remarkable and glorious effects of the gospel." The Philadelphia Association in 1778 "voted to raise a fund for the particular and express purpose of preaching the Gosepl among the back settlements."[3] The struggle for liberty was not to continue long enough to nationalize Baptists, the fields of education and missions were. Other New England Associations took up the

[1] Hovey, *op. cit.*, pp. 228-229.
[2] *Ibid.*, pp. 229-231.
[3] Burrage, *op. cit.*, pp. 134-154.

mission work[1] and the Massachusetts Baptist Missionary Society held its first meeting in the First Baptist Church of Boston, May 26, 1802. A national society was achieved in 1814 when delegates met in Philadelphia "to organize a plan for electing, combining and directing the energies of the whole denomination in one sacred effort for the sending the glad tidings of salvation to the heathen and to nations destitute of pure gospel light." This meeting organized "The General Missionary Convention of the Baptist Denomination in the United States of America for foreign Missions."

The effect of the War and independence upon the organization of Baptists can best be traced in Virginia where it appears most clear cut, in the leading Baptist union, The General Association of the Separate Baptists, and the organization into which this society grew.

The first meeting of the Virginia Separate Baptist Association was held in Craig's Meeting-house in May 1771. A moderator and a clerk were chosen and the following agreements were entered into:

"1. It is unanimously agreed that the association has no power or authority, to impose anything upon the churches; but that we act as an advisory council.

2. We believe we have a right to withdraw ourselves from any church that may neglect to correspond with us, and justify their conduct.

3. (Constitution of Churches). Any number of members that live at a distance too far to assemble with ease . . . . . at their monthly meeting, having first obtained leave from their church, have a right to petition any ordained minister of the same faith and order . . . . . to look into their stability, and if found ripe, to constitute them a church . .

4. (Ordination). Every ordained minister of the same faith . . . . . may administer the sacraments among them and with the help of their church ordain their elders and deacons . . . . . and in case they have made choice of a minister whom they desire to be examined and ordained, they may petition neighboring ministers to proceed in said

[1] Vedder, *op. cit.*, p. 135.

work, and on special occasions . . . . . one ordained minister with an ordained elder or elders may proceed in the ordination.

7. All matters brought before the association for their advice to be determined by a majority of voices.

8. It is agreed, that an itinerant minister may be ordained without applying to the association, by a presbytery of ministers . . . . . upon their examination and a recommendation of his doctrine and manner of life, from the church he is a member of.

9. It is agreed that a circular letter be sent by the Association to each church, informing them something of the heads of their business . . ."[1]

The Association of 1773, Dover, Goochland county, represented 34 churches and 3,195 members. It appointed four ministers to visit the Kehukee Regular Association and churches in order to investigate and report on their standing.[2]

The nationalizing movement is well exhibited in the 1774 meeting at Walker's Meeting-house in Amelia county. A letter was received from the Philadelphia Association together with a copy of their minutes; likewise the minutes of the Charleston Association were received and read. A radical effort at centralization was also attempted; Samuel Harris, for the Southern District, and John Waller and Elijah Craig, for the Northern District, were appointed "Apostles" to superintend the churches and report to the next Association. Semple gravely observes:

"The Apostles made their report to the next Association rather in discouraging terms, and no others ever were appointed. The judicious reader will quickly discover that this is only the old plan of bishops, etc., under a new name. In the last decision it was agreed that the office of Apostles, like that of prophets, was the effect of miraculous inspiration, and did not belong to ordinary times."[3]

[1] Semple, *History of the Rise and Progress of the Baptists in Virginia*, pp. 49-53.

[2] *Ibid.*, pp. 54-55.

[3] *Ibid.*, p. 59.

Thus the Virginia Baptists essayed a form of bishop and discarded this means of centralization, a form corresponding to the New England "Agent." This was radical procedure but they were preparing for great things; in 1775 they were to begin their campaign with the General Assembly for religious liberty.[1]

Committees were found effective and for a time the Association acted through such agencies. "A committee of seven members was appointed to take into consideration the civil grievances of Baptists, and make report," at the October meeting, 1778, Dupuy's Meeting-house, Powhatan county.[2] They noted certain abuses and recommended, "that two persons be appointed to wait on the next General Assembly and lay these grievances before them."

Further unification was also urged by this meeting, 1778, in a resolution,

> "That a society of churches combined to seek the mutual good of the whole is desirable: That it also promotes acquaintance among brethren, and affords opportunity to consult, respecting the best modes of counteracting national grievances: But Assoications are not to interfere with the internal concerns of churches, except where their advice is required by any church, in the way of query."

Herein is advocated a means of "national" action.[3]

In 1779 upon the report of the associational delegate to the General Assembly, Jeremiah Walker, it was; "Ordered, That our approbation of the said bill (For Religious Freedom), be transmitted to the public printers, to be inserted in the gazette."[4] The association was beginning to realize how much might be accomplished through

[1] *Supra.*, pp. 334-335; *Infra*, p. 364.
[2] Semple, *op. cit.*, p. 64.
[3] *Ibid.*, p. 65.
[4] *Ibid.*, p. 65; *infra*, p. 388.

memorial, petition and effective lobbyist. Jeremiah Walker, Reuben Ford, John Waller, and John Leland seem to have fulfilled all the requirements of the latter.

The October meeting at Sandy Creek Meeting-house in 1780 received a letter from a committee of the Regular Baptists, requesting that a similar committee be appointed by this, the Separate Association, to consider national grievances, in conjunction. Reuben Ford, John Williams, and E. Craig were accordingly appointed.[1]

A delegate from the Strawberry Association, Robert Stockton, was in attendance at the October meeting at the Dover Meeting-house, Goochland county, in 1782.[2] At this meeting it was decided that "having already secured their most important civil rights, they would hold only one more General Association, and then divide into districts but "to form some plan, to keep a standing sentinel for political purposes."

The Last General Association met at Dupuy's Meeting-house, Powhatan county, in October 1783. The war was over and it seemed essential that a new form of government be instituted; a General Committee was accordingly substituted for the General Association. It was resolved:

> "That our General, or Annual, Association cease, and that a General Committee be instituted, composed of not more than four delegates from each district association; to meet annually, to consider matters that may be for the good of the whole society, and that the present association be divided into four districts: Upper and Lower Districts, on each side of the James River."[3]

A motion was made by John Williams: "That as they were now about to divide into sections, they ought to adopt a confession of faith; by way of affording a standard

[1] Semple, *op. cit.*, p. 66.
[2] *Ibid.*, p. 67.
[3] *Ibid.*, p. 68.

of principles to subsequent times." It was then agreed to adopt the Philadelphia Confession of Faith, upon the following explanation:

"To prevent its usurping a tyrannical power, over the consciences of any; we do not mean that every person is to be bound to the strict observance of everything therein contained, nor do we mean to make it, in any respect superior or equal to the Scriptures, in matters of faith and practice; although we think it the best human composition of the kind now extant; yet it shall be liable to alterations, whenever the General Committee, in behalf of the Association, shall think fit."[1]

The General Committee of the Virginia Baptists was in existence from 1784 to 1799. It was at first composed of delegations from four associations; it was organized with a moderator and clerk and it adopted the following plan of government:

"1. The General Committee shall be composed of delegates, sent from all the district associations, that desire to correspond with each other.

2. No Association shall be represented in the General Committee by more than four delegates.

3. The Committee thus composed, shall consider all the political grievances of the whole Baptist Society in Virginia, and all references from the district associations, respecting matters which concern the Baptist society at large.

4. No petition, memorial or remonstrance, shall be presented to the General Assembly from any Association in connection with the General Committee, — All things of that kind shall originate with the General Committee."[2]

It appears that the General Committee was very well satisfied with the results of its modes of procedure as a rule. At its August meeting at Anderson's Meeting-house, Buckingham county, 1786, "Reuben Ford, who was appointed to wait upon the Assembly, with a memorial and petition against the bill for a general assessment; Reported, that he waited on the house of Assembly

[2] Semple, *op. cit.*, pp. 68-69.
[1] *Ibid.*, p. 70.

according to appointment; that the law for assessment did not pass; but, on the contrary, an act passed explaining the nature of religious liberty." "The Committee concurred in the report and declared themselves well pleased with the law above mentioned."[1]

The Ketocton or Regular Baptist Association sent delegates to this General Committee at this Anderson's Meeting-house gathering and they were received upon equal footing with those from the other associations. This gave rise to the following recommendation:

"It is recommended to the different Associations to appoint delegates to attend the next General Committee, for the purpose of forming a union with the Regular Baptists."[2]

Agreeable to appointment, the subject of the union of the Regular and Separate Baptists was taken up at the Dover Meeting-house session of the General Committee in August 1787. A happy and effectual reconciliation was accomplished and the distinction between Regulars and Separates disappeared, — all became the *United Baptist Churches* of *Virginia*.

Objections to the union on the part of the Separates related chiefly to matters which concern the communion. The Regulars complained that the Separates were not sufficiently explicit in their principles, having never published or sanctioned any confession of faith, and that they kept within their communion many who were professed Arminians.

Terms of the union were entered on the minutes in the following record:

"The committee appointed to consider the terms of union with our Regular Brethren, Reported; that they conceive the manner in which the

[2] Semple, *op. cit.*, p. 72.
[1] *Ibid.*, p. 73.

Regular Baptist Confession of Faith has been received by a former association, is the ground work for such union.

To prevent the confession of faith from usurping a tyrannical power over the conscience of any, we do not mean, that every person is bound to the strict observance of every thing therein contained; yet that it holds forth the essential truths of the gospel and that the doctrine of salvation by Christ and free unmerited Grace alone, ought to be believed by every Christian and maintained by every minister of the Gospel. Upon these terms we are united, — and desire hereafter that the names Regular and Separate, be buried in oblivion; and that, from henceforth, we should be known by the name of the *United Baptist Churches in Christ in Virginia*."[1]

The fame and power of the General Committee was increasing rapidly. At the March meeting of 1788 held in Williams' Meeting-house, Goochland county, the following religious political subjects were taken up:

"1. Whether the new Federal Constitution, which had now lately made its appearance in public, made sufficient provision for the secure enjoyment of religious liberty; on which, it was agreed unanimously, that, in the opinion of the General Committee, it did not.

2. Whether a petition shall be offered to the next General Assembly, praying the sale of the vacant glebes, ... as being public property; and accordingly, four persons were chosen from the General Committee to present their memorial, viz., Eli Clay, Reuben Ford, John Waller, and John Williams. (This object was gained in 1799).

3. Whether a petition should be offered to the General Assembly, praying that the yoke of slavery may be made more tolerable. Referred to the next session."[2]

It appears from the minutes of this session that a letter had been received from the Rev. Asa Hunt of Massachusetts, and the Rev. Lemuel Powers of New York, proposing a correspondence between the General Committee and the Northern Associations, to which proposal the General Committee readily agreed, and appointed Mr. Leland to visit as many of them as he could con-

[1] Semple, *op. cit.*, p. 74.
[2] *Ibid.*, pp. 76-77.

veniently. Letters of correspondence were also prepared. Hopes were entertained by some, about this time, of forming a general meeting to be composed of delegates from all the states in the union. This session also proposed the publication of *A History of the Rise and Progress of the Baptists in Virginia.*[1]

The August session of the General Committee, Dupuy's Meeting-house, Powhatan county (1788), received a letter from the Rev. James Manning, President of Rhode Island College, recommending and encouraging the Baptists of Virginia to erect a seminary of learning. This subject was taken up and the following decision was reached:

"Resolved, That a committee of five persons on each side of the James River, be appointed to forward the business respecting a seminary of learning; accordingly Samuel Harris, John Williams, Eli Clay, Simeon Walton and David Barrow were appointed on the South; and Robert Carter, John Waller, Wm. Fristoe, John Leland and Reuben Ford on the North side of the said river."[2]

The year of the establishment of the federal government for the United States marks the high-water influence of the General Committee. The August session of that year met in Richmond. Delegates from several associations were present. Letters and minutes of correspondence were received from various quarters. The usefulness of this General Committee in keeping up intercourse among the Baptists throughout the United States was recognized as inconceivable. From Georgia to Massachusetts they were known and they received occasionally from some and statedly from others, letters, minutes and other tokens of unity. The General Committee did in a sense represent the united Baptists of America. And in that capacity,

[1] Semple, *op. cit.*, p. 77.
[2] *Ibid.*, p. 78.

in fact if not officially, they prepared their address to the newly elected President of the United States and through them President Washington replied to the Baptists in general of the United States.[1]

This session proceeded with its plans for a seminary of learning and for the collection of documents of its history. Furthermore it legislated on the question of slavery as follows:

"Resolved, That slavery is a violent deprivation of the rights of nature, and inconsistent with a republican government, and therefore recommend it to our brethren, to make use of every legal measure to extirpate this horrid evil from the land; and pray Almighty God that our honorable legislature may have it in their power to proclaim the great jubilee consistent with the principles of good policy."[2]

The prestige of the General Committee fell much more rapidly than it had been created, the prey to the jealousy of fundamental Baptist principles. Baptist centralization throve on persecution by external enemies; these once removed, it was destroyed by internal forces.

The first business of the Nuckol's Meeting-house session in May 1791, Goochland county, was to consider whether they had not departed from their former plan. This question produced a long debate and it was determined that they had deviated from their original plan; that the original design was to consider only religious political grievances, and to seek for their redress. Therefore it was Resolved, That that part of the third article which contains these words, "And all references from the district associations respecting matters that may concern the whole body," be struck out.

This decision proved fatal to the rising prosperity of the General Committee. For from this session it declined in

[1] *Infra.*, pp. 507-508.
[2] Semple, *op. cit.*, pp. 79-80.

power so rapidly, that it was finally dissolved in 1799. This decision also seems the more mysterious as the Nuckol session was the fullest and the most respectable of any that had been held; all of the greatest of the Virginia Baptist preachers were present in addition to two or three from Georgia.[1]

The Tomahawk Meeting-house session of May 1792, Chesterfield county, completed the work of destruction begun by the Nuckol session. It was made a question whether the last meeting had not cramped the General Committee by the amendment to the constitution. In order to decide this point a committee was appointed to frame a resolution, which after some amendments, was adopted in the following words:

> After maturely deliberating on a variety of circumstances, your committee suppose that the business of the General Committee is to consider all the political grievances of the whole Baptist Society in Virginia, and all references from associations; as also other circumstances, which evidently relate to the external interest of the whole body of Baptists, and no other concerns whatever."[2]

After this self-denying ordinance there is no need to follow the Virginia Baptists further. They had built up a most powerful state politico-religious organism. This in turn had assumed considerable national power. Apparently it was the jealousy of the states-rights idea as applied to religion that caused the destruction of the General Committee. It continued to function feebly until 1799, when as a last act its Waller's Meeting-house session, Spottsylvania county, recommended to the associations that they form a plan for a general meeting of correspondence, to promote and preserve union and harmony among the churches.[3]

[1] Semple, *op. cit.*, pp. 80-83.
[2] *Ibid.*, pp. 83-84.
[3] *Ibid.*, p. 86.

Semple observes, "The War, though very propitious to the liberty of the Baptists, had an opposite effect upon the life of religion among them. As if persecution was more favorable to vital piety, than unrestrained liberty, they seem to have abated in their zeal, upon being unshackled from their manacles . . . . . God sent them liberty, and with it, leanness of soul."[1]

Congregationalists must be classed in the same "independent" group as Baptists.

To speak of the "nationalization" of denominations so "independent" in character may seem a Hiberianism. From the very earliest days of America's settlement, Puritanism was styled by the English observers "Independency or The American Way." This shows that even in the very spirit of individual congregational autonomy there lay an American or national characteristic. Congregational nationalism did not work itself out in hierarchical centralized institutions but in the new United States the New England Way grew into An American Way, no less loyal to the State than were the more braced-up centrally managed organizations. We will find, moreover, that nationalism caused a strengthening of central institutions even with Congregationalism.

No one has better phrased the New England view of centralization in religion than did Nathaniel Emmons in 1803. Emmons stands with Jonathan Edwards the Younger, John Smalley, and Timothy Dwight as the leaders of Congregational thought for this period. A native of East Haddam, Connecticut, Emmons was graduated from Yale in 1767. From 1773 to 1827 he was pastor of the Congregational Church at Franklin, Massachusetts. During this period he trained more than a hundred young

[1] Semple, *op. cit.*, p. 35.

men for the ministry. No man of the period exerted a greater influence on New England's religious thought. In opposing the establishment of State Associations for Massachusetts similar to those of Connecticut, in 1803, he said:

"Association leads to Consociation; Consociation leads to Presbyterianism; Presbyterianism leads to Episcopacy; Episcopacy leads to Roman Catholicism; and Roman Catholicism is an ultimate fact."

He declared that a Congregational Church was a "pure democracy," which placed every member of the church upon the same level, and gave "perfect liberty with order." The pastor was "but a mere moderator"; and, in respect to a voting, "stands upon the same ground as a private brother." "One church has as much power as another" and "there is no appeal from the authority of a particular church to any higher ecclesiastical tribunal."

The Reverend Philips Payson of Chelsea thus stated the theological basis of Congregational individualism, in debate on the subject of religious tests before the Massachusetts convention for ratifying the Federal Constitution, in 1788:

"The great object of religion being God Supreme, and the seat of religion in man being the heart or conscience, that is, the reason God has given us, employed on our moral actions, in their most important consequences, as related to the tribunal of God, hence I infer, that God alone is the God of conscience, and, consequently, attempts to erect human tribunals for the consciences of men are impious encroachments upon the prerogatives of God."[1]

This theory, however, did not lead New England Congregationalism to complete individualism or even to an advocacy of the separation of church and state. It did not even reduce in any way the exalted position of the

[1] *Debates in Convention*, p. 148; Backus, *op. cit.*, edition of 1871, p. 336.

ministry. For according to the Reverend Ezra Stiles, President of Yale College, "the pastors are orderly and regularly set apart to the ministry by the laying on of the hands of the presbytery, or of those who have regularly derived office power, in a lineal succession, from the apostles and Jesus Christ."[1] Individualism might prevail as to dogma or rather as to lack of dogma, but the church continued to remain an established state institution. With the state as its sponsor there was not much need for a separate strong centralized institution. The Reverend Isaac Backus, that New England Baptist apostle of religious liberty, could complain, "Great Britain has lost all her power here and our rulers have sworn to renounce all foreign power over America, and yet they compel the people to support ministers (Congregational) who claim a power of office from England. How shocking is this."[2] He adds, "In the year 1784, ... laws were made in Connecticut to force people to support such ministers, and the like was soon done in Massachusetts. The chief rulers of New Hampshire, for many years, were not of the Congregational denomination, and therefore the people did not suffer so much from them, as they did in Massachusetts and Connecticut, and so I have passed them over."[3]

When Emmons was arguing against centralism for the church in Massachusetts, he was but opposing institutions similar to those which the Connecticut clergy had used for a great many years. At the "Synod" of Saybrook in 1708 there had been adopted an organization consisting of "parishes" grouped into "consociations" for

[1] Stiles, Ezra, *Election Sermon, Preached May 8, 1783,* pp. 58-61; Thornton, *op. cit.*, pp. 474-475.

[2] Backus, *op. cit.*, abridged edition of 1804, p. 217.

[3] Backus, *op. cit.*, abridged edition of 1804, p. 218.

mutual counsel and help. The ministers were to meet in "Associations" for consultation, licensure, ordination and recommendation. Associations elected delegates to the annual "General Association," representative of the entire colony. True, the legal establishment of this Saybrook Platform was silently but finally repealed in the 1784 revision of the statute book, and the individual churches left free to adopt whatever scheme of doctrine, discipline, or organization they might severally elect and to alter the same at discretion. This did not much change the traditional state of Congregationalism. The organism remained as before, the establishment was continued until 1818.

Even the doctrines of the church were under the control largely of their central educational institution, Yale College, "The School of Prophets." In 1783 Ezra Stiles saw the power of Yale; he observed, "The colleges have been of singular advantage in the present day. When Great Britain withdrew all her wisdom from America, this Revolution found above two thousand in New England only, who had been educated in the colonies, intermixed among the people, and communicating knowledge among them."[1]

Each year in an election sermon the clergy told the legislators of the state what the Church would expect of its lawmakers; as it were, a religious petition was annually presented to the legislature, and the most powerful kind of a petition, — so much is exhortation greater than a written petition. And yearly the ministers of the state were called together at Yale College to listen to a sermon, the *conscio ad clericum*, representative of the latest wisdom of the beacon of congregationalism.

[1] Thornton, *op. cit.*, p. xxxiv.

We find the General Association of Connecticut, in its post-Revolutionary anxiety about religion, taking thought to this *conscio ad clericum.* At Norwich in 1785 the following minute was adopted:

"Upon representation that the lecture the day after commencement at New Haven is not attended upon by ministers in general and thereby the design thereof is, much frustrated, the opinion of this association is asked, whether it is advisable, said lecture be continued? This Association taking into consideration the general design thereof, are unwilling it should be discontinued; therefore would earnestly recommend it to the particular associations to desire those of their body who may attend commencements, not to suffer any little inconveniences to prevent their attendance upon a service designed for their profit; lest they give occasion to its being said that ministers are as unmindful of obligation to attend religious services as others." [1]

And at Berlin in 1787 it was,

"Voted that it be a standing rule that the preacher of the *conscio ad clericum* at Yale College, the day after commencement, be appointed in that association where the General Association shall set the preceding June." [2]

In 1770 the General Association of Connecticut "earnestly recommend it to the several Associations to prosecute such measures as they shall think most expedient to revive brotherly watchfulness and Church Discipline,"[3] and in 1771, "finding that no return from any association hath been made . . . . . and being desirous of promoting so good a design and observing with grief and concern the declining state of our church for want of Gospel Discipline, do recommend to the several associations to take this matter into serious consideration; and desire they would send to the next General Association

[1] *Records of the General Association,* p. 18.
[2] *Ibid,* p. 123.
[3] *Ibid.,* p. 68.

their resolutions or opinion on the following questions, viz:

Whether it is not the indispensable duty of Christian churches to maintain Gospel discipline?

What can be done to restore Gospel discipline in our churches?"[1]

Action was slow; in 1772 "but three of them have returned answers."[2] However in 1773 "papers were read on the subject . . . . . sent in from several of the particular associations," and a committee was voted "to collect some general things into form from said papers or exhibits, and prepare the same to be laid before the next General Association."[3] The report of the committee was read at the 1774 General Association[4] and another committee was appointed to "draw up something upon the subject . . . . . to be recommended to the several churches of this colony."[5] The report of this committee was soon ready, and upon being read was ordered filed.[6] Another committee was then appointed to draw up a Draft upon Church Government, to be presented to the General Association at an adjourned meeting in September.[7]

The report on Church Discipline was brought in by the committee at the special meeting at New Haven in 1774;[8] and the General Association adopted certain "thoughts upon that subject" and recommended their practice to the churches. Chief of these was in the fourth section of their recommendations which reads, ...

"We propose, that each church choose a small number of the Brethren as a Committee of Inspection, Inquiry and Information, to act with or by

[1] *Records of the General Association*, p. 70.
[2] *Ibid.*, p. 71.
[3] *Ibid.*, pp. 73-74.
[4] *Ibid.*, p. 75.
[5] *Ibid.*, pp. 75-76.
[6] *Ibid.*, p. 76.
[7] *Ibid.*, p. 76.
[8] *Ibid.*, p. 81.

direction of the Pastor, who upon hearing anything of their members, which they apprehend to be matter of scandal and church censure, are to consider themselves as under obligations to make inquiry, examine evidence, etc. . . . . . If they find it necessary . . . . . to exhibit a formal written complaint to the church and support the charge with . . . . . light and evidence . . . . . that the church may proceed against such offenders according to the Laws of Christ's Kingdom."[1]

The sum total of all the activity of the General Association in four years of agitation (1770-1774) on the subjects of church discipline and government was a mild recommendation to the several churches and pastors. The condition of the churches was not improved thereby; and the matter was soon again before the body for consideration.

In 1779, "A motion from the West Association in New London County, was . . . . . laid before the association by their delegates to this effect, 'Considering the dark aspect upon our churches in the discouragement lying upon candidates entering into the ministry, and the present distress and difficulties of them that are already in office — from whence we fear these churches may be left without lights in the candlestick — we instruct our delegates to lay our sentiments before the General Association, and join (if it be thought proper) to call a convention of the clergy of the state, appointing time and place where it may be thought most convenient to deliberate upon these subjects. Two things have been upon our minds: viz, That an address be made to the rulers and people of this state, showing our apprehension of the danger and the propriety of some exertion to save the churches from ruin, or that a modest, dutiful representation be made to the Honorable Assembly of this state, in their next session in October, of these our apprehensions, praying their honors to take the same into consideration and do as wisdom may direct."[2]

This motion was considered and after much discussion a proposal for a convention of the clergy of the state was negated:[3] and it was decided "that they make an address to the people at large" and a committee was named to

[1] *Records of the General Association*, pp. 81-84.
[2] *Ibid.*, p. 102.
[3] *Ibid.*, p. 103.

prepare this. The committee reported and their draft was approved, and it was ordered that it be printed, and it was recommended that it be publicly read in the several congregations of the state.[1] Also a committee was appointed to draft an address in the General Assembly.[2] In 1783,

"The General Association is . . . . . . of opinion that the matter is of so great and serious importance as to require the attention of ministers and people in general, and therefore the General Association appoint . . a committee to consider the matter at large. The committee is desired to obtain the best advice they can of ministers and other gentlemen of character in this state, as to what further measures may be expedient, and make report to the next General Association. The first meeting of the committee is appointed to be at Yale College, in New Haven, the day after Commencement."[3]

Again as earlier, the result of all this deliberation was but a feeble recommendation made by the General Association in 1784:

"This association, after deliberating and conversing largely upon the subject, is of opinion, that in cases where there may be reason to apprehend a faulty neglect of proper endeavors, in any destitute church to settle a minister over them in the Lord, it is the duty of those pastors, who are in the vicinity, to take with them some respectable characters from among the brethren of their churches, and obtain a conference with the members of such destitute church, and in a candid Christian manner enquire into the causes of their neglect; and if they shall find them guilty of censurable negligence, to inculcate upon them the importance of Gospel ordinances, and (if possible) to persuade them to pay a proper attention to the matter and if such measures should prove ineffectual, and said church continue criminally negligent, after due pains taken, that it is the duty of such neighboring pastors and brethren, to exhibit a complaint against such church to the moderator of the Consociation to which it belongs, if consociated, that it may be dealt with as walking disorderly, and cut off from the Body if irreclaimable; and if said church be unconsociated that it is the duty of the churches in communion with it, to

[1] *Records of the General Association*, p. 103.
[2] *Ibid.*, p. 103.
[3] *Ibid.*, pp. 114-115.

withdraw communion from it, if found pertinaciously offending against the Laws of Christ in the above particular. But that those individuals of such offending church, as appear disposed to walk orderly, if any such there be, ought to be taken under the protection of neighboring sister churches, or the consociation, if consociated."[1]

Apparently the Congregationalists would do very little to strengthen their existing central organization. It is in the line of missionary activity alone, that such a movement is evidenced as successful. Here again Connecticut was in the lead through its General Association. At the Mansfield meeting of 1774 the following minute was recorded,

"The Association taking into consideration the state of the Settlements now forming in the wilderness to the Westward and Northwestward of us, who are most destitute of a preached Gospel, many of which are of our Brethren Emigrants from this Colony, think it advisable that an attempt should be made to send missionaries among them, and for obtaining a support for such missionaries would recommend it to the several ministers in this colony to promote a subscription among their people for this purpose. Upon which it was voted that the preceding conclusion together with the form of subscription be printed and sent to the several ministers in this colony."[2]

A missionary organization was established by the special session of the General Association at New Haven in the Fall. It was decided that two pastors go for a tour of from five to six months . . . . . "if the committee are able to provide for their support so long." "That one person be appointed in each county to receive the subscription or donation made, ... and give their receipt to the person from whom they receive them." "That a committee of three persons be appointed to receive these donations from the receivers in the several counties, and to give their receipts therefor. This com-

[1] *Records of the General Association*, pp. 116-117.
[2] *Ibid.*, p. 76.

mittee to appoint to the missionaries their support; to pay such sums to them, as they may see proper to appoint from the donations received by them; to direct the missionaries in any thing they shall judge necessary where not particularly directed by the General Association; (to) appoint other missionaries in case of the failure of any appointed by this body; . . . . . to account to the General Association yearly for the disposal of the monies received by them; to lay before this body the proceedings of the missionaries . . . . . their success . . . . . the state of the place wherein they may discharge their mission, etc. This committee to continue during the pleasure of the Association."[1] Receivers were named, the committee appointed, and three missionaries were named, "any two to go as missionaries as agreed." According to instruction given by the General Association;

"These missionaries are directed to travel through the Settlements in the wilderness to the Northwestward of this colony; but not to proceed further Northward than the Northern boundary of the Province of New York, where they shall judge their services may be most likely to be beneficial, excepting so far as they shall be more particularly instructed by this committee. They are directed to perform all parts of the ministerial office as Providence shall open the door. They are directed to set out upon their mission sometime next Spring . . . . . to keep an exact journal of their proceedings, and give as accurate an account as possible of the state of the several places they pass through that the General Association may be better able to determine where to send their missionaries in coming times."[2]

It was moreover, "Voted that the following advertisement be published in the several newspapers in this colony" wherein the names of the various authorized agents for collection of the funds were designated."[3]

[1] *Records of the General Association*, pp. 79-80.
[2] *Ibid.*, p. 80.
[3] *Ibid.*, p. 81.

Concord and Lexington interfered seriously with this prerevolutionary plan for missions. At various times during the war and immediately thereafter the matter was mentioned in the General Association, but it was not until 1788 that there was serious thought given to active resumption of the effort. Then it is recorded that, —

"A committee (was appointed) to take into consideration the address of the Association of the Western District in New Haven County, respecting the state and circumstances of the New Settlements in the States of Vermont and New York, with respect to the preaching of the Gospel, and the necessity of there being some measures taken to send suitable missionaries to preach the Gospel, gather churches, and administer Gospel ordinances among them; and to report what is proper to be done thereon." [1]

In 1791 a missionary was approved; in 1798 the General Association organized a Missionary Society; and in 1802 this was chartered by the Connecticut legislature. Even that champion of extreme Congregationalism, Emmons, succumbed to the force of the movement and in 1799 accepted the presidency of the Massachusetts Missionary Society.

[1] *Records of the General Association*, p. 125.

PART THREE

THE STATE AND RELIGION

CHAPTER XIII

SEPARATION OF CHURCH AND STATE

Separation of Church and State is one of America's greatest contributions to modern religion and politics. The adoption of this as a political principle marks an epoch in the history of mankind. Previously at least half the wars of Europe and half the internal troubles since the founding of Christianity had had a religious basis.[1] America put an end to religious wars: for herself through the acts of the period on constitution-making; for the world at large through the power of the example thus set.

The epochal significance of this can only be grasped when one stops to realize that Christianity was thereby surrendering a privilege which it had held for nearly fifteen hundred years. In 1786 Christianity in Virginia voluntarily renounced a state position which had existed for Christianity at large ever since Constantine in 313 A.D. had admitted Christianity into the "Trust of State Religions."

It should not be thought that this separation of state and church was in any way a blow aimed at American religion, although this has frequently been asserted. Baird holds that, "now none of Mr. Jefferson's admirers will consider it slanderous to assert that he was a very bitter enemy to Christianity, and we may even assume that he wished to see not only the Episcopalian Church separated from the state in Virginia, but the utter overthrow of everything in the shape of a church

[1] Bryce, *American Commonwealth,* 1st edition, vol. ii, p. 554.

throughout the country.[1] It was not through hostility to religion but because of a new phase of religious conviction that the issue rose in America. It resulted from the rivalry of many religious enthusiasts, all of whom were Christians. Judge Story was of the opinion that: "The real object of the amendment (first) was not to countenance, much less to advance Mahometanism, or Judaism, or infidelity, by prostrating Christianity; but to exclude all rivalry among Christian sects, and to prevent any national ecclesiastical establishment, which should give to an hierarchy the exclusive patronage of the national government. It thus sought to cut off the means of religious persecution (the vice and pest of former ages), and the power of subverting the rights of conscience in matters of religion, which have been trampled upon almost from the days of the Apostles to the present age."[2] Separation of church and state was to promote the Christian character of the American nation. Here again we must recall that "nation" is greater than "state" and that "religion" is above "church". The separation was merely intended to keep the church out of politics and vice versa.

Many seem to think that separation was a natural and inevitable result of the separation of the colonies from the mother country. But the establishments in America had always been colonial rather than imperial. The political connections of the churches were with the colonial governments rather than with the mother country. Their political ties with England were incidental, resulting from the fact that the colonies themselves were supposed to

[1] Baird, *op. cit.*, p. 106.
[2] Story, *Commentary on the Constitution*, abridged edition, 1833, pp. 701-702.

operate under English law. So when the colonies became independent states, the alliance that had subsisted between certain colonies and certain churches was not necessarily affected. Churches remained, as previously, part and parcel of those states, and we have the spectacle of fights for religious freedom going on not only in the various states but also in the nation as a whole.

Dissolution of the connections between church and state was not primarily an act of the national government; rather it fell chiefly within the province of state jurisdiction. As we shall see Continental Congress evaded the issue of religious freedom when it was first presented.[1] In fact even after the Federal Constitution had been adopted, the matter of the place of religion was still undecided. The Magna Charta of religious freedom in America, in so far as it affects the nation as a whole, is to be found in the first amendment to the Constitution. This was the price for ratification demanded by certain states, where the issue had already been met in its state form. It came in response to the demand that the Central Government should not have the power to interfere with that religious freedom which had already been extorted from the State Government. In a sense the guarantee contained in the Federal Constitution is a negative one, as it protects against interference only on the part of the Central Government; it does not guarantee religious freedom to the individual, each state is left at liberty to adopt whatever policy it wishes relative to the question. There is still nothing in the Federal Constitution to prevent the individual states from establishing religion if they so desire.

Separation of church and state was not exclusively or

[1] *Infra*, pp. 415-416.

even principally the work of Thomas Jefferson, as is so often stated. Jeffersonians are apt to appropriate the works of others to their patron saint; and his enemies have at times charges him with this as a crime.[1] Jefferson was himself a skillful phrase-maker and composed his own epitaph, "Here was buried Thomas Jefferson, author of the Declaration of Independence, of the statute of Virginia for religious freedom, and father of the University of Virginia." This still does not constitute Jefferson the foremost champion of religious freedom in America. It is true that the Virginia law was the first of its kind in America, — even in Christendom; it is equally true that it was phrased by Jefferson. But as students of historic origins, we will find that the issue of "religious liberty" was brought forward by James Madison in Virginia. And even Madison, rather than originating the idea, learned it from his Baptist neighbors of Orange County, Virginia. He had witnessed their persecution, had listened to their pleas for freedom, and had decided to champion their cause. Primarily then, separation of church and state in America, resulted from the initial efforts of small bodies of persecuted sects; Baptists, Presbyterians, Catholics, Quakers, etc., who made use of the spirit of the Revolution to demand religious freedom in exchange for another, — to the majority a more important natural right, political freedom.

[1] Baird, *op. cit.*, p. 111, ascribes authorship of this act to Jefferson but imputes his interest therein to the basest motives: "It (the Act) gave its author great satisfaction, not because it embodied the principle of eternal justice, but because, by putting all religious sects on an equality, it seemed to degrade Christianity, and 'to comprehend', to use his own words, 'within the mantel of protection the Jew and the Gentile, the Christian and the Mohammedan, the Hindoo and infidel of every denomination,' It was this that made the arch-infidel chuckle with satisfaction— not, we repeat, that the great principles imbodied in the measure were right."

To the Baptists of Massachusetts and Rhode Island belongs the glory of initiating the American conflict for religious liberty. The most serious advocate of religious freedom in America, and the man to make the first onslaught for it, was Isaac Backus, Agent for the Baptists of Massachusetts and Rhode Island. We have already[1] told of his assault upon Continental Congress, and of the methods employed by the skillful Massachusetts politicians to prevent any official notice being taken of the matter. But even though no Congressional action resulted, the Baptists had, indeed, succeeded in giving to the cause of religious freedom in America a semi-official national political standing.

Evaded in Philadelphia, Backus took his fight back to the stronghold of Congregationalism. Early in 1774 he had expressed his views as follows in a letter to John Adams, January 19, 1774 . . . . .

"I fully concur with your grand maxim, that it is essential to liberty that representation and taxation go together. Well, then, since people do not vote for representatives in our legislature from ecclesiastical qualifications, but only, by virtue of those which are of a civil and worldly nature, how can representatives thus chosen have any right to impose ecclesiastical taxes? Yet they have assumed and long exercised such a power. For they assume a power to compel each town and parish in this Province to settle a minister, and have empowered the majority of the inhabitants to give away as much of their neighbor's estates as they please to their minister; and if they refuse to yield it to them, then to take it by force. And I am bold in it that taxes laid by the British Parliament upon America are not more contrary to civil freedom, than these taxes are to the very nature of liberty of conscience, which is an essential article in our character . . . . . Two thousand dollars will not make good the damages that the Baptists in this Province have sustained within these ten years, by being taxed to the other party, and by suing for their rights before judges and jurors who were of that party." [2]

[1] *Supra.*, pp. 117-120, 330-334.
[2] Hovey, *op. cit.*, pp. 196-197.

The Provincial Congress at Cambridge, December 9, 1774, "on reading the memorial of the Rev. Isaac Backus, Agent to the Baptist churches in this government: Resolved, That the establishment of civil and religious liberty, to each denomination in the province, is the sincere wish of this Congress; but being by no means vested with powers of civil government, whereby they can redress the grievances of any person whatever; they therefore recommend to the Baptist churches, that when a General Assembly shall be convened in this colony, they lay the real grievances of said church before the same, when and where this petition will most certainly be met with all that attention due to the memorial of a denomination of Christians, so well disposed to the public weal of their country.

(Signed) By order of the Congress,

JOHN HANCOCK, President."[1]

Backus came before the regular Congress of Massachusetts in 1775 again with his *Memorial*; which *Memorial* was submitted to the Assembly, read, and referred to a committee. The committee's report was favorable and a time was set for a second reading; but other more pressing matters of 1775, crowded it out and nothing more was done about the matter. Whereupon the Warren Association sent out an address "To all Christian people in the American Colonies, and especially to those who are of the Baptist denomination."[2]

The Baptists of Massachusetts, led by Backus, continued their fight for years. The constitution of 1778

[1] *Journal of Each Provincial Congress of Massachusetts in 1774 and 1775*, edition of Lincoln, Boston, 1838, pp. 65-67; Hovey, *op. cit.*, pp. 222-223.

[2] Hovey, *op. cit.*, pp. 229-231; *supra*, pp. 334-335.

contained as its thirty-fourth article, "The free exercise and enjoyment of religious profession and worship shall forever be allowed to every denomination of Protestants in this state." This constitution was rejected by a large majority. The constitution of 1779, adopted what we may consider the Massachusetts principle, which "withheld authority for the legislature, and asserted *the right and duty of the legislature to authorize and require the several towns, parishes, precincts, and other bodies, politic, or religious societies to make suitable provision at their own expense, for the instruction of the public worship of God.*" Baptists continued to protest; the Warren Association asserted, September 1780, "We . . . . . enter our protest against the power claimed in the Third Article of the declaration of rights in the new plan of government, introduced among us."[1]

The Massachusetts form of establishment was not given up until 1833. Massachusetts' Baptists had fought a good fight but the honor of working out the principle of separation of church and state was to belong to Virginia. Backus was to envy the completeness of the triumph of the Baptists over Virginia Episcopalians. Writing from Middleborough, Massachusetts, for the July-October, 1 . . . . number of the Rippon *Register* he said: "Now their power is so gone that Episcopalian worshippers are but a small sect in that state, and have no power to demand a farthing from any man for the maintenance of their ministers; nor has any tax been gathered by force to support any denomination of Christians for three years past. Equal Liberty of Conscience is established as fully as words can express it. O! when shall it be so in New England! However, God is working wonders here."[2]

[1] Backus, edition of 1871, *op. cit.*, p. 229. [2] *Rippon Register*, p. 94.

The American principle of separation of church and state was first adopted by the state of Virginia. There were numerous main reasons for this separation.

First and foremost as a cause for disestablishment was the prevalence of dissent even in Virginia; it has been estimated that from one-half to two-thirds of the population were non-Episcopalians.

Again, the official clergy were not even in harmony with their own laity. In the first place the clergy were, as some one remarked, "a gentlemen's club," which remained Tory, attached to the mother country, "by the circumstance of birth and bond . . . . . by the oath of allegiance,"[1] while the laity was preponderately patriotic. Also the religion and morality of many of the clergy was repellent to the high type of Virginia manhood. "Had the doctrines of the Gospel," wrote the Reverend Samuel Davis, a Presbyterian clergyman in Virginia, "been solemnly and faithfully preached of the Established Church, I am persuaded there would have been but few dissenters in these parts of Virginia; for their first objections were not against the peculiar rites and ceremonies of that Church, much less against her excellent articles, but against the general strain of the doctrines delivered from the pulpit, in which the articles were opposed, or (which was more common) not mentioned at all; so that, at first, they were not properly dissenters from the original constitution of the Church of England, but the most strict adherents of it, and only dissented from those who had forsaken it.[2] Reverend Davis does not condemn quite all of the clergy. "I have reason to hope," he writes,

[1] Hawks, *op. cit.*, p. 135-136.
[2] Davis, *Narrative of the State of Religion among Dissenters in Virginia*, p. 6.

"there are and have been a few names in various parts of the colony, who are sincerely seeking the Lord, and groping after religion in the communion of the Church of England."[1] The historian of the early Virginia Church, Hawks, gives an excellent exposition of the low morality of the clergymen of the colony. While a law passed by the assembly of 1776 read: "that such ministers as shall become notoriously scandalous by . . . . drunkenness, swearing, fornication, or other heinous and crying sins, and shall thereof be lawfully convicted, shall for each such heinous crime and wickedness, etc."[2] Distrust of their clergy undoubtedly aided disestablishment. It went even farther; in the post-Revolutionary reorganization of Episcopalianism the Southerners were to be the champions of the layman, lay-representation even to the point where it practically eliminated the clergy.[3]

Baptist polity aided its Americanization case. The Baptist organization was the most democratic of the Protestant bodies. Each church was a little republic in which each member possessed and maintained equal rights with his fellow. Such a system appealed powerfully to the political instincts of the Virginia leaders, Henry, Mason, Jefferson, and Madison. Baptists had inherited the will to freedom. They were the first and only religious denomination to strike for independence from Great Britain and for religious liberty previous to the declaration of national independence.[4]

This honor has been claimed for the Presbyterians of Virginia; Baird writes, "The first body of clergymen of

[1] Davis, *op. cit.*, p. 5; cf. Muzzey, *Thomas Jefferson*, p. 61.

[2] Hawks, *Protestant Episcopal Church in Virginia*, pp. 64-65; Hening, *op. cit.*, vol. ii, p. 384.

[3] *Supra*, p. 201.

[4] James, *Struggle for Religious Freedom in Virginia*, p. 197.

any denomination in America that . . . . . identified themselves with the cause of freedom, and independence was the comparatively numerous and very influential Presbytery of Hanover in Virginia in a memorial recommending the separation of Church and State."[1] Virginia Presbyterians, previous to the Declaration of Independence contented themselves with a demand for their rights under the Act of Toleration; it was not until the Revolution had been accomplished and Virginia had thrown off her allegiance to Great Britain that they united with the Baptists in an effort to pull down the establishment. Even this they did in an opportunistic manner for when they thought they saw a chance for themselves to become a part of an establishment they wavered, and for the moment deserted the cause of religious liberty. This delayed the achievement of the ultimate victory. But this wavering is not surprising in view of Presbyterian polity which since the days of Calvin had heartily approved of an establishment, providing they were it.

Establishment had been accompanied in Virginia by heresy laws of such extreme severity as to defeat their own ends. They could not be enforced, and they were the best possible object lesson of the dangers of establishment. Had they been enforced they would have brought Thomas Jefferson to the stake. To deny the Trinity was punishable with three years imprisonment and a Unitarian or Free-thinker was an unfit custodian for his own children.

The Baptists especially had been subject to violent persecutions. During the co-called "Period of the Great Persecution," 1768 to 1774, they had been whipped, beaten, arrested, fined, imprisoned (sometimes on bread

[1] Baird, *Religion in America*, p. 106; *supra*, pp. 78-81.

and water), and in other ways shamefully abused. The evidence for this is overwhelming. Semple, the Baptist historian records,

"The rage of the persecutors had in no wise abated (1771); they seemed sometimes to strive to treat the Baptists and their worship with as much rudeness and indecency as was possible. They often insulted the preachers in time of service, and would ride into the water and make sport when they administered baptism. They frequently fabricated and spread the most groundless reports, which were injurious to the character of the Baptists." "But," he adds, "it is worthy to remark, that generally the Baptist cause has flourished most extensively where it met with most severe opposition." [1]

Some were whipped by individuals, several fined. "They (Chesterfield County) kept up their persecution after other counties had laid it aside."[2] It seems by no means certain that any law in force in Virginia authorized the imprisonment of any person for preaching. The law for the preservation of peace, however, was so interpreted, as to answer this purpose, and accordingly, whenever, the preachers were apprehended, it was done by a peace warrant."[3]

Fristoe writes, "The enemy, not contented with ridicule and defamation, manifested their abhorrence to the Baptists in another way. By a law then in force in Virginia, all were under obligations to go to church, several times in the year; the failure subjected them to fine. Little notice was taken of this omission, of members of the Established church; but so soon as the 'New Lights' were absent, they were presented by the Grand Jury, and fined according to law."[4] "When persecutors found religion

[1] Semple, *History of the Rise and Progress of the Baptists in Virginia*, p. 19.
[2] Semple, *op. cit.*, p. 207.
[3] *Ibid.*, p. 14.
[4] Fristoe, *History of the Ketocton Baptist Association*, p. 69.

could not be stopped in its progress by ridicule, defamation, and abusive language, the resolution was to take a different step and see what that would do; and the preachers in different places were apprehended by magisterial authority, some of whom were imprisoned."[1] "They were charged with design . . . . . when once they supposed themselves sufficiently strong, that they would fall on their fellow subjects, massacre the inhabitants and take possession of the country."[2]

Leland notes that, "About thirty of the preachers were honored with a dungeon, and a few others besides. Some of them were imprisoned as often as four times, besides all the mobs and perils they went through."[3] And we are informed by Dr. Bailey that, "the father of Henry Clay was thus imprisoned."[4]

The *Journals of the House of Delegates* disclose, November 14, 1778, a petition from Jeremiah Walker, one of the most prominent Baptist preachers, praying for the reconsideration of "his being taxed with prison charges" for his time in jail "for preaching." To which the Committee for Religion responded with a resolution, November 20; "That the petition be rejected as Walker's offence had been a breach of the Peace."[5]

The Episcopalian, Hawks, admits that, "No dissenters in Virginia experienced for a time harsher treatment than did the Baptists. They were beaten and imprisoned; and cruelty taxed its ingenuity to devise new modes of punishments and annoyance."[6]

[1] Fristoe, *op. cit.* pp. 79-80.
[2] *Ibid.*, p. 65.
[3] Leland, *Writings*, p. 107.
[4] Bailey, *The Trials and Victories of Religious Liberty in America.*
[5] *Journals of House of Delegates*, Nov. 14 and 20, 1778.
[6] Hawks, *op. cit.*, p. 121.

One of the most convincing indictments of the establishment was written by James Madison, January 24, 1774, in a letter to a college classmate, Bradford of Philadelphia, of the New Jersey College (Princeton). This letter is evidence of why Madison, the neighbor of the persecuted Baptists of Brown County, became the early champion of "religious liberty."

"If the Church of England had been the established and general religion in all the Northern colonies, as it has been among us here, and uninterrupted tranquillity had prevailed throughout the continent, it is clear to me that slavery and subjection might and would have been gradually insinuated among us. Union of religious sentiments begets a surprising confidence, and ecclesiastical establishments tend to great ignorance and corruption; all of which facilitates the execution of mischievous projects . . . . . .

I want again to breath your free air . . . . . Poverty and luxury prevail (in Virginia) among all sorts: pride, ignorance, and knavery among the priesthood, and vice and wickedness among the laity. This is bad enough, but it is not the worst I have to tell you. That diabolical, hell-conceived principle of persecution rages among some; and, to their eternal infamy, the clergy can furnish their quota of imps for such business. This vexes me the worst of anything whatever. There are at this time in the adjacent county not less than five or six well-meaning men in close jail for publishing their religious sentiments, which, in the main, are very orthodox. I have neither patience to hear, talk, or think of anything relative to this matter; for I have squabbled and scolded, abused and ridiculed, so long about it, to little purpose, that I am without common patience. So I must beg you to pity me, and pray for the liberty of conscience."[1]

The Baptists were not slow to discover the advantageous position in which the political situation had placed them. Their numerical strength was such as to make it important for either side to secure their influence. Fristoe writes, "The business then (1776) was to unite, as an oppressed

[1] *Writings of James Madison,* edition of 1865, vol. i, pp. 1-12; Hunt edition, vol. i, pp. 19-21; Rives, *Life and Times of Madison,* vol. i, p. 43.

people, in using our influence and give our voices in electing members of the State Legislature — members favorable to religious liberty and the rights of conscience. Although the Baptists were not numerous, when there was anything near a division among other inhabitants in a country, the Baptists, together with their influence, gave caste to the scale, by which means many a worthy and useful member was lodged in the House of Assembly and answered a valuable purpose."[1] To the Church of England the course of the Baptists seemed vindictive and relentless; yet it was but the relentless vindictiveness of the logic of the situation, the battle for religious freedom.

The establishment fortified itself behind the barricade of "religious toleration" which had been granted only a few years previously through the efforts of the Presbyterians, 1763-1768.[2] To be sure it was not a liberal toleration but under certain onerous conditions dissenters might obtain legal toleration. From 1758 to 1775, efforts were made to liberalize this act of toleration. A new bill was brought forward in the assembly of 1772; from 1772 to 1775 Virginia waged a war of petitions, for and against this new toleration bill. But among all the petitions presented, up to 1775, not one asked for the abolition of the establishment; not one protests state taxation for the support of religion; not one sought religious liberty. Plainly the struggle for "Religious Liberty" resulted from the struggle for "Political Freedom." No amount of ingenious argument can make of the Hanover Petition, November 1774, "Praying that no bill may pass into a law but such as will secure to the petitioners equal liberties and

[1] Fristoe, *op. cit.*, p. 90.
[2] McIllwaine, *Struggle for Religious Toleration in Virginia.*

advantages with their fellow subjects,"[1] an attack on the establishment or a memorial for religious liberty.

In 1775 the Church of England was most carefully guarded by the statutes of Virginia. Acts of the Assembly provided for: services according to the laws and orders of the Church of England; a ministry conformable to the canons; compulsory attendance upon services; regulation of non-conformists; glebe lands for the support of the clergy; vestries, empowered to levy tithes for the salaries of the ministers; vestrymen who should subscribe to the doctrines and discipline of the Church and bound by the oath of supremacy. Vestries were closed corporations and irresponsible; they were charged with the support of the poor and they fixed the assessments for that purpose as well as for general church expenses.

The first breach in the exclusive privileges of the Anglican establishment and the first step toward religious equality came with the organization of the Revolutionary Army. The Convention at Richmond in 1775, granted to each denomination of dissenters the privilege of performing divine service for its respective adherents in the army, "for the ease of such scrupulous consciences as may not choose to attend divine services as celebrated by the chaplain." This much was accomplished by the Baptists in 1775, "the first step towards placing the clergy for all denominations upon an equal footing in Virginia."[2] At the meeting of their Association at Dupuy's Meeting-house, Powhatan County, in August they resolved to petition for the abolition of the establishment and to send a patriotic address to the convention, offering their

[1] *Journal of the House of Delegates,* June 5, 1775; Henry, *Life of Patrick Henry,* calls this "the advance guard of . . . . . remonstrance, which so vigorously attacked the establishment."

[2] Hawks, *op. cit.,* p. 138; *Journal of Convention,* August 16, 1775.

services for the army, and requesting that their ministers be allowed to preach to the soldiers. Semple gives us the following account of this important meeting:

"It seems that one great object of uniting together the two districts (of Baptists in Virginia) at this time was to strive together for the abolition of the hierarchy, or church establishment, in Virginia. The discontents in America, arising from British oppression, were now drawing to a crisis; most of the colonies had determined to resist, and some were for independence. This was a very favorable season for the Baptists. Having been much ground under by the British laws, or at least by the interpretation of them in Virginia, they were to a man favorable to any revolution by which they could obtain freedom of religion. They had known from experience that mere toleration was not a sufficient check, having been imprisoned at a time when that law was considered by many as being in force. It was, therefore, resolved at this session to circulate petitions to the Virginia Convention, or General Assembly, throughout the State, in order to obtain signatures. The prayer of these was that the church establishment should be abolished, and religion left to stand on its own merits; and that all religious societies should be protected in the peaceable enjoyment of their own religious principles and modes of worship. They appointed Jeremiah Walker, John Williams, and George Roberts to wait on the Legislature with these petitions. They also determined to petition the Assembly for leave to preach to the army, which was granted."[1]

The petition did not reach the Convention this year, but the committee arrived with the address from the Association. The records of the Convention show, August 16, 1775, that:

"An address from the Baptists in this colony was presented and read setting forth that, however distinguished from the body of their countrymen by appellations and sentiments of a religious nature, they, nevertheless, considered themselves as members of the same community in respect to matters of a civil nature, and embarked in the same common cause; that, alarmed at the oppression which hangs over America, they have considered what part it would be proper to take in the unhappy contest, and had determined that in some cases it was lawful to go to war; and that they ought to make a military resistance against Great Britain in her unjust invasion, tyrannical oppression, and repeated hostilities; that

[1] Semple, *op. cit.*, p. 62.

their brethren were left at discretion to enlist without incurring the censure of their religious community; and, under these circumstances, many had enlisted as soldiers, and many more were ready to do so, who had an earnest desire that their ministers should preach to them during the campaigns; that they had, therefore, appointed four of their brethren to make application to this Convention for the liberty of preaching to the troops at convenient times, without molestation or abuse, and praying the same may be granted to them.

Resolved, That it be an instruction to the commanding officers of the regiments of troops to be raised, that they permit the dissenting clergymen to celebrate divine worship, and to preach to the soldiers, or exhort, from time to time, as the various operations of the military service may permit, for the ease of such scrupulous consciences as may not choose to attend divine services as celebrated by the chaplains." [1]

The year 1776 was a great one for religious liberty as it was for political emancipation. The Virginia Convention incorporated into the organic law of the state the philosophy of religious liberty; the first Legislature assembled under the new republic, declared against all laws punishing men for religious opinions, and exempted dissenters from taxation for the support of the establishment.

The philosophy of religious liberty was incorporated into the Virginia Bill of Rights by the Constitutional Convention at Williamsburg. It was the work of James Madison, taught as we have noted[2] by the sufferings of his Orange County neighbors. The original article (16) drawn by George Mason was as follows:

"That religion, or the duty we owe to our Creator, and the manner of discharging it, can be directed only by reason and conviction, and not by force or violence; and, therefore, that all men should enjoy the fullest toleration in the exercises of religion, according to the dictates of conscience, unpunished and unrestrained by the magistrate, unless, under the color of religion, any man disturb the peace, the happiness, or the safety of society; and that it is the mutual duty of all to practice Christian forbearance, love, and charity towards each other." [3]

[1] *Journal of the Convention*, August 6, 1775.
[2] *Supra*, p. 371.
[3] Rowland, *Life of George Mason*, vol. i, appendix x.

Upon the motion of James Madison, June 12, 1776, in the "Committee of the Whole," this article was amended to read:

"That religion, or the duty which we owe to our Creator, and the manner of discharging it, can be directed only by reason and conviction, not by force or violence; and therefore, all men are equally entitled to the free exercise of religion according to the dictates of conscience; and that it is the mutual duty of all to practice Christian forbearance, love, and charity towards each other." [1]

Madison had changed "toleration" to "equality." Thus originated the "Religious Freedom" clause of the Bill of Rights of Virginia.

A petition from the Baptists of Prince William County brought to the attention of the legislature, the question of the practical application of this philosophy of religious equality. The problem was stated as follows; June 20, 1776:

"A petition of sundry persons of the Baptist church, in the county of Prince William, ... was presented to the Convention, and read, setting forth that at a time when this colony, with others, is contending for the civil rights of mankind, against the enslaving schemes of a powerful enemy, they are persuaded the strictest unanimity is necessary among ourselves and that every remaining cause of division may, if possible, be removed, they think it their duty to petition for the following religious privileges, which they have not yet been indulged with in this part of the world — to wit: That they be allowed to worship God in their own way, without interruption; that they be permitted to maintain their own ministers, and none others; that they be married, buried, and the like, without paying the clergy of other denominations; that, these things granted they will gladly unite with their brethren, and to the utmost of their ability promote the common cause.

"Ordered, That the said petition be referred to the Committee of Propositions and Grievances; that they inquire into the allegations thereof and report the same, with their opinion thereupon to the Convention." [2]

[1] Hening, *Statutes*, vol. ix. pp. 111-112; Bitting, *Strawberry Association*, p. 18.

[2] *Journals of the Convention*, June 20, 1776.

Thus the practical issue was phrased. From the fact that it begs religious indulgences, we may infer that the petitioners had drawn the document before they were familiarized with Madison's "religious equality" phrase of the Bill of Rights. The *questo vexata* for the next three years, 1776-1779, was to be the one of "support of the clergy."

When the first republican legislative assembly met, October 7, 1776, petitions came pouring in from all denominations; Anglicans and Methodists supported the establishment whilst Baptists, Presbyterians, Lutherans and others prayed for its abolition.

The petitioners, in general, argued against the church on the grounds: that they had been living in ecclesiastical bondage, under restrictions inconsistent with equal rights, especially in that they must pay for the support of a church which they could not conscientiously attend:[1] that even in the frontier settlements where very few Anglicans were to be found, glebes and church support were to be provided;[2] that the temporal interest of the country would be advanced by making "Virginia an asylum for free inquiry, knowledge and the virtuous of every denomination;"[3] that Christianity might safely be left to its own force for its preservation; that only the Creator himself could prescribe the mode of worship;[4] and that such severity as had been practiced was unworthy of a Christian people.

Arguments advanced by the proponents of the establishment cited the justice, wisdom, and expediency of the

[1] *Journal of the Convention*, Oct. 22, 1776, Petitions of Various Dissenters, Albemarle, Amherst & Buckingham Counties.

[2] *Ibid.*, Oct. 24, 1776, Petition of Presbytery of Hanover, Nov. 9, 1776, Petition of August County.

[3] *Ibid.*, Oct. 11, 1776, Petition of Prince Edward County.

[4] *Ibid*, Petition from Presbytery of Hanover, Oct. 24, 1776.

existing polity. "It would be inconsistent with justice either to deprive the present incumbents of parishes or of any right or profits they hold or enjoy, or to cut off from such as are now in orders and unbeneficed those expectations which originated from the laws of the land." It would be unwise to change because of "the experience of 150 years, during which . . . . . order and internal tranquillity, true piety and virtue have prevailed." "A religious establishment is conducive to . . . . . peace and happiness . . . . . . virtue . . . . . and study." And as a matter of practical politics, "the hardships which such a regulation might impose on individuals, or even bodies of men, ought not to be considered," that "the mildness of the church establishment has heretofore been acknowledged by those very dissenters who now aim at its ruin," and finally "they cannot suppose, should all denominations . . . . . be placed upon a level, that this equality will continue . . . . . and they dread the ascendancy of that religion which permits its professors to threaten destruction to the Commonwealth, in order to serve their own private ends."[1]

Thomas Jefferson wrote,

"The first republican legislature . . . . . was crowded with petitions to abolish . . . . . spiritual tyranny. These brought on the severest contests in which I have ever been engaged. Our greatest opponents were, Mr. Pendleton and Robert Carter Nicholas, honest men, but zealous churchmen. The petitions were referred to the Committee of the Whole House on the State of the Country; and, after desperate contests in that committee almost daily from the 11th of October to the 5th of December, we prevailed so far only as to repeal the laws which rendered criminal the maintenance of any religious opinions (other than those of the Episcopalians), the forbearance of repairing to (Episcopal) Church, or the exercise of any (other than the

[1] *Journal of Congress*, Nov. 8, 1776, Memorial from clergy of the Established Church.

Episcopal) mode of worship; and further, to exempt dissenters from contributions to the support of the Established Church; and to suspend, only until the next session, levies on the members of that church for the salaries of their own incumbents. For, although the majority of our citizens were dissenters . . . . a majority of the Legislature were churchmen. Among these, however, were some reasonable and liberal men, who enabled us, on some points, to obtain feeble majorities. But *our opponents carried,* in the general resolutions of committee of November 19th, *a declaration that religious assemblies ought to be regulated, and that provision ought to be made for continuing the succession of the clergy and superintending their conduct.* And in the bill now passed, was inserted an express reservation of the question whether a general assessment should not be established by law on every one to the support of the pastor of his choice; or whether all should be left to voluntary contribution: and on this question, debated at every session from 1776 to 1779, (some of our dissenting allies, having now secured their particular object, going over to the advocates of a general assessment), we could only obtain a suspension from session to session until 1779, when the question against a general assessment was finally carried and the establishment of the Anglican Church entirely put down."[1]

The bill which repealed the laws which made heresy or absence from worship a crime and forced dissenters to contribute to the support of the church, was adopted as resolutions of the Committee of the Whole House on November 19, and was passed by the House, December 5, 1776. It read:

"1. Resolved, As the opinion of this Committee, that all and every act or statute, either of the Parliament of England or of Great Britain, by whatever title known or distinguished, which renders criminal the maintaining any opinions in matters of religion, forbearing to repair to church, or the exercising any mode of worship whatsoever, or which prescribes punishment for the same, ought to be declared henceforth of no validity or force within this Commonwealth.

2. Resolved, That so much of an act of Assembly made in the fourth year of the reign of Queen Anne, intitled, 'An act for the Effectual Suppression of Vice, and Restraint and Punishment of Blasphemous, wicked, and dissolute Persons,' as inflicts certain additional penalties on any

[1] *Works of Thomas Jefferson,* Ford edition, vol. i, pp. 53-54. Washington edition, vol. 1, pp. 9-40. Cf. Foote, *Sketches of Virginia,* pp. 322-323.

person or persons convicted a second time of any of the offences described in the first clause of the said act, ought to be repealed.

3. Resolved, That so much of the petitions of the several dissenters from the church established by law within this Commonwealth as desires an exemption from all taxes and contributions whatever towards supporting the said church, and the ministers thereof or towards the support of their respective societies in any other way than themselves shall voluntarily agree, is reasonable.

4. Resolved, That, although the maintaining any opinions in matters of religion ought not to be restricted, yet that public assemblies of societies for divine worship ought to be regulated, and that proper provision should be made for continuing the succession of the clergy and superintending their conduct.

5. Resolved, That the several acts of Assembly making provision for the support of the clergy ought to be repealed, securing to the present incumbents all arrears of salary, and to the vestries a power of levying for performance of their contracts.

6. Resolved, That a reservation ought to be made to the use of the said church, in all times coming, of the several tracts of glebe lands already purchased, the churches and chapels already built for the use of the several parishes, and of all plats belonging to or appropriated to the use of the said church, and all arrears of money or tobacco arising from former assessments; and that there should be reserved to such parishes as have received private donations for the support of the said church and its ministers the perpetual benefit of such donations." [1]

Dissenters were but slightly mollified by this act; they wanted religious equality; religious liberty would not suffice. So for the next three years petitions continued to roll in, from Baptists, Anglicans, Methodists and Presbyterians, Presbyteries, Parishes and Associations, by counties and by groups, from dissenters and from supporters of the general assessment. Finally, November 15, 1779, the House,

"Ordered. That leave be given to bring in a bill for 'repealing so much of the act of Assembly entitled, "An Act for the Support of the Clergy, etc." as relates to the payment of salaries heretofore given to the clergy of the Church of England; and that Messrs. Mason, Strother and Randolph, do prepare and bring in the same'." [2]

[1] *Journal of House*, November 19, December 5, 1776.
[2] *Ibid.*, November 15, 1779.

Mr. Mason presented the bill, November 18, 1779. It was read and ordered read a second time. On the next day it was given a second reading, and turned over to the Committee of the Whole House. December 11, it was ordered engrossed. December 13, it was passed to a third reading and the following act was carried,

"Be it enacted by the General Assembly, That so much of the act entitled — 'An Act for the Support of the Clergy, and for the regular collecting and paying the Parish Levies,' and of all and every other Act or Acts providing salaries for the Ministers, and authorizing the vestries to levy the same, shall be, and the same is hereby repealed." [1]

The question had been decided against the system of a general assessment, and the establishment was finally put down. Its purse strings had been cut and the important economic bond between church and state in Virginia was severed.

Hawks tells us that, "The Baptists were the principal promoters of this work, and in truth aided more than any other denomination in its accomplishment."[2] And Semple explains,

"It is said, however, and probably not without truth, that many of the Episcopalians who voted for abolishing the Establishment did it upon an expectation that it would be succeeded by a general assessment; and, considering that most of the men of wealth were on that side, they supposed that their funds would be lessened very little. This, it appeared in the sequel, was a vain expectation. The people having once shaken off their fetters, would not again permit themselves to be bound. Moreover, the war now rising to its height, they were in too much need of funds to permit any of their resources to be devoted to any other purpose during that period; and we shall see that when it was attempted, a few years after the expiration of the war, the people set their faces against it." [3]

[1] Hening, *Statutes*, x, p. 197; *Journal of House*, November 18, 19, and December 11 and 13, 1779.

[2] Hawks, *Protestant Episcopal Church in Virginia*, p. 152.

[3] Semple, *op. cit.*, p. 27.

Virginia Baptists in their politico-religious semi-yearly associations had by 1779 discovered new points of religious equality. While the Assembly was threshing over the assessment bill, the Baptists had discovered other points wherein religious equality was being denied them. At this General Association of 1777:

"A committee was appointed, charged with the duty of examining the laws of the Commonwealth and designating all such as were justly considered offensive; of recommending the method to be pursued to obtain their removal from the statute book; to propose in form such laws, to be laid before the Legislature, as should firmly establish and maintain 'religious freedom' in all its extent and bearings, and to report at the earliest moment practicable.

In that report numerous laws were designated as offensive, prominent among which was the law which required all marriages to be performed by Episcopal clergymen, with the ceremonies of the Established Church, and made all otherwise performed illegal and void; and all the laws establishing the Episcopal Church as the religion of the State, and providing for its support from the public purse. As the best method to procure their removal from the statute book, continued agitation among the people, and petitions to the Legislature were recommended; and, as expressive of such government action as was desired, a law was drawn up in form and reported, entitled, 'Act for the Establishment of Religious Freedom' to be presented to the Legislature, with an earnest petition that it might be adopted as a law of the state.

This report was received, amply discussed, and adopted. An address was prepared, embodying all the suggestions of the report, especially the proposed law to establish religious liberty; commissioners were appointed, to whose fidelity it was confided, and they were instructed to remain with the Legislature and give their attention to these interests during the approaching session." [1]

The Baptists had learned the expediency of petitions, publicity, agitation, commissions and lobbying.

Continuous agitation was not without results. In October 1777, Virginia decreed that Baptists and Methodists might raise their own companies, troops, regiments,

[1] Howell, *Early Baptists in Virginia,* p. 164.

or other units of soldiery and provided them with their own field-officers, chaplains, etc.[1]

At the May meeting of the General Association of the Baptists in 1778, the committee "appointed to enquire whether any grievances existed in the civil laws that were oppressive to the Baptists," reported on the marriage laws as "partial and oppressive." "Upon which it was agreed to present to the next General Assembly a memorial praying for a law affording equal privileges to all ordained ministers of every denomination."[2]

The October meeting of this association, held at Dupuy's Meeting-house "recommend that two persons be appointed to wait on the next General Assembly and lay these grievances before them." Jeremiah Walker and Elijah Craig (and in case of the failure of either), John Williams were appointed to attend the General Assembly.[3]

The bill "declaring marriages solemnized by dissenting ministers lawful" was presented on December 5, and read a first time. Two days later the bill was rejected.[4] But the Baptists were not dismayed, they went on marrying and trusting that their political activities would ultimately win. In fact they seem deliberately to have augmented the number of these illegal marriages as an argument for their legalization.

At the October meeting of 1779, Nottoway in Amelia County, the following entry was agreed to unanimously:

"It seems that many of the Baptists preachers, presuming upon a future sanction, had gone on to marry such people as applied for marriage. It was determined that a memorial should be sent from this Association requesting that all such marriages should be sanctioned by a law for

[1] Hening, *Statutes*, ix, p. 348.
[2] Semple, *op. cit.*, p. 64.
[3] *Ibid.*, p. 64.
[4] *Journal of the House*, December 5 and 7, 1778.

that purpose . . . . . For a set of preachers to proceed to solemnize the rites of matrimony without any law to authorize them, might at first view appear incorrect and indeed censurable; but we are informed that they were advised to this measure by Mr. Patrick Henry, as being the most certain of obtaining the law. It succeeded."[1]

The petition from the Baptist Association, "praying that an act may pass to declare such marriages (those solemnized by dissenting ministers) lawful" was read in the House on October 25, 1779. On the 25th, Mr. Henry accordingly presented a bill but again this failed.[2] Whereupon the Baptists fairly flooded the 1780 General Assembly with petitions upon the subject.

On December 2, 1780, the Committee for Religion reported a bill declaring "what shall be a lawful marriage" which was passed on the 18th. It was as follows:

> "For encouraging marriage and for removing doubts concerning the validity of marriages celebrated by ministers other than the Church of England, be it enacted by the General Assembly — That it shall and may be lawful for any minister of any society or congregation of Christians, and for the Society of Christians called Quakers and Mennonites, to celebrate the rites of matrimony, and to join together as man and wife, those who may apply to them agreeable to the rules and usage of the respective societies to which the parties to be married respectively belong, and such marriages, as well as those heretofore celebrated by dissenting ministers, shall be, and they are hereby, declared good and valid in law."[3]

This act, clogged with "provisos" as it was, marks an advance in religious liberty, the solemn vows to live together as husband and wife might now be uttered in words and with forms agreeable to the consciences of the contracting parties.

Then the Baptists had machinery for remedying

[1] Semple, *op. cit.*, pp. 55-66; Howell, *op. cit.*, p. 167.
[2] *Journal of House*, 1779, October 25, 26, November 29.
[3] Hening, *Statutes*, x, pp. 361-362; *Journal of House*, November 21, December 2, 18, 1780.

unsatisfactory laws. By 1784, the restrictive features of the act of 1780 had been removed.

In 1782 the Committee on Religion reported favorably on petitions, the first of which asked for "the repeal of that part of the law defining lawful marriages which kept dissenting ministers from marrying people beyond the limits of their own counties"; and the second of which called for "the repeal also of the clause limiting the number of dissenting ministers who were to be licensed in each county to perform the marriage ceremony."[1]

In response to a petition "to authorize marriage by civil authorities" for "the relief of settlers on Western waters," a bill for "Marriages in certain cases" was passed June 27, 1783.[2] This provided that county courts on the Western waters might license "sober and discreet laymen" to perform the marriage ceremony in the absence of accessible ministers under certain conditions, and it legalized all such marriages previously made.

In 1783 the Assembly received numerous memorials and petitions for the repeal and amendment of parts of the marriage act.[3] The Baptist General Association in 1784 sent a commissioner, Reuben Ford, to the General Assembly to attend to this and other matters for them[4] and the General Assembly was deluged with petitions.[5]

Accordingly on December 16, a bill amending the Acts Concerning Marriage, passed the house and soon became a law. This provided, "It shall and may be lawful for any ordained minister of the Gospel in regular communion

[1] *Journal of House*, November 22, 1782.
[2] *Ibid.*, 1783, May 30, June 25 and 27.
[3] *Ibid.*, 1783, May 30, 31, June 19, November 6.
[4] Fristoe, *History of the Ketocton Association*, p. 92.
[5] *Journal of House*, 1784, May 24, 26, June 8, Nov. 11, etc.

with any society of Christians, and every such minister is hereby authorized to celebrate the rites of matrimony according to the forms and customs of the Church to which he belongs."[1] Freedom had been achieved in another point of religious ceremonial.

Baptists next assaulted the vestries, Episcopalian closed corporations. A petition from Amelia County, May 12, 1780, prayed "that vestries be dissolved."[2] A bill for dissolving several vestries and electing overseers of the poor became a law, July 5, 1780.[3] But the Baptists wanted a root and branch policy; November 8, 1780, the General Association petitioned for the abolition of the existing vestry law;[4] and a petition in 1781, November 22, asks that "all vestries be dissolved by Act of Assembly, and new ones elected by the body of the community at large, dissenters to be equally competent with conformists to the post of vestrymen, and the sole proviso to be attachment to the present form of government."[5] The vestry question was swallowed up in the climax of the struggle for religious freedom which developed in the years 1784 and 1785: the petition just mentioned was rejected by the next assembly, June 9, 1782.

The close of the Revolutionary War in 1783, left religion in Virginia in a deplorable state and was followed by a grand effort at revival. Revival for the Churchmen took the form of an effort at restoration of the establishment. The parties thereto were the Churchmen against the Baptists. In the struggle the Presbyterians wavered,

[1] Hening, *op. cit.*, xi, p. 503.
[2] *Journal of the House*, May 12, 1780.
[3] Hening, *op. cit.*, vol. x, p. 288.
[4] *Journal of House*, November 8, 1780.
[5] *Ibid.*, November 22, 1781; June 9, 1782; May 30, 31, 1783; November 6, 15, 1783; May 24, 26 and June 8, November 11, 17, 1784.

and for a time supported the Anglicans. Every effort was put forth on both sides; the adoption of Thomas Jefferson's statute of Religious Freedom was the final outcome. Jefferson has left us his own account of the steps which led up to the adoption of this bill:

"Early . . . . . in the session of 1776 . . . . . I moved and presented a bill for the revision of the laws, which was passed on the twenty-fourth day of October, and on the fifth of November, Mr. Pendleton, Mr. Wythe, George Mason, Thomas Lee and myself were appointed a committee to execute the work . . . . . We met . . . . . on the thirteenth of January 1777. The first question was whether we should propose to abolish the whole existing system of laws and prepare a new and complete Institute, or preserve the general system, and only modify it to the present state of things. Mr. Pendleton, contrary to his usual disposition in favor of ancient things, was for the former proposition in which he was joined by Mr. Lee . . . . . This last was the opinion of Mr. Wythe, Mr. Mason and myself. When we proceeded to the distribution of the work, Mr Mason excused himself, as, being no lawyer, he felt himself unqualified for the work, and he resigned soon after. Mr. Lee excused himself on the same ground, and died indeed in a short time. The other two gentlemen, therefore, and myself divided the work among us . . . . . We were employed in this work from that time to February, 1779, when we met at Williamsburg . . . . . and meeting day by day, we examined critically our several parts, sentence by sentence, scrutinizing and amending, until we had agreed on the whole. We then returned home, had fair copies made of our several parts which were reported to the General Assembly, June 18th, 1779, by Mr. Wythe and myself, Mr. Pendleton's residence being distant, and he having authorized us by letter to declare his approbation. We had in this work brought so much of the Common law as it was thought necessary to alter, all the British statutes from Magna Charta to the present day, and all the laws of Virginia, from the establishment of our Legislature, in the 4th Jac 1 (James 1) to the present time, which we thought should be retained, within the compass of one hundred and twenty-six bills, making a printed folio of ninety pages only. Some bills were taken out, occasionally, from time to time and passed; but the main body of the work was not entered on by the Legislature, until after the general peace, in 1785, when by the unwearied exertions of Mr. Madison, in opposition to the endless quibbles, chicaneries, perversions, vexations and delays of lawyers and demi-lawyers, most of the bills were passed by the Legislature, with little alteration.

The bill for establishing religious freedom, the principles of which had, to a certain degree, been enacted before, I had drawn in all the latitude of reason and right. It still met with opposition, but with some mutilations in the preamble, it was finally passed."[1]

The fight over Mr. Jefferson's bill lasted from 1779 to 1786. Other bills were offered and considered, as those of Messrs. Harvie, Mason, and Baker of June 12, 1779,[2] and of Patrick Henry, of October 25, 1779.[3] The whole matter was given fullest publicity and the various religious assemblies considered it carefully and worked for its acceptance or rejection, accordingly as it met their ideas.

The meeting of the Baptist Association held at the Nottoway Meeting-house, Amelia County, October 1779, decided that the report of Jeremiah Walker, as delegate to the General Assembly, was highly gratifying. Upon which the following entry was unanimously agreed to,

"On consideration of the bill establishing religious freedom, agreed: That the said bill, in our opinion, puts religious freedom upon its proper basis, prescribes the just limits of the power of the State with regard to religion, and properly guards against partiality towards any religious denomination; We, therefore, heartily approve of the same, and wish it may pass into a law. Ordered, That this our approbation of the said bill be transmitted to the public printers to be inserted in the Gazettes."[4]

November 1, the House records a petition from Amherst county for the passage of the bill of the last Assembly for Religious Freedom.[5] November 10, "Divers of the freeholders and other free inhabitants of Amherst," who afterwards describe themselves as "composed of Church of England men, Presbyterians, Baptists and Methodists,"

[1] Jefferson, *Works*, Ford edition, vol. i, pp. 58-62.
[2] *Journal of House*, 1779, June 4, 12, 14.
[3] *Ibid.*, 1779, October 25, 26, etc.
[4] Semple, *op. cit.*, p. 65.
[5] *Journal of House*, November 1, 1779; October 20, 21, 22, 27. November 3, 10.

"unanimously and with one voice, declare their hearty assent, concurrence, and approbation of the Act of January, 1779, declaring all church laws null, and the Act of Religious Freedom the true exposition of the Bill of Rights." [1]

The bill for Religious Freedom was to be greatly confused with another bill, dealing with the question of the church property. November 15, 1779, the bill concerning religion was put off till the first of the next March, and Messrs. Mason, Henry, and General Nelson, were ordered to bring in a bill "For saving and securing the property of the Church heretofore by law established."[2] The deplorable state of the country without religion was causing a mass of petitions relative to the subject. One from Essex was read, October 22, 1779, to the effect that:

"The great confusion and disorder that hath arisen, and is likely to continue in this county on account of Religion, since the Old Establishment has been interrupted, convinces us of the great and absolute necessity there is for the Legislative body of this State, to take it under their most serious consideration . . . . . A General Assessment for the support of Religious worship would be most agreeable to your Petitioners, that all licensed and Itinerate Preachers be forbid collecting or Assembling of Negroes and others at unseasonable times. That every Minister of every Christian Denomination have his stated place of Worship. That no insults, or interruptions be suffered to any Christian Congregation assembled at proper times for Worship. That no doctrine be permitted to be preached, which may tend to subvert Government or disturb Civil Society. That there be a general Election of Vestry Men in every Parish, and that they may have power to assess or levy upon the Tythables of their respective Parishes, what they may think reasonable for the support of the Ministers of every Denomination and to be paid to any profession that the occupiers of such Tythes may think proper." [3]

From 1780 to 1783 the engagement between the forces of religious freedom and those of religious support was but desultory. The General Assembly did but little for or

[1] *Journal of House*, 1779, November 10; Thom, *op. cit.*, pp. 66-67.
[2] *Ibid.*, November 15, 1779.
[3] *Ibid.*, October 22, 1779; Eckenrode, *op. cit.*, pp. 57-58.

against these respective causes; it merely listened respectfully to the memorials and petitions of the parties. Throughout these were numerous, showing that interest in the matter had not waned. At the 1780 meeting of the Presbytery of Hanover, "A memorial to the Assembly of Virginia . . . . . to abstain from interfering in the government of the church," was prepared, "and being read in Presbytery, is appointed and directed to be transmitted to the House. The Presbytery to request Colonel McDowell and Captain Johnson to present their memorial to the Assembly, and to second it by their influence, and Mr. Wadell and Mr. Graham are appointed to inform these gentlemen of the request of Presbytery."[1]

The General Assembly ordered, June 4, 1780; That leave be given to bring in a bill "for saving the property of the church heretofore by law established," and that the committee appointed to prepare and bring in a bill "for religious freedom" do prepare and bring in the same.[2] On the 14th a "bill for establishing religious freedom was read a second time." Its third reading was deferred till August. On that same date a bill "for saving the property, etc." was read a second time.[3] On July 5, a bill for dissolving several vestries and electing overseers of the poor was passed; it became a law on the 11th.[4]

At the Fall Assembly the Baptist Association petitioned for the abolition of the existing vestry law.[5] Buckingham, Prince Edward and Cumberland Counties request the silencing of all non-jurors and a double tax on them.[6] This continues to be the situation; in 1783,

[1] Foote, *op. cit.*, p. 332.
[2] *Journal of House*, June 4, 1780.
[3] *Ibid.*, June 14, 1780.
[4] *Ibid.*, July 5, 11; Hening, *op. cit.*, x. p. 288.
[5] *Ibid.*, November 8, 1780.
[6] *Ibid.*, November 7, 10, 23.

November 6, "the ministers and messengers of the several Baptist churches petition for religious freedom[1] while requests come from Lunenburg and Amherst counties for "a general and equal constitution for the support of the clergy."[2]

In 1784, the War being over, the twin questions of support of religion and religious freedom were attacked in earnest. The Assemblies of that year were flooded with petitions from both sides. One from Amelia county, read on November 8, recited:

"That your Petitioners have with much concern observed a general Declension of Religion for a number of years past, occasioned in Part, we conceive by the late war, but chiefly by its not being duly aided and patronized by the Civil Power; that should it decline with nearly the same rapidity in the Future, your Petitioners apprehend consequences dangerous, if not fatal to the Strength and Stability of Civil Government . . . . . Were all Sense of Religion rooted out of the Minds of Men, scarce anything would be left on which human laws would take hold . . . . . Your Petitioners therefore think that those who legislate, not only have a right, founded upon the Principle of Public Utility, but as they wish to promote the Virtue and Happiness of their Constituents and the Good People of the State in general; as they wish well to the strength and Stability of Government, they ought to aid and patronize Religion . . . . . As every man of the state partakes of the Blessings of Peace and Order . . . . . (so) every man should contribute as well to the support of Religion, as that of Civil Government; nor has he any Reason to complain of this, as an Encroachment upon his religious Liberty, if he is permitted to worship God according to the dictates of his Conscience."[3]

Similar petitions for the support of religions were received from Warwick county, the Isle of Wight, etc.[4]

The opposition to this idea of a renewed general assessment was best expressed by the Baptists. When their

[1] *Journal of House*, November 6, 1783.
[2] *Ibid.*, 1783, November 8, 27.
[3] *Ibid.*, 1784, November 8; Eckenrode, *op. cit.* p. 84.
[4] *Journal of House*, 1784, May 15, 27, November 4, 12.

General Committee met in October it drew a memorial to the General Assembly and "Resolved to oppose the law for a general assessment and that for the incorporation of religious societies, which are now in agitation.

First, it was contrary to their principles and avowed sentiments, the making provision for the support of religion by law; that the distinction between civil and ecclesiastical governments ought to be kept up without blending them together; that Christ Jesus hath given laws for the government of his Kingdom and direction of his subjects, and gave instruction concerning collections for the various purposes of religion, and therefore needs not legislative interference.

Secondly, should a legislative body undertake to pass laws for the government of the church, for them to say what doctrines shall be believed, in what mode worship shall be performed, and what the sum collected shall be, what a dreadful precedent it would establish; for when such a right is claimed by a legislature, and given up by the people, by the same rule that they decide in one instance they may in every instance. Religion in this is like the press; if government limits the press, and says this shall be printed and that shall not, in the event it will destroy the freedom of the press; so when legislatures undertake to pass laws about religion, religion loses its form, and Christianity is reduced to a system of worldly policy.

Thirdly, it has been believed by us that that Almighty Power that instituted religion will support His own cause; that in the course of divine Providence events will be overruled, and the influence of grace on the hearts of the Lord's people will incline them to afford and contribute what is necessary for the support of religion, and therefore there is no need for compulsory measures.

Fourthly, it would give an opportunity to the party that were numerous (and, of course, possessed the ruling power) to use their influence and exercise their art and cunning, and multiply signers to their own favorite party. And, last, the most deserving, the faithful preacher, who in a pointed manner reproved sin and bore testimony against every species of vice and dissipation, would, in all probability, have been profited very little by such a law, while men-pleasers, the gay and fashionable, who can wink at sin and daub his hearers with untempered mortar, saying, 'Peace, peace,' when there is no peace, who can lay out his oratory in dealing out smooth things mingled with deception, the wicked, it is clear, would like to have it so; and it follows the irreligious and carnal part of the people would richly reward them for their flattery, and the undeserving go off with the gain." [1]

[1] Fristoe, *op. cit.*, p. 92.

A similar petition against the assessment was received from Rockingham county.[1]

June 8, 1784, the Committee on Religion reported to the House, "That . . . . . . so much of the memorial from the clergy of the Protestant Episcopal Church, and the United Clergy of the Presbyterian Church in Virginia, as relates to an incorporation of their Societies is reasonable; and that a like incorporation ought to be extended to all other religious Societies within this Commonwealth which may apply for the same."[2] A bill was accordingly ordered, but it was put off until the November session of the legislature. On November 11, it was resolved in the Committee of the Whole, "That the people of this Commonwealth, according to their respective abilities, ought to pay a moderate tax or contribution annually for the support of the Christian religion, or of some Christian Church, denomination, or communion of Christians, or of some form of Christian worship;"[3] and a special committee with Patrick Henry as chairman was appointed to draft a bill, the vote being 47 to 32.

November 17, the House ordered bills brought in regulating the laws as to marriage and the vestries and also one to incorporate the clergy of the Protestant Episcopal Church. It also adopted a resolution, "that acts ought to pass for the incorporation of all societies of the Christian religion, which may apply for the same."[4] Patrick Henry voted for this bill, James Madison against it. On December 20, the Senate finally passed the amended bill for the incorporation of the Protestant Episcopal Church. By this act each vestry could hold property up to the value

[1] *Journal of House*, November 18, 1784; Eckenrode, *op. cit.*, pp. 95-96.
[2] *Journal of House*, June 8, 16, 25, 1784.
[3] *Ibid.*, November 11, 1784.
[4] *Ibid.*, November 17, 1784.

of a certain yearly income, could sue and be sued, like any other corporation, and could retain the glebe lands and the churches.

"A Bill establishing a provision for the teachers of the Christian religion, or a general assessment bill," was brought in, December 2, 1784. On the third, it was read a second time and recommitted to the Committee of the Whole House. Its preamble stated: "Whereas the general diffusion of Christian knowledge hath a natural tendency to correct the morals of men, restrain their vices, and preserve the peace of society, which cannot be effected without a competent provision for learned teachers, who may be thereby enabled to devote their time and attention to the duty of instructing such citizens as from their circumstances and want of education cannot otherwise attain such knowledge; and it is judged such provision may be made by the Legislature, without counteracting the liberal principle theretofore adopted and intended to be preserved, by abolishing all distinctions of pre-eminence amongst the different societies or communities of Christian."[1]

Then followed the provisions that a general assessment was to be established and persons in giving in taxes should declare the denomination to which they wished their assessment to go. If no such a declaration were made, the money would go to encourage seminaries of learning in their respective counties. December 24, by a vote of 45 to 38, the engrossing of this bill was postponed to the fourth Thursday of November, 1785. In the *interim* the bill together with the vote thereon was to be printed and distributed in order that the sentiments of the people might be ascertained.

As a part of this discussion, James Madison drew up and circulated his famous *Memorial and Remonstrance against Religious Assessments. To the Honorable the General Assembly of the Commonwealth of Virginia.*

"We, the subscribers, citizens of the said Commonwealth, having taken into serious consideration, a Bill printed by order of the last Session

[1] *Journal of House*, November 17, December 2, 3, and 4, 1784.

of General Assembly, entitled, 'A Bill establishing a provision for Teachers of the Christian Religion,' and conceiving that the same, if finally armed with the sanctions of a law, will be a dangerous abuse of power, are bound as faithful members of a free state, to remonstrate against it, and to declare the reasons by which we are determined. We remonstrate against the said Bill,

1. Because we hold it for a fundamental and undeniable truth, 'that religion, or the duty which we owe to our Creator and the Manner of discharging it, can be directed only by reason and conviction, not by force or violence.' The Religion then of every man must be left to the conviction and conscience of every man; and it is the right of every man to exercise it as these may dictate. This right is in its nature an unalienable right. It is unalienable; because the opinions of men, depending only on evidence contemplated by their own minds, cannot follow the dictates of other men: It is unalienable also; because what is here a right towards men, is a duty towards the Creator. It is the duty of every man to render to the Creator such homage, and such only, as he believes to be acceptable to Him. This duty is precedent, both in order of time and in degree of obligation, to the claims of Civil Society. Before any man can be considered as a member of Civil Society, he must be considered as a subject of the Governor of the Universe: And if a member of Civil Society, who enters into any subordinate Association, must always do it with a reservation of his duty to the general authority; much more must every man who becomes a member of any particular Civil Society, do it with a saving of his allegiance to the Universal Sovereign. We maintain, therefore, that in matters of Religion, no man's right is abridged by the institution of Civil Society, and that religion is wholly exempt from its cognizance. True, it is, that no other rule exists, by which any question which may divide a Society, can be ultimately determined than the will of the majority; but it is also true, that the majority may trespass on the rights of the minority . . . . .

4. Because the bill violates that equality which ought to be the basis of every law, and which is more indispensable, in proportion as the validity or expediency of any law is more liable to be impeached. 'If all men are by nature equally free and independent,' all men are to be considered as entering into Society, on equal conditions; as relinquishing no more, and therefore retaining no less, one than another of their natural rights. Above all are they to be considered as retaining an 'equal title to the free exercise of Religion according to the dictates of conscience.' Whilst we assert for ourselves a freedom to embrace, to profess, and to observe the Religion which we believe to be of divine origin, we cannot deny an equal freedom to those whose minds have not yielded to the evidence which has convinced us. If this freedom be

abused, it is an offence against God, not against man. To God, therefore, not to man, must an account of it be rendered . . . . . .

5. Because the bill implies either that the Civil Magistrate is a competent Judge of Religious truth, or that he may employ Religion as an engine of Civil policy. The first is an arrogant pretention falsified by the contradictory opinions of Rulers in all ages, and throughout the world: the Second, an unhallowed perversion of the means of salvation!

6. Because the establishment proposed by the Bill is not requisite for the support of the Christian Religion. To say that it is, is a contradiction to the Christian Religion itself, for every page of it disavows a dependence on the powers of this world. It is a contradiction to fact; for it is known that this Religion both existed and flourished, not only without the support of human laws, but in spite of every opposition from them, and not only during the period of miraculous aid, but long after it had been left to its own evidence and the ordinary care of Providence: Nay, it is a contradiction in terms: for a Religion not invented by human policy, must have pre-existed and been supported before it was established by human policy. It is, moreover, to weaken in those who profess this Religion a pious confidence in its innate excellence and the patronage of its Author; and to foster in those who still reject it a suspicion that its friends are too conscious of its fallacies to trust to its own merits.

7. Because experience witnesseth that ecclesiastical establishments, instead of maintaining the purity and efficacy of Religion, have had a contrary operation. During almost fifteen centuries, has the legal establishment of Christianity been on trial. What have been its fruits? More or less in all places, pride and indolence in the Clergy; ignorance and servility in the laity; in both, superstitution, bigotry and persecution. Enquire of the Teachers of Christianity for the ages in which it appeared in its greatest lustre; those of every sect, point to the ages prior to its incorporation with Civil policy. Propose a restoration of this primitive state in which its Teachers depended on the voluntary rewards of their flocks; many of them predict its downfall. On which side ought their testimony to have greatest weight, when for or when against their interest?

8. Because the establishment in question is not necessary for the support of Civil Government. If it be urged as necessary for the support of Civil Government only as it is a means of supporting Religion, and it be not necessary for the latter purpose, it cannot be necessary for the former. If Religion be not within cognizance of Civil Government, how can its legal establishment be said to be necessary to civil government? What influence, in fact, have ecclesiastical establishments had on Civil Society? In some instances they have been seen to erect a spiritual

tyranny on the ruins of Civil authority; in many instances have they been seen upholding the thrones of political tyranny; in no instance have they been seen the guardians of the liberties of the people. Rulers who wished to subvert the public liberty, may have found an established clergy convenient auxiliaries. A just government, instituted to secure and perpetuate it, needs them not. Such a government will be best supported by protecting every citizen in the enjoyment of his Religion with the same equal hand which protects his person and his property; by neither invading the equal rights of any Sect, nor suffering any Sect to invade those of another.

9. Because the proposed establishment is a departure from that generous policy, which, offering an asylum to the persecuted and oppressed of every Nation and Religion, promised a lustre to our country, and an accession to the number of its citizens. What a melancholy mark is the Bill of sudden degeneracy! Instead of holding forth an asylum to the persecuted, it is itself a signal of persecution. It degrades from the equal rank of Citizens all those whose opinions in Religion do not bend to those of the Legislative authority. Distant as it may be, in its present form, from the Inquisition, it differs from it only in degree. The one is the first step, the other the last in the career of intolerance. The magnanimous sufferer under this cruel scourge in foreign Regions, must view the Bill as a Beacon on our Coast, warning him to seek some other haven, where liberty and philanthropy in their due extent may offer a more certain repose from his troubles . . . . .

12. Because, the policy of the bill is adverse to the diffusion of the light of Christianity. The first wish of those who ought to enjoy this precious gift, ought to be, that it may be imparted to the whole race of mankind. Compare the number of those who have as yet received it with the number still remainging under the dominion of false Religions; and how small is the former! Does the policy of the Bill tend to lessen the disproportion? No; it at once discourages those who are strangers to the light (of revelation) from coming into the Region of it; and countenances, by example the nations who continue in darkness, in shutting out those who might convey it to them. Instead of leveling as far as possible, every obstacle to the victorious progress of truth, the Bill with an ignoble and unchristian timidity would circumscribe it, with a wall of defence against the encroachments of error . . . . .

15. Because, finally, 'the equal right of every citizen to the free exercise of his religion according to the dictates of conscience,' is held by the same tenure with all our other rights. It we recur to its origin, it is equally the gift of nature; if we weigh its importance, it cannot be less dear to us; if we consult the Declaration of those rights 'which pertain to the good people of Virginia, as the basis and foundation of government,' it is

enumerated with equal solemnity, or rather with studied emphasis. Either, then, we must say, that the will of the Legislature is the only measure of their authority; and that in the plenitude of this authority, they may sweep away all our fundamental rights; or that they are bound to leave this particular right untouched and sacred. Either we must say that they may control the freedom of the press, may abolish the trial by jury, may swallow up the Executive and Judiciary Powers of the State; nay that they may despoil us of our very right of suffrage, and erect themselves into an independent and hereditary assembly; or we must say, that they have no authority to enact into a law the Bill under con-consideration. We the subscribers say, that the General Assembly of this Commonwealth have no such authority: And that no effort may be omitted on our part against so dangerous a usurpation, we oppose to it, this remonstrance; earnestly praying, as we are in duty bound, that the Supreme Lawgiver of the Universe, by illuminating those to whom it is addressed, may on one hand, turn their councils from every act which would affront His holy prerogative or violate the trust committed to them: and on the other, guide them into every measure which may be worthy of His blessing, redound to their own praise, and establish more firmly the liberties, the prosperity, and the happiness of this Commonwealth."[1]

Madison, writing to James Monroe from his home in Orange, April 12, 1785, could say, "The only proceeding of the late Session of Assembly which makes a noise through the country is that which relates to a General Assessment. The Episcopal people are generally for it, though I think the zeal of some of them has cooled. The laity of the other sects are equally unanimous on the other side. So are all the Clergy, except the Presbyterian, who seem as ready to set up an establishment which is to take them in as they were to pull down that which shuts them out. I do not know a more shameful contrast than might be found between their memorials on the latter and former occasion."[2] The Presbyterian clergy could not hold out

[1] *Writings of James Madison*, edition of 1865, vol. 1, pp. 162-169; Hunt edition, edition of 1865, vol. ii, pp. 183-191.

[2] *Ibid.*, edition of 1865, vol. i, p. 144; Hunt edition, vol. ii, pp. 131-132.

against the protests of their laity and all the other dissenters. By May 29, Madison could write to Monroe, "The Presbyterian clergy, too, who were in general friends of the scheme, are already in another tone, either compelled by the laity of that sect, or alarmed at the probability of farther interference of the Legislature, if they once begin to dictate in matters of Religion.[1] And on August 20, he wrote to Jefferson,

"The Presbyterian clergy have at length espoused the side of the opposition, being moved either by a fear of their laity or a jealousy of the Episcopalians. The mutual hatred of these sects has been much inflamed by the late Act incorporating the latter. I am far from being sorry for it, as a coalition between them could alone endanger our religious rights, and a tendency to such an event had been suspected."[2]

The Baptists stood firm as usual. Their General Committee, August 13, 1785, heard with alarm through the report of their Agent, Reuben Ford, of the engrossing of the bill for a general assessment, and;

"Resolved, That it be recommended to those counties which have not yet prepared petitions to be presented to the General Assembly against the engrossed bill for a general assessment for the support of the teachers of the Christian religion, to proceed thereon as soon as possible; that it is believed to be repugnant to the spirit of the Gospel for the Legislature thus to proceed in matters of religion, that no human laws ought to be established for this purpose, but that every person ought to be left entirely free in respect to matters of religion; that the Holy Author of our religion needs no such compulsive measures for the promotion of His cause; that the gospel wants not the feeble arm of man for its support; that it has made, and will again through divine power, make its way against all opposition; and that, should the Legislature assume the right of taxing the people for the support of the Gospel, it will be destructive to religious liberty. Therefore, This Committee agrees, unanimously, that it will be expedient to appoint a delegate to wait on the General Assembly with a

[1] Madison, *op. cit.*, edition of 1865, vol. i, p. 154, Hunt edition, vol. ii, p. 145; Rives, *op. cit.*, vol. i, p. 630.

[2] Madison, *op. cit.*, edition of 1865, vol. i, p. 175; Hunt edition, vol. i, p. 175.

remonstrance and petition against such assessment. Accordingly, the Reverend Reuben Ford was appointed."[1]

The Presbytery of Hanover, May 19, 1785, decided, unanimously, in opposition to the measure;[2] and the Convention of the Presbyterian Church in Virginia, August 10, approved this stand. On the thirteenth, the Convention adopted the following *Memorial:*

"To the Honorable the General Assembly of the Commonwealth of Virginia:

The Ministers and Lay Representatives of the Presbyterian Church in Virginia, assembled in convention, beg leave to address you . . . . . The engrossed bill for establishing a provision for the teaching of the Christian religion and the act for incorporating the Protestant Episcopal Church, so far as it secures to that church, the churches, glebes, etc., procured at the expense of the whole community are not only evidence of this but of an impolitic partiality which we are sorry to have observed so long. We therefore in the name of the Presbyterian Church in Virginia, beg leave to exercise our privilege as freemen in remonstrating against the former absolutely, and against the latter under the restrictions above expressed.

We oppose the Bill: Because it is a departure from the proper line of legislation; Because it is unnecessary, and inadequate to its professed end — impolitic, in many respects — and a direct violation of the Declaration of Rights.

The end of civil government is security to the temporal liberty and property of mankind, and to protect them in the free exercise of religion. Legislators are invested with powers from their constitutents, for this purpose only, and their duty extends no farther. Religion is altogether personal, and the right of exercising it unalienable; and it is not, cannot, and ought not to be, resigned to the will of the society at large; and much less to the Legislature, which derives its authority wholly from the consent of the people, and is limited by the original intention of civil associations.

We never resigned to the control of government, our right of determining for ourselves, in this important article; and acting agreeably to the convictions of reason and conscience, in discharging our duty to our Creator. And therefore, it would be an unwarrantable stretch of prerogative, in the legislature, to make laws concerning it, except for

[1] Semple, *op. cit.*, p. 71.
[2] Foote, *op. cit.*, p. 341.

protection. And it would be a fatal sympton of abject slavery in us, were we to submit to the usurpation . . . . .

We farther remonstrate against the bill as an impolitic measure;

It disgusts so large a proportion of the Citizens, that it would weaken the influence of government in other respects, and diffuse a spirit of opposition to the rightful exercises of constitutional authority, if enacted into law.

It partially supposes the Quakers and Mennonites to be more faithful in conducting the religious interests of their societies, than the other sects, which we apprehend to be contrary to fact.

It unjustly subjects men who may be good citizens but who have not embraced our common faith, to the hardship of supporting a system they have not as yet believed the truth of; and deprives them of their property, for what they do not suppose to be of importance to them.

It establishes a precedent for further encroachments, by making the Legislature judges of religious truth. If the Assembly have a right to determine the preference between Christianity, and the other systems of religion that prevail in the world, they may also, at a convenient time, give a preference to some favored sect among Christians.

It discourages the population of our country by alarming those who may have been oppressed by religious establishments in other countries, with fears of the same in this: and by exciting our own citizens to emigrate to other lands of greater freedom.

It revives the principle which our ancestors contested to blood, of attempting to reduce all religions to one standard by force of civil authority.

And it naturally opens a door for contention among citizens of different creeds, and different opinions respecting the extent of the powers of Government."[1]

Washington could see no harm in the bill. He wrote to Mason, 1785: "Although no man's sentiments are more opposed to any kind of restraint upon religious principles than mine, yet I confess, I am not among the number of those who are so alarmed at making men pay toward the support of that which they profess."

When the Fall session of the Assembly met, October, 1785, the mass of petitions received indicated the intensity of the feeling relative to the question. Fifty-five

[1] *Sketches of Virginia*, pp. 342-343.

were hostile to the measure; these represented forty-eight counties. Twenty-two counties sent no petitions; only seven counties favored the bill. Yet so strong was ecclesiasticism that Dr. Foote informs us the General Assessment Bill was defeated only by a majority of three votes.[1] This indicates the magnitude of the strategic victory involved which apparently would have been won on no other issue than that of the assessment.

As a fruit of this victory the Jefferson's "Bill for Establishing Religious Freedom" which had been under consideration since 1779 was passed, December 17, 1785, and signed by the Speaker of the House, January 19, 1786, as an enrolled bill:

"Section I. Well aware that the opinions and beliefs of men depend not on their own will, but follow involuntarily the evidence proposed to their minds; that Almighty God hath created the mind free, and manifested his supreme will that it shall remain by making it altogether insusceptible of restraints; that all attempts to influence it by temporal punishments, or burdens, or by civil incapacitations, tend only to beget habits of hypocrisy and meanness, and are a departure from the plan of the holy author of religion, who being lord both of body and mind, yet chose not to propagate it by coercion on either, as was in his Almighty power to do, but to extend it by its influence on reason alone; that the impious presumption of legislators and rulers, civil as well as ecclesiastical, who being themselves but fallible and uninspired men, have assumed dominion over the faith of others, setting up their own opinions and modes of thinking as the only true, and infallible, and as such endeavoring to impose them on others, hath established and maintained false religions over the greatest part of the world and through all times; that to compel a man to furnish contributions of money for the propagation of opinions which he disbelieves and abhors, is sinful and tyrannical; that even the forcing him to support this or that teacher of his own religious persuasion is depriving him of the comfortable liberty of giving his contributions to the particular pastor whose morals he would make his pattern, and whose powers he feels most persuasive to righteousness; and is withdrawing from the ministry those temporary rewards, which proceeding from an approbation of their personal conduct, are an additional incitement to earnest and unremitting labors for the instruction of mankind; that our civil

[1] Foote, *op. cit.*, p. 431.

rights have no dependence on our religious opinions, any more than on opinions in physics or geometry; that therefore the prescribing any citizen as unworthy the public confidence by laying upon him an incapacity of being called to offices of trust and emolument, unless he profess or renounce this or that religious opinion, is depriving him injuriously of those privileges and advantages to which, in common with his fellow citizens, he has a natural right; that it tends also to corrupt the principles of that very religion it is meant to encourage, by bribing with a monopoly of worldly honors and emoluments those who will externally profess and conform to it; that though indeed those are criminal who do not withstand such temptations, yet neither are those innocent who lay the bait in their way; that the opinions of men are not the object of civil government, nor under its jurisdiction; that to suffer the civil magistrate to intrude his powers into the field of opinion and to restrain the profession or propagation of principles on supposition of their ill tendency is a dangerous fallacy, which at once destroys all religious liberty, because he being of course judge of that tendency, will make his opinions the rule of judgment, and approve or condemn the sentiments of others only as they shall square with or differ from his own; that it is enough for the rightful purposes of Civil Government for its officers to interfere when principles break out into overt acts against peace and good order; and, finally, that truth is great and will prevail if left to herself, that she is the proper and sufficient antagonist to error, and has nothing to fear from the conflict unless by human interposition disarmed of her natural weapons, free argument and debate; errors ceasing to be dangerous when it is permitted freely to contradict them.

Section II. *We, the General Assembly of Virginia, do enact that no man shall be compelled to frequent or support any religious worship, place or ministry whatsoever, nor shall be enforced, restrained, molested or burdened in his body or goods, nor shall otherwise suffer on account of his religious opinions or belief; but that all men shall be free to profess, and by argument to maintain, their opinions in matters of religion, and that the same shall in no wise diminish, enlarge or affect their civil capacities.*

Section III. And though we all know that this Assembly, elected by the people for the ordinary purposes of legislation only, have no power to restrain the acts of succeeding Assemblies, constituted with powers equal to our own, and that, therefore, to declare this act irrevocable would be of no effect in law; yet we are free to declare, and do declare, that the rights hereby asserted are of the nature of natural rights of mankind, and that if any act shall be hereafter passed to repeal the present or to narrow its operation, such act will be an infringement of natural right."[1]

[1] *Report of Committee of Revisors appointed by the General Assembly of Virginia in 1776*, published by order of the General Assembly, Richmond, 1784; Hening, *op. cit.*, vol. xii, p. 84-86; *Journal of the House* December 17, 1785, January 19, 1786.

By this the "Act of 1785," as it is generally known, Virginia became the first government in the world to establish the absolute divorce of Church and State, "the greatest distinctive contribution of America to the sum of Western Christianized Civilization."[1] Thomas Jefferson was our minister to France when this bill finally became a law. He clearly foresaw its importance to the European world. He had it printed both in English and in French and circulated as a part of that pamphlet literature which was so influential in advancing the French Revolution. In a letter to James Madison, December 16, 1786, he wrote:

"The Virginia Act for Religious Freedom has been received with infinite approbation in Europe, and propagated with enthusiasm. I do not mean by the governments, but by the individuals who compose them. It has been translated into French and Italian, has been sent to most of the courts of Europe, and has been the best evidence of the falsehood of those reports which stated us to be in anarchy. It is inserted in the new Encyclopedia, and is appearing in most of the publication respecting America. In fact, it is comfortable to see the standard of reason at length erected, after so many ages during which the human mind has been held in vassalage by kings, priests, and nobles; and it is honorable for us to have produced the first legislature who had the courage to declare that the reason of man may be trusted with the formation of his own opinions."[2]

In the following year, 1787, we find Count Mirabeau discussing this act in his essay on *Moses Mendelssohn and the Political Reform of the Jews.* French Jews addressed the French National Assembly as follows, January 29, 1790:

"America, to which politics will owe so many useful lessons, has rejected the word toleration from its code, as a term tending to compromise individual liberty and to sacrifice certain classes of men to other classes. To tolerate is, in fact, to suffer that which you could, if you wish, prevent and prohibit."

[1] Thom, *Struggle for Religious Freedom in Virginia,* p. 73.
[2] *Writings of Thomas Jefferson,* Ford edition, vol. iv, p. 334.

With the passage of the "Act of 1785" the real struggle for religious freedom had been won, — the principle of "Religious Liberty" had assumed legal form. Yet, religious strife was not at an end for, even in Virginia, there were still points for friction. The General Assembly of 1787 repealed the Act incorporating the Protestant Episcopal Church but provided, January 9, that each religious society should be secured in its property and authorized to regulate its own discipline.[1] The Assembly still regarded the Protestant Episcopal Church as the legal successor to the Established Church and entitled to its property. However, this was partly remedied in 1799 when the Assembly, January 24, passed "An Act to Repeal Certain Acts and to Declare the Construction of the Bill of Rights and Constitution Concerning Religion." This act recites that the acts of 1776, 1779, 1784, etc. "do admit the church established under the regal government to have continued so, subsequently to the Constitution; have asserted a legislative right to establish any religious sect, and have incorporated religious sects, all of which is inconsistent with the principles of the Constitution and of religious freedom, and manifestly tends to the establishment of a national church." The Act of 1799, accordingly, repealed the acts mentioned; but it contained no order for the sale of the glebes.[2]

It was not until 1802 that the General Assembly repealed all the laws relative to the late Protestant Episcopal Church, and declared a true exposition of the principles of the Bill of Rights and Constitution respecting the same to be contained in the act entitled, "An act for Establishing Religious Freedom (Jefferson's Law of

[1] Hening, *op. cit.*, vol. xii, p. 266; Semple, *op. cit.*, p. 74.
[2] *Code of Virginia*, Articles under "Churches".

1785)"; thereby recognizing the principle that all property formerly belonging to the said Church, of every description, devolved on the good people of this Commonwealth on the dissolution of the British Government here in the same degree in which the right and interest of the said Church was therein derived from them; and that although the General Assembly had the right to authorize the sale of all such property indiscriminately, yet being desirous to reconcile all the good people of this Commonwealth, it was deemed inexpedient at that time to disturb the present incumbents. Accordingly it was enacted that in any county where any glebe was or should become vacant, the overseers of the poor should have full power to sell the same. The proceeds were to be appropriated to the poor of the parish, or to any other object which a majority of freeholders and housekeepers in the parish might by writing direct, provided, that nothing should authorize an appropriation of it, "to any religious purpose whatever." The church buildings with the property contained in them, and the churchyards were not to be sold under the law, neither were any private donations made before the year 1777 to be sold, if there were any person in being entitled to hold property under the original donor. Gifts of any kind made after the year 1777 were left untouched.[1]

The Episcopalian historian Hawks can write, "The warfare begun by the Baptists seven-and-twenty years before was now finished."[2] Religious Freedom had triumphed in Virginia, whence it spread to the nation. The principles of the "Act of 1785" were to be made a part also of the national Bill of Rights by the First Amendment to the Constitution.

[1] *Code of Virginia*, "Churches"; Fristoe, *op. cit.*, p. 95; Semple, *op. cit.*, p. 74.

[2] Hawks, *op. cit.*, p. 233.

CHAPTER XIV

CONTINENTAL CONGRESS AND RELIGION

Separation of Church and State had been effected only at the close of the period under consideration; throughout the period, 1774 to 1789, Religion was one of the chief concerns of the State. From the first meeting of a committee working for American rights through to the final session of Continental Congress, we find the political assemblies imbued with a profound appreciation of their religious responsibilities. The founders of the republic invoked God in their civil assemblies, sought guidance for their political actions from their religious leaders and recognized the precepts of their Bible as sound political maxims.

The proclamations and other state papers of Continental Congress are so filled with Biblical phrases as to resemble Old Testament ecclesiastical documents. They unabashedly exhibit a belief in a Protestant Christianity and they invoke, as a sanction for their acts, the name of "God," "Almighty God," "Nature's God," "God of Armies," "Lord of Hosts," "His Goodness," "God's Superintending Providence," "Providence of God," "Providence," "Supreme and Universal Providence," "Overruling Providence of God," "Creator of All," "Indulgent Creator," "Great Governor of the World," "The Divinity," "Supreme Judge of the Universe," "Supreme Disposer of All Events," "Holy Ghost," "Christian Religion," "Jesus Christ," "God and the Constitution," and "Free Protestant Colonies." Their extreme insistence upon the religious sanction may be explained in part by the fact that the Government was without definite legislative authority; this deficiency could be remedied in no other way so well as by a reliance upon religion.

Just as there was no legally limited authority for their acts, so too there was no constitutional limitation upon the scope of their legislation. We find them legislating upon such subjects as morality, sins, repentance, humiliation, divine service, fasting, prayer, reformation, mourning, public worship, funerals, chaplains, true religion, and Thanksgiving. The Sabbath is recognized to a degree rarely exhibited in other countries; Congress adjourns, and all official business is suspended.

Almost every denomination was represented in Congress; Episcopalians by Washington, Jay, Duane, Randolph; Congregationalists by the Adamses; Quakers by Mifflin and Dickinson; Lutherans by Muhlenberg; Baptists by Manning and Ward; Presbyterians by Witherspoon, etc. Clergy as well as laymen were represented; in Zubly, Manning, Muhlenberg and Witherspoon. In fact the preëminence of some of them seems to have given cause for uneasiness and we find an effort being made to exclude them from participation in the civil affairs of the nation. On July 25, 1778, "a motion was made, that the sense of the house be taken, whether it is proper that Congress should appoint any person of an ecclesiastical character to any civil office under the United States."[1] It is evident that little support was found for the motion as when the previous question was put it was carried and the matter was never again brought forward. It is not difficult, however, to see how the commanding influence of such men as

[1] *Journals of Congress*, vol. xi, p. 718.

Manning, Witherspoon and Muhlenberg might have caused a feeling to have arisen that the clergy were a dominating power in Congress.

In so far as Congress was possessed of any delegated authority it was empowered to deal with religious matters. The credentials of the first delegates from Massachusetts Bay instructed them "to deliberate and determine upon wise and proper measures . . . . . for the recovery and establishment of their just rights and liberties, civil and religious."[1] And the Suffolk Resolutions which that colony placed before Congress on September 17, 1774, resolved among other things:

"1. That it is an indispensable duty which we owe to God, our Country, ourselves, and posterity, by all lawful ways and means in our power to maintain, defend and preserve those civil and religious rights and liberties, for which many of our fathers fought, bled and died, and to hand them down entire to future generations.

10. That the late act of Parliament for establishing the Roman Catholic religion and the French laws, in that extensive country, now called Canada, is dangerous in an extreme degree to the Protestant religion and to the civil rights and liberties of all America: and, therefore, as men and Protestant Christians, we are indispensably obliged to take all proper measures for our security.

17. That this country, confiding in the wisdom and integrity of the Continental Congress, now sitting in Philadelphia, pay all due respect and submission to such measures as may be recommended by them to the colonies for the restoration and establishment of our just rights, civil and religious." [2]

These resolutions were addressed to Gage personally with a dedication, "We are resolved, by Divine assistance, never to submit."[3] Congress replied to the resolutions with a vote of sympathy. In describing this vote John Adams wrote to his wife, "These votes were passed in full

[1] *Journals of Congress,* vol. i, p. 16.
[2] *Ibid.*, vol. i, pp. 33-36
[3] *Ibid.*, vol. i, p. 38.

Congress with perfect unanimity . . . . . the fixed determination . . . . . was enough to melt a heart of stone. I saw the tears gush into the eyes of the old, grave pacific Quakers of Pennsylvania."[1]

The First Continental Congress assembled September 5, 1774. The next day Cushing of Massachusetts moved that the daily sessions be opened with prayer. To this an objection was made by John Jay of New York and another by Rutledge of South Carolina, on the ground that, proper as the act would be, it was rendered impractical by the diversity on religious sentiments and usages of the members of Congress, — some being Congregationalists, some Presbyterians, some Anabaptists, some Episcopalians, some Quakers, etc. Whereupon Samuel Adams spoke, "I am no bigot. I can hear a prayer from a man of piety and virtue, who is at the same time a friend of his country. I am a stranger in Philadelphia, but I have heard that Mr. Duché deserves that character; and therefore I move that Mr. Duché, an Episcopalian clergyman, be desired to read prayers to the Congress tomorrow morning."[2] This motion prevailed and it was "Resolved: That the Reverend Mr. Duché be desired to open the Congress, tomorrow morning with Prayers, at the Carpenters' Hall, at 9 o'clock."[3] Mr. Adams later explained the politics of his motion as follows: "As many of our warmest friends are members of the Church of England, I thought it prudent, as well on that as on some other accounts, to move that the service should be performed by a clergyman of that denomination."[4]

The first religious service of Continental Congress is

[1] *Journals of Congress,* vol. i, p. 39.
[2] *Letters of John Adams,* vol. i, p. 23.
[3] *Journals of Congress,* vol. i, p. 26.
[4] *Ibid.,* vol. i, p. 26, footnote gives letter of Adams to John Warren.

well worth recounting in detail. Peyton Randolph, the president of Continental Congress, waited upon the Reverend Jacob Duché, rector of the united parishes of Christ Church and St. Peter's, who readily acceded to the wishes of Congress. The following morning the rector "appeared with his clerk and in his pontificals and read several prayers in the established form, and read the collect (Psalter) for the seventh of September, which was the thirty-fifth (also thirty-sixth) Psalm, 'Plead thou my cause, O Lord, with them that strive with me.' 'Bring forth the spear and stop the way against them that persecute me. Let them that imagine mischief for me be as dust before the wind. Who is like unto thee, who deliverest the poor from him that is too strong for him? Lord, how long wilt thou look on? Awake, and stand up, to judge my quarrel; avenge thou my cause, My God and my Lord.' "You must remember," continues John Adams, whose description of the event we are quoting, "this was the next morning after we heard the horrible rumor of the cannonade of Boston (Putnam's Express had brought word that the British had opened fire on the city). I never saw a greater effect upon an audience. It seemed as if Heaven had ordained that Psalm to be read on that morning. After this, Mr. Duché, unexpectedly to everybody, struck out into an extemporary prayer, which filled the bosom of every man present. I must confess, I never heard a better prayer, or one so well pronounced . . . . . Dr. Cooper himself never prayed with such fervor, such ardor, such earnestness and pathos, and in language so elegant and sublime, for America, for the Congress, for the Province of Massachusetts, and especially the town of Boston. It has had an excellent effect upon everybody . . . . . Mr. Duché is one of the most ingenious men, and the best characters, and greatest orators, in the Episcopalian order upon this continent — yet a zealous friend of liberty and his country."[1]

Mr. Duché continued in his post as chaplain of Congress for about three years; upon the Declaration of Independence his appointment was renewed.[2] His official duties were numerous. July 7, 1775, he preached in Christ Church before the First Battalion a sermon on *The Duty of Standing Fast in our Spiritual and Temporal Liberties*, which was published both in Philadelphia and in London.[3]

July 20, 1775, marks the first general fast ever proclaimed for America. On that day Continental Congress, "considering the present critical, alarming and calamitous state . . . . . for the English colonies on this continent, as a day of public humiliation, fasting and prayer" assembled at their usual place of meeting at half-past nine and went in a body "to attend divine service at Mr. Duché's church."[4] Mr. Duché took for his subject "The American Vine." In the afternoon they attended divine service at Doctor Alison's Church.[5]

In notifying Mr. Duché of his re-election to the chaplaincy in 1776, John Hancock stated that it was because of his "piety" and "uniform and zealous attachment to the rights of America."[6] Mr. Duché's prayer upon the morrow

[1] *Letters of John Adams*, vol. i, pp. 23-24. *Journals*, vol. i, p. 27.

[2] *Journals of Congress*, vol. v, p. 530, vol. vi, pp. 886-887, 911.

[3] Duché, Jacob, *The Duty of Standing Fast in our Spiritual and Temporal Liberties. A Sermon in Christ Church, Philadelphia, July 7, 1775, before the first Battalion, etc.*, Philadelphia, 1775.

[4] *Journals of Congress*, vol. ii, pp. 81, 87, 192.

[5] Duché, Jacob, *The American Vine. A Sermon Preached before Congress, 20 July 1775.* Philadelphia, 1775.

[6] *Pennsylvania Magazine*, vol. ii, p. 67 for reprint of the letter of John Hancock.

of this reappointment was a strong plea for America. It ran, in part:

"Look down in mercy, we beseech Thee, on these our American States, who have fled to Thee from the rod of the oppressor, and thrown themselves on Thy gracious protection, desiring to be henceforth dependent only on Thee. To Thee do they now look up for that countenance and support which Thou alone canst give. Take them therefore, Heavenly Father, under Thy nurturing care. Give them wisdom in council, and valor in the field; defeat the malicious designs of our cruel adversaries; convince them of the unrighteousness of their cause; and if they still persist in their sanguinary purposes, Oh! let the voice of Thine own unerring justice, sounding in their hearts, constrain them to drop the weapons of war from their unnerved hands in the day of battle."[1]

Mr. Duché possessed a gift of oratory but his enthusiasm for liberty lost its novelty and his resignation as chaplain of Congress was accepted, October 17, 1776. "Mr. Duché," so reads the *Journal*, "having, by letter, informed the president, that the state of his health, and his parochial duties, were such as obliged him to decline the honor of continuing Chaplain to the Congress, Resolved, That Mr. President be desired to return the thanks of this house to Mr. Duché, for the devout and acceptable manner in which he discharged his duty during the time he officiated as Chaplain to it; and that $150 be presented to him, as an acknowldgement from the house for his services."[2] Mr. Duché, by letter to the president acknowledged his obligation for the kind manner in which Congress had expressed its approbation of his services and requested, "as he accepted their appointment from motives perfectly disinterested, that the $150 voted to him, may be applied to the relief of the widows and children of such of

[1] Sabine, Lorenzo, *Biographical Sketches of Loyalists of the American Revolution, with an Historical Essay*, vol. i, p. 389.
[2] *Journals of Congress*, vol. vi, pp. 886-887.

the Pennsylvania officers, as have fallen in battle in the service of their country."[1]

Duché's resignation was the prelude to a still greater defection; he was to become the Benedict Arnold of the American clergy. When the British occupied Philadelphia in 1777 he remained in that city, opened his church to them and restored to the service such portions of the Prayer Book as he had recently omitted.[2] Soon he addressed a letter to his former friend, George Washington, the commander-in-chief of the American Army, exhorting him by all that was sacred and prudent, "to represent to Congress the indispensable necessity of rescinding the hasty and ill-advised Declaration of Independence." "Your interposition and advice," he continued, "I am confident, would meet with a favorable reception from the authority under which you act; if it should not, you have an infallible recourse left — negotiate for your country at the head of your army."[3] General Washington promptly referred this letter to Congress;[4] Duché was ruined. He went to England with Lord Cornwallis and the defeated British army and only returned to his native country in 1792, — old, paralytic and harmless.

A resolution of December 21, provided, "That two Chaplains be appointed."[5] On December 23, 1776, the Reverend Mr. P. Alison and the Reverend Mr. William White were selected.[6] The former having declined the appointment, the Reverend Dr. George Duffield was

[1] *Journals of Congress*, vol. vi, p. 911.
[2] *Pennsylvania Magazine*, vol. ii, p. 69.
[3] *Washington's Writings*, vol. vi, p. 114; Sparkes, Jared, *Correspondence of the American Revolution*, vol. i, pp. 448-458.
[4] *Journals of Congress*, vol. iv, p. 822.
[5] *Ibid.*, vol, vi, p. 1033.
[6] *Ibid.*, vol. vi, p. 1034.

elected in his stead, and accepted the honor.[1] These two, Dr. White, an Episcopalian,[2] and Dr. Duffield, a Presbyterian,[3] were both Philadelphia clergymen. They continued in the service of Congress for some time, conducting services for its dead, preparing and delivering sermons and memorials for days of fast, prayer, humiliation and thanksgiving, assisting in patriotic celebrations, supervising the preparation and publication of an American Bible, — in general acting as spiritual guides to the new nation, the officially constituted leaders of American Christianity.

In 1784 the Reverend Mr. Daniel Jones was elected chaplain of Congress,[4] and it was resolved that appointments be made annually.[5] But nothing seems to have gone regularly and according to law in the later days of Continental Congress. Mr. Jones was reëlected in 1784 for 1785;[6] but he having resigned in January, 1785, Mr. Provoost was elected.[7] Later in that same year the Rev. Mr. Provoost and the Reverend Dr. Rodgers were elected.[8] They continued to be reëlected until the termination of Congress.[9] In 1788 an effort to regularize their offices was made by the provision for an annual salary of "not to exceed three hundred dollars."[10]

The Baptists of New England sent their representative, the Reverend Isaac Backus, to Philadelphia to interest the First Continental Congress in the question of religious

[1] *Journals of Congress,* vol. viii, pp. 756, vol. ix, 822.
[2] *Supra.,* pp. 43-44.
[3] *Supra,* pp. 96-98.
[4] *Journals of Congress,* vol. iv, p. 331 (Washington edition 1823).
[5] *Ibid.,* vol. iv, p. 454.
[6] *Ibid.,* vol. iv, p. 456.
[7] *Ibid.,* vol. iv, p. 462.
[8] *Ibid.,* vol. iv, pp. 461-607.
[9] *Ibid.,* vol. iv, pp. 720, 811.
[10] *Ibid.,* vol. iv, p. 811.

freedom. We have already noted how the political skill of the Massachusetts politicians prevailed over the Baptists and Quakers[1] and prevented the discussion from reaching the floor of Congress. The question of the relinquishment of control over religious matters did not come before Continental Congress.

In fact Congress acted as though it possessed plenary powers in matters touching religious questions. The non-importation agreement of October 14, 1774, demanded that Parliament speedily and absolutely repeal certain abuses, prominent among which was the following, "Also the Act passed in the same session for establishing the Roman Catholic Religion in the Province of Quebec."[2] The Act of Association, October 20, 1774, reiterated as a cause for union, "an act for extending the Province of Quebec . . . . thus . . . . . . to dispose the inhabitants to act with hostility against the free Protestant colonies."[3] The Address to the People of Great Britain, October 21, 1774, stated,

"That we think the Legislature of Great Britain is not authorized by the Constitution to establish a religion fraught with sanguinary and impious tenets . . . . . in any quarter of the globe . . . . .

And by another Act the dominion of Canada is to be so extended, modelled, and governed, as that by being disunited from us, detached from our interests, by civil as well as religious prejudices, that by their numbers daily swelling with Catholic emigrants from Europe, and by their devotion to an administration, so friendly to their religion they might become formidable to us, and on occasion be fit instruments in the hands of power, to reduce the ancient free Protestant Colonies to the same state of slavery with themselves.

Nor can we suppress our astonishment, that a British Parliament should ever consent to establish in that country a religion that has deluged your island in blood, and dispersed impiety, bigotry, persecution, murder and rebellion throughout every part of the world.

[1] *Supra.*, pp. 117-120, 330-334, 361, 363.
[2] *Journals of Congress*, Ford edition, vol. i, p. 72.
[3] *Ibid.*, vol. i, p. 76.

Admit that the Ministry, by the powers of Britain, and the aid of our Roman Catholic neighbors, should be able to carry the point of taxation, and reduce us to a state of perfect humiliation and slavery . . . . . remember the taxes from America, the wealth and, we may add, the men, and particularly the Roman Catholics of this vast continent will then be in the power of your enemies."[1]

The Memorial to the Inhabitants of the Colonies, October 21, 1774, contained similar clauses:

"Duty to Almighty God, the creator of all, requires . . .
In the session of parliament last mentioned, an act was passed, for changing the government of Quebec, by which act the Roman Catholic religion, instead of being tolerated, as stipulated by the treaty of peace, is established . . . . .
The authors of this arbitrary arrangement flatter themselves, that the inhabitants, deprived of liberty, and artfully provoked against those of another religion, will be proper instruments for assisting in the oppression of such as differ from them in modes of government and faith.
We . . . . . cannot . . . . . be persuaded that they (the people of England), the defenders of true religion, and the asserters of the rights of mankind, will take part against their affectionate Protestant brethren in the colonies, in favor of our open and their own secret enemies, whose intrigues, for several years past, have been wholly exercised in sapping the foundations of civil and religious liberty."[2]

In their Petition to the King, October 26, 1774, they complain, that:

"In the last session of parliament an act was passed . . . . . for extending the limits of Quebec, abolishing the English and restoring the French law, whereby great numbers of the British freemen are subjected to the latter, and establishing an absolute government and the Roman Catholic religion throughout those vast regions."[3]

At the same time that Congress was composing the foregoing addresses, memorials and petitions, it was drawing up a Letter to the Inhabitants of Quebec. This letter appears to the American historian, Bancroft, "a

[1] *Journals of Congress*, vol. i, pp. 83-88.
[2] *Ibid.*, vol. i, pp. 90-100.
[3] *Ibid.*, vol. i, p. 117.

masterly address, drawn by Dickinson;"[1] and to the English historian, Lecky, "an ingenious address . . . . . to alienate (the Canadians) from England."[2] It contains the following articles with respect to the religious question:

"These are the rights you are entitled to and ought at this moment in perfection, to exercise. And what is offered to you by the late Act of Parliament in their place? Liberty of Conscience in your religion? No. God gave it to you; and the temporal powers with which you have been and are connected, firmly stipulated for your enjoyment of it . . . Such is the precarious tenure of mere will, by which you hold your lives and religion. The Crown and its Ministers are empowered as far as they could be by Parliament, to establish even the Inquisition itself among you.

We are too well acquainted with the liberality of sentiment distinguishing your nation, to imagine, that differences of religion will prejudice you against a hearty amity with us. You know, that the transcendent nature of freedom elevates those, who unite in her cause, above all such low-minded infirmities. The Swiss Cantons, furnish a memorable proof of this truth. Their union is composed of Roman Catholic and Protestant States, living in the utmost concord and peace with one another, and thereby enabled, ever since they bravely vindicated their freedom, to defy and defeat every tyrant that has invaded them.

That Almighty God may incline your minds to approve our equitable and blessed measures, to add yourself to us, to put your fate . . . . . on the consolidated powers of North America . . . . . is the fervent prayer of us, your sincere and affectionate friends and fellow-subjects." [3]

The foregoing series of documents relative to American Catholicism is not so disingenuous as it might seem on first reading; certainly they did not give offense to that body of Catholics in the Colonies led by Charles Carroll. American Catholicism had been fighting a battle for the principles of "freedom" as against the English principle

[1] Bancroft, *op. cit.*, vol. vii, p. 159.

[2] Lecky, *England in the 18th Century*, vol. iii, p. 446.

[3] *Journals of Congress*, vol. i, pp. 108-117; Cobb, *Rise of Religious Liberty*, p. 490, says of this address, "This was the sole reference to the subject of religion until the Convention of 1787, embedded in the Federal Constitution, the principle of full religious liberty." Bancroft, *op. cit.*, vol. vii, p. 159.

of an establishment which had "dispersed impiety, bigotry, persecution, murder, and rebellion."

The temper of the Second Continental Congress, which met May 10, 1775, was far different from that of the First Congress; American blood had been shed at Lexington. This new body was assembled to carry on active warfare and to organize a nation for victory. Even in this temper they were not unmindful of their reliance on Diety. On their opening day it was ordered, "That Mr. Duché be requested to open the Congress with prayers to-morrow morning."[1] This he did, agreeable to the desire of the Congress, with an "excellent prayer so well adapted to the present occasion."[2]

On June 7, it was resolved, "That Thursday the 20th of July next, be observed throughout the twelve United Colonies (Georgia has not as yet sent delegates to the Congress), as a day of humiliation, fasting and prayer: and that Mr. Hooper, Mr. J. Adams, and Mr. Paine, be a committee to bring in a resolve for that purpose."[3] As supplications to Divine Providence continue a frequent recourse of Continental Congress it is well to note carefully the character of this its first one:

"As the great Governor of the World, by his supreme and universal Providence, not only conducts the course of nature with unerring wisdom and rectitude, but frequently influences the minds of men to serve the wise and gracious purposes of His providential government; and it being at all times, our indispensable duty devoutly to acknowledge his superintending providence, especially in times of impending danger and public calamity, to reverence and adore his immutable justice as well as to implore his merciful interposition for our deliverance:

This Congress, therefore, considering the present critical, alarming and calamitous state of these colonies, do earnestly recommend, that Thurs-

[1] *Journals of Congress*, vol. ii, p. 12.
[2] *Ibid.*, vol. ii, pp. 13, 22.
[3] *Ibid.*, vol. ii, p. 81.

day, the 20th day of July next, be observed, by the inhabitants of all the English colonies on this continent, as a day of public humiliation, fasting and prayer; that we may, with united hearts and voices, unfeignedly confess and deplore our many sins; and offer up our joint supplications to the all-wise, omnipotent, and merciful disposer of all events; humbly beseeching Him to forgive our iniquities, to remove our present calamities, to avert those desolating judgments, with which we are threatened, and to bless our rightful sovereign, King George the Third, and inspire him with wisdom to discern and pursue the true interest of all his subjects, that a speedy end may be put to the civil discord between Great Britain and the American colonies, without farther effusion of blood: And that the British nation may be influenced to regard the things that belong to her peace, before they be hid from her eyes: That these colonies may be ever under the care and protection of a kind Providence, and be prospered in all their interests; That the divine blessing may descend and rest upon all our civil rulers, and upon the representatives of the people, in their several assemblies and conventions, that they may be directed to wise and effectual measures for preserving the union, and securing the just rights and privileges of the colonies: That virtue and true religion may revive and flourish throughout our land; And that all America may soon behold a gracious interposition of Heaven, for the redress of her many grievances, the restoration of her invaded rights, a reconciliation with the parent state, on terms constitutional and honorable to both; And that the civil and religious privileges may be secured to the latest posterity.

And it is recommended to Christians, of all denominations, to assemble for public worship, and to abstain from servile labor and recreation on said day.

Ordered, That a copy of the above be signed by the President and attested by the Secretary and published in the newspapers, and in hand bills."[1]

Congress renewed its appeal to Canada, May 29, 1775, saying, "We perceived the fate of the Protestant and Catholic colonies to be strongly linked together." A thousand copies of this were sent to Canada to be dispersed among the inhabitants.[2] The Congressional Address to their constituency, July 8, was an invocation: "Let us entreat Heaven to avert our ruin, and the

[1] *Journals of Congress*, vol. ii, pp. 87-88.
[2] *Ibid.*, vol. ii, pp. 68-69.

destruction that threatens our friends, brethren, and countrymen."[1] The Declaration setting forth the causes and necessities for taking up arms reads:

"Our cause is just. Our union is perfect . . . . . We gratefully acknowledge, as signal instances of Divine favor towards us, that His Providence would not permit us to be called into this severe controversy until . . . . .

With an humble confidence in the mercies of the supreme and impartial Judge and Ruler of the universe, we most devoutly implore His Divine Goodness."[2]

In An Address to the People of Ireland, they assert their determination, "to enjoy that degree of Liberty, to which God and the Constitution have given them an undoubted right."[3]

Religion proved an excellent weapon with which to keep the Indians friendly. Captain White Eyes, a Delaware Chief, who had come down with the Commissioners for Indian Affairs in the Middle Department, was introduced into Congress. Whereupon the President addressed him in the following manner:

"Brother White Eyes . . .

We have heard of your friendship for your Brethren, the White People, and how useful you have been in preserving peace and harmony between your nation and us . . . . .

We are pleased that the Delawares intend to embrace Christianity. We will send you, according to your desire, a minister and a schoolmaster to instruct you in the principles of religion and other parts of useful knowledge."[4]

In pursuance of this promise Congress resolves, April 10, 1776:

"That the commissioners for Indian Affairs, in the Middle Department, or anyone of them, be desired to employ, for reasonable salaries, a minister

[1] *Journals of Congress*, vol. ii, pp. 163-170.
[2] *Ibid.*, vol. ii, pp. 140-157.
[3] *Ibid.*, vol. ii, p. 217.
[4] *Ibid.*, vol. iii, p. 433.

of the gospel, to reside among the Delaware Indians, and instruct their youth reading, writing, and arithmetic; and also, a blacksmith to do the work of the Indians in the Middle Department." [1]

Chief White Eyes had entered upon this negotiation without authorization from his tribe, — he had transgressed an Indian law. The Delawares when they learned of these plans, feared that a minister of some denomination other than the Moravian Brethren might be placed over them. White Eyes had acted independently of Zeisberger and his Christian Indians. The Council of the Indians accordingly disapproved of such action and the new Indian agent for the Middle Department was informed that the Delawares would abide by the Moravian Church.[2]

While providing for the Delawares, Congress at first refused aid to Dartmouth College for its work with the Indians, saying that "Although the prosperity of Dartmouth College . . . . . is a desirable object, it is neither seasonable nor prudent to contribute towards its relief or support out of the public treasury."[3] However, later, January 21, 1778, the Board of War brought in another report on Indian Affairs, which contained a clause to the effect, "that the Commissioners be authorized, and directed, to comply with Mr. Wheelock's request, as to the maintenance and education of the Indian children."[4] And on December 18, 1778;

"A report of the Board of Treasury was read: Whereupon, Congress came to the following order and resolution: Whereas Dr. Wheelock has incurred expense in supporting a number of Indian youths, of the Caghnawage tribe, at his school, which in times past has been the means of conciliating the friendship of that tribe: Ordered, That a warrant be issued on the treasurer in favor of Lieutenant Colonel Wheelock for nine

[1] *Journals of Congress*, vol. iv, pp. 267-269.
[2] De Schweinitz, *op. cit.*, pp. 431, 436-439.
[3] *Journals of Congress*, vol. iv, p. 267.
[4] *Ibid.*, vol. xii, p. 1230.

hundred and twenty five dollars, for the use of the said Dr. Eleazar Wheelock."[1]

Thenceforth, appropriations for Dartmouth College are regular Congressional expenses.[2] Dr. Witherspoon also was emboldened to seek similar support for his College of New Jersey (Princeton).[3] New England missionaries seem to have been especially effective in alienating Indians from British allegiance.[4]

The interest of Congress in religion and education kept on the increase and in 1778, October 12, we find that:

"Congress came to the following resolution: Whereas true religion and good morals are the only solid foundation of public liberty and happiness: Resolved, That it is, hereby earnestly recommended to the several states, to take the most effectual measures for the encouragement thereof, and for the suppression of theatrical entertainments, horse racing, and such other diversions as are productive of idleness, dissipation, and general depravity of principles and manners. Resolved, That all officers in the Army of the United States, be, and hereby are, strictly enjoined to see that the good and wholesome rules provided for the discountenancing of prophaneness and vice, and the preservation of morals among the soldiers, are duly and punctually observed."[5]

Opposition developed to the first clause of this resolution, but New Hampshire, Massachusetts, Rhode Island, Connecticut, New Jersey, and South Carolina supported it; Pennsylvania, Virginia, and Georgia were divided on the subject, and Maryland and North Carolina were the only two states wholly opposed. It was accordingly adopted and may be considered as the original federal educational action which was to assert itself next in the "religion and education" clause of the North-West Ordinance.[6]

[1] *Journals of Congress*, vol. x, p. 106.
[2] *Ibid.*, vol. xvi, pp. 162-163.
[3] *Ibid.*, vol. xxi, pp. 820, 841, 1051.
[4] *Washington's Works*, vol. iii, p. 495; *Documents Relating to the Colonial History of New York*, vol. viii, pp. 656-657.
[5] *Journals of Congress*, vol. xii, p. 1001.
[6] *Infra.*, p. 438.

In the matter of army organization and regulation Congress kept a religious point of view well to the fore. Chaplains were provided for with a pay equivalent to that of Captains.[1] The Articles of War, as agreed to June 30, 1775, provided:

"Article 2. It is earnestly recommended to all officers and soldiers, diligently to attend Divine Service; and all officers and soldiers who shall behave indecently or irreverently at any place of Divine Worship, shall, if commissioned officers, be brought before a court martial, there to be publicly and severely reprimanded by the President; if non-commissioned officers or soldiers, every person so offending, shall, for the first offence, forfeit one sixth of a dollar, to be deducted out of his next pay; for the second offence, he shall not only forfeit a like sum, but be confined for twenty-four hours, and for every like offence, shall suffer and pay in like manner; which money so forfeited, shall be applied to the use of the sick soldiers of the troop or company to which the offender belongs.

Article 3. Whatsoever non-commissioned officer or soldier shall use any profane oath or execration, shall incur the penalty expressed in the second article; and if a commissioned officer be thus guilty of profane cursing or swearing, he shall forfeit and pay for each and every such offence, the sum of four shillings, lawful money."[2]

The revised Articles of War, as adopted by Congress in 1776, reaffirm these provisions, merely changing the fine to one sixth of a dollar. But they add the following article on Chaplains:

"Section 1, article 4: Every Chaplain who is commissioned to a regiment, company, troop, or garrison, and shall absent himself from the said regiment, company, troop, or garrison (excepting in case of sickness or leave of absence), shall be brought to a court-martial, and be fined not exceeding one month's pay, besides the loss of his pay during his absence, or be discharged, as the said court-martial shall judge most proper."[3]

The Rules for the Regulation of the Navy as agreed upon November 28, 1775, decreed:

"If any shall be heard to swear, curse, or blaspheme the name of God, the Commander is strictly enjoined to punish them for every offence, by

[1] *Journals of Congress*, vol. ii, pp. 220. [2] *Ibid.*, vol. ii, p. 111.
[3] *Ibid.*, vol. v, p. 789.

causing them to wear a wooden collar, or some other shameful badge or distinction, for so long time as he shall judge proper. If he be a commissioned officer, he shall forfeit one shilling for each offence, and a warrant or inferior officer six pence." [1]

The navy chaplain was to receive the same pay as a navy captain, a rate slightly higher than that paid in the army.

We have reason to doubt the effectiveness of army and navy regulations respecting profanity, morality or religion. John Gano, the Baptist chaplain, records,

> "We lay here on the fourth of July, and the officers insisted on my preaching, which I did . . . . . On this occasion, the soldiery behaved with the most decency that I ever knew them to, during the war. Some of them usually absented themselves from worship on Lord's-day, and the only punishment they were subjected to, was the digging up of stumps, which in some instances, had a good effect." [2]

And the candid Baptist historian, Semple, tells us, "Jeremiah Walker and John Williams, being appointed by the Association, went and preached to the soldiers, when encamped in the lower parts of Virginia; they, not meeting with much encouragement, declined it after a short time."[3]

We have noted that the Roman Catholics remained firm in the allegiance to the cause of liberty even at the time when Congress was addressing anti-Catholic proclamations. A striking example of their service is to be found in the mission to Canada in 1776. The members first chosen for this commission were Dr. Benjamin Franklin, Mr. Samuel Chase and Mr. Charles Carroll. It was also resolved: "That Mr. Carroll be requested to prevail on Mr. John Carroll (a priest, later to be the first Catholic bishop in the United States) to accompany the

[1] *Journals of Congress,* vol. iii, p. 378.
[2] *Biographical Memoirs of the Late Rev. John Gano,* p. 104.
[3] Semple, *op. cit.,* p. 62.

committee to Canada, to assist them in such matters as they shall think useful."[1] The Reverend John Carroll accepted the commission and the committee thus composed proceeded to Canada, under the injunctions from Congress, dated March 20, 1776, the religious part of which was as follows:

> "You are further to declare, that we hold sacred the rights of conscience, and may promise to the whole people, solemnly in our name, the free and undisturbed exercise of their religion; and, to the clergy the full, perfect, and peaceable possession and enjoyment of all their estates; that the government of everything relating to their religion and clergy shall be left entirely in the hands of the good people of that province, and such legislature as they shall constitute; Provided, however, that all other denominations of Christians be equally entitled to hold offices, and enjoy civil privileges and the free exercise of their religion, and be totally exempt from the payment of any tythes or taxes for the support of any religion.
>
> Inform them, that you are vested by this Congress with full powers to effect these purposes." [2]

We note, from the multitude of proclamations which Congress composed, the great part which propaganda played in the War for American Independence; in fact, it was the first great war in which this element played its full part. Since the Protestant Revolt of the sixteenth century, the churches had known the use of this element of warfare, as a means of breaking or creating morale. It is not surprising to find the new state relying largely upon the religious element as an instrument of propaganda and upon the churches as means of promulgating the same.

On August 14, 1776, a committee appointed to devise a plan for encouraging the Hessians, and other foreigners, to

[1] *Journals of Congress*, vol. iv, p. 152.
[2] *Ibid.*, vol. iv, pp. 215-218.

desert the British service, brought in a report which resulted in the adoption of the following resolution:

"Whereas it has been the wise policy of these states to extend the protection of their laws to all those who should settle among them, of whatever nation or religion they might be, and to admit them to a participation of the benefits of civil and religious freedom; and, the benevolence of this practice, as well as its salutary effects, have rendered it worthy of being continued in future times . . . . . .

Resolved, Therefore, that these states will receive all such foreigners who shall leave the armies of his Britannic majesty in America, and shall choose to become members of any of these states; and that they shall be protected in the free exercise of their respective religions." [1]

Congress was to learn that assumption of ecclesiastical powers entailed responsibilities and might ultimately raise difficulties which were hard to settle. We have seen how their actions with relation to the Quakers tended to convince them that it would be just as well to leave some religious matters to state jurisdictions.[2] This episode contributed not a little toward the ultimate willingness with which the Federal Government renounced those powers over religious matters which it had assumed during the Revolutionary period.

Then too not all questions of religious policy could meet with unanimous decisions. April 2, 1777, Mr. Gouverneur Morris moved, "that as this day is Good Friday, the House adjourn until tomorrow, agreeable to the former practice in the years 1776 and 1777."[3] This motion was carried: Muhlenberg, John Jay, Samuel Adams, and Morris voted for it, Witherspoon against it. It is quite evident from the fact that business was usually suspended on Good Friday that the champions of that holiday were numerous in Congress.

[1] *Journals of Congress*, vol. v, p. 653.
[2] *Supra.*, pp. 145-151.
[3] *Journals of Congress*, vol. xiii, pp. 409-410.

In March 1781, the Articles of Confederation, duly ratified by the States, were put into effect through the Declaration of Congress which began:

"The delegates of the States, in promulgating the Articles of Confederation, do for themselves make the following acknowledgment:

And whereas, it hath pleased the Great Governor of the World to incline the hearts of the legislatures we respectively represent in Congress, to approve and to authorize us to ratify the said . . . . . [1]"

One of the first acts of Congress under the Articles was the procurement of an American Bible. No edition of the Bible in the English language had been published in America up to the time of the Revolution. Ministers experienced a shortage of Bibles for their services as a result of the war and Congress had accordingly been petitioned to secure the publication of the book. A resolution was adopted, October 26, 1780, "That it be recommended to such of the States who may think it convenient for them that they take proper measures to procure one or more new and correct editions of the Old and New Testament to be printed and that such states regulate their printers by law so as to secure effectually the said books from being misprinted."[2]

In the meantime Robert Aitken of Philadelphia had gone ahead on his own initiative and finished an edition of the Bible. He accordingly memorialized Congress for an official endorsement of his work.

On September 12, 1782, the committee consisting of Mr. Duane, Mr. McKean, and Mr. Witherspoon, to whom had been referred the memorial from Robert Aitken, dated January 21, 1781, respecting an edition of the Holy Scriptures, reported:

"That Mr. Aiken has at a great expense now finished an American edition of the Holy Scriptures in English; that the committee have,

[1] *Journals of Congress*, vol. xix, p. 221.
[2] *Ibid.*, vol. xxiii, pp. 572-577.

from time to time, attended to his progress in the work; that they also recommend it to the two chaplains of Congress to examine and give their opinion of the execution, who have accordingly reported thereon. The recommendation and report being as follows:

Philadelphia, September 1, 1782.

Reverend Gentlemen, Our knowledge of your piety and public spirit leads us without apology to recommend to your particular attention the edition of the Holy Scriptures publishing by Mr. Aitken. He undertook this expensive work at a time, when from the circumstances of the war, an English edition of the bible could not be imported, nor any opinion formed how long the obstruction might continue. On this account particularly he deserves applause and encouragement. We therefore wish you, reverend gentlemen, to examine the execution of the work, and if approved, to give it the sanction of your judgment and the weight of your recommendation. We are with every great respect your most obedient humble servants.

James Duane, Chairman.

Rev. Dr. White and Rev. Mr. Duffield, chaplains of the United States in Congress assembled

Report September 10, 1782.

Gentlemen. Agreeably to your desire, we have paid attention to Mr. Robert Aitken's impression of the Holy Scriptures, of the Old and New Testament. Having selected and examined a variety of passages throughout the work we are of opinion, that it is executed with great accuracy as to the sense, and with as few grammatical and typographical errors as could be expected in an undertaking of such magnitude. Being ourselves witnesses of the demand for this invaluable book, we rejoice in the present prospect of a supply, hoping that it will prove as advantageous as it is honorable to the gentleman, who has exerted himself to furnish it at the evident risk of private fortune. We are, gentlemen, your very respectful and humble servants.

William White
George Duffield

Whereupon it was resolved: That the United States in Congress assembled, highly approve the pious and laudable undertaking of Mr. Aitken, as subservient to the interest of religion as well as an instance of the progress of arts in this country, and being satisfied from the above report, of his care and accuracy in the execution of the work, they recommend this edition of the Bible to the inhabitants of the United States and hereby authorize him to publish this recommendation in the manner he shall think proper."[1]

[1] *Journals of Congress*, vol. xxiii, pp. 572-574.

After the adoption of the Articles of Confederation and the close of the war the usefulness of Congress rapidly declined. Its two greatest achievements were the Treaty of Peace with Great Britain and the North-West Ordinance. Both of these documents disclose a Congress still reliant upon Christianity.

The Treaty of Peace was proclaimed January 14, 1783, "In the name of the Most Holy and Undivided Trinity," and its opening phrase was, "It having pleased the Divine Providence to dispose the hearts."[1]

Congress, through its diplomatic agents, was forced to take a stand on the religious questions as it affected foreign relations. No sooner was peace established than the Papal Nuncio at Paris, July 28, 1783, addressed to Benjamin Franklin the following note, in which the idea of a French superior for American Catholicism is clearly advocated and in which the question of the government of American Catholicism is viewed as a matter to be settled by the King of France and Congress.

"The Nuncio Apostolic has the honor to transmit to Mr. Franklin the subjoined note. He requests him to cause it to be presented to the Congress of the United States of North America, and to support it with his influence.

Note, — Previous to the revolution which has just been completed in the United States of North America, the Catholics and missionaries of those provinces depended, in spiritual matters, on the Vicar-Apostolic residing in London. It is now evident that this arrangement can be no longer maintained, but, as it is necessary that the Catholic Christians of the United States should have an ecclesiastic to govern them in matters pertaining to religion, the *Congregation de Propaganda Fide*, existing at Rome, for the establishment and preservation of missions, have come to the determination to propose to Congress to establish, in one of the cities of the United States of North America, one of their Catholic brethren, with the authority and power of Vicar-Apostolic and dignity of

[1] *Treaties and Conventions Concluded between the United States of America and Other Powers, Since July 4, 1776*, p. 375.

Bishop, or simply with the rank of Apostolic Prefect. The institution of a Bishop-Apostolic appears the most suitable, inasmuch as the Catholics of the United States may have within their reach the reception of Confirmation and Orders in their own country. And as it may sometimes happen that among the members of the Catholic body in the United States, no one may be found qualified to undertake the charge of the spiritual government, either as Bishop or Prefect-Apostolic, it may be necessary under the circumstances, that Congress should consent to have one selected from some foreign nation on close terms of friendship with the United States." [1]

Dr. Franklin seems to have been willing to lend his support to the plan. On December 15, 1783, he wrote the Count de Vergennes:

"Sir: — I understand that the Bishop or Spiritual persons who superintends or governs the Roman Catholic clergy in the United States of America, resides in London, and is supposed to be under obligations to that Court, and subject to be influenced by its Ministers. This gives me some uneasiness, and I cannot but wish that one should be appointed to that office, who is of this nation and who may reside here among our friends. I beg your Excellency to think a little of this matter and to afford me your counsels upon it." [2]

The memorandum of Vergennes on this matter shows that he was keener than Franklin as to national character of American Catholicism. He wrote:

"Mr. Franklin represente que l'Evêque de la direction du clergé Catholique, en Amerique résidant a Londres, il est de notre interret de nommer à cette place une personne qui puisse demeurer dans les Etats Unis." [3]

We have no record, though, that Franklin did more than to transmit to the Continental Congress, without personal comment, the documents submitted to him. Unfortunately at that moment Congress contained no Catholics as both Daniel Carroll and Thomas Fitz-

[1] *Diplomatic Correspondence of the American Revolution*, vol. iv, pp. 158-159.

[2] Shea, *Life and Times of Archbishop Carroll*, vol. ii, pp. 214-215.

[3] *Ibid.*, vol. ii, p. 216.

simons had retired. The reply of Congress was without the knowledge of American Catholics; it does, however, embody a great American principle.

> "Resolved, That Doctor Franklin be desired to notify to the Apostolic Nuncio at Versaille, that Congress will always be pleased to testify their respect to his sovereign and state; but that the subject of his application to Doctor Franklin, being purely spiritual, it is without the jurisdiction and powers of Congress, who have no authority to permit or refuse it, these powers being reserved to the several states individually." [1]

As Professor W. F. Johnson points out, "The importance and value of this action, to all the subsequent history of the nation, are scarcely to be overestimated . . . . . It was a priceless precaution against our being drawn into complications with alien powers in which, — as at that time was all but universally the case, — church and state were united to the detriment of both."[2]

An American principle had been established by this action but this does not preclude the possibility of diplomatic influence working along religious lines. A very delicate international problem was presented by the American desire for Anglican ordination for their bishops; and it was managed with tact to a successful issue, thanks to the discretion of several American officials, both civil and ecclesiastical.

The Episcopalian Convention of 1785, in agreeing to a plan for obtaining consecration through addressing the Archbishops and Bishops of England, decided, October 5, 1785:

> "In order to assure their Lordships of the legality of the present proposed application, that the Deputies now assembled be desired to make a respectful address to the civil rulers of the States in which they

[1] *Secret Journals of the Acts and Proceedings of Congress*, vol. iii, p. 493.
[2] Johnson, *America's Foreign Relations*, vol. i, pp. 135-136.

respectively reside, to certify that the said application is not contrary to the Constitutions and laws of the same." [1]

In the address to the English clergy they inserted the following significant passage:

"It may be of consequence to observe, that in these States there is a separation between the concerns of policy and those of religion; that, accordingly, our civil rulers cannot officially join in the present application; that, however, we are far from apprehending the opposition or even displeasure of any of those honorable personages; and finally, that in this business we are justified by the Constitutions of the States, which are the foundations and control of all our laws." [2]

American Episcopalians were far too skilled in the politics of church and state not to utilize whatever influence there was available. The Episcopalian members of Congress were able to procure unofficial aid from the officials of the national government. William White wrote to Dr. Smith, November 1, 1785:

"Mr. Provoost has enclosed to me a Copy of a Letter from the President of Congress to the Minister at the Court of Great Britain. After stating our late proceedings and the political hinderances on a former occasion, he says, that if our application to the Bishops should come before the King and Ministry, it is the wish of 'the Church of England Members of Congress' that Mr. Adams may assure them of our right to take the said step and that the granting our petition would not be an intermeddling in the affairs of these states." [3]

The governors of several of the states were induced to intercede. Upon the adjournment of the Episcopalian Convention on 1785 the Pennsylvania delegates, composed the following:

"To the Honorable the Supreme Executive Council of the Commonwealth of Pennsylvania.

The petition of the subscribers, late Deputies of the Protestant Episco-

[1] Perry, *Journals*, vol. pp. 24-25.
[2] *Ibid.*, vol. i, pp. 26-27.
[3] *Ibid.*, vol. iii, p. 138.

pal Church in the said Commonwealth to a general ecclesiastical Convention of the said church, held in this City:

Humbly sheweth;

That the said Church has taken sundry measures for the obtaining within itself the powers of ordination, agreeably to its ancient institutions of usage, in order that it may exist independently of all foreign authority, civil or ecclesiastical;

That for the accomplishing of this purpose the said ecclesiastical convention have addressed the Archbishops and Bishops of the Church of England, requesting them to confer the Episcopal character on such persons, as shall be chosen and sent to their Lordships by the said church in any of the United States; a copy of which address your petitioners now lay before your Honorable Council.

That the said ecclesiastical convention had received undoubted information (which your petitioners are ready to lay before the Honorable Council) that the English prelates, on a similar application from the clergy of the said church in one of the United States, were not able to take measures for the granting of the request, because the British Ministry were apprehensive that might be offensive to the civil authority of the said state;

That in consequence of the above information, the said ecclesiastical convention instructed the deputies composing their body, that on their return to their respective states, they should make a respectful application to their civil rulers requesting them to certify, that the said Address to the Archbishops and Bishops of the Church of England is not contrary to our laws or constitutions, and that a compliance with it will not be offensive to the civil powers under which we live; and

That your petitioners do accordingly now make the said application to your honorable body, and as it has been uniformly the endeavor of the Episcopal Church in this State, and in the other states represented in the late convention, so to form their ecclesiastical system, as that it may harmonize with our civil duties and the interests and happiness of the United States; so they trust, that your Honorable Body will condescend to their request; and think it not unworthy of your wisdom or beneath your dignity to remove the political obstacle which may prevent their obtaining the Episcopal Succession in a way, which they hope will be thought reputable to themselves and safe to their country."[1]

A document similar to this had been furnished by the governor of Maryland, upon the application of Dr. Smith. Certificates of the desired form were obtained

[1] Perry, *op. cit.*, vol. iii, pp. 279-280.

from the chief officers of Pennsylvania, New York and Virginia.

The Pennsylvania certificate is as follows:

"The Supreme Executive Council of the Commonwealth of Pennsylvania, do hereby certify and make known to all whom it may concern, that agreeable to the frame of government and laws of this Commonwealth, — the clergy and others, members of the Church of England in Pennsylvania, are at liberty to take such means as they may think proper for keeping up a succession of religious teachers — Provided only, that the measures they adopt for this purpose do not induce a subjection to any foreign jurisdiction, civil or ecclesiastical." [1]

The New York certificate, signed by Governor George Clinton read: December 28, 1785:

"To All to Whom these Presents Shall Come or May Concern.

It is certified and made known that by the constitution of the said state, it is ordained and declared that the free exercises and enjoyment of religious profession and worship, without discrimination or preference, shall forever be allowed within this state to all mankind, and that there is nothing in the said constitution, or in any of the laws of the said state, to prohibit the clergy and others of the Episcopal Churches or of any other church in the said state, to take such measures as they shall judge proper, for keeping up a succession of religious teachers, Provided, that the means they may adopt for this purpose be not inconsistent with the peace or safety of the state and do not induce a subjection or allegiance to any foreign jurisdiction or power, civil or ecclesiastical whatever." [2]

At the request of Dr. Griffith, Patrick Henry, the Governor of Virginia, furnished the certificate from that state as follows: June 1, 1786:

"It is certified and made known to all whom it may concern — That the Protestant Episcopal Church is incorporated by an Act of the Legislature of this Commonwealth, for that purpose made and provided: that there is no law existing in the Commonwealth, which in any manner forbids the admission of Bishops, or the exercise of their office; on the contrary, by the 16th Article of the Declaration of Rights, it is provided in the words following, viz., — 'That religion, or the duty which we owe to our Creator, and the manner of discharging it, can be directed only by

[1] Perry, *op. cit.*, vol. iii, p. 281.
[2] *Ibid.*, vol. iii, pp. 281-282.

reason and conviction, not by force or violence, and therefore all men are equally entitled to the free exercise of religion, according to the dictates of conscience; and that it is the mutual duty of all to practice Christian forbearance, love and charity towards each other,' — which said Article is now in full force." [1]

Dr. Provoost wrote to Dr. White, November 7, 1785:

"The Address was sent by the Packet with recommendatory letters from the President of Congress and John Jay, Esqr., who have interested themselves much in our business." [2]

Mr. Adams wrote to John Jay the following account of his activities in this matter, January 4, 1786:

"Dear Sir: A day or two after the receipt of your letter of November 1, and that of President Lee which came with it, I wrote to the Archbishop of Canterbury, by Col. Smith, for an hour when I might have the honor to pay my respects to his Grace, and was answered very politely that he would be glad to have the honor of seeing me next day, between 11 and 12. Accordingly I went yesterday, and was very agreeably received, by a venerable and candid prelate, with whom I had before only exchanged visits of ceremony.

I told his Grace, that at the desire of two very respectable characters in America, the late President of Congress, and the present Secretary of State for the Department of Foreign Affairs, I had the honor to be the bearer to his Grace, of a letter from a convention of delegates from the Episcopal Churches in most of the Southern States, which had been transmitted to me open, that I might be acquainted with its contents. That in this business, however, I acted in no official character, having no instructions from Congress, or indeed from the convention, but that I thought it most respectful to them, as well as to his Grace, to present the letter in person. The Archbishop answered, that all that he could say at present was that he was himself very well disposed to give the satisfaction desired, for he was by no means one of those, who wished that contentions should be kept up between the two countries, but on the contrary was desirous of doing everything in his power to promote harmony and good humor.

I then said that if his Grace would take the trouble of reading two letters, from Mr. Lee and Mr. Jay, he would perceive the motives of those gentlemen in sending the letter to my care. I gave him the letters which he read attentively and returned, and added that it was a great satisfaction to him to see, that gentlemen of character and reputation

[1] Perry, *op. cit.*, vol. iii, pp. 281-282.
[2] *Ibid.*, vol. iii, pp. 283-284.

interested themselves in it, for that the Episcopalians in the United States could not have the full and complete enjoyment of their religious liberties without it, and he subjoined that it was a great satisfaction to him to have received this visit from me upon this occasion — and that he would take the liberty to ask me, if it were not an improper question, whether the interposition of the Episcopal bishops would not give uneasiness and dissatisfaction in America. I replied that my answer could be only that of a private citizen, and in that capacity, I had no scruple to say that the people of the United States, in general were for a liberal and generous toleration, I might employ a stronger word and call it a right and the first right of mankind to worship God according to their consciences; and therefore, I could not see any reasonable ground for dissatisfaction, and that I hoped, and believed there would be none of any consequence.

His Grace was then pleased to say, that religion in all countries, especially in a young one, ought to be attended to, as it was the foundation of government. He hoped the characters which should be recommended would be good ones.

I replied, that there were in the churches in America able men, of character altogether irreproachable, and that such and such only, I presumed, would be recommended. I then rose to take my leave, and his Grace, then asked me, if he might be at liberty to mention that I had made him this visit on this occasion. I answered, certainly, if his Grace should judge it proper. Thus, Sir, I have fulfilled my commission and remain as usual, etc." [1]

Mr. Adams had previously interested himself in obtaining ordination for several candidates for orders in the Episcopalian Church who, after the acknowledgment of American independence, had found difficulty in obtaining it from the Bishop of London. Mr. Adams had taken the matter up with the Danish minister, who had succeeded in obtaining a promise from Denmark that they would gladly perform the ceremony. The proceedings in this matter were made known by Mr. Adams in letters to the president of the Continental Congress and to Dr. White.[2] And when Doctors White and Provoost reached London for their consecration, they immediately waited

[1] Perry, *op. cit.*, vol. iii, pp. 191-193.
[2] White, *Memoirs of the Church*, pp. 20-21; Tiffany, *op. cit.*, p. 351.

on Mr. Adams, November 29, 1786. The next day he accompanied them to Lambeth and presented them to the Archbishop of Canterbury. Thus we see that though all of it was done unofficially, yet American public officials played a very important part in the diplomatic ceremonies whereby the American Episcopal Church re-established connections with its parent in Europe.

The North-West Ordinance, July 13, 1787, pledged the government to a permanent support of religion in that territory in the following manner:

> "And for extending the fundamental principles of civil and religious liberty, which form the basis whereon these republics, their laws and constitutions are erected; to fix and establish those principles as the basis of all laws, constitutions and governments, which forever hereafter shall be formed in the said territory . . . . .
>
> It is hereby ordained and declared, ... That the following articles shall be considered as articles of compact between the original States and the people and the States in said territory, and forever remain unalterable unless by common consent, to wit:
>
> Article 1. No person demeaning himself in a peaceable and orderly manner, shall ever be molested on account of his mode of worship or religious sentiments in the said territory.
>
> Article 3. Religion, morality and knowledge, being necessary to good government and the happiness of mankind, schools and the means of education shall forever be encouraged."[1]

For a long time it was the prevailing opinion that these articles were perpetually binding on the states formed out of the North-West territory; court decisions, however, have not always held uniformly to this point of view. There should be no doubt that the United States pledged itself and also required the people of this territory to compact to promote "religion, morality and knowledge."[2]

Congress also proceeded to make reparations to the Christian Indians who had been so grievously maltreated

[1] *Journals of Congress,* (edition of 1823), vol. iv, p. 753.

[2] Cornelison, *Religion and Civil Government in the United States*, p. 113.

by the federal troops during the Revolution. In 1783 Ettwein delivered to Charles Thomson, the secretary of Congress, a memorial, setting forth the claims of these Indians. Ettwein appeared personally before Congress in 1785 and in 1786, on the report of a committee consisting of Mr. Johnson, Mr. Symmes and Mr. Manning, to whom was referred a letter from Lieutenant-Colonel Harmar to the Secretary at War, together with another letter from Mr. Ettwein to the Secretary of Congress, both relative to the Moravian Indians, it was resolved:

"That the Secretary at War give orders to Lieutenant-Colonel Harmar that he signify to the Moravian Indians, lately come from the River Huron to Cayahoga, that it afford pleasure to Congress to hear of their arrival, and that they have permission to return to their former settlement on the Muskingum, where they may be assured of the friendship and protection of the United States."[1] And the Board of the Treasury ruled "that each of the three towns should be allotted 4,000 acres of land, and that each tract might be surveyed in an oblong square, twice as long as broad; and that a free deed without any expense should be given to the society."[2]

We have noted the extent to which Congress depended upon religion for its sanction, and we have considered the phraseology and content of its more important acts. It is clear that Congress rested heavily upon a religious authority and intended in every way possible to promote as a basis for a well-ordered government a dependence upon Protestant Christianity. There is no evidence that it for a moment contemplated a possible separation of the state and religion. This makes all the more intense the process by which, so soon after the adoption of the Federal Constitution and its new government, separation of church and state became a national characteristic.

[1] *Journals of Congress*, (Washington edition of 1823,) vol. iv, p. 688.
[2] *Archives of the Moravian Church at Guadenhütten, Ohio. Supra*, p. 163.

CHAPTER XV

THE CHURCHES AND THE FEDERAL CONSTITUTION

Enthusiasm for ecclesiastical nationalism helped to develop a zeal for political nationalism on the part of the leaders of the churches of America; many of these leaders found time to engage actively in those political battles which were to create a real government for the state. The championing of the cause of "strong government" by such men as Witherspoon, Manning, Rodgers, Muhlenberg, and the Carrolls did a great deal toward saving the day for American political nationalism.

Presbyterianism and politics have always been notoriously intermingled, and it is not surprising that after independence had been won the Presbyterian leaders actively undertook the next logical step, — the creation of a real government for the independent people, and that a unified central government. We cannot but repeat that the centralized governing body of the Presbyterian Church in America during the colonial period, the Synod of New York and Philadelphia, was the most influential of all colonial institutions towards the development of a centralized national conscience.

We have noted that, at the outbreak of the war, one of the first official acts of this body was directed against that reign of anarchy which the fall of the old government must entail. "We cannot but recommend," ran their official pastoral letter of 1775, "and urge in the warmest manner, a regard to order and public peace; and as in many places, during the confusions that prevail, legal proceedings have been difficult, it is hoped, that all persons will conscientiously pay their just debts, and to the utmost of their power serve one another, so that the evils inseparable from a civil war may not be augmented by wantonness and irregularity."[1]

As a member of Continental Congress John Witherspoon, the premier of American Presbyterianism, was among the first to realize the defects of the articles and to work for a stronger government. "For what," said he, "would it signify to risk our possessions and shed our blood to set ourselves free from the encroachments and oppressions of Great Britain, with a certainty, as soon as peace was settled with them, of a more lasting war, a more unnatural, more bloody, and much more hopeless war, among ourselves."[2] In Congress on the third day of February, 1781, he proposed to clothe that body with authority to regulate commerce and to lay duties upon imported articles. Congress accepted this idea and it was agreed that it was indispensably necessary for the states to vest a power in Congress to levy a duty of five per cent on imports of articles of foreign growth and manufacture. But as the concurrence of all of the thirteen states was, under the Articles of Confederation, necessary before any act of Congress could become a law, Witherspoon's bill for strengthening the central government failed of acceptance.[3]

Witherspoon was one of the earliest champions of a sound financial policy for the nation. As a member of Congress he opposed every emission of paper currency, after the first or second, and after he had retired from that body, at the instance of his opponents, he published his

[1] *Supra.*, p. 77. [2] *Works of Witherspoon,* vol. iv, p. 348.
[3] Bancroft, *op. cit.,* vol. v, p. 453.

ideas on the nature, value and uses of money, in his *Essay on Money, as a Medium of commerce, with remarks on the advantages and disadvantages of paper admitted into general circulation, by a citizen of the United States.* (Philadelphia, 1786.) His biographer, Breed, says that, "He pronounced inefficacy upon it (the general government). But he complained and remonstrated in vain."[1] Fruitless as were his concrete proposals, the ideas which they involved prevailed and his championship added great weight to the cause of strong central government.

Dr. John Rodgers, that powerful leader of New York Presbyterianism, was another of the early champions of a stronger central government. In a sermon preached December 11, 1783, on *The Divine Goodness displayed in the American Revolution*, he said:

"The eyes of the nations of the earth, and particularly the eyes of all Europe, are upon these States, to see what use they will make of the great things God has done for us . . . . . . Would you reap the fruits of your toils, your losses and your blood; *it is indispensably necessary that the federal union of these States be cemented and strengthened — that the honor of the Great Council of the nation be supported, and its salutary measures carried into execution, with unanimity and dispatch without regard to partial views, or local interests* — that the credit of this new empire be established, on the principles of strictest justice — and its faith maintained sacred and inviolable, in whatever way, or to whatever description of persons it has been pledged, or may at any time be pledged. Alas! that its glory has suffered so much already, by the failure of our currency. Let us carefully repair this waste of honor, if we cannot repair the waste of property, by the most sacred adherence to our engagements, in all future time.

You will please to remember farther, that the virtue I recommend, both political and moral, is essential to the preservation of the clear-earned privileges in which we rejoice this day. This is especially the case in a democratic government, and the more democratic the government, the more necessary."[2]

[1] Breed, *Witherspoon*, p. 35.

[2] Rodgers, J., *The Divine Goodness displayed in the American Revolution. A Sermon preached December 11, 1783.*

As official Presbyteriandom had aided the colonial cause of independence, so it contributed to the formation of that more perfect and perpetual union under the constitution. It championed strong government for state as well as for church. Its influence was especially noticeable in New Jersey, Pennsylvania and the West.

Baptists, owing to the nature of their ecclesiastical polity, may object to having a single individual named as their leader. But the very nature of their organization, without centralization, made for greater power in the case of their spiritual and intellectual leader, Dr. James Manning, President of the College of Rhode Island. No other man stood so close to the whole body of American Baptists. He was a member of the Philadelphia Association as well as of the Warren Association and he regularly attended the annual meetings of both, where he filled at various times the offices of moderator, clerk and preacher. Then too he was seeking the support of all American Baptists for their national college. Dr. Manning's influence was great in winning Baptists to a support of centralized institutions, — hardly an orthodox Baptist point of view. His chief Baptist opponent was Isaac Backus, a New England exponent of the principle of complete local autonomy, — a Baptist Anti-Federalist.

In 1786 Dr. Manning accepted an appointment from his state as delegate to Continental Congress. This brought him into direct contact with the national political problem. To his religious co-worker, the Rev. Dr. Smith, he wrote, May 17, 1786:

"The savages have begun their barbarous depredations on our Western frontiers . . . . . The wretched, deranged finances of the Federal Government, will allow us, if disposed, to afford these people but feeble aid.

I am treated with respect by Congress and the heads of departments. The present Congress possesses great integrity, and a good share of ability; but for want of more States on the floor the public and important business is from from day to day neglected. We are, however, in daily expectation of a fuller delegation. If personal matters could be so adjusted that I were not disquieted, I should be very happy in my situation here; for I commonly preach once or twice on Lord's Day, either in town, on Long or Staten Island, or in the Jerseys."[1]

Dr. Manning's correspondence with his absent colleague, Brigadier General Nathan Miller, gives an incisive view of the state of Congressional affairs. He wrote, June 7, 1786:

"Dear Sir: I think if for a moment you would figure to yourself my situation, alone here for more than a month, reduced to the very last guinea and a trifle of change (which is the case); my lodging, washing, barber's, hatter's, tailor's bills, etc., not paid; without the favor of a single line from you advising me whether you mean to come or not, or sending forward the one hundred dollars on hand, which you proposed doing from the election if you were not likely to follow me soon, — if, I say, you would but realize my situation, you could not but pity me from your heart. I wrote you long since. I begged an answer from you, one way or another, that I might know what measures to take. But as I am now situated, I can neither stay nor go, except to the new City Hall, if my creditors exact it; and strangers have no more compassion on me than the State that appointed me. I must interest you to forward that sum of one hundred dollars, if no more can be had, by the first opportunity, with a line advising me of your real intentions. Matters highly interesting to this Confederacy, and indeed I think the question whether the Federal Government shall long exist, are now before Congress, and there are not States sufficient to transact the necessary business, as we now have barely nine States on the floor. Our affairs are come very much to a point, and if the States continue to neglect keeping up their delegations in Congress, the Federal Government must *ipso facto* dissolve. I have written the Governor on these subjects, and desired his answer, whether we should keep up our delegation, or not. I shall wait till a reasonable time for an answer from you, and quit if I do not receive it. Send me by the post or packets. Frank your letters by the post. I shall impatiently wait the event, and with sentiments of esteem, I have the honor to be sir, etc., etc."[2]

[1] Guild, *Life, Times and Correspondence of James Manning, and the Early History of Brown University*, p. 390.

[2] Guild, *op. cit.*, pp. 391-392.

This letter was followed by a much sharper one, June 12:

"Sir: — Yours of the 27th ult. came to hand two days ago. Am mortified exceedingly that you have not come forward, nor sent on the money on hand; for I am reduced to but a few shillings, and my bills are not paid. My situation — without a colleague, without money, and without any instructions or favorable prospects from the government — is painful. Rhode Island has not many more strides to make to complete her disgrace and ruin too; but that is not all. She is likely to hold a distinguished rank amongst the contributors to the ruin of the Federal Government. Never probably was a full delegation of the States more necessary than now, for you may rest assured that in the opinion of every member of Congress, and in the several departments, things are come to a crisis with the Federal Government. You say you think the present House do not want a Congress; they may, it is more than probable, very soon see the accomplishment of their wishes; for without a speedy reform in the policy of the States, the Federal Government must be no more. The flagrant violations of the public faith, solemnly plighted, in the late emission of paper money, on the conditions on which it is emitted, is here considered as the completion of our ruin as a nation: but I wrote you before on this subject; it is too painful to repeat. Pray send me on the money on hand, or come and bring it yourself, without loss of time; at least write me by every vessel. With sentiments of esteem, etc., etc." [1]

Dr. Manning had come to hold a very low regard for the attitude of the Rhode Island legislature towards its fellow states; upon his return to his college duties, we find him writing to the Rev. Dr. Smith, January 18, 1787:

"The paper money of this State has run down to six for one, notwithstanding which the Legislature continue it as a tender, and means to do so, and to pay off all the State debts with it, be it as bad as it may. At the last session I petitioned them to pay my advances, and the remainder of my salary as delegate, amounting to upwards of four hundred dollars. This they offered to do in their paper, but in no other way. Besides, they have ordered all the import orders brought in and exchanged at the treasury for paper at par, so that I must lose five sixths of my salary so paid to me. A more imfamous set of men under the character of a legislature, never, I believe, disgraced the annals of the world. And there is no prospect of a change for the better . . . . . Confusion in State matters seems to increase." [2]

[1] Guild, *op. cit.*, p. 392.
[2] *Ibid.*, pp. 398-399.

It was General Varnum, one of Dr. Manning's graduates from the College of Rhode Island, Class of 1769, who won the first victory in the fight for sound money in that state. Contending for the illegality of the paper currency act, he won the case of *Trevett vs. Weeden* wherein the Rhode Island court adjudged the amended acts of the state legislature unconstitutional and void. And it could hardly have been in opposition to the wishes of President Manning that Nathaniel Lambert at the Commencement of 1787 delivered the oration, "The Present Appearance of Public Affairs in the United States of America, portraying the superior advantages to be enjoyed by this country and the public happiness rationally to be expected, in case the States harmoniously agree on the great federal measures necessary for the good of the whole, whereon the convention had been for some time deliberating at Philadelphia, and recommending industry, the manufactures of our country and the disuse of foreign goods; and soliciting the fair daughters of America to set the patriotic example by banishing from their dress costly gewgaws and articles of foreign production."[1] Under Dr. Manning Rhode Island College and its alumni stood for a stronger national government.

In Connecticut the election sermons, delivered before the magistrates and general assembly annually, give a convincing picture of the national political sentiments of Congregational Clergy. Next after Presbyterians, they had had the greatest colonial national experience. For together with their Presbyterian brethren, they had known the power of unity as expressed in the Congregational-Presbyterian Confederation of the years 1766 to 1775. Timothy Dwight began a correspondence looking toward the renewal of this organization in 1788. The General

[1] Guild, *op. cit.*, pp. 400.

Association of Connecticut spoke of this as a "Scheme for Union of the Presbyterians in America." Dwight's plan resulted in an agreement between the General Assembly of the Presbyterians and the Connecticut General Association of the Congregationalists to the effect that delegates from each body be sent regularly to the sessions of the other. At the request of the Presbyterians, in 1794 these representatives were given full power of voting in the meetings to which they were accredited. Similar exchange relations were effected between the Presbyterian General Assembly and the Congregational state organizations in Massachusetts, Vermont, and New Hampshire and continued in force until 1837. The spirit of cooperation and consolidation exhibited in the organization of these national unions was reflected in the election sermons wherein the Congregational clergy advised the state officials as to their politico-religious duties.

Samuel Wales, D.D., Professor of Divinity in Yale College, delivering the sermon in 1785, spoke on "The Dangers of our National Prosperity." In addressing the Clergy present he remarked, "No order of men have equal advantages with you, to warn the people against the encroachment of power on the one hand, and the evils of anarchy on the other; and at the same time to instruct them in all those various duties which they owe to civil rulers and to their country."[1]

"National Justice" is the theme of the sermon of 1784 by Joseph Huntington, D.D., from the text, "God ruling the Nations for the most glorious end." Dr. Huntington observed:

"Your Honors know what demands on this state, and on the nation are justly made, by those who have lent us their livings to support the

[1] Wales, Samuel, D.D., *The Dangers of our National Prosperity. A Sermon delivered . . . . . May 12th, 1785.* Hartford, 1785.

war, or have served in it. You know likewise what just obligations we are under to nations beyond the water who have lent us their aid. Most certainly it is high time this state, and every state, and all in conjunction, so far as demands are national, make full provision to pay every honest debt, and till this is done public guilt lies upon us . . . . . Those who fought our battles for us are our brethren . . . . . To be just, righteous and faithful is humanity . . . . . A state or a nation ought to be as upright and faithful, in dealing with individuals or a community, as one neighbor with another. It lies with your Honors to concert effectual measures, that this state, and, as far as to us appertains, the whole nation may be so."[1]

This ideal of "justice" is repeated by Dr. Wales in the election sermon of 1785, mentioned above:

"Another particular evil into which we have fallen, and by which we are endangered, is injustice, injustice to the best and most deserving friends of our country. Those certainly are to be esteemed some of the most deserving friends of the country, who have willingly lent her either their lives or their property in the late important struggle. To such persons we are under obligations not only of gratitude but of justice. Their voluntary sacrifices have, through divine blessing, purchased for us our lives and fortunes, our liberties, our independence, our peace, and in a great measure all our temporal happiness . . . . .

The least that we can do for them, according to strict justice, is to afford them a reward equal to the full import of our promises. Gladly would I draw a veil over this part of our national conduct, were it possible, and could it be done with propriety. But it cannot be done, it ought not to be attempted. The best and wisest thing which we can now do with regard to this matter, is to reprobate our own conduct and reform it for the future . . . . . Our public injustice is attended with consequences most deplorable and alarming . . . . . It tends to render public faith contemptible and is highly injurious to our national character. It gives too much countenance to the reproach of our enemies who have stigmatized us with the character of a knavish, faithless people; covering the most iniquitous designs under the garb of liberty and the cloak of religion . . . . .

This public injustice destroys some of the most important ends of civil society; such as the equal administration of justice . . . . . It tends to destroy all confidence in the Public and to create a distrust of Government . . . . . It is a fatal influence upon the morals of the people at large.

[1] Huntington, Joseph, D.D., *National Justice. A Sermon delivered May 13th, 1874.* Hartford, 1784.

By true patriotism I mean a real concern for the welfare of our whole country in general . . . . . There is danger that our union will not be so great as will be necessary for the general good . . . . . In this view we may see how much it concerns us to support our grand bond of union, or, in other words, to maintain the rights of our honorable Congress, and even to enlarge their power, should this be proved necessary . . . . .

Fellow Citizens and Fellow Christians! Great are the benefits of good government. But let us not imagine that these benefits are to be expected by us, unless, as a people and as individuals, we are willing to perform those duties which we owe to our civil rulers and to the public in general." [1]

Levi Hart, A. M., Pastor of a Church in Preston, gave the election sermon of 1786 on the subject "A Description of a Good Character Attempted and Applied to the Subject of Jurisdiction and Civil Government." He observed:

"Through the good of our God upon us, in the peace of 1783, our freedom and independence are recognized, by the British court . . . . . We rank among the other nations . . . . . have an immense territory extending through a variety of climates . . . . . a wide field is opened for the cultivation of the arts of peace . . . . . and opportunity for perfecting and perpetuating the most happy constitution of government, in the federal union. And, by the divine blessing on proper civil and military discipline, we shall be secure from the attacks, or, at least, from the ravages of an enemy.

That we may enjoy the proffered blessings much is yet to be done . . . the various and complicated interests of the state are to be fixed and secured. The energy of the government, enfeebled by the revolution, and other causes, is to be restored . . . . . the principles of union improved, and confirmed . . . . . the public credit established . . . . and the whole system of the finances placed on a wise and respectable footing." [2]

"The Principles of Civil Union and Happiness considered and recommended" was the subject of the 1787 sermon by Elizur Goodrich, D.D., Pastor of the Church of Christ in

[1] *Supra.*, p. 447.

[2] Hart, Levi, A.M., *Description of a Good Character Attempted and Applied to the Subject of Jurisdiction and Civil Government. A Sermon delivered . . . . . May 11th, 1786.* Hartford, 1786.

Durham, from the text, "Jerusalem is builded as a city that is compact together," *Psalms* cxxii, 3:

"Its (Jerusalem's) inhabitants were not a loose, disconnected people, but most strictly united, not only among themselves, but with all the tribes of Israel, into a holy nation and commonwealth . . . . . We enjoy all the privileges of a free government, the blessings of the gospel of peace, and the honors of the Church of God. This is our Jerusalem . . . Civil Government . . . . . must have for its foundations the principles of laws, of truth, justice, and righteousness. Civil society can exist no longer than while connected by its laws and constitution . . . . . Regular support of authority is the only security a people can have against violence and injustice, feuds and animosities. . . . . . Hence the very end of civil society demands that the orders of government be enforced . . . . . the state defended against all internal and foreign violence.

I exhort the several orders of men present, that in their several places they use their best and most faithful endeavors for promoting the public peace and prosperity that this and the United States may be 'builded as a city compact together'.

Never was union in counsel and in public exertions more necessary in America than at the present day . . . . . If we forget the God of our Salvation, and neglect the means of virtue and religion, with which we are favored above any people on earth, if we are divided and contend about every plan devised for strengthening the national union and restoring the national honor and safety, — if the several states, losing sight of the great end of the confederation, are influenced by mere local and partial motives, and if, in their respective and distinct jurisdictions, they forsake the paths of righteousness, we shall become the scorn and contempt of foreign nations, a prey to every bold invader; or fall by intestine divisions, till we sink into general ruin, and universal wretchedness.

If the national union by concentrating the wisdom and force of America was the means of our salvation from conquest and slavery — if the existence, liberty and independence of these states, and their national character, importance and glory depend still upon their united firmness and strength — if this union be necessary for the decision of controversies, which might otherwise endanger war among ourselves, and be the only probable means of their safety and defence against foreign nations . . . If these things are true . . . . . certainly there are no objects of greater magnitude and importance, more loudly calling the attention of America, than the national union, the necessity of supporting the national honor, and to give the federal government energy at home and respectability abroad . . . . . I own, Gentlemen, I am concerned for the national honor and happiness and were I to consult my own feelings, I might hold up to your view, the dying languors of the national union, as forboding ruin, division, or some dreadful convulsion to these states.

My most sincere prayer is that heaven . . . . . would collect and unite the wisdom and patriotism of America, in the proposed convention of the States, in some just and equal system of federal subordination." [1]

These excerpts from various election sermons will suffice to illustrate the broad national concern of the Congregational Church in Connecticut. The clergy advise the legislators that stronger federal union is essential to the honor, justice, peace, security, law, order and general welfare of the country. In general we may say that they were federalists. In Massachusetts at the time of Shays' Rebellion they were able to exert considerable influence on the side of the Government.[2]

We have noted the political activity of certain members representing Presbyterian, Congregational, and Baptist denominations. These sects were perhaps the most openly active in the interest of a stronger central government. There were good reasons why the clergy of the Quakers, Methodists and Episcopalians would shun active participation in politics. Wilson in his *Memoir of the Life of William White*, thus summarizes the attitude of that leader of American Episcopalianism. Speaking of the local situation in Pennsylvania in 1776 he remarks:

"Dr. White's own sentiments were favorable to the republican party, though maintained with moderation and calmness. He was independent in forming his political opinions, and reflected upon them for himself. And though he freely expressed them, with his reasons for maintaining them, and also constantly, and from a sense of duty as a citizen, gave his

[1] Goodrich, Elizur, D.D., *The Principles of Civil Union and Happiness Considered and Recommended, A Sermon delivered . . . . . May 10th, 1787*. Hartford, 1787.

[2] Morse, *Federal Party in Massachusetts*, p. 95; *Jefferson's Writings*, Ford edition, vol. viii, p. 48; Robinson, *Jeffersonian Democracy in New England*, in *Yale Historical Publications*, Miscellany vol. iii.

vote at elections, he would never condescend to become an active political partisan; much less to make religious profession an instrument of policy. He was decidedly opposed to the combination of religion with politics, and desired that the members of the Episcopal church should harmoniously unite, in conducting their ecclesiastical affairs, without regard to their differences in political opinions." [1]

Dr. White leaves us the following letter of January 31, 1783, addressed to General Joseph Reed, President of the Supreme Executive Council of Pennsylvania.

"I hope that you will not think me impertinent in requesting your attention to a distinction, which was perhaps obscurely expressed in my last, between your being opposed, on account of your religious profession, and the opposition on this principle proceeding principally, if not exclusively, from the members of the Episcopal churches: the former, I told you, I had no reason to believe, though it was not my intention to remark on it; and the latter, I was sure, you never meant to assert; the reason for both was my observing among the opponents of the late administration, many members of the Presbyterian church, and my knowing many of its advocates in the churches with which I am connected. There never existed a dispute, in this state or province, in which these societies were, as such, in opposition.

I believe that you abhor the introduction of religious ideas into politics, and can add, with truth, that so do I. No doubt, it is necessary, in public elections, to have a mixture of men of different religious societies; but this is to avert the evil which we abhor; because we know there are men of every society, who, if they had the power, would apoint none but those of their own to places of power and profit . . . . .

Having always endeavored, in my ecclesiastical employment, to impress the idea of an agreement, in religious concerns, where differences exist as to the civil, and having observed our church members of opposite parties harmoniously promoting the good of our communion, it hurt me to see even an apparent imputation of mixing religion and politics, applied chiefly, if not only, to this quarter; for the churches which I serve contain a great majority of the Episcopalians in this city; the only part of the state in which any considerable society of them is to be found." [2]

Following the lead of Bishop White the clergy of the Episcopalian church seem to have avoided politics, but the

[1] Wilson, *Memoir of the Life of William White*, p. 75.
[2] *Ibid.*, pp. 76-77.

laity of this denomination more than made up for any inactivity on the part of their religious leaders; Episcopalians were not esteemed non-political beings, as the names of Washington, Hamilton, Madison, Duane, Jay, etc., testify. Even in Connecticut, the historian Robinson finds them to be the balance of power in early politics; he says, "While the dissenters were numerous and active the Federalists had the support of the strong Episcopalian body, and until they had alienated that support were able to hold their ground."[1] The Episcopalians of that state were wealthy and of the same social class as the Congregationalists,[2] and even the bigoted Dwight can make a complimentary reference to Episcopalian ministers.[3]

The Constitutional Convention which met in Philadelphia, May 25 to September 17, 1787, put into form the governmental theories which the new nation was developing. At various times fifty-five delegates were in attendance, though but thirty-five signed the completed constitution. These men were sufficiently representative of the various religious interests of the United States. There was that "religious enthusiast, lately turned Methodist," Richard Bassett of Delaware, friend of Wesley.[4] There were the Quakers, Thomas Mifflin of Pennsylvania[5] and John Dickinson of Delaware.[6] Catholics were represented by Daniel Carroll of Maryland, brother of Bishop Carroll,[7] and Thomas Fitzsimons of Pennsylvania. Presbyterian influence was strong, as we should expect to

[1] Robinson, *op. cit.*, p. 148.
[2] Greene, *Religious Liberty in Connecticut*, pp. 405, 417, 441, 444.
[3] Dwight, *Travels*, vol. i, p. 177.
[4] *Supra.*, p. 185.
[5] *Supra.*, pp. 135-136.
[6] *Supra.*, pp. 134-135.
[7] *Supra.*, p. 237.

find it, keeping in mind the politico-religious activities of their College of New Jersey, Representing that institution were Oliver Ellsworth of Connecticut, James Madison of Virginia, Edmund Randolph of Virginia, Gunning Bedford of Delaware, William Patterson of New Jersey, William Davie of North Carolina, and Luther Martin of Maryland.[1]

Besides these college men were that ex-preacher, Hugh Williamson of North Carolina and Governor William Livingston of New Jersey, Thomas McKean and Charles Thomson, both of Pennsylvania.[2] William C. Houston of Georgia was later to be appointed a professor at the College of New Jersey.

Of course not all of the students of the College of New Jersey were Presbyterians. James Madison and Edmund Randolph were Episcopalians and Oliver Ellsworth was a Congregationalist. In addition to Madison and Randolph, Episcopalianism was represented by General Washington, John Blair, George Wythe, and George Mason in the Virginia delegation, by C. C. Pinckney of South Carolina and by Charles Pinckney of that same state who had assisted in the formation of the national Episcopalian constitution,[3] and by Alexander Hamilton of New York, a King's College man. Perhaps the most learned man of the convention was the Episcopalian William Samuel Johnson of Connecticut. A son of the Reverend Samuel Johnson, the Tory president of King's College, he had received his education at Yale and Oxford. For a time he had worked for the Society for the Propagation of the Gospel. During the war he had remained at home, at its close he became the first president of the re-opened Columbia (King's) College.[4]

[1] *Supra.*, p. 82. [2] *Supra.*, p. 83. [3] *Supra.*, p. 215.
[4] Beardsley, *Life of William Samuel Johnson*, Boston, 1876.

Congregationalism was represented by delegates from states as far apart as Georgia and New Hampshire. Abraham Baldwin of Georgia was an alumnus of Yale. New Hampshire was represented by Nicholas Gilman and John Langdon; Massachusetts by Caleb Strong, Elbridge Gerry, Nathaniel Gorham, and Rufus King. Rhode Island, the seat of the Baptist political influence, was unrepresented. The Connecticut delegation was divided between Congregationalism and Episcopalianism.

Edmund Randolph speaks from the experience of sitting with the representatives of these various sects when, arguing for freedom of religion before the Virginia Convention for Ratification, he remarked, "How many different sects will be in Congress? We cannot enumerate the sects that may be in Congress."[1]

Diversity of religious beliefs made the Convention cautious about the introduction of any subject that might tend to raise purely religious controversy, while at the same time it led to the very broadest possible point of view when the question of the politico-religious powers of Congress had to be established.

Benjamin Franklin nearly precipitated a religious controversey when, June 25, he proposed the employment of prayers and a chaplain for the Convention. He made the following plea:

"Mr. President! The small progress we have made after four weeks' close attendance and continual reasoning with each other; our different sentiments on almost every question, several of the last producing as many noes as ayes, is, methinks, a melancholy proof of the imperfection of the human understanding. We indeed seem to feel our want of political wisdom, since we have been running about in search of it. We have gone back to ancient history for models of government, and examined the different forms of those republics, which having been formed with

[1] Farrand, *Records*, vol. iii, p. 310.

the seeds of their own dissolution, now no longer exist. And we have viewed modern States all round Europe, but find none of their Constitutions suited to our circumstances.

In this situation of this Assembly, groping, as it were, in the dark, to find political truth, and scarce able to distinguish it when presented to us, how has it happened, Sir, that we have not hitherto once thought of humbly applying to the Father of Light to illuminate our understandings. In the beginning of the contest with Great Britain, when we were sensible of danger, we had daily prayer in this room for the divine protection. Our prayers, Sir, were heard and they were graciously answered. All of us who were engaged in the struggle must have observed frequent instances of a superintending Providence in our favor. To that kind Providence we owe this happy opportunity of consulting in peace on the means of establishing our future national felicity. And have we now forgotten that powerful friend? I have lived, Sir, a long time, and the longer I live the more convincing proofs I see of this truth, that God governs in the affairs of men. And if a sparrow cannot fall to the ground without His notice, is it probable that an Empire can arise without His aid? We have been assured, Sir, in the sacred writings, that 'except the Lord build the house they labor in vain that build it'. I firmly believe this, and I also believe that without His concurring aid we shall succeed in this political building no better than the builders of Babel. We shall be divided by our little partial local interests; our projects will be confounded, and we ourselves shall become a reproach and by-word down to future ages. And what is worse, mankind may hereafter from this unfortunate instance, despair of establishing governments by human wisdom and leave it to chance, war and conquest.

I, therefore, beg leave to move that hereafter prayers, imploring the assistance of Heaven and its blessings on our deliberations, be held in this assembly every morning before we proceed to business, and that one or more of the clergy of this city be requested to officiate in that service". [1]

Mr. Sherman seconded Franklin's motion. Hamilton and several others expressed apprehension that, however proper such a resolution might have been at the beginning of the convention, it might at this late day, in the first place, bring on it some disagreeable animadversions; and in the second place, lead the public to believe that the embarrassments and dissentions within the convention had suggested the measure. It was answered by Dr. Franklin, Mr. Sherman and others that the past omission of a duty

[1] Farrand, *op. cit.*, vol. i, pp. 450-452, 457-458; Schaff, *op. cit.*, p. 423.

could not justify a further omission; that the rejection of such a proposition would expose the convention to more unpleasant animadversions than the adoption of it; and that the alarm out of doors that might be excited for the state of things within would at least be as likely to do good as ill.[1] Mr. Williamson observed that the true cause of omission could not be mistaken; the convention had no funds. Mr. Randolph proposed, in order to give a favorable aspect to the measure, that a sermon be preached at the request of the convention on the fourth of July, the Anniversary of Independence, and thenceforth prayers, etc., be read in the convention every morning. Dr. Franklin seconded this motion. But adjournment was carried without any vote of the motion.[2] Writing in 1834 Madison states:

"The proposition was received and treated with the respect due to it; but the lapse of time which had preceded, with considerations growing out of it, had the effect of limiting what was done, to a reference of the proposition to a highly respectable committee. The Quaker usage, never discontinued in the State, and the place where the convention held its sittings, might not have been without an influence, as might also the discord of religious opinions within the convention, as well as among the clergy of the spot." [3]

Religious controversy, aside from that just mentioned in connection with the Franklin motion, centered about the question of the oath. The fourteenth resolution of the Virginia plan as introduced in the Committee of the Whole, May 29, was:

"Resolved, that the Legislative, Executive and Judicial powers within the several States ought to be bound by oath to support the Articles of Union." [4]

[1] Farrand, *op. cit.*, Appendix A. ccclv, cxcv, ccclxvii, ccclxxxix, cccxciii.
[2] *Journal of the Federal Convention, James Madison*, edition of E. H. Scott, Chicago, 1893, pp. 259-261.
[3] Farrand, *op. cit.*, vol. iii, Appendix A, cccxciii.
[4] *Ibid.*, vol. i, pp. 22, 28, 117.

Debate of this resolution at first assumed an exclusively political nature. June 11, Mr. Luther Martin moved to strike out "within the several states," but his motion was lost seven to four. Thereupon the Committee of the Whole accepted the resolution by a vote of six to five; Massachusetts, Pennsylvania, Virginia, North Carolina, South Carolina, and Georgia voting against Connecticut, New York, New Jersey, Maryland, and Delaware.[1] July 23, after unanimously inserting "and of the national government" the resolution passed the convention unanimously.[2]

The distinctively religious phase of this matter appeared, August 20, when Mr. Charles Pinckney moved to add "that no religious test or qualification shall ever be annexed to any oath of office under the authority of the United States."[3] In his draft of a constitution as submitted to the Convention, May 29, Mr. Pinckney had included a clause (Article vi), "The legislature of the United States shall pass no law on the subject of religion."[4] August 30, Pinckney's motion came to a vote. It was agreed to insert "or affirmation" after the word "oath," whereupon the whole passed, 8 to 1, with two states divided; North Carolina voted in the negative and Maryland and Connecticut were divided. Mr. Gouverneur Morris and General C. C. Pinckney spoke for the resolution while Mr. Sherman argued against it, "that it was unnecessary, the prevailing liberality being a sufficient security against tests."[5]

[1] Farrand, *op. cit.*, vol. i, pp. 194, 203, 204, 207, 227, 231.
[2] *Ibid.*, vol. ii, pp. 87, 133.
[3] *Ibid.*, vol. ii, p. 335.
[4] Elliot, *Debates*, vol. v, supplementary, p. 131, Philadelphia, 1859.
[5] Farrand, *op. cit.*, vol. ii, pp. 461, 468; Elliot, *Debates*, vol. v, p. 49.

As it finally emerges from the Committee on Style we find that the Constitution provides, Article vii, section 3:

"The Senators and Representatives before mentioned, and the members of the several State legislatures, and all executive and judicial officers both of the United States and of the several States, shall be bound by oath or affirmation to support this Constitution; but no religious test shall ever be required as a qualification to any office or public trust under the Unites States."[1]

It is quite impossible to give a definite quantitative estimate of the contribution of each religious denomination to the separate clauses of the Constitution. It is clear that the device for the election of the chief executive by an indirect election is derived from the Catholic model, the College of Cardinals. And resemblances are numerous between many of its features and various ecclesiastical institutions. Yet it is not by any copying of external features that the church and state governments of America are most related. Certain great national impulses had arisen in America to give expression to phases of a new order of government. The Presbyterian Synod of Colonial times stood alone as the first expression of this spirit. It developed the method by which, through Republican organization, the collective wisdom of the entire church, lay as well as clerical, could be focused continuously upon church affairs. The Congregational churches of Connecticut made an approach to this but doubtlessly through their contact with the Presbyterial organization. The task of American constitution-building was to create for all the denominations and for all political units means whereby the common affairs of the various social groups were placed in the hands of conferences, synods, conventions,

[1] Farrand, *op. cit.*, vol. ii, pp. 579, 603, 663.

legislatures, congresses, assemblies, and the like, meeting periodically. This was the American impulse.

And during the period which we are considering we have found all denominations giving free rein to this impulse. The Presbyterian Synod was debating and amending Witherspoon's report at the very same time, and in the very same city with the Constitutional Convention.

The paramount issue in the campaign which ensued for the ratification of the Federal Constitution was the one of personal rights. The Constitution made no provision for guaranteeing individual rights and foremost among such rights demanded was the one of religious freedom.

The first states to ratify were Delaware, December 7, 1787, and Pennsylvania, December 12, the homes of the Quakers and the Presbyterians. McMaster and Stone say of the Pennsylvania convention,

> "Scarcely a sect, or creed . . . . . in the Commonwealth, but had at least one representative on the floor of the convention. Some were Moravians; some were Lutherans; some were Episcopalians; some were Quakers; most were Presbyterians." [1]

The Lutheran Frederick Augustus Muhlenberg was president of this convention. We find Mr. Wilson, in the convention, replying to the charge "that there is no security for the rights of conscience," with the query, "I ask the honorable gentleman, what part of this system puts it in the power of Congress to attack those rights? When there is no power to attack, it is idle to prepare the means of defence."[2] Ratification was carried with a majority of fifteen votes and the dissenting minority issued

[1] McMaster and Stone, *Pennsylvania and the Federal Constitution*, p. 13

[2] Elliot, *Debates*, vol. iii, p. 252.

an address to their constituents, *Reasons of Dissent*, proposing fourteen amendments, the first being,

"The right of conscience shall be held inviolable, and neither the legislative, executive, or judicial powers of the United States, shall have power to alter, abrogate or infringe any part of the constitutions of the several states, which provide for the preservation of liberty in matters of religion." [1]

Trench Coxe of Pennsylvania was one of the writers in support of the Constitution. He expressed admiration for the religious clause already in the Constitution;

"No religious test is ever to be required . . . . . The convention has the honor of proposing the first public act, by which any nation has ever divested itself of a power, every exercise of which is a trespass on the Majesty of Heaven." [2]

Archbishop Carroll claims that the American Catholics concurred with perhaps greater unanimity than any other body of men in recommending and promoting the Constitution "from whose influence America anticipates all the blessings of justice, peace, plenty, good order and civil and religious liberty."[3] Robinson finds that the New England clergy "were, as a rule, strongly in favor of the adoption."[4] Two small Presbyterian bodies, the Associated Church and the Reformed Presbyterian Church, decided to abstain from voting until the Constitution was so amended as to acknowledge the sovereignty of God

[1] *The Reasons of Dissent.* Philadelphia, 1787, Reprinted in Carey, *American Museum*, vol. ii, no. v, pp. 536-553.

[2] Coxe, Trench, *An Examination of the Constitution for the United States of America, Submitted to the People by the General Convention, At Philadelphia, the 17th Day of September, 1787, and since adopted and ratified by the Conventions of Eleven States, chosen for the purpose of considering it, being all that have yet decided on the subject. By an American Citizen.* Philadelphia, 1788, pp. 15-16. Quoted in Ford, *Pamphlets on the Constitution*, p. 146.

[3] O'Gorman, *The Roman Catholics*, pp. 255-256.

[4] Robinson, *op. cit.*, p. 129.

and the subserviency of the state to the kingdom of Christ.[1]

Luther Martin in his *Genuine Information, delivered to the Legislature of the State of Maryland, relating to the proceedings of the General Convention* sets forth that:

"The part of the system which provides, that no religious test shall ever be required as a qualification to any office or public trust under the United States was adopted by a great majority of the Convention and without much debate: however, there were some members so unfashionable as to think, that a belief in the existence of a Deity, and of a state of future rewards and punishments would be some security for the good conduct of our rulers, and that, in a Christian Country, it would be at least decent to hold out some distinction between the professors of Christianity and downright infidelity or paganism."[2]

Opposition to the Constitution on religious grounds was strong in New England where Congregationalism was established. In Connecticut we find that at the June Meeting held in West Hartford, in 1788:

"A request from the Association of Windham County was laid before this Association, requesting that some suitable Testimony might be borne against a sinful omission in the late Federal Constitution, in not looking to God for direction, and of omitting the mention of the name of God in the Constitution they proposed to the people for their approbation."[3]

This request was laid over and at the September Meeting it was found to be unauthentic.[4] In *The American Mercury* (No. 88), February 11, 1788, we find a letter from William Williams to "A Landholder" (Oliver Ellsworth), which reads in part:

"When the clause in the 6th article . . . . . came under consideration, I observed I should have chose that sentence and anything relating to a religious test, had been totally omitted rather than stand as it did,

[1] Schaff, *op. cit.*, p. 433.
[2] Farrand, *op. cit.*, vol. iii, p. 227.
[3] *Records of the General Association*, p. 126.
[4] *Ibid.*, p. 129.

but still more wished something of the kind should have been inserted, but with a reverse sense, so far as to require an explicit acknowledgement of the being of God, his perfections and his providence, and to have been prefixed to, and stand as, the first introductory words of the Constitution, in the following or similar terms, viz. *We the people of the United States, in a firm belief of the being and perfections of the one living and true God, the creator and supreme Governor of the world, in his universal providence and the authority of his laws; that he will require of all moral agents an account of their conduct; that all rightful powers among men are ordained of, and mediately derived from God; therefore in a dependence on his blessing and acknowledgement of his efficient protection in establishing our Independence, whereby it is become necessary to agree upon and settle a Constitution of federal government for ourselves,* . . . . . do ordain, etc. . . . . . that no other religious test should ever be required." [1]

Oliver Ellsworth, later Chief Justice of the United States, gave in *The Connecticut Courant*, December 17, 1787 (Number 1195), under the pseudonym "The Landholder," the following discussion of the legal position of the religious clause:

"Some very worthy persons, who have not had great advantages for information, have objected against that clause in the Constitution which provides, that no religious test shall ever be required as a qualification to any office or public trust under the United States. They have been afraid that this clause is unfavorable to religion. But my countrymen, the sole purpose and effect of it is to exclude persecution, and to secure to you the important right of religious liberty. We are almost the only people in the world, who have a full enjoyment of this important right of human nature. In our country every man has a right to worship God in that way which is most agreeable to his conscience. If he be a good and peaceable person he is liable to no penalties or incapacities on account of his religious sentiments; or in other words, he is not subject to persecution.

But in other parts of the world, it has been, and still is, far different . .

A religious test is an act to be done, or profession to be made, relating to religion (such as partaking of the sacrament according to certain rites and forms, or declaring one's belief of certain doctrines) for the purpose of determining whether his religious opinions are such, that he is admissible to a public office. A test in favor of any one denomination of

[1] Ford, *Essays on the Constitution*, pp. 207-209; *Connecticut Courant*, February 4, 1788 (Number 1202).

Christians would be to the last degree absurd in the United States. If it were in favor of either Congregationalists, Presbyterians, Episcopalians, Baptists, or Quakers, it would incapacitate more than three-fourths of the American citizens for any public office; and thus degrade them from the rank of freemen. There need be no argument to prove that the majority of our citizens would never submit to this indignity.

If any test-act were to be made, perhaps the least exceptionable would be one requiring all persons appointed to office to declare, at the time of their admission, their belief in the being of God, and in the divine authority of the Scriptures. In favor of such a test it may be said, that one who believes these great truths will not be so likely to violate his obligations to his country, as one who disbelieves them; we may have greater confidence in his integrity. But, I answer: His making a declaration of such a belief is no security at all. For suppose him to be an unprincipled man, who believes neither the word nor the being of God; and to be governed merely by selfish motives; how easy it is for him to dissemble! how easy for him to make a public declaration of his belief in the creed which the law prescribes; and excuse himself by calling it a mere formality. This is the case with the test-laws and creeds in England . . . . . In short, test-laws are utterly ineffectual; they are no security at all; because men of loose principles will, by an external compliance, evade them. If they exclude any persons, it will be honest men, men of principle, who will rather suffer an injury, than act contrary to the dictates of their consciences. If we mean to have those appointed to public office, who are sincere friends to religion, we, the people who appoint them, must take care to choose such characters; and not rely upon such cob-web barriers as test-laws are.

But to come, to the true principle by which this question ought to be determined; the business of civil government is to protect the citizen in his rights, to defend the community from hostile powers, and to promote the general welfare. Civil government has no business to meddle with the private opinions of the people. If I demean myself as a good citizen, I am accountable, not to man, but to God, for the religious opinions which I embrace, and the manner in which I worship the Supreme Being. If such had been the universal sentiments of mankind, and they had acted accordingly, persecution, the bane of truth and nurse of error, with her bloody axe and flaming hand, would never have turned so great a part of the world into a field of blood.

But while I assert the rights of religious liberty, I would not deny that the civil power has a right, in some cases, to interfere in matters of religion. It has a right to prohibit and punish gross immoralities and impieties; because the open practice of these is of evil example and detriment. For this reason, I heartily approve of our laws against drunkness, profane swearing, blasphemy, and professed atheism. But in this state, we have never thought it expedient to adopt a test-law; and yet I sincerely believe we have as great a proportion of religion and morality, as they have in England, where every person who holds a public office, must either be a saint by law, or a hypocrite by practice. A test-law is the parent of hypocrisy, and the off-spring of error and the spirit of persecution. Legislatures have no right to set up an inquisition, and examine into the private opinions of men. Test-laws are useless and ineffectual, unjust and tyrannical; therefore the Convention have done wisely in excluding this engine of persecution, and providing that no religious test shall ever be required."[1]

In Connecticut, as we see, the absence of a test-law seems to have furnished a serious argument against the Constitution. Oliver Wolcott, in the ratifying convention argued:

"I do not see the necessity of such a test as some gentlemen wish for. The Constitution enjoins an oath upon all the officers of the United States. This is a direct appeal to that God who is the avenger of perjury. Such an appeal to him is a full acknowledgment of His Being and Providence. An acknowledgment of these great truths is all that the gentleman contends for. For myself, I should be content either with or without that clause in the Constitution which excludes test laws. Knowledge and liberty are so prevalent in this country, that I do not believe that the United States would ever be disposed to establish one religious sect, and lay all others under legal disabilities. But as we know not what may take place hereafter, and any such test would be exceedingly injurious to the rights of free citizens, I cannot think it altogether superfluous to have added a clause, which secures us from the possibility of such oppression."[2]

Connecticut ratified the Constitution January 9, 1788, being the fifth state to do so.

In Massachusetts the religious clause evoked even more discussion than in Connecticut, so much so that it attracted Dr. Manning from Rhode Island to the convention and

[1] *The Connecticut Courant*, Monday, Dec. 17, 1787, "To the Landholders and Farmers" by "A Landholder" (Oliver Ellsworth). Quoted in Ford, *Essays on the Constitution*, pp. 167-171.

[2] Elliot, *Debates*, Philadelphia, 1859, vol. ii, p. 202.

his influence was necessary in order to secure that slim majority by which ratification was finally secured.

Here, too, the liberalism of the clause was attacked. Major Lusk "concluded by saying, that he shuddered at the idea that Roman Catholics, Papists and Pagans might be introduced into office; and that Popery and the Inquisition may be established in America."[1] While Colonel Jones "thought, that the rulers ought to believe in God or Christ; and that, however a test may be prostituted in England, yet he thought if our public men were to be of those who had a good standing in the Church, it would be happy for the United States; and that a person could not be a good man without being a good Christian."[2]

Mr. Isaac Backus, though opposed to ratification, yet spoke in favor of the religious clause:

"I shall begin with the exclusion of any religious test. Many appear to be much concerned about it, but nothing is more evident, both in reason and the Holy Scriptures, than that religion is ever a matter between God and individuals, and therefore no man or men can impose any religious test without invading the essential prerogatives of the Lord Jesus Christ . . . . . Let the history of all nations be searched from that day (Constantine's) to this, and it will appear that the imposing of religious tests hath been the greatest engine of tyranny in the world. And I rejoice to see so many gentlemen who are now giving in their rights of conscience in this great and important matter. Some serious minds discover a concern lest if all religious tests be excluded, the Congress would hereafter establish Popery or some other tyrannical way of worship. But it is most certain that no such way of worship can be established without any religious test." [3]

Mr. Parsons, of Newburyport, was among those who gave in their testimony for the clause. He observed:

"It has been objected that the Constitution provides no religious test by oath, and we may have in power unprincipled men, atheists and

[1] Elliot, *Debates*, vol. ii, p. 148.
[2] *Ibid.*, vol. ii, p. 119.
[3] *Ibid.*, vol. ii, pp. 148-149.

pagans. No man can wish more ardently than I do that all our public offices may be filled by men who fear God and hate wickedness, but it must remain with the electors to give the government this security. An oath will not do it. Will an unprincipled man be entangled by an oath? Will an atheist or a pagan dread the vengeance of the Christian God, a Being in his opinion the creature of fancy and credulity? It is a solecism in expression. No man is so illiberal as to wish the confining places of honor or profit to any one sect of Christians, but what security is it to the government that every public officer shall swear that he is a Christian? . . . Sir, the only evidence we can have of the sincerity of a man's religion is a good life, and I trust that such evidence will be required of every candidate by every elector."[1]

The Reverend Mr. Shute spoke as follows for the clause:

"To establish a religious test as a qualification for offices in the proposed Federal Constitution it appears to me, sir, would be attended with injurious consequences to some individuals, and with no advantage to the whole.

By the injurious consequences to individuals, I mean, that some who in every other respect are qualified to fill some important post in the government, will be excluded by their not being able to stand the religious test; which I take to be a privation of part of their civil rights.

Nor is there to me any conceivable advantage, sir, that would result to the whole from such a test. Unprincipled and dishonest men will not hesitate to subscribe to anything, that may open the way for their advancement, and put them into a situation the better to execute their base and iniquitous designs. Honest men alone, therefore, however well qualified to serve the public, would be excluded by it, and their country be deprived of the benefit of their abilities.

In this great and extensive empire, there is and will be a great variety of sentiments in religion among its inhabitants. Upon the plan of a religious test, the question I think must be, who shall be excluded from national trusts? Whatever answer bigotry may suggest, the dictates of candor and equity, I conceive, will be none.

Far from limiting my charity and confidence to men of my own denomination in religion, I suppose, and I believe, sir, that there are worthy characters among men of every denomination — among the Quakers — the Baptists — the Church of England — the Papists — and even among those who have no other guide, in the way to virtue and heaven, than the dictates of natural religion.

The presumption is, that the eyes of the people will be upon the faithful in the land, and, from a regard to their own safety, they will choose

[1] Elliot, *Debates,* vol. ii, p. 90.

for their rulers men of known abilities — of known probity — of good moral characters . . . . . I know of no reason, why men of such a character, in a community, of whatever denomination, in religion, *coeteris paribus*, with other suitable qualifications, should not be acceptable to the people, and why they may not be employed by them with safety and advantage in the important offices of government. The exclusion of a religious test in the Proposed Constitution, therefore, clearly appears to me, sir, to be in favor of its adoption."[1]

The Reverend Mr. Payson, of the Congregational Church, said:

"The great object of religion being God supreme, and the seat of religion in man being the heart or conscience, that is the reason God has given us, employed on our moral actions, in their most important consequences, as related to the tribunal of God; hence, I infer, that God alone is the God of conscience, and, consequently, attempts to erect human tribunals for the consciences of men, are impious encroachments upon the prerogatives of God. Upon these principles, had there been a religious test, as a qualification for office, it would, in my opinion, have been a great blemish upon the instrument."[2]

Twelve of the four hundred delegates to this convention were Baptists. Dr. Manning was so interested in the issue that he came to the convention and labored for ratification. He wrote, February 11, 1788:

"I felt so deeply interested in the adoption of the new Federal Constitution by your state, that I attended the debates in convention more than a fortnight . . . . . I considered Massachusetts the hinge on which the whole must turn, and am happy in congratulating you on the favorable issue of their deliberations. I am mortified to find Father (Noah) Alden among the nays."[3]

Isaac Backus, as well as Father Alden, were Baptists who remained Bitter-enders in their opposition to the Constitution. But other Baptists like the influential Stillman of Boston supported it. Ratification carried by the vote of 187 to 168. The Governor, therefore, asked Dr.

[1] Elliot, *Debates*, vol. ii, pp. 118-119.
[2] *Ibid.*, vol. ii, p. 120.
[3] Guild, *op. cit.*, p. 406.

Manning to "close the solemn convocation with thanksgiving and prayer,"[1] and Dr. Waterhouse, who dined in a large company after the adjournment, said "the praise of the Reverend Dr. Manning was in every mouth. Nothing but the popularity of Dr. Stillman prevented the rich men of Boston from building a church for Dr. Manning's acceptance."[2]

With the possible exception of his fellow Baptist, John Brown, Dr. Manning was the strongest single influence in causing a final acceptance of the Federal Constitution by the State of Rhode Island. That state at first rejected the instrument and Manning wrote to the Reverend Dr. Smith June 10, 1788:

"Our wicked State has rejected the Constitution by the town meetings to which the Legislature sent it, instead of complying with the recommendation of the General Convention. Our rulers are deliberately wicked but the people of some of the towns begin to wake up since South Carolina has adopted the new Constitution, and Massachusetts has so effectually crushed Shayism." [3]

Providence and Dr. Manning finally led the way to ratification:

"At an adjourned meeting of the town (Providence) on Thursday (August 27, 1789), a committee, that had been appointed on Tuesday for the purpose, reported a draft of a petition to be presented to the Congress of the United States, setting forth the distressed situation of this State, the probability of our soon joining the Union, and praying that vessels belonging to our citizens may be exempted from foreign tonnage and goods shipped from this State from foreign duties, for such time and under such regulations and restrictions as Congress in their wisdom shall think proper.

This petition was unanimously voted: and after having been signed by the moderator and town clerk, the Rev. Dr. Manning and Benjamin Bourne, Esq., were appointed to proceed to New York and present the same." [4]

[1] Burrage, *op. cit.*, pp. 121-122.
[2] Guild, *op. cit.*, p. 405.
[3] *Ibid.*, p. 411.
[4] *Ibid.*, p. 424.

President Manning had been one of the committee to draft this petition.[1]

May 24, 1790, a State Convention on the Federal Constitution was held at Newport, where, after three days of debate in the Second Baptist Church, adoption was carried by a vote of thirty-four to thirty-two. In August of that year President Washington visited Brown University and publicly expressed his appreciation of the zeal of that corporation "for the success of the cause of your country."[2]

New Hampshire, the ninth state to ratify, did so, June 21, 1788, and proposed twelve amendments, the eleventh of which read:

> "Congress shall make no laws touching religion, or to infringe the rights of conscience."[3]

Perhaps the fight over the religious clause was fiercest in Virginia where so much had already been done for religious liberty. Champions of religious freedom did not wish to see their gains lost through federal interference and Patrick Henry, George Mason, and others knew just how to take advantage of this sentiment. Nine states had ratified when the Virginia Convention met, June 22, 1788. Ratification was voted, June 25.

When the General Committee of the Baptists met at William's Meeting-house, Goochland County, March 7, 1788, it was considered:

> "Whether the new Federal Constitution, which had now lately made its appearance in public, made sufficient provision for the secure enjoyment of religious liberty; on which it was agreed unanimously that, in the opinion of the General Committee, it did not."[4]

[1] Staples, *Annals of Providence*.
[2] Guild, *op. cit.*, p. 435.
[3] *Provincial and State Papers, New Hampshire*, vol. x, p. 17.
[4] Semple, *op. cit.*, p. 76.

Accordingly they resolved to oppose ratification and Elder John Leland, the most popular Baptist in Virginia, was nominated as a delegate from Orange County, — the home county of James Madison. Madison's father wrote his son, "The Baptists are now generally opposed to it (the Constitution)."[1] On the day of election Elder Leland withdrew in favor of Madison, a fact of great significance for the cause of ratification and to be accounted for, doubtlessly, by Madison's well-known championship of religious liberty.

James Madison wrote to Edmund Randolph, April 10, 1788:

> "As to the religious test, I should conceive that it can imply at most nothing more than that without that exception, a power would have been given to impose an oath involving a religious test as a qualification for office."[2]

Randolph had at first felt that dangerous powers respecting religion had been conferred upon Congress by the Constitution. But he altered his opinion and on June 10, 1788, in the Virginia Convention, he announced this:

> "Freedom of religion is said to be in danger. I will candidly say, I once thought that it was, and felt great repugnance to the Constitution for that reason. I am willing to acknowledge my apprehensions removed — and I will inform you by what process of reasoning I did remove them. The Constitution provides, that 'The Senators and Representatives . . shall be bound by oath or affirmation to support this Constitution; but no religious test shall ever be required as a qualification to any office or public trust under the United States.' It has been said, that if the exclusion of the religious test were an exception from the general power of Congress, the power over religion would remain. I inform those who are of this opinion, that no power is given expressly to Congress over religion. The senators and representatives, members of the state

[1] *Writings of James Madison*, Hunt edition, vol. v., p. 105; James, *op. cit.*, p. 152.

[2] Farrand, *op. cit.*, vol. iii, p. 297; Robertson, *Debates of the Convention of Virginia*, 1788, (second edition, 1805), pp. 151-152.

legislatures and executive and judicial officers, are bound by oath, or affirmation, to support this Constitution. This only binds them to support it in the exercise of the powers constitutionally given it. The exclusion of a religious test is an exception from this general provision, with respect to oaths or affirmations. Although officers, etc., are to swear that they will support this Constitution, yet they are not bound to support one mode of worship, or to adhere to one particular sect. It puts all sects on the same footing. A man of abilities and character, of any sect, whatever, may be admitted to any office or public trust under the United States. I am a friend to a variety of sects, because they keep one another in order. How many different sects are we composed of throughout the United States? How many different sects will be in Congress? We cannot enumerate the sects that may be in Congress. And there are so many now in the United States, that they will prevent the establishment of any one sect in prejudice to the rest, and will forever oppose all attempts to infringe religious liberty. If such an attempt be made, will not the alarm be sounded throughout America? If Congress be as wicked as we are foretold they will, they would not run the risk of exciting the resentment of all, or most of the religious sects of America."[1]

Such was the judicious opinion of that Randolph whom President Washington was to name as the first attorney-general of the United States.

But Jefferson was writing from abroad, February 7, 1788, urging a declaration of rights which shall stipulate freedom of religion, freedom of the press, freedom of commerce against monopolies, trial by juries in all cases, etc., etc. And in the convention Patrick Henry, who well knew how to utilize public sentiment to the limit, declaimed:

"That sacred and lovely thing, religion, ought not to rest on the ingenuity of logical deduction. Holy religion, Sir, will be prostituted to the lowest purposes of human policy. What has been more productive of mischief among mankind than religious disputes? Then here, Sir, is a foundation for such disputes, when it required learning and logical deduction to perceive that religious liberty is secure."[2]

[1] Farrand, *op. cit.*, vol. iii, p. 310.
[2] Elliot, *Debates,* vol. iii, p. 318.

Mr. Madison replied:

"The honorable member has introduced the subject of religion. Religion is not guarded — there is no bill of rights declaring that religion should be secure. Is a bill of rights a security for religion? Would the bill of rights, in this state, exempt the people from paying for the support of one particular sect, if such sect were exclusively established by law? If there were a majority of one sect, a bill of rights would be a poor protection for liberty. Happily for the states, they enjoy the utmost freedom of religion. This freedom arises from that multiplicity of sects, which pervades America, and which is the best and only security for religious liberty in any society. For where there is such a variety of sects, there cannot be a majority of any one sect to oppress and persecute the rest. Fortunately for this commonwealth, a majority of the people are decidedly against any establishment — I believe it to be so in the other states. There is not a shadow of right in the general government to intermeddle with religion. Its least interference with it would be a most flagrant usurpation. I can appeal to my uniform conduct on this subject, that I have warmly supported religious freedom. It is better that this security should be depended upon from the general legislature than from one particular state. A particular state might concur in one religious project. But the United States abound in such a variety of sects, that it is a strong security against religious persecution, and is sufficient to authorize a conclusion, that no one sect will ever be able to outnumber or depress the rest . . . . .

I confess to you, Sir, were uniformity of religion to be introduced by this system, it would, in my opinion, be ineligible; but I have no reason to conclude, that uniformity of government will produce that of religion. This subject is, for the honor of America, perfectly free and unshackled. The government has no jurisdiction over it — the least reflection will convince us, there is no danger to be feared on this ground." [1]

Virginia accompanied its ratification with a list of proposed amendments and a Bill of Rights, Number 20 of which read (see Article 16 of the Virginia Bill of Rights):

"That religion, or the duty which we owe to our Creator, and the manner of discharging it, can be directed only by reason and conviction, not by force or violence, and therefore all men have an equal, natural and unalienable right to the free exercise of religion according to the dictates of conscience, and that no particular religious sect or society ought to be favored or established by law in preference to others." [2]

[1] Elliot, *op. cit.*, vol. iii, pp. 93, 330.
[2] *Supra.*, p. 376; Elliot, *op. cit.*, vol. iii, p. 659.

This same declaration regarding religion was adopted by North Carolina when she ratified, November 21, 1789, after a most protracted debate relative to "the last clause of the sixth article."

Mr. Henry Abbot voiced the fear of many as follows:

"Some are afraid, Mr. Chairman, that should the Constitution be received, they would be deprived of the privilege of worshipping God according to their consciences, which would be taking from them a benefit they enjoy under the present Constitution. They wish to know if their religious and civil liberties be secured under this system, or whether the General Government may not make laws infringing their religious liberties. The worthy member from Edenton mentioned sundry political reasons why treaties should be the supreme law of the land. It is feared by some people, that by the power of making treaties, they might make a treaty engaging with foreign powers to adopt the Roman Catholic religion in the United States, which would prevent the people from worshipping God according to their own consciences. — The worthy member from Halifax has in some measure satisfied my mind on this subject. But others may be dissatisfied. Many wish to know what religion shall be established. I believe a majority of the community are Presbyterians. I am for my part against any exclusive establishment, but if there were any, I would prefer the Episcopal. The exclusion of religious tests is by many thought dangerous and impolitic. They suppose that if there be no religious test required, pagans, deists and Mahometans might obtain offices among us, and that the senators and representatives might all be pagans. Every person employed by the general and state governments is to take an oath to support the former. Some are desirous to know how, and by whom they are to swear, since no religious tests are required — Whether they are to swear by Jupiter, Juno, Minerva, Proserpine, or Pluto . . . . . I would be glad some gentleman would endeavor to obviate these objections, in order to satisfy the religious part of the society. . . . . . ."[1]

Mr. Iredell replied at length:

"Under the color of religious tests the utmost cruelties have been exercised . . . . . America has set an example to mankind to think more modestly and reasonably; that a man may be of different religious sentiments from our own, without being a bad member of society . . . . I should be sorry to find, when examples of toleration are set even by

[1] Elliot, *Debates*, vol. iv, pp. 189-190.

arbitrary governments, that this country, so impressed with the highest sense of liberty, should adopt principles on this subject, that are narrow and illiberal. I consider the clause under consideration as one of the strongest proofs that could be adduced, that it was the intention of those who formed this system, to establish a general religious liberty in America . . . . . . I confess the restriction on the power of congress in this particular has my hearty approbation. They certainly have no authority to interfere in the establishment of any religion whatsoever and I am astonished that any gentleman should conceive they have. Is there any power given to congress in matters of religion? Can they pass a single act to impair our religious liberties? If they could it would be a just cause of alarm. If the could, Sir, no man would have more horror against it than myself. Happily no sect here is superior to another. As long as this is the case, we shall be free from those persecutions and distractions with which other countries have been torn. If any future congress should pass an act concerning the religion of the country, it would be an act which they are not authorized to pass by the Constitution, and which the people would not obey. Every one would ask, 'Who authorized the Government to pass such an act? It is not warranted by the Constitution, and is a barefaced usurpation.' The power to make treaties can never be supposed to include a right to establish foreign religion among ourselves, though it might authorize a toleration of others.

But it is objected, that the people of America may perhaps, choose representatives who have no religion at all, and that Pagans and Mahometans may be admitted into offices. But how is it possible to exclude any set of men, without taking away that principle of religious freedom which we ourselves so warmly contend for. — This is the foundation on which persecution has been raised in every part of the world. The people in power were always in the right, and everybody else wrong. If you admit the least difference, the door to persecution is opened. Nor would it answer the purpose, for the worst part of the excluded sects would comply with the test, and the best man only be kept out of our counsels. — But it is never to be supposed that the people of America will trust their dearest rights to persons who have no religion at all, or a religion materially different from their own. It would be happy for mankind if religion was permitted to take its own course, and maintain itself by the excellence of its own doctrines. The divine Author of our religion never wished for its support by worldly authority . . . . It made much greater progress for itself, than when supported by the greatest authority upon earth.

It has been asked . . . . . what is the meaning of that part, where it is said, that the United States shall guarantee to every state in the union a republican form of government, and why a guarantee of religious freedom was not included . . . . . Had Congress undertaken to guarantee religious freedom, or any particular species of it, they would then have had a pretence to interfere in a subject they have nothing to do with. Each state, so far as the clause in question does not interfere, must be left to the operation of its own principles.

. . . . . I met by accident with a pamphlet this morning, in which the author states as a very serious danger, that the Pope of Rome might be elected president. I confess that this never struck me before, and if the author had read all the qualifications of a president perhaps his fears might have been quieted . . . . . Sir, it is impossible to treat such idle fears with any degree of gravity . . . . .

. . . . . This article is calculated to secure universal religious liberty, by putting all sects on a level, the only way to prevent persecution. I thought nobody would have objected to this clause, which deserves in my opinion the highest approbation. This country has already had the honor of setting an example of civil freedom, and I trust it will likewise have the honor of teaching the rest of the world the way to religious freedom also."[1]

In continuing his exposition of the clause, Iredell said:

"It has been universally considered, that in administering an oath, it is only necessary to enquire if the person who is to take it, believes in a Supreme Being, and in a future state of rewards and punishments . . . We may, I think, very safely leave religion to itself; and as to the form of the oath, I think this may well be trusted to the General Government, to be applied on the principles I have mentioned."[2]

Governor Johnston expressed great astonishment that the people were alarmed on the subject of religion. This he said, must have arisen from the great pains which had been taken to prejudice men's minds against the Constitution. He begged leave to add the following observations:

"When I heard there were apprehensions that the pope of Rome could be the president of the United States, I was greatly astonished. . . . . . It appears to me that it would have been dangerous, if Congress could intermeddle with the subject of religion . . . . . When any attempt is made by any government to restrain men's consciences, no good consequences can possibly follow . . . . .

[1] Elliot, *op. cit.*, vol. iv, pp. 195-196.
[2] *Ibid.*, vol. v, 197-198.

But great apprehensions have been raised as to the influence of the Eastern states. When you attend to circumstances, this will have no weight. I know but two or three states where there is the least chance of establishing any particular religion. The people of Massachusetts and Connecticut are mostly Presbyterians. In every other state, the people are divided into a great number of sects. In Rhode Island, the tenets of the Baptists I believe prevail. In New York they are divided very much; the most numerous are the Episcopalians and the Baptists. In New Jersey they are as much divided as we are. In Pennsylvania, if any sect prevails more than others, it is that of the Quakers. In Maryland the Episcopalians are most numerous, though there are other sects. In Virginia there are many sects; you all know what their religious sentiments are. So in all the Southern States they differ; as also in New Hampshire. I hope therefore that the gentlemen will see there is no cause of fear that any one religion shall be exclusively established." [1]

Mr. Caldwell thought some danger might arise. He imagined the clause might be objected to in a political as well as in a religious way. He remarked:

"In the first place there was an invitation for Jews and Pagans of every kind to come among us. At some future period this might endanger the character of the United States . . . . . Even those who do not regard religion acknowledge that the Christian religion is best calculated of all religions to make good members of society, on account of its morality. I think that, in a political view, those gentlemen who formed this Constitution, should not have given this invitation to Jews and Heathens. All those who have any religion are against the emigration of those people from the Eastern Hemisphere." [2]

Mr. Spencer spoke as follows:

"He thought that no one particular religion should be established. Religious tests have been the foundation of persecutions in all countries . . . . . It is feared that persons of bad principles, deists, atheists, etc., may come into this country, and there is nothing to restrain them from being eligible to offices. He asked if it was reasonable to suppose that the people would choose men without regarding their character. Tests would not keep unscrupulous men out of office but would exclude some truly conscientious and religious men. This would be a great cause of objection to a religious test. But in this case as there is not a

[1] Elliot, *op. cit.*, vol. iii, pp. 175-176.
[2] *Ibid.*, vol. iv, pp. 198-199.

religious test required, it leaves religion on the solid foundation of its own inherent validity, without any connection with temporal authority, and no kind of oppression can take place . . . . . He could not object to this part of the Constitution and wished that every other part was as good and proper."[1]

Governor Johnston admitted that Jews, Pagans, etc., might emigrate to the United States but said they could not be in proportion to the emigration of Christians who should come from other countries and that in all probability the children even of such would be Christians, and that this, with the rapid population of the United States, their zeal for religion and love of liberty, would, he trusted, add to the progress of Christian religion among us.[2]

Mr. Lenoir feared that there being no provision against infringement of the rights of conscience, ecclesiastical courts might be established;[3] and Mr. Wilson wished that the Constitution had excluded popish priests from office for "As there was no test required, and nothing to govern them but honor, when their interest clashed with their honor the latter would fly before the former."[4] Mr. Lancaster insisted that there was a real danger that papists might occupy the presidential chair.[5]

The conclusion of this debate was the suggestion of a bill of rights wherein the Virginia article on religious freedom was incorporated.

In all, six states suggested an amendment bearing upon the religious questions; the First Amendment to the Constitution was the result. On June 8, 1789, Madison proposed nine amendments, others were suggested and agreed to by the two houses, September 25. The one

[1] Elliot, *op. cit.*, vol. iv, p. 200.
[2] *Ibid.*, vol. iv, p. 200.
[3] *Ibid.*, vol. iv, p. 203.
[4] *Ibid.*, vol. iv, p. 212.
[5] *Ibid.*, vol. iv, p. 215.

covering religion provides that "Congress shall make no law respecting any establishment of religion, or prohibiting the free exercise thereof."[1]

In the meantime the Baptist General Committee of Virginia had opened correspondence with the Baptists in other states, especially in Massachusetts, Rhode Island, and New York, the object being to secure coöperation in the matter of the procurement of this amendment. Elder John Leland was at the head of this committee. At its session in Richmond, August 8, 1789, it addressed a patriotic letter to President Washington, invoking his aid in the movement which they sponsored.[2] They were much pleased with the amendments and James Madison wrote from his home among them in Orange County, to President Washington, November 20, 1789, "One of the principal leaders of the Baptists lately sent me word that the amendments had entirely satisfied the disaffected of his sect and that it would appear in their subsequent conduct."[3]

Not all on the contrary were satisfied. At least nine times since that date a resolution proposing an amendment to the preamble has been introduced into Congress. However, it has never got beyond the committee to which it had been referred. The following is the pioneer resolution as it was introduced by Mr. Frye of Maine:

"We, the people of the United States, devoutly acknowledging the supreme authority and just government of God in all the affairs of men and nations, and grateful to Him for our civil and religious liberty, and encouraged by the assurances of His Word, invoke His Guidance, as a Christian nation, according to His appointed way, through Jesus Christ, in order to form, etc."

[1] *Annals of Congress*, vol. i, pp. 440 sqq., 448, 685-692, 699, 730 sqq., 796, 758.

[2] James, *op. cit.*, pp. 159-168; Catchcart, *Centennial Offering*, p. 109.

[3] *Writings of James Madison*, vol. v. p. 429.

"Thus" says Story, "the whole power over the subject of religion was left exclusively to the state government, to be acted on according to their own sense of justice and the state constitutions."[1] "Probably," he remarks elsewhere, "at the time of the adoption of the Constitution and of the Amendment to it . . . . . the general, if not the universal sentiment in America was that Christianity ought to receive encouragement from the state, so far as it is not imcompatible with the private rights of conscience and the freedom of religious worship. An attempt to level all religions and to make it a matter of state policy to hold all in utter indifference would have created universal disapprobation, if not universal indignation."[2]

Slavery has been the one great issue thus far in the history of the United States to threaten the destruction of the Union. This question was present in the Constitutional Convention, largely as the result of actions taken by certain religious denominations. The churches of America assumed the leadership of the forces for emancipation and in the Constitution they already secured recognition of the issue. The triumph of the churches in this moral issue is a splendid illustration of the control of American religious principles over both the principle of separation of church and state and over purely economic interests.

To the Quakers we owe the beginning of anti-slavery sentiment in America. William Penn, like Friends in general, seems to have owned slaves. German Friends, at Germantown, April 1688, first addressed a protest "against the traffic in the bodies of men," and against handling "men as cattle." The Yearly Meeting of that year recorded that a "paper was presented by some German Friends concerning the lawfulness and unlawfulness of buying and keeping negroes. It was judged not to be proper for this meeting to give a positive judgment in the

[1] Story, *Commentary*, pp. 702-703.
[2] *Ibid.*, p. 700; Cooley, *Constitutional Limitations*, p. 371.

case, it having so general a relation to many other parts; and therefore at present they forbear it."[1] This document is believed to be the first official protest of any religious body in America against slavery.

In 1693 the Friends' Meeting of Philadelphia advised that no slaves should be bought "except to be set free."[2] The 1696 Yearly Meeting advised Friends "not to encourage the bringing in of any more negroes," and also that they should be brought to meetings, and in other respects well cared for.[3] In 1711 importation of slaves was absolutely forbidden. This law was vetoed by the Council in England as was another imposing the prohibitive duty of twenty pounds per head on every slave imported.[4] In 1758 the Yearly Meeting at Philadelphia directed a "visitation" of all who held slaves, and decided that all who should "be concerned in importing, selling, or purchasing slaves" should be forbidden to sit in meetings for discipline.[5] And the year of the Declaration of Independence this Yearly Meeting took final action:

"Where any members continue to reject the advice of their brethren, and refuse to execute proper instruments in writing for releasing from a state of slavery such as are in their power, or to whom they have any claim, whether arrived at full age or in their minority, and no hopes of the continuance of Friends' labor being profitable to them; that Monthly Meeting after having discharged a Christian duty to such, should testify their disunion with them." In accordance with this resolution, subordinate meetings were directed to "deny the right of membership to such as persist in holding their fellow men as property."[6]

[1] Thomas, *History of the Friends in America*, 5th edition, pp. 112-115; *Pennsylvania Magazine of History and Biography*, vol. iv, p. 28: Bowden, *op. cit.*, vol. ii, p. 193.

[2] Bowden, *op. cit.*, vol. ii, p. 195.

[3] *Ibid.*, vol. ii, p. 196.

[4] *Ibid.*, vol. ii, p. 197.

[5] *Ibid.*, vol. ii, p. 212.

[6] Applegarth, *Quakers in Pennsylvania*, in *Johns Hopkins University Studies*, 10th series, vols. vii-ix, chapter iv, "Attitude of the Quakers towards Slavery."

The Yearly Meeting of Pennsylvania, 1783, addressed Congress on the iniquity of the slave trade. A special delegation waited on Congress with a petition signed by more than five hundred members, earnestly soliciting the interposition of the Federal Government, for the suppression of this atrocity.[1]

New England Friends in 1758 and 1769 passed strong "minutes" in regard to slavery and in 1772 Friends were "disowned" for not setting their slaves free: New York Friends made it a disciplinary offence to buy, sell, or hold slaves in 1776. And the Virginia Meetings were to disown those who refused to manumit after 1784. This was the action taken by the Baltimore Yearly Meeting for Maryland in 1777. By the close of the eighteenth century there was not a slave in the possession of a Friend in good standing except where they were held by trustees, and state laws did not allow them to be set free.[2]

The Methodists soon took up the cause of the Blacks. A minute of the Baltimore Meeting of 1780 asks and answers the following questions:

"16. Ought not this Conference to require those travelling preachers who hold slaves to give promise to set them free? Yes.

17. Does the Conference acknowledge that slavery is contrary to the laws of God, man and nature, and hurtful to society; contrary to the dictates of conscience and pure religion, and doing that which we would not that others should do to us and ours? Do we pass our disapprobation on all our friends who keep slaves? and advise their freedom? Yes."[3]

In 1783 the following was answered (Question 10):

"What shall be done with our local preachers who hold slaves contrary to the laws which authorize their freedom in any of the United States? We will try them another year. In the meantime let every assistant

[1] Bowden, *op. cit.*, vol. ii, p. 217.

[2] *Ibid.*, vol. ii, ch. viii.

[3] *Minutes of the Annual Conferences of the Methodist Church for the Years, 1773-1823*, N. Y., 1840, p. 12.

deal faithfully and plainly with every one, and report to the next conference. It may then be necessary to suspend them."[1]

And in 1784 the following action was taken:

"Question 12, What Shall we do with our friends that buy and sell slaves? Answer, If they buy with no other design than to hold them as slaves, and have been previously warned they shall be expelled, and permitted to sell on no consideration.

Question 13, What shall we do with our local preachers who will not emancipate their slaves in the states where the laws admit it? Answer, Try those in Virginia another year, and suspend the preachers in Maryland, Delaware, Pennsylvania and New Jersey.

Question 22, What shall be done with our travelling preachers that now are, or hereafter shall be, possessed of slaves, and refuse to manumit them where the law permits? Answer, Employ them no more."[2]

The conference of 1785 noted: "We do hold in the deepest abhorrence the practice of slavery and shall not cease to seek its destruction by all wise and prudent means."[3]

The Baptists of the South in 1789 resolved, "That slavery is a violent deprivation of the rights of nature, and inconsistent with a republican government, and we therefore recommend it to our brethren to make use of every legal measure to extirpate this horrid evil from the land."[4]

In 1787 a committee of Presbyterians brought in the following overture at the annual meeting of the joint synod:

"The Creator of the world having made of one flesh all the children of men, it becomes them as members of the same family, to consult and promote each other's happiness. It is more especially the duty of those who maintain the rights of humanity, and who acknowledge and teach the obligations of Christianity, to use such means as are in their power to extend the blessings of equal freedom to every part of the human race.

[1] *Minutes*, p. 18. [2] *Ibid.*, p. 20.

[3] *British Minutes of 1785*, edition of 1812, vol. i, p. 181.

[4] Newman, *The Baptists*, p. 305.

From a full conviction of these truths, and sensible that the rights of human nature are too well understood to admit of debate, Overture, that the Synod of New York and Philadelphia recommend, in the warmest terms, to every member of their body, and to all the churches and families under their care, to do everything in their power consistent with the rights of civil society, to promote the abolition of slavery and the instruction of negroes, whether bond or free."[1]

Two days later, May 28, the Synod came to the following judgment:

"The Synod of New York and Philadelphia do highly approve of the general principles in favor of universal liberty, that prevail in America, and the interest which many of the states have taken in promoting the abolition of slavery; yet, inasmuch as men introduced from a servile state to a participation of all the privileges of civil society, without a proper education, and without previous habits of industry, may be, in many respects, dangerous to the community, therefore they earnestly recommend it to all the members belonging to their communion, to give those persons who are at present held in servitude, such good education as to prepare them for the better enjoyment of freedom; and they moreover recommend that masters, wherever they find servants disposed to make a just improvement of the privilege, would give them a *peculium*, or grant them sufficient time and sufficient means of procuring their own liberty at a moderate rate, that thereby, they may be brought into society with the habits of industry that may render them useful citizens; and, finally, they recommend it to all their people to use the most prudent measures, consistent with the interest and the state of civil society, in the counties where they live, to procure eventually the final abolition of slavery in America."[2]

The General Association of the Connecticut Congregationalists took up the question at their meeting in West Hartford, June, 1788:

"On motion made by the Association in the Western District of New Haven County, the association voted that the Slave Trade be unjust, and that every justifiable means ought to be taken to suppress it.

Voted, also, that Drs. Goodrich, Edwards and Wales be a committee to draw up an address and petition to the General Assembly, that some effectual laws may be made for the total abolition of the slave trade.

[1] *Records*, p. 539.
[2] *Ibid.*, p. 540.

The committee . . . . . made a draft of a petition, etc., which was accepted, and one for the total abolition of the slave trade, connected with it. Drs. Edwards and Wales were appointed a committee to forward said petition to the General Assembly at their session in October next."[1]

That the churches had taken up the question of slavery as a moral issue, had a great deal to do with the character of the slavery clause inserted in the Federal Constitution. Randolph, speaking of the slavery clause, noted, that "By agreeing to the clause (as it then stood), it would revolt the Quakers and the Methodists."[2] Quaker principles were represented in the convention, as we have noted, by Mifflin and Dickinson; Methodist ideals by Bassett. A prospective abolition of the slave trade was secured.

During this period various states abolished slavery: Vermont in 1777, Pennsylvania in 1780, New Hampshire in 1783, Connecticut and Rhode Island (gradual emancipation) in 1784; and Massachusetts in 1780 by a clause in the Constitution which the courts later interpreted as signifying emancipation.

Writing to their brethren in England in 1785, the Friends of Pennsylvania and New Jersey remarked: "The silence of Congress on the subject-matter of our Yearly Meeting's address in 1783, relative to the slave-trade engaged us to revive that important affair in their view by a letter to the President."[3] In 1789, they memorialized Congress again on the subject.

As soon as the emancipation of slaves had been accomplished in Pennsylvania, the Quakers were confronted with the issue of the legal status of migratory slaves. In 1786, April 12, General Washington wrote, relative to a slave

[1] *Records of the General Association*, pp. 126-127.
[2] *Records of the Federal Convention*, vol. ii, p. 374.
[3] Bowden, *op. cit.*, vol. ii, p. 361.

of a Mr. Dably of Alexandria, who had escaped to Philadelphia, "Whom a sect of Quakers in the city, formed for such purposes, have attempted to liberate." From Mr. Dably's account of the occurrence, General Washington concluded, "that this society is not only acting repugnantly to justice, so far as its conduct concerns strangers, but in my opinion impoliticly with respect to the state, the city in particular, without being able, by acts of tyranny and oppression to accomplish its own ends."[1]

[1] Washington, *op. cit.*, Sparks edition, vol. ix, p. 158.

CHAPTER XVI

"AMERICAN CIVIL CHURCH LAW" IN THE STATE CONSTITUTIONS

As we have noted, Oliver Ellsworth asserted, during the campaign for the ratification of the Federal Constitution, through the *Connecticut Courant*, that he "would not deny that the civil power has a right, in some cases, to interfere in matters of religion. It has a right to prohibit and punish gross immoralities and impieties."[1]

This view has been subsequently upheld by the Supreme Court of the United States. In the case of *Reynolds vs. The United States*, October, 1878, Chief Justice White defined the bounds of religious liberty as guaranteed by the Constitution as follows:

"Laws are made for the government of actions, and while they cannot interfere with mere religious beliefs and opinions, they may with practices. Suppose one believed that human sacrifices were a necessary part of religious worship, would it be seriously contended that the civil government under which he lived could not interfere to prevent a sacrifice? Or if a wife religiously believed it her duty to burn herself upon the funeral pile of her dead husband, would it be beyond the power of civil government to prevent her carrying her belief into practice?

So here, as a law of the organization of society under the exclusive dominion of the United States, it is provided that plural marriages shall not be allowed. Can a man excuse his practices to the contrary because of his religious belief? To permit this would be to make the professed doctrines of religious belief superior to the law of the land, and in effect to permit every citizen to become a law unto himself. Government could exist only in name under such circumstances."[2]

The government, state and national, through its executives, legislature and courts, has had to deal with a great

[1] *Supra.*, p. 464.

[2] *United States Supreme Court Reports*, vol. 98, pp. 166-177.

variety of matters pertaining to religion; such as, the appropriation of public funds to charitable institutions managed by some particular denomination, church properties, Sunday observance, marriage rights, etc. In fact Carl Zollman has worked out a very substantial treatise on *American Civil Church Law*. His first chapter is devoted to an interpretation of the phrase "Religious Liberty." He concludes:

"The American citizen is protected in his religious liberty against any act of the Federal Government by the United States constitution and against any act of his state government by his state constitution. Under both he is entirely free to formulate any opinion whatsoever in regard to religion, to practice and teach it to others, provided he respects their rights and does not incite to crime or breach of the peace. In defining forbidden acts the law recognizes the Christian religion as the prevailing religion in this country and punishes blasphemers, Mormons, Christian Scientists, fortune-hunters, members of the Salvation Army and others, though the acts which have brought them into conflict with the law have been performed with a religious motive. It fosters religion by affording churches the right to become corporations, by protecting their worship against disturbance, by exempting their property from taxation and by providing for a cessation from work on Sunday. It permits (Illinois excepted) the Bible, or portions of it, to be read in the public schools.[1] It allows the use of public-school buildings for Sunday schools and other forms of religious worship where such use does not conflict with the school laws or regulations and permits churches to lease their buildings to

[1] A recent survey of the Bible in schools, Mr. Fleming in *The Christian Statesman*, summarized in *The Literary Digest*, vol. 78, no. 11, September 15, 1923, p. 36 finds that: "By the opinion of the Attorney-General or the State Superintendent of Public Instruction, the Bible is not used in the schools of Minnesota, Idaho, Utah, Arizona, New Mexico, Montana, New York (outside of New York City), and possibly Louisiana." Wisconsin, "excluded the Bible as a whole" but "plainly asserts that parts of it might and should be used." "The Bible is read by law every morning in every schoolroom in Massachusetts, New Jersey, Pennsylvania, Tennessee, Alabama, Georgia, and probably Mississippi." "Excepting Massachusetts, these states have all passed the mandatory law within the last ten years." "With the Bible definitely excluded from the schools of twelve states and legally required to be read daily in the schools of seven states, there remain twenty-nine states, with just about half the national population, in which its daily use is permitted."

school districts for a consideration. It frowns upon the wearing of denominational garments in the public school by teachers and does not suffer pupils to break up the school discipline by absenting themselves from public school on purely religious holidays."[1]

The effect of the Third Section of Article Six in the Constitution and the First Amendment was to throw religious responsibility back upon the state governments. It appears that in the various colonial governments, toleration, when secured, had meant only the separation of some particular sect of Christians, not Christianity itself, from the civil institutions. Even in the fundamental law of Rhode Island a Christian purpose was expressly stated and a particular form of Christianity (Protestantism) was required as a qualification for office holding. The American Revolution was followed by an alarming increase in irreligion and the influence of the French Revolution added to the worries of those who were interested in the preservation of true religion in America. Such was the battle thrown back upon the Christian state in the United States.

In Virginia the Court of Appeal in the case of *Kemper vs. Hawkins*, 1793, decided that the Bill of Rights was a part of the Constitution and that all laws contrary to it were null and void.[2] An act of 1799 repealed every law in seeming contradiction with the Bill of Rights, the Constitution and the Act for Establishing Religious Freedom, on the ground that "the several acts presently recited do admit the Church established under the regal government to have continued so subsequently to the Constitution."[3] An act of January 12, 1802, to sell vacant glebe lands but

[1] Zollman, *American Civil Church Law,* pp. 36-37; Bryce, *op. cit.*, first edition, vol. ii, chapter 103, "The Churches and the Clergy."
[2] *Virginia Cases*, Philadelphia, 1815, vols. i and ii, pp. 20-108.
[3] Shepherd, *Statutes at Large*, vol. ii, p. 149.

not to disturb any incumbent, the proceeds to go to the parish debt and the remainder to the poor,[1] was unanimously sustained by the Court of Appeal in 1840. "Not until then," says Howison, "was the divorce between Church and State in Virginia complete."[2]

The New York Constitution of 1777 (Article 35) abrogated all laws and parts of law, common or statute, which "may be construed to establish or maintain any particular denomination of Christians or their ministers;" and ordained (Article 38), "The free exercise and enjoyment of religious profession and worship without discrimination or preference shall forever hereafter be allowed within this State to all mankind."[3] In 1784 the legislature repealed the "Settling Act" of 1693 and all subsequent acts "which do grant certain emoluments and privileges to the Episcopal Church," with two restrictions; first, that all persons naturalized by the state should take an oath of abjuration of all foreign allegiance and subjection in all matters, "ecclesiastical as well as civil," and second, that clergymen were excluded from office as they "ought not to be diverted from their great duties of the service of God and the care of souls." These clauses were repealed by the Constitution of 1821, which however (Article 7, section 4), again forbad ministers or priests to hold office.[4]

The New Jersey Constitution of 1776 (Article 18) decreed to every one "the inestimable privilege of worshipping Almighty God in a manner agreeable to the dictates of his own conscience," but at the same time (Article 19) imposed a religious test for office, which was

[1] Shepherd, *op. cit.*, vol. ii, pp. 314-316.

[2] Howison, *History of Virginia*, vol. ii, pp. 396-405.

[3] Thorpe, *Constitutions and Charters*, vol. v, pp. 2636-2637; Hoffman, Murray, *Ecclesiastical Law of the State of New York*, p. 40.

[4] Thorpe, *op. cit.*, vol. v, p. 2648.

confined to "Protestant inhabitants of the Colony."[1] Bancroft deduces from this that "When the constitution of that state (New Jersey) was framed by a convention composed chiefly of Presbyterians, they established perfect liberty of conscience without the blemish of a test."[2]

The Delaware Constitution of 1776 (Article 29) forbad the "establishment of any one religious sect" and also "civil office" to clergymen or preachers.[3] And the holder of any office or public trust must subscribe to the following oath (Article 22):

"I do profess faith in God the Father, and in Jesus Christ His only son, and in the Holy Ghost, one God, blessed for evermore; and I do acknowledge the Holy Scriptures of the Old and New Testament to be given by divine inspiration."[4]

The Constitution of 1792 fixed the standards for religion in Delaware in the following terms, which have been repeated in the Constitutions of 1831 and 1897:

Preamble; "Through divine goodness all men have, by nature, the rights of worshipping and serving their Creator according to the dictates of their conscience."[5]

Bill of Rights, Article One, Sections one and two:

"Although it is the duty of all men frequently to assemble together for the public worship of the Author of the universe, and piety and morality, on which the prosperity of communities depends, are thereby promoted; yet no man shall or ought to be compelled to attend any religious worship, to contribute to the erection or support of any place of worship, or to the maintenance of any ministry, against his own free will and consent; and no power shall or ought to be vested in or assumed by any magistrate that shall in any case interfere with, or in any manner control, the rights of conscience, in the free exercise of religious worship, nor a preference be given by law to any religious societies, denominations, or modes of worship.

[1] Thorpe, *op. cit*, vol. v, pp. 2597-2598; Baird, *Religion in America*, p. 268.
[2] Bancroft, *op. cit.*, vol. v, p. 123.
[3] Thorpe, *op. cit.*, vol. i, pp. 567-568.
[4] *Ibid.*, vol. 1, p. 566.
[5] *Ibid.*, vol. i, pp. 568, 582, 600.

No religious test shall be required as a qualification to any office, or public trust, under this State."[1]

In Pennsylvania by the Constitution of 1776 (Article 2 of the Declaration of Rights), "All men have a natural and inalienable right to worship Almighty God according to the dictates of their own consciences and understanding," but civil rights were restricted to persons "who acknowledge the being of a God." Office holders were required, (section 10) to swear, or affirm, "I do believe in one God, the creator and Governor of the Universe, the rewarder of the good and punisher of the wicked. And I do acknowledge the Scriptures of the Old and New Testament to be by Divine inspiration."[2] In the 1790 Constitution (Article 9, section 4) there was added to the previous test a belief in "a future state of rewards and punishments."[3] The Constitution of 1838 repeats this[4] and there it stands to-day.[5] The state has never repealed the law of 1700 which imposed a penalty upon anyone who should "wilfully, premeditatedly, and despitefully blaspheme, or speak lightly or profanely of Almighty God, Jesus Christ, the Holy Spirit, or the Scriptures of Truth," and the Supreme Court in 1824, *Updegraph vs. Commonwealth*, declared this law still in force.[6]

Charles Carroll of Carrollton wrote, February 20, 1829:

"When I signed the Declaration of Independence I had in view not only our independence of England, but the toleration of all sects professing the Christian religion, and communicating to them all equal rights. Happily this wise and salutary measure has taken place for

[1] Thorpe, *op. cit.*, vol. i, pp. 568, 582, 601; McMaster, *op. cit.*, vol. iii, p .149.
[2] Thorpe, *op. cit.*, vol. v, pp. 3082, 3085; Baird, *op. cit.*, p. 270.
[3] Thorpe, *op. cit.*, vol. v, p. 3100.
[4] *Ibid.*, vol. v, p. 3113.
[5] *Ibid.*, vol. v, p. 3121.
[6] *Updegraph vs. Commonwealth*, 11 Sergeant and Rowle, pp. 394, 404.

eradicating religious feuds and persecution, and become a useful lesson to all governments. Reflecting, as you must, on the disabilities, I may truly say on the proscription of the Roman Catholics in Maryland, you will not be surprised that I had much at heart this grand design founded on mutual charity, the basis of our holy religion." [1]

The Maryland Bill of Rights of 1776 (Article 23) made "persons professing the Christian religion . . . . . . equally entitled to protection in their religious liberty."[2] It forbad compelling any person to attend or support any particular form of worship and "Yet the legislature may in their discretion lay a general and equal tax for the support of the Christian religion, leaving to each individual the power" of indicating the direction of his own tax, to any Church or to the poor. The property held by the Church of England was to remain theirs forever. A form of prayer for the new government was adopted which the majority of the clergy of the Church of England refused to use and these were consequently required to pay a "treble tax" or to leave the country. Most of them went and their churches were closed or used by other bodies."[3]

The North Carolina Constitution of 1776 (Article 19, of the Declaration of Rights), claimed that "All men have a natural and unalienable right to worship Almighty God according to the dictates of their own consciences."[4] And yet, although it did not go so far as to support any particular church or religion, it laid down that (Article 32, of the Constitution):

"No person who shall deny the being of God, or the truth of the Protestant religion, or the Divine authority of either the Old or New

[1] O'Gorman, *op. cit.*, p. 257.
[2] Thorpe, *op. cit.*, vol. iii, p. 1689.
[3] Hawks, *Ecclesiastical Contributions*, vol. ii, p. 283.
[4] Thorpe, *op. cit.*, vol. v, p. 2788.

Testament, or who shall hold religious opinions incompatible with the freedom or safety of the State, shall be capable of holding any office or place of trust in the civil department within this state."[1] An amendment of 1835 changed the word "Protestant" to "Christian."[2]

No religious provisions were to be found in the South Carolina Constitution of 1776 but the one of 1778 more than compensated for this omission. It excluded from the offices of governor, lieutenant governor, and membership in the privy council or legislature all clergymen "until two years after demitting the ministry." And Chapter xxxviii. read:

"All persons and religious societies, who acknowledge that there is one God, and a future state of rewards and punishments, and that God is publicly to be worshipped, shall be freely tolerated. The Christian Protestant religion shall be deemed and is hereby constituted and declared to be, the established religion of this State. All denominations of Christian Protestants in this State . . . . . shall enjoy equal religious and civil privileges." Security of ownership for property held by the Protestant Episcopal Church is ordered and provision for the incorporation of other religious bodies is made as follows, "when ever fifteen or more male persons, not under twenty-one years of age" shall agree together for religious worship. Every such society "shall have agreed to and subscribed in a book the following five articles, without which no agreement or union of men, upon pretence of religion, shall entitle them to be incorporated and esteemed as a church of the established religion of this State:

1. That there is one Eternal God and a future state of rewards and punishments.
2. That God is publicly to be worshipped.
3. That the Christian Religion is the true religion.
4. That the Holy Scriptures of the Old and New Testament are of divine inspiration, and are the rules of faith and practice.
5. That it is lawful, and the duty of every man, being thereunto called by those that govern, to bear witness to the truth."

Pastors were to be chosen by a majority of the church, and no minister might enter upon a pastorate until he had subscribed to a declaration, "that he is determined by God's grace out of the holy scriptures to

[1] Thorpe, *op. cit.*, vol. v, p. 2793.
[2] *Ibid.*, vol. v, pp. 2798-2799.

instruct the people committed to his charge, and to teach nothing as required of necessity to eternal salvation, but that which he shall be persuaded may be concluded and proved from the scripture; that he will use both public and private admonition, as well to the sick as to the whole within his care, as need shall require and occasion shall be given; and that he will be diligent in prayers and in reading of the scriptures and in such studies as help to the knowledge of the same; that he will be diligent to frame and fashion his own self and his family according to the doctrine of Christ and to make both himself and them, as much as in him lieth, wholesome examples and patterns to the flock of Christ; that he will maintain and set forward, as much as he can, quietness, peace, and love among all people, and especially among those that are, or shall be committed to his charge.

No person shall, by law, be obliged to pay towards the maintenance and support of a religious worship, that he does not freely join in, or has not voluntarily engaged to support." [1]

The Constitution of 1790 put aside these elaborate provisions and decreed (Article 8, Article 1, section 23), religious freedom "without distinction or preference,"[2] but maintained the exclusion of clergymen from civil office.

Georgia, by the Constitution of 1777 (Article 56), established freedom of conscience; but required (Article 6) that all members of the legislature "shall be of the Protestant religion,"[3] and forbad (Article 62) clergymen seats in the legislature.[4]

Disestablishment was a slow process in New England. Connecticut, by an act of 1729, had exempted Baptists from the tax for ministers and meeting houses, when they could present certificates signed by two magistrates. In 1784 an "Act for Securing the Rights of Conscience" was passed, which read,

"No persons professing the Christian religion, who soberly dissent from the worship and ministry established by law, and attend worship by

[1] Thorpe, *op. cit.*, vol. vi, pp. 3255-3257.
[2] *Ibid.*, vol. vi, pp. 3264, 3261.
[3] *Ibid.*, vol. ii, pp. 779, 784; Baird, *op. cit.*, p. 272.
[4] *Ibid.*, vol. ii, p. 785.

themselves, shall incur a penalty by not attending the established worship; that Christians of other denominations, who attend and help maintain worship according to their consciences shall not be taxed for the support of other worship; that those who do not belong to any other society are to be taxed for the support of the State-Church; and that all Protestant dissenters shall have liberty to use the same powers for maintaining their respective societies, as belongs to societies established by law." [1]

As modified in 1791 this law read;

"In future, whenever any person shall differ in sentiments from the worship and ministry, in the ecclesiastical societies in this state, constituted by law within certain bounds, and shall choose to join himself to any other denomination of Christians, which shall have formed themselves into distinct churches or congregations, for the maintenance and support of the public worship of God, and shall manifest such his choice, by a certificate thereof, under his hand lodged in the office of the clerk of the society to which he belongs—such person shall thereupon, and so long as he shall continue ordinarily to attend on the worship and ministry in the church or congregation, be exempted from being taxed for the future support of the worship, and ministry in such society." [2]

The state still required every citizen to contribute to the support of the Gospel, and taxes of all unconnected with any church were turned over to the standing order. An act of 1816 repealed the penalty for non-attendance upon church. Governor Oliver Wolcott was placed in power in 1817 by all the opponents of the state church.[3] An act was thereupon passed that any person of any Christian denomination should have full power to change his church relations at will and that every Christian society should have power to tax its own members only. A Constitutional Convention was called and the new

[1] *Connecticut State Records*, vol. i, p. 11; *New Haven Historical Papers*, vol. iii, p. 400; Lauer, *Church and State in New England*, p. 84.
[2] Lauer, *op. cit.*, p. 99.
[3] Johnston, *History of Connecticut*, p. 352.

constitution of 1818 provided (Article 1, sections 3-4 and Article 7, sections 1-2):

"The exercise and enjoyment of religious profession and worship, without distinction, shall forever be free to all persons in this state . . . No preference shall be given by law to any Christian sect or mode of worship . . . . . No person should be compelled to join or support nor be classed with, or associated to any congregation, church or religious association."[1]

This was drafted by a Baptist minister, Rev. Asahel Morse of Suffield. Dr. Lyman Beecher wrote of this day:

"It was as dark a day as I ever saw. The odium thrown on the ministry was inconceivable. The injury done to the cause of Christ, as we then supposed, was irreparable. For several days I suffered what no tongue can tell for the best thing that ever happened to the State of Connecticut. It cut the churches loose from dependence on State support. It threw them wholly on their own resources and on God."[2]

New Hampshire laws for the support of religion were similar to those of Connecticut. The Constitutions of 1776, 1784, and 1792 left unchanged the old colonial law which made the church a town institution and its support a matter of public tax, and discriminated in favor of the Protestant religion.[3] Legislative acts of 1792, 1804, 1805, and 1807 recognized Baptists and Episcopalians, Universalists and Methodists respectively as legal sects.[4] Complete religious liberty was achieved by the Toleration Act of 1819 for *All Christian Sects*. Still, the colonial idea remains in the Constitution of 1902, wherein it is provided that "Every denomination of Protestant Christians, demeaning themselves quietly and as good subjects of the state, shall be equally under the

[1] Thorpe, *op. cit.*, vol. i, pp. 537, 545.
[2] Beecher, *Autobiography*, vol. i, p. 344.
[3] Thorpe, *op. cit.*, vol. iv, pp. 2451, 2470; *New Hampshire Historical Society*, vol. v, p. 175; Cobb, *op. cit.*, p. 500.
[4] Lauer, *op. cit.*, p. 101.

protection of the law."[1] Though another provision states: "No person of any one particular religious sect or denomination, shall ever be compelled to pay toward the support of the teacher or teachers of another persuasion, sect, or denomination."[2]

Vermont passed the following law in 1801:

> "That every person of adult age, being a legal voter in any town or parish, shall be considered as of the religious opinion and sentiment of such society as is mentioned in said act, and be liable to be taxed for the purpose mentioned in said act, unless he shall, previous to any vote, authorized in and by said act, deliver to the clerk of said town or parish, a declaration in writing, with his name thereto subscribed, in the following words, to wit: I do not agree in religious opinion, with a majority of the inhabitants of this town."[3]

The Legislature in 1807 deprived the towns of the power to support ministers or to build meeting houses by tax levies; religion was placed upon a purely voluntary basis; it was left to the individual to support the gospel of his choice.

Complete separation of church and state in Massachusetts did not come until 1833.[4] Article 3 of the Bill of Rights of the Constitution of 1780 provided:

> "As the happiness of a people and the good order and preservation of civil government, essentially depend upon piety, religion, and morality; and as these cannot be generally diffused through a community but by the institution of the public worship of God, and of public instructions in piety, religion, and morality; therefore, to promote their government, the people of this commonwealth have a right to invest their legislature with power to authorize and require the several towns, parishes, precincts, and other bodies politic, or religious societies, to make suitable provision at their own expense, for the institution of the public worship of God and for the support and maintenance of public Protestant teachers

[1] Thorpe, *op. cit.*, vol. iv, pp. 2494-2495.
[2] Burrage, *op. cit.*, pp. 129-130; Thorpe, *loc. cit.*
[3] *Records of the Governor and Council of the State of Vermont*, Appendix E, p. 402.
[4] Lauer, *op. cit.*, p. 104.

of piety, religion, and morality, in all cases where such provision is not made voluntarily.

And the people of this commonwealth have a right and do invest their legislature with authority to enjoin upon all the subjects an attendance upon the instructions of the public teachers aforesaid at stated times and seasons, if there be any on whose instructions they can conscientiously and conveniently attend." [1]

Dedham, by a majority vote, chose a Unitarian minister. Many of the church members refused to attend worship and the case was carried to the Supreme Court. There Chief Justice Parker decided, 1820, *The Dedham Case*, that the Constitution, "Bill of Rights of 1780 secures to towns not to churches, the right to elect the ministers in the last resort."[2] The Constitution as amended in 1820, (Articles 6-7), abolished religious tests for office-holding;[3] and in 1833 (Article 11), the church was finally disestablished, a voluntary system of worship was made universal and towns were discharged from all concern and power over church affairs.[4]

Cobb, in his *Rise of Religious Liberty in America*, tabulates the following statistics relative to ecclesiastical laws found in the first state constitutions:

two out of thirteen, Virginia and Rhode Island, conceded full and perfect freedom;
six, New Hampshire, Connecticut, New Jersey, Georgia, North and South Carolina, insisted on Protestantism;
two, Delaware and Maryland, demanded Christianity;
four, Pennsylvania, Delaware, North and South Carolina, required assent to the divine inspiration of the Bible;
two, Pennsylvania and South Carolina, imposed a belief in heaven and hell;
three, New York, Maryland, and South Carolina, excluded ministers from civil offices;

[1] Thorpe, *op. cit.*, vol. iii, pp. 1889-1890; Cobb, *op. cit.*, p. 500.
[2] *Baker vs. Fales*, 16 Massachusetts, p. 488; Lauer, *op. cit.*, p. 105; Buck, *Massachusetts Ecclesiastical Law*, p. 52.
[3] Thorpe, *op. cit.*, vol. iii, pp. 1912-1913.
[4] *Ibid.*, vol. iii, p. 1914.

two, Pennsylvania and South Carolina, emphasized belief in one eternal God;
one, Delaware, required assent to the doctrine of the Trinity;
five, New Hampshire, Massachusetts, Connecticut, Maryland, and South Carolina, adhered to religious establishment;
one, South Carolina, still spoke of religious "toleration". [1]

The same author finds the following characteristics of state constitutions as a whole:

thirty-one use in their preambles the phrase "grateful to Almighty God";
three substitute for this "invoking the favor and guidance — or the blessing — of Almighty God";
two only, Michigan and West Virginia, do not mention the name of God;
twenty-six declare that it is the privilege of "every man to worship God according to the dictates of his own conscience";
eleven say that "the free enjoyment of religious sentiments and forms of worship shall ever be held sacred";
five assert a "duty of the legislature to pass laws for the protection" of religious freedom;
nineteen declare that "no human authority ought to control, or interfere with the rights of conscience."
nine ordain that "no person may be molested in person or estate on account of religion";
thirteen state that this liberty is "not to excuse licentiousnes or justify practices inconsistent with the peace and safety" of society;
seven say that it is "not to excuse disturbances of the public peace";
three, that it is "not to justify practices inconsistent with the rights of others";
three require that "no person may disturb others in worship";
twenty-four forbid compulsion of any person to attend worship "contrary to his own faith";
one, New Hampshire, says that "no person of one sect may be compelled to support a minister of another";
one, New Jersey, forbids compulsion of any person to attend the worship "contrary to his own faith";
five forbid "an established Church";
twenty-nine forbid the civil government to show any "preference" for any sect;
three forbid any "subordination" of one sect to another;

[1] Cobb, *Rise of Religious Liberty in America*, p. 507.

two, Delaware and Vermont, say that "every sect ought to observe the Lord's day and keep up some sort of religious worship."
fourteen forbid the appropriation of state money for the support of sectarian institutions;
seven include municipal money in this prohibition;
six apply the prohibition to any property of the state;
four, to any property of any municipality;
two, Michigan and Oregon, forbid even the appropriation of public money to pay for chaplains to the legislature;
one, New Hampshire, says that the legislature may authorize towns and parishes to provide for the support of religious teachers;
two, Massachusetts and Missouri, permit this authorization to parishes;
one, Maine, gives this power to "religious societies";
two, Virginia and West Virginia, forbid any such action on the part of the legislature;
twenty-three declare that no religious test shall be required for office;
eighteen add to this "for any public trust";
four include voting as exempt from tests;
six forbid tests for jury duty;
seventeen for witnesses;
two, Oregon and Wyoming, forbid the questioning of a witness as to his religious belief;
eleven declare that no man can "be deprived of any civil right on account of religious sentiments":
five, Arkansas, Mississippi, Texas, North Carolina and South Carolina, provide that no person may hold office "who denies the being of Almighty God or the existence of a Supreme Being";
one, Arkansas, makes the denier of God incompetent as a witness;
two, Pennsylvania and Tennessee, restrict office to such as "believe in God and a future state of reward and punishment";
one, Maryland, requires this belief in a juror or witness, but for the office holder demands only a belief in God;
two, Mississippi and Tennessee, though requiring some religious qualification for office holding, yet forbid a religious test.[1]

"In a certain sense and for certain purposes it is true," says Judge Cooley, "that Christianity is a part of the law of the land."[2] Or as Bryce puts it, "Christianity is in

[1] Cobb, *op. cit.*, pp. 517-520; Bryce, *op. cit.*, edition of 1911, vol. ii, pp 736-766; Stimson, *American Statute Law*.

[2] Cooley, *Constitutional Limitations*, p. 579; Cornelison, *The Relation of Religion to Civil Government in the United States of America: A State*

fact understood to be, though not the legally established religion, yet the national religion."[1]

The *Index*, organ of the Liberal League, published, January 4, 1873, the following League demands:

"1. We demand that churches and other ecclesiastical property shall no longer be exempt from taxation.

2. We demand that the employment of chaplains in Congress, in State legislatures, in the navy and militia, and in prisons, asylums, and all other institutions supported by public money, shall be discontinued.

3. We demand that all public appropriations for education and charitable institutions of a sectarian character shall cease.

4. We demand that all religious services now sustained by the government shall be abolished, and especially that the use of the Bible in the public schools, whether ostensibly as a text-book or avowedly as a book of religious worship, shall be prohibited.

5. We demand that the appointment by the President of the United States or by the Governors of the various States of all religious festivals and fasts shall cease.[2]

6. We demand that the judicial oath in the courts and in all other departments of the government shall be abolished, and that simple affirmation under the pains and penalties of perjury shall be established in its stead.

7. We demand that all laws, directly or indirectly enforcing the observance of Sunday as the Sabbath shall be repealed.

8. We demand that all laws looking to the enforcement of 'Christian' morality shall be abrogated, and that all laws shall be conformed to the requirements of natural morality, equal rights, and impartial liberty.

9. We demand that, not only in the Constitution of the United States and of the several states, but also in the practical administration of the same, no privilege or advantage shall be conceded to Christianity or any other religion; that our entire political system shall be founded and administered on a purely secular basis, and that whatever changes shall prove necessary to this end be consistently, unflinchingly and promptly made."

without a Church, but not without a Religion; Cobb, *op. cit.;* Morris, *Christian Life and Character of Civil Institutions of the United States, developed in the official and historical annals of the Republic.*

[1] Bryce, *op. cit.*, edition of 1911, p. 770.

[2] Congress in the crisis of the Civil War, July 1863, requested the President to appoint a day for humiliation and prayer.

CHAPTER XVII

AMERICAN CHURCHES GREET NEW NATIONAL GOVERNMENT AT THE INAUGURATION OF PRESIDENT WASHINGTON

Inauguration of a new national government under President Washington found the churches of America well organized and conscious of the duties and responsibilities which rested upon them in connection with the civic life of the nation. The addresses which they presented, in the names of their various denominations, to the new head of the nation, show how conscious they were of their part in the achievement of a successful statehood. And their promises of a hearty coöperation in the maintenance and promotion of religion and morality among the people augured well for the future character of the new state.

To express the sentiments of the Roman Catholics, John Carroll, Bishop-elect of Baltimore, on behalf of the clergy, and Charles Carroll, Daniel Carroll, Dominick Lynch, and Thomas Fitzsimons for the laity, presented President Washington with the following address (in part):

"You encourage respect for religion; and inculcate by words and actions, that principle, on which the welfare of nations so much depends, that a Superintending Providence governs the events of the world, and watches over the conduct of men. Your exalted maxims and unwearied attention to the moral and physical improvement of our country, have produced already the happiest effects. Under your administration, America is animated with zeal for the attainment and encouragement of useful literature. She improves her agriculture; extends her commerce; and acquires with foreign nation dignity unknown to her before . . . .

Whilst our country preserves her freedom and independence, we shall have a well founded title to claim from her justice, the equal rights of citizenship, as the price of our blood spilt under your eyes . . . . . rights rendered more dear to us by the remembrance of former hardships. When we pray for the preservation of them, where they have been granted — and expect the full extension of them from the justice of those states, which still restrict (New Jersey and South Carolina [1]) . . . We recommend your preservation to the single care of Divine Providence." [2]

Washington's reply was as follows (in part):

"To the Roman Catholics in the United States of America.

America, under the smiles of Divine Providence — the protection of a good government — and the cultivation of manners, morals, and piety. cannot fail of attaining an uncommon degree of eminence, in literature, commerce, agriculture, improvements at home and respectability abroad . . . . . I hope ever to see America among the foremost nations in examples of justice and liberality. And, I presume, that your fellow-citizens will not forget the patriotic part, which you took in the accomplishment of their revolution, and the establishment of your government, or the important assistance, which they received from a nation in which tne Roman Catholic faith is professed . . . . .

May the members of your society in America, animated alone by the pure spirit of Christianity, and still conducting themselves as the faithful subjects of our free government, enjoy every temporal and spiritual felicity." [3]

The Coetus of the German Reformed Church despatched the following *Letter*:

"To the President of the United States:

The address of the ministers and elders of the German Reformed Church in the United States, at their general meeting, held at Philadelphia, the tenth of June, 1789.

As it is our most firm purpose to support in our persons a government founded in justice and equality, so it shall be our constant duty to impress the minds of the people entrusted to our care with a due sense of the

[1] *Supra*, p. 499.

[2] Shea, *op. cit.*, vol. ii, pp. 348-350; *An Address from the Roman Catholics of American to George Washington, Esq., President of the United States.* London, 1790.

[3] Shea, *op. cit.*, vol. ii, pp. 350-351; *Washington's Writings,* (Sparks edition), vol. xii, pp. 177-179.

necessity of uniting reverence to such a government and obedience to its laws with the duties and exercises of religion. Thus we hope, by the blessing of God, to be, in some measure, instrumental in alleviating the burden of that weighty and important charge to which you have been called by the unanimous voice of your fellow-citizens, and which your love to your country has constrained you to take upon you.

Deeply possessed of a sense of the goodness of God in the appointment of your person to the highest station in the national government, we shall continue, in our public worship and all our devotions before the throne of grace, to pray that it may please God to bless you in your person, in your family, and in your government, with all temporal and spiritual blessings in Christ Jesus."[1]

Washington replied:

"I am happy . . . . . in believing that I shall always find in you and the German Reformed Congregations in the United States a conduct corresponding to such worthy and pious expression.

At the same time I return you my thanks for the manifestation of your firm purpose to support in your persons a government founded in justice and equity, and for the promise that it will be your constant study to impress the minds of the people entrusted to your care with a due sense of the necessity of uniting reverence to such a government and obedience to its laws with the duties and exercises of religion.

Be assured, Gentlemen, it is by such conduct very much in the power of the virtuous members of the community to alleviate the burden of the important office which I have accepted . . . . ."[2]

The General Assembly of the Presbyterian Church sent the following address (in part):

"Your military achievements insured safety and glory to America, in the late arduous conflict for freedom; while your disinterested conduct, and uniformly just discernment of the public interest, gained you the entire confidence of the people: And in the present interesting period of public affairs, the influence of your personal character moderates the divisions of political parties, and promises a permanent establishment of the civil government.

We are happy that God has inclined your heart to give yourself once more to the public. And we derive a favorable presage of the event from the zeal of all classes of the people, and their confidence in your virtues;

[1] *Minutes and Letters*, pp. 428-434.

[2] *Ibid.*, p. 435; a German translation appeared in the Philadelphia *Gemeinneutzige Correspondenze*, number 4268, July 7, 1789; *Washington's Writings*, Sparks edition, vol. xii, p. 156.

as well as from the knowledge and dignity with which the federal councils are filled. But we derive a presage, even more flattering, from the piety of your character. Public virtue is the most certain means of public felicity; and religion is the surest basis of virtue. We therefore esteem it a peculiar happiness to behold in our chief magistrate, a steady, uniform, avowed friend of the Christian religion; who has commenced his administration in rational and exalted sentiments of piety; and who, in his private conduct, adorns the doctrines of the gospel of Christ; and, on the most public and solemn occasions, devoutly acknowledges the government of Divine Providence.

The example of distinguished characters will ever possess a powerful and extensive influence on the public mind; and when we see, in such a conspicuous station, the amiable example of piety to God, of benevolence to men, and of a pure and virtuous patriotism, we naturally hope that it will diffuse its influence; and that, eventually, the most happy consequences will result from it. To the force of imitation, we will endeavor to add the wholesome instructions of religion. We shall consider ourselves as doing an acceptable service to God, in our profession, when we contribute to render men sober. honest, and industrious citizens, and the obedient subjects of a lawful government. In these pious labors, we hope to imitate the most worthy of our brethren of other Christian denominations, and to be imitated by them; assured that if we can, by mutual and generous emulation, promote truth and virtue, we shall render a great and important service to the republic; shall receive encouragement from every wise and good citizen; and, above all, meet the approbation of our Divine Master.

We pray Almighty God, to have you always in His holy keeping. May He prolong your valuable life, an ornament and a blessing to your country, and at last bestow on you the glorious reward of a faithful servant.

Signed by order of the General Assembly, John Rodgers, Moderator." May 25, 1789.[1]

Washington's reply ran (in part):

"I will observe that the general prevalence of piety, philanthropy, honesty, industry, and economy seems in the ordinary course of human affairs, particularly necessary for advancing and confirming the happiness of our country. While all men within our territories are protected in worshipping the Deity according to the dictates of their consciences, it is rationally to be expected form them in return that they will all be emulous in evincing the sincerity of their professions by the innocence of their lives and the beneficence of their actions; for no man who is profligate in

[1] *Acts and Proceedings of the General Assembly of the Presbyterian Church in the United States of America, A. D., 1789*, pp. 4-6.

his morals, or a bad member of the civil community, can possibly be a true Christian, or a credit to his own religious society.

I desire you to accept my acknowledgements for your laudable endeavors to render men sober, honest, and good citizens, and the obedient subjects of a lawful government; as well as for your prayers to Almighty God for His blessings on our common country, and the humble instrument which He has pleased to make use of in the administration of its government."[1]

The Address from the Committee on the United Baptist Churches of Virginia was as follows (in part):

"We wish to take an active part . . . . . in expressing our great satisfaction in your appointment to the first office in the nation . . . .

The want of efficacy in the Confederation, the redundancy of laws, and their partial administration in the States, called aloud for a new arrangement in our systems. The widsom of the States for that purpose was collected in a grand convention, over which you, Sir, had the honor to preside. A national government, in all its parts, was recommended as the only preservation of the Union, which plan of government is now in actual operation.

When the Constitution first made its appearance in Virginia, we as a society, had unusual strugglings of mind, fearing that the liberty of conscience, dearer to us than property or life, was not sufficiently secured. Perhaps our jealousies were heightened by the usage we received in Virginia under the regal government, when mobs, fines, bonds, and prisons were our frequent repast.

Convinced, on the one hand, that without an effective national government the States would fall into disunion and all the consequent evils, and on the other hand, fearing that we should be accessory to some religious oppression, should any religious society predominate over the rest; amidst all these inquietudes of mind our consolation arose from this consideration — viz., the plan must be good, for it has the signature of a tried, trusty friend, and if religious liberty is rather insecure in the Constitution, the administration will certainly prevent all oppressions, for a Washington will preside. According to our wishes, the unanimous voice of the Union has called you, Sir, from your beloved retreat, to launch forth again into the faithless seas of human affairs, to guide the helm of the States.

By order of the Committee,
REUBEN FORD, Clerk. SAMUEL HARRIS, Chairman."[2]

[1] *Washington's Writings*, Sparks edition, vol. xii, pp. 152-153.

[2] James, *op. cit.*, pp. 171-173; Leland, *Works*, pp. 52-54; Bitting, *Notes on the Century History of the Strawberry Association.*

The reply to this was (in part):

"If I could have entertained the slightest apprehension that the Constitution framed in the Convention, where I had the honor to preside, might possibly endanger the religious rights of any ecclesiastical society, certainly I would never have placed my signature to it; and, if I could now conceive that the general government might ever be so administered as to render the liberty of conscience insecure, I beg you will be persuaded, that no one would be more zealous than myself to establish effectual barriers against the horrors of spiritual tyranny, and every species of religious persecution. For you doubtless remember, that I have often expressed my sentiments, that every man, conducting himself as a good citizen, and being accountable to God alone for his religious opinions, ought to be protected in worshipping the Deity according to the dictates of his own conscience.

When I recollect with satisfaction, that the religious society of which you are members have been, throughout America, uniformly and almost unanimously the firm friends to civil liberty, and the persevering promoters of our glorious revolution, I cannot hesitate to believe that they will be the faithful supporters of a free, yet efficient, general government. Under this pleasing expectation, I rejoice to assure them that they may rely upon my best wishes and endeavors to advance their prosperity.

In the meantime, be assured, gentlemen, that I entertain a proper sense of your fervent supplications to God for my temporal and eternal happiness." [1]

The Address of the Religious Society called Quakers, from their Yearly Meeting for Pennsylvania, New Jersey, Delaware, and the Western Parts of Maryland and Virginia was as follows (in part):

"Being met in this our annual assembly, for the well ordering of the affairs of our religious Society, and the promotion of universal righteousness, our minds have been drawn to consider, that the Almighty . . has permitted a great revolution to take place in the government of this country . . . . .

We are sensible thou hast obtained great place in the esteem and affection of people of all denominations over whom thou presidest; and many eminent talents being committed to thy trust, we much desire they may be fully devoted to the Lord's honor and service, — that thus thou mayst be a happy instrument in his hand, for the suppression of vice,

[1] James, *op. cit.*, pp. 173-174; Backus, *op. cit.*, pp. 224-225; *Writings of Washington*, Sparks edition, vol, xii, pp. 154-155; Leland, *Virginia Chronicle*, pp. 47-48.

infidelity, and irreligion, and every species of oppression on the persons or consciences of man, so that righteousness and peace, which truly exalt a nation, may prevail throughout the land, as the only solid foundation that can be laid for the prosperity and happiness of this or any country.

The free toleration which the citizens of these States enjoy, in the public worship of the Almighty, agreeable to the dictates of their consciences, we esteem among the choicest of blessings; and as we desire to be filled with fervent charity for those who differ from us in matters of faith and practice, believing that the general assembly of saints is composed of the sincere and upright-hearted of all nations, kingdoms, and people; so, we trust, we may justly claim it from others: and in a full persuasion that the divine principle we profess, leads unto harmony and concord, we can take no part in carrying on war on any occasion, or under any power, but are bound in conscience to lead quiet and peaceable lives, in godliness and honesty among men, contributing freely our portion to the indigencies of the poor, and to the necessary support of civil government, acknowledging those who rule well to be worthy of double honor; and if any professing with us are, or have been, of a contrary disposition and conduct, we own them not therein; having never been chargeable from our first establishments as a religious Society, with fomenting or countenancing tumults or conspiracies, or disrespect to those who are placed in authority over us.

We wish not improperly to intrude on thy time or patience, nor is it our practice to offer adulation to any; but as we are, a people whose principles and conduct have been misrepresented and traduced, we take the liberty to assure thee, that we feel our hearts affectionately drawn towards thee, and those in authority over us, with prayers, that thy presidency may, under the blessing of Heaven, be happy to thyself and to the people; that through the increase of morality and religion, Divine Providence may condescend to look down upon our land with a propitious eye, and bless the inhabitants with the continuance of peace, the dew of Heaven, and the fatness of the earth, and enable us gratefully to acknowledge his manifold mercies; and it is our earnest concern, that He may be pleased to grant thee every necessary qualification to fill thy weighty and important station to His glory . . . . . ."[1]

Washington replied (in part):

"We have reason to rejoice for the prospect, that the present national government, which, by the favor of Divine Providence, was formed by the common counsels, and peaceably established with the common consent of the people, will prove a blessing to every denomination . . .; to render it such, my best endeavors shall not be wanting.

[1] Bowden, *op. cit.*, vol. ii, pp. 346-348.

Government being, among other purposes instituted to protect the persons and consciences of men from oppression, it certainly is the duty of rulers, not only to abstain from it themselves, but according to their stations to prevent it in others.

The liberty enjoyed by the people of these States of worshipping Almighty God agreeably to their consciences, is not only among the choicest of their blessings, but also of their rights. While men perform their social duties faithfully, they do all that society or the state can with propriety demand or expect, and remain responsible only to their Maker for the religion or mode of faith which they may prefer or profess.

Your principles and conduct are well known to me; and it is doing the people called Quakers no more than justice to say, that (except their declining to share with others, the burden of the common defence) there is no denomination among us who are more exemplary and useful citizens.

I assure you very explicitly, that in my opinion, the conscientious scruples of all men should be treated with great delicacy and tenderness; and it is my wish and desire, that the laws may always be as extensively accommodated to them, as a due regard to the protection and essential interests of the nation may justify and permit."[1]

The address of the Bishops of the Methodist Episcopal Church reads (in part):

"We are conscious from the signal proofs you have already given, that you are a friend of mankind; and, under this established idea, place as full confidence in your wisdom and integrity for the preservation of those civil and religious liberties which have been transmitted to us by the providence of God and the glorious Revolution, as we believe ought to be reposed in man.

We have received the most grateful satisfaction from the humble and entire dependence on the great Governor of the Universe which you have repeatedly expressed, acknowledging Him the source of blessing, and particularly of the most excellent Constitution of these States, which is at present the admiration of the world, and may in future become its great exemplar for imitation; and hence we enjoy a holy expectation that you will always prove a faithful and impartial patron of genuine, vital religion, the grand end of our creation and present probationary existence.

Signed, in behalf of the Methodist Episcopal Church,

THOMAS COKE,
FRANCIS ASBURY."[2]

[1] *Washington's Writings*, Sparks, vol. xii, pp. 168-169; Bowden, *op. cit.*, vol. ii, pp. 348-349.

[2] Buckley, *History of the Methodists*, pp. 265-266.

The response of Washington was as follows (in part):

"To the Bishops of the Methodist Episcopal Church in the United States of America.

It shall still be my endeavor to manifest . . . . . the sincerity of my desires to contribute whatever may be in my power toward the preservation of the civil and religious liberties of the American people.

I trust the people of every denomination who demean themselves as good citizens, will have occasion to be convinced that I shall always strive to prove a faithful and impartial patron of genuine, vital religion." [1]

A letter from President Washington, acknowledging the congratulation sent him is addressed "To the Ministers, Church wardens, and Vestrymen of the German Lutheran Congregation in and near Philadelphia"; in it he testifies to the patriotism of the German Americans during the War and says, among other things:

"From the excellent character for diligence, sobriety and virtue which the Germans in general who are settled in America have ever maintained, I cannot forbear felicitating myself on receiving from so respectable a number of them such strong assurances of their affection for my person, confidence in my integrity, and zeal to support me in my endeavors for promoting the welfare of our common country." [2]

Washington replied to the Synod of The Reformed Dutch Church in North America:

"You, gentlemen, act the part of pious Christians and good citizens by your prayers and exertions to preserve that harmony and good will towards men, which must be the basis of every political establishment; and I readily join with you that '*while just government protects all in their religious rights, true religion affords to government its surest support*'." [3]

"To the Directors of the Society of the United Brethren for Propagating The Gospel among the Heathen," he wrote:

[1] Buckley, *op. cit.*, pp. 266-267; *Washington's Writings*, Sparks edition, vol. xii, pp. 153-154; Bangs, *History of Methodism*, vol. i, p. 284.

[2] *Washington's Writings*, Sparks edition, vol. xii, pp. 147-148; Jacobs, *History of the Evangelical Lutheran Church in the United States*, p. 346.

[3] *Washington's Writings*, Sparks edition, vol. xii, pp. 166-167.

"I received with satisfaction the congratulations of your society and of the Brethren's congregations in the United States of America. For you may be persuaded, that the approbation and good wishes of such a peaceable and virtuous community cannot be indifferent to me.

You will also be pleased to accept my thanks for the treaties (*An Account of the Manner, in which the Protestant Church of the Unitas Fratrum, or United Brethren, preach the Gospel and Carry on their Mission among the Heathen*) you presented, and be assured of my patronage of your laudable undertakings.

In proportion as the general government of the United States shall acquire strength by duration, it is probable they may have it in their power to extend a salutary influence to the aborigines in the extremities of their territory. In the meantime, it will be a desirable thing, for the protection of the Union, to cooperate, as far as the circumstances may conventiently admit, with the disinterested endeavors of your society to civilize and Christianize the savages of the wilderness." [1]

"To the Convention of the Universal Church Lately Assembled in Philadelphia," Washington wrote in 1790:

"I thank you for your congratulations.

It gives me the most sensible pleasure to find that, in our nation, however different are the sentiments of citizens on religious doctrines, they generally concur in one thing; for their political professions and practices are almost universally friendly to the order and happiness of our civil institutions. I am also happy in finding this disposition particularly evinced by your society. It is, moreover, my earnest desire, that all the members of every association or community, throughout the United States, may make such use of the auspicious years of peace, liberty and free inquiry, with which they are now favored, as they shall hereafter find occasion to rejoice for having done." [2]

Even the non-Christian Hebrews are included in the list of acclaimers of the new nation. President Washington sent the following response:

"To the Hebrew Congregation of the City of Savannah:

I thank you, with great sincerity, for your congratulations. I rejoice that a spirit of liberality and philanthropy is much more prevalent than

[1] *Washington's Writings*, vol. xii, p. 160.

[2] *Ibid.*, Sparks edition, vol. xii, pp. 193-194.

it formerly was among the enlightened nations of the earth, and that your brethren will benefit thereby in proportion as it shall become still more extensive. Happily, the people of the United States of America have, in many instances, exhibited examples worthy of imitation, the salutary influence of which will doubtless extend much farther, if, gratefully enjoying those blessings of peace, which, under the favor of Heaven, have been obtained by fortitude in war, they shall conduct themselves with reverence to the Deity, and charity towards their fellow-creatures.

May the same wonder-working Deity, who long since delivered the Hebrews from their Egyptian oppressors, and planted them in the promised land, whose providential agency has lately been conspicuous in establishing these United States as an independent nation, still continue to water them with the dews of Heaven, and to make the inhabitants of every denomination participate in the temporal and spiritual blessings of that people, whose God is Jehovah." [1]

We must not pass over the felicitations sent by that individualist of individualists, Isaac Backus, to the new civil head of a centralized nation:

"To George Washington, Esq., President of the United States.

Sir, Among the many addresses to your Excellency since your advancement to the highest seat of government in America, I suppose you have received none from any community of Baptists in the State of Massachusetts . . . . . An obscure individual begs your acceptance

[1] *Washington's Writings*, vol. xii, pp. 185-186. Mention has not previously been made of the part played by the Hebrews in the American Revolution because their support was individual rather than official. It should be noted that considering their numbers in America (about three thousand in all) their service to the cause of freedom was considerable. More than fifty Jews fought in the Revolution, twenty-four of whom were officers, the names of Colonel Isaac Franks and Colonel David Salisbury Franks being prominent. Haym Salomon sacrificed his fortune and his life for independence. A friend of Pulaski and Kosciusko, he generously supported Robert Morris in his struggle for funds, giving in all about $350,000. He died in a British prison. Aaron Levy of Philadelphia, Benjamin Jacobs of New York, Isaac Moses of Philadelphia, Samuel Lyon of New York, and Manuel Mordecai Noah of Savannah, all gave large sums. In the active service were such men as Mordecai Sheftall, Benjamin Nones, Jacob de la Motta, Jacob de Leon, Philip Moses Russell, Solomen Bush, Emanuel de la Motta, Benjamin Ezekiel, Jason Sampson, Ascher Levy, Nathaniel Levy, David Hays, Jacob Hays, Reuben Etting, Jacob Cohen, Lewis Bush, Aaron Benjamin, Isaac Israel, and Benjamin Moses. See Peters, *Justice to the Jew*, pp. 90-94; Wolf, *The American Jew as Patriot, Soldier, and Citizen*; Wiernik,

of a private token of love, which may be of more real service than many flattering public addresses . . . . .

The continuation of tax and compulsion for religious ministers in New England, while it is abolished in Virginia, is a clear demonstration of the narrow selfishness of mankind. The continuance of it here for Congregationalists, and the abolishing of it there for Episcopalians, are both commended by Dr. Gordon in his *History of the American Revolution*, in which is much impartiality about civil and military affairs. But religious ministers, when supported by force, are the most dangerous men upon earth; while no men are more necessary and useful to human society than faithful teachers. Of this further evidence is given in two late pieces which I here send you.

That your Excellency may still be guided and preserved in your exalted and difficult station until righteous government shall be well established in this land; that your latter days may be peaceful and happy, and your end be eternal life, is the earnest prayer of

Your humble servant,

November 15, 1790."[1] ISAAC BACKUS

Most illuminating is the reply which President Washington addressed to his co-religionists:

"To the Bishops, Clergy and Laity of the Protestant Episcopal Church in the States of New York, New Jersey, Pennsylvania, Delaware, Maryland, Virginia and North Carolina, in General Convention Assembled:

August 19, 1789.

Gentlemen,

I sincerely thank you for your affectionate congratulations on my election to the chief magistracy of the United States.

The satisfaction arising from the indulgent opinion entertained by the American people of my conduct will, I trust, be some security for preventing me from doing anything, which might justly incur the forfeiture of that opinion. And the consideration, that human happiness and moral duty are inseparably connected, will always continue to prompt me to promote the progress of the former by inculcating the practice of the latter.

On this occasion, it would ill become me to conceal the joy I have felt in perceiving the fraternal affection. which appears to increase every day

History of the Jews in America, chapter xii. President Washington also sent answers to addresses from "The Hebrew Congregation of Newport, Rhode Island", and "The Hebrew Congregations in the Cities of Philadelphia, Richmond, and Charleston," Wiernik, *op. cit.*, pp. 100-103.

[1] Hovey, *op. cit.*, pp. 251-252.

among the friends of genuine religion. It affords edifying prospects, indeed, to see Christians of different denominations dwell together in more charity and conduct themselves in respect to each other with a more Christian-like spirit, than ever they have done in any former age, or in any other nation.

I receive with the greater satisfaction your congratulations on the establishment of the new Constitution of government, because I believe its mild yet efficient operations will tend to remove every remaining apprehension of those, with whose opinions it may not entirely coincide, as well as to confirm the hopes of its numerous friends; and because the moderation, patriotism, and wisdom of the present Federal Legislature seem to promise the restoration of order, and our ancient virtues, the extension of genuine religion, and the consequent advancement of our respectability abroad, and of our substantial happiness at home." [1]

President Washington also replied to addresses from the Congregational Church and Society at Medway, formerly St. John's Parish, in the State of Georgia;[2] and to the Members of the New Church in Baltimore.[3]

While these addresses were pouring in on the chief executive of the new nation, the First Congress was proceeding to organize the administration of the New Government in a spirit of "moderation, patriotism, and wisdom," which to President Washington seemed "to promise the restoration of order, and our ancient virtues, the extension of genuine religion, and the consequent advancement of our respectability abroad, and of our substantial happiness at home." September 25, 1789, Mr. Boudinot, a Presbyterian member of the House, from New Jersey, moved a resolution to request the President to recommend "a day of public thanksgiving and prayer . . . . . for the many signal favors of Almighty God, especially by affording them an opportunity peaceably to establish a Consti-

[1] *Washington's Writings,* Sparks edition, vol. xii, pp. 162-163.
[2] *Ibid.*, vol. xii, pp. 198-199.
[3] *Ibid.*, vol. xii, pp. 201-202.

tution of government for their safety and happiness." Mr. Burke did not like this mimicking of European customs, while Mr. Tucker objected to the idea of returning thanks for a Constitution before they had experienced that it did actually promote safety and happiness. Mr. Sherman, however, supported the resolution and Mr. Boudinot was able to quote precedents from the practices of the late Congress. Accordingly it was passed.[1]

Congress under the new constitution, following tradition, the precedent of previous American legislative bodies, and the leadership of President Washington, thus officially recognized those national churches which had so enthusiastically greeted the new government and pledged it wholehearted support. State and church mutually agreed to accept each other, to work together in harmony for their common ideals of politics and religion, the basis for our American Civil Church Law.

[1] *Annals of Congress,* vol. i, pp. 914-915, 923.

BIBLIOGRAPHY

Acts and Proceedings of the General Assembly of the Presbyterian Church in the United States of America, A. D. 1789. Philadelphia, 1803.

Acts and Proceedings of the General Synod of the Reformed Protestant Dutch Church in North America. Vol. i, 1771-1812: Preceded by the Minutes of the Coetus (1738-1754) and the Proceedings of the Conferantie (1755-1767) and followed by the Minutes of the Original Particular Synod (1794-1799). New York, 1859.

Adams, James Truslow, *Revolutionary New England,* 1691-1776. Boston, 1923.

Adams, John. Works of, with a Life of the Author. Notes and Illustrations by Charles Francis Adams. 10 vols. Boston, 1850-1856.

Adams, John and Abigail, Familiar Letters of John Adams and His Wife. Edited by His Grandson, Charles Francis Adams. 2 vols. Boston, 1875.

Adams, Zabdiel, *Election Sermon, Preached . . . . . May 29, 1782.* Boston, 1782.

Address from the Roman Catholics of America to George Washington, Esq., President of the United States. London, 1790.

Andrews, C. N., *Colonial Folk Ways. Chronicles of America Series,* vol. 9. New Haven, 1919.

Applegarth, A. C., *Quakers in Pennsylvania. Johns Hopkins University Studies.* 10th Series. vols. 7-9. Baltimore, 1892.

Armitage, Thomas, *History of the Baptists.* New York, 1887.

Asbury, Francis, *Journal.* 3 vols. New York, 1821.

Aspund, John, *The Annual Register of the Baptist Denomination in North America to November 1, 1790.*

Backus, Isaac, *History of New England, with Particular Reference to the Denomination Called Baptists.* 3 vols. 1777, 1784, 1796. Abridgement 1804. Second edition, with notes by David Weston, Newton, 1871.

Bachus, Isaac, *An Appeal to the Public For Religious Liberty, against the Oppressors of the Present Day . . . . .* Boston, 1773.

Bacon, L. W., *A History of American Christianity.* New York, 1900.

Bailey, G. S., *The Trials and Victories of Religious Liberty in America; A Centennial Memorial, 1876.* Philadelphia, 1876.

Baird, Robert, *Religion in America: or, An Account of Origin, Relation to the State, and Present Conditions of the Evangelical Churches in the United States, With Notices of the Evangelical Denominations.* New York, 1844; second edition, 1856.

Baird, Robert, *Progress and Prospects of Christianity in the United States.* London, 1851.

Balch, Thomas, *Calvinism and American Independence.* Philadelphia, 1909

Bancroft, G., *History of the United States.* 10 vols. Boston, 1834-1874.

Bandot, Seraphin, *Discours pronouncé le 4 Juillet, Jour de l'anniversaire de l' indepéndence, dans l'église catholique, par le Reverend Père Seraphin Bandot, Recollet, Aumonier de son Excellence Mr. Gerard Ministre Plénipoteniaire de France auprès des États Unis de l'Amerique Suptentrionale.* Philadelphia, 1779.

Bangs, Nathan, *Life of the Reverend Freeborn Garrettson, Compiled from his Printed and Manuscript Journals and other Authentic Documents.* New York, 1832.

Bascom, Bishop H. B., *Methodism and Slavery.* Nashville, 1846.

Bates, F. G., *Rhode Island and the Formation of the Union.* New York, 1898.

Beard, Charles A., *An Economic Interpretation of the Constitution.* New York, 1913.

Beardsley, E. E., *Life and Correspondence of Samuel Johnson, D.D., Missionary of the Church of England in Connecticut and First President of King's College.* Boston, 1881.

Beardsley, E. E., *Life of William Samuel Johnson.* Boston, 1876.

Beardsley, E. E., *History of the Episcopal Church in Connecticut, from 1635 to 1865.* 2 vols. 4th edition, New York, 1883.

Beecher, Lyman, Autobiography, Correspondence, etc. Edited by Charles Beecher. 2 vols. New York, 1864-1865.

Benedict, David, *History of the Baptist Denomination.* 2 vols. Boston, 1813.

Benson, Allen, *Our Dishonest Constitution.* New York, 1914.

Bentley, W. J., *Diary, 1783-1819.* Published by Essex Institute. Salem, 1905-1914.

Bernheim, G. D., *History of the German Settlements and of the Lutheran Church in North and South Carolina.* Philadelphia, 1872.

Bitting, C. C., *Notes on the Century History of the Strawberry Association of Virginia for One Hundred Years from 1776 to 1876.*

Bitting, C. C., *Religious Liberty and the Baptists.* Philadelphia, 1879.

Black, J. W., *Maryland's Attitude in the Struggle for Canada,* in *Johns Hopkins University Studies,* vol. vii, tenth series. Baltimore, 1892.

Blaikie, Alexander, *History of Presbyterianism in New England.* Boston, 1881.

Boucher, Jonathan, *A View of the Causes and Consequences of the American Revolution; in Thirteen Discourses, preached in North America between the years 1763 and 1775, with an Historical Preface.* London, 1797.

Boucher, Jonathan, *Autobiography* in *Notes and Queries*, 5th Series, vol. vi.

Boudinot, J. J., *The Life and Public Services, Addresses and Letters of Elias Boudinot*. 2 vols. New York, 1896.

Bowden, James, *The History of the Society of Friends in America*. 2 vols. London, 1854.

Brackenridge, Hugh Montgomery, *Six Political Discourses Founded on the Scripture*. Lancaster, n.d.

Brackett, J. R., "The Status of the Slave, 1775-1789" in *Essays in the Constitutional History of the United States*. New York, 1899.

Breckinridge, R. J., *Presbyterian Government Not a Hierarchy, but a Commonwealth*, and *Presbyterian Ordination*. Baltimore, 1843.

Breed, Wm. P., *An Historical Discourse on Presbyterians and the Revolution*. Philadelphia, 1876.

Breed, Wm. P., *Proceedings and Addresses at the Laying of the Cornerstone and at the Unveiling of the Statue to John Witherspoon in Fairmont Park, Philadelphia*. Compiled by Rev. Wm. P. Breed. Philadelphia, 1877.

Briggs, C. A., *American Presbyterianism, Its Origin and Early History*. New York, 1885.

Briggs, F. W., *Bishop Asbury: A Biographical Study for Christian Workers*. London, 1879.

Bryce, James, *American Commonwealth*. 2 vols. New York, 1886.

Bryce, James, *Modern Democracies*. 2 vols. New York, 1921.

Buckley, J. M., *A History of Methodism in the United States*. 2 vols. New York, 1898.

Buckley, J. M., *A History of Methodists in the United States*. Fourth edition, New York, 1900.

Burrage, Henry S., *A History of the Baptists in New England*. Philadelphia, 1894.

Carey, Mathey, editor, *American Museum, January 1787-December 1792*. 12 vols. Philadelphia, 1787-1792.

Chamberlain, Mellen, *John Adams*. Boston, 1898.

Chauncy, Charles, *A Discourse on the Good News from a Far Country*. Boston, 1766.

Chauncy, Charles, *Trust in God, the Duty of a People in a Day of Trouble*. . . . . . Boston, 1770.

Chauncy, Charles, *The Accursed Thing must be taken away from among the People if they would reasonably hope to stand before their Enemies* . . Boston, 1782.

Clark, Jonas, *A Sermon Preached at Lexington, April 19, 1776* . . . . . *To which is added a Brief Narrative of the Principal Transactions of that Day*. Boston, 1777.

Clark, Jonas, *Election Sermon, Preached . . . . . 1781.* Boston, 1781.

Cobb, Sandford, H., *Rise of Religious Liberty in America.* New York, 1902.

Cole, G. D. R., *Social Theory.* New York, 1920.

Combe, Thomas Edwin, *A Sermon, Preached July 20th, 1775.* Philadelphia, 1775.

Connecticut Courant for December 17, 1787 (Number 1195). Hartford,

Connecticut, The Public Records of the Colony of Connecticut, 1636-1776. 15 vols. Hartford, 1850-1890.

Connecticut, The Public Records of the State of Connecticut, Hartford, 1894-1895.

Constitution of the Reformed Dutch Church in the United States. New York, 1793. Second edition, 1815.

Cooley, T. M., *A Treatise on the Constitutional Limitations which rest upon the Legislative Power of the States of the American Union.* 6th edition, Boston, 1890.

Cooper, Samuel, *The Crisis.* Boston, 1754.

Cooper, Samuel, *A Sermon . . . . . on the Commencement of the Constitution and Inauguration of the New Government.* Boston, 1780.

Cornelison, I. A., *The Relation of Religion to Civil Government in the United States: A State Without a Church, but not Without a Religion.* New York, 1895.

Corwin, E. F., *History of the Reformed Church (Dutch).* New York, 1895.

Corwin, E. F., *Manual of the Reformed Church in America.* 3rd edition, New York, 1879.

Coxe, Trench, *An Examination of the Constitution for the United States of America, Submitted to the People by the General Convention at Philadelphia, etc. By An American Citizen.* Philadelphia, 1788.

Cross, Arthur Lyon, *The Anglican Episcopate and the American Colonies,* in *Harvard Historical Studies,* vol. ix. New York, 1902.

Davis, *Narrative of the State of Religion among Dissenters in Virginia.*

de Tocqueville, Alexis, *Democracy in America.* Translated by Henry Reeve. New York, 1835.

De Schweinitz, Bishop Edmund, *Life and Times of David Zeisberger.* Philadelphia, 1880.

DeWarville, Brissot, J. P., *Citoyen Francais, Noveau Voyage dans les États-Unis de l'Amerique Septentrional fait en 1788.*

De Witte, Cornelius, *La Vie de Thomas Jefferson.* Paris, 1861.

DeWitt, John *First General Assembly of the Presbyterian Church in the United States of America.* Philadelphia, 1881.

Dickinson, John, The Writings of, edited by Paul Leicester Ford. Philadelphia, 1895.

Diplomatic Correspondence of the American Revolution. Boston, 1829.

Documentary History of New York. 4 vols. Albany, 1849-1851.

Douglass, William, *A Summary, historical and political, of the first planting, progressive improvements, and present state of the British Settlements in North America.* 2 vols. Boston, 1749-1753.

Drake, *Acts and Proceedings of the Synod of New York and Philadelphia, A. D., 1787-1788.* Philadelphia, 1788.

Draught of the Form of the Government and Discipline of the Presbyterian Church in the United States of America. New York, 1787.

Draught of a Plan of Government and Discipline for the Presbyterian Church in North America, Proposed by a Committee Appointed for that Purpose. Philadelphia, 1786.

Drew, Samuel, *The Life of the Reverend Thomas Coke, D.D.* New York, 1818.

Dubbs, J. H., *A History of the Reformed (German) Church in the United States.* New York, 1895.

Duché, Jacob, *The American Vine: A Sermon Preached before Congress, 20 July, 1775.* Philadelphia, 1775.

Duché, Jacob, *The Duty of Standing Fast in our Spiritual and Temporal Liberties. A Sermon, in Christ Church . . . . . 7 July, 1775, before the First Battalion, etc.* Philadelphia, 1775.

Duffield, George *A Sermon Preached in the Third Presbyterian Church in the City of Philadelphia, Thursday, December 11, 1783 . . . . .* Philadelphia, 1784. Reprinted in *The Patriotic Preachers of the American Revolution*, pp. 344-368.

Dwight, Timothy, *Travels in New England and New York.* 4 vols. New Haven, 1821-1822.

Ecclesiastical Records of the State of New York, edited by E. F. Corwin, 7 vols. Albany, 1901-1916.

Eckenrode, H. J., *Separation of Church and State in Virginia.* Richmond, 1910.

Elliot, Jonathan, *The Debates in the Several State Conventions on the Adoption of the Federal Constitution, etc.* 5 vols. Philadelphia, 1836-1859.

Elmer, L. Q. C., *History of New Jersey, with Biographical Sketches of the Governors and Reminiscences of the Bench and Bar.* Newark, 1872.

Emory, Robert, *History of the Discipline of the Methodist Episcopal Church.* Revised and brought down to 1858 by W. P. Strickland.

Farrand, Max, *The Records of the Federal Convention of 1787.* 3 vols. New Haven, 1911.

Faulkner, J. A., *The Methodists in America.* New York, 1903; 3rd edition, New York, 1913.

Fischer, S. G., *Struggle for American Independence.* 2 vols. Philadelphia, 1908.

Foote, W. H., *Sketches of Virginia: History and Biography.* 1st series Philadelphia, 1849; 2nd series, Philadelphia, 1855.
Ford, H. J., *The Scotch-Irish in America.* Princeton, 1915.
Ford, P. L., *Pamphlets on the Constitution of the United States, published during its discussion by the people, 1787-1788.* Brooklyn, 1888.
Ford, P. L., *Essays on the Constitution of the United States, published during its discussion by the people, 1787-1788.* Brooklyn, 1892.
Four Dissertations on the Reciprocal Advantages of a Perpetual Union between Great Britain and her American Colonies. London, 1766.
Fristoe, William, *History of the Ketocton Baptist Association.* Staunton, Virginia, 1808.
Galloway, Joseph, *The Examination of Joseph Galloway, Esq., Late Speaker of the House of Assembly of Pennsylvania, before the House of Commons in a Committee on the American Papers, etc.* London, 1779.
Galloway, Joseph, *Historical and Political Reflections on the Rise and Progress of the American Revolution.* London, 1780.
Gano, John of Frankfort, —formerly of New York, Biographical Memoirs of the Late Reverend. New York, 1806.
Garrettson, Mr. Freeborn, Experiences and Travels of. Philadelphia, 1791.
Gillette, E. H., *History of the Presbyterian Church in the United States.* 2 vols. Philadelphia, 1864. Revised edition, Philadelphia, 1873.
Goodrich, Elizur, D.D., *The Principles of Civil Union and Happiness Considered and Recommended. A sermon . . . . . May 10th, 1787.* Hartford, 1787.
Gordon, William, *History of the Rise, Progress and Establishment of the United States of America: Including an account of the Late War and of the Thirteen Colonies from their Origin to that Period.* 4 vols. London, 1788.
Gordon, William, *Election Sermon, Preached . . . . . July 19, 1775.*
Greene, G. W., *Life of Nathaniel Greene.* 3 vols. 1867-1871.
Greene, M. L., *The Development of Religious Liberty in Connecticut.* Cambridge, 1905.
Grigsby, H. B., *History of the Virginia Federal Convention of 1788,* with *Some Account of the Eminent Virginians of the Body.* 2 vols. Richmond, 1890-1891.
Guild, R. A., *Life, Times, and Correspondence of James Manning and the Early History of Brown University.* Boston, 1864.
Gunning, *Election Sermon, Preached . . . . . May 28, 1783.* Boston, 1783.
Gunn, Alexander, *Memoir of Reverend John H. Livingston.* 1829; 2nd edition, 1856.
Haltigan, James, *The Irish in the American Revolution and their Early Influence in the Colonies.* Washington, 1908.

Hamilton, Alexander, *A Full Vindication of the Measures of the Congress, from the Calumnies of their Enemies: in Answer to a Letter under the Signature of A W. Farmer. Whereby his Sophistry is exposed, his cavils confuted, and his Wit ridiculed.* New York, 1774.

Hamilton, Alexander, *The Farmer Refuted: or, A More impartial and comprehensive View of the Dispute between Great Britain and the Colonies; intended as a further vindication of Congress, in answer to a Letter from A W. Farmer, entitled a View of the Controversy, etc.* New York, 1775.

Hamilton, J. L., *History of the Unitas Fratrum, or Moravian Church in the United States of America.* New York, 1895.

Hart, Levi, *Description of A Good Character Attempted and Applied to the Subject of Jurisdiction and Civil Government. A Sermon delivered . . . May 11th, 1786.* Hartford, 1786.

Hawkins, E., *Historical Notices of the Missions of the Church of England in the North American Colonies, Previous to the Independence of the United States: Chiefly from the Manuscript Documents of the Society for the Propagation of the Gospel in Foreign Parts.* London, 1845.

Hawks, F. L., *Contributions to the Ecclesiastical History of the United States of America.* 2 vols., 1, *Virginia;* 2, *Maryland.* New York, 1836-39.

Hawks, F. L., *Efforts to Obtain a Colonial Episcopate before the Revolution.* In *Protestant Episcopal Historical Society Collection,* vol. i. New York, 1851.

Hawks, F. L. and Perry, W. S., *Journals of the General Convention of the Protestant Episcopal Church, 1785-1853.* Philadelphia, 1861.

Headley, J. T., *The Chaplains and Clergy of the American Revolution.* New York, 1864.

Hening, W. W., *Statutes at large, being a Collection of all the laws of Virginia, from the first session of the legislature in the year 1619-1792.* 13 vols. 1809-1823.

Henry, W. W., *Patrick Henry: Life, Correspondence and Speeches.* New York, 1890-1891.

Hildreth, Richard, *History of the United States.* 6 vols. New York, 1849-1856.

Hitchcock, Gad, *Election Sermon . . . . . May 25, 1774.* Boston, 1774.

Hodge, Charles, *The Constitutional History of the Presbyterian Church in the United States of America.* Parts i and ii, 1705-1788. Philadelphia, 1839-1840.

Hoffman, Murray, *Ecclesiastical Law of the State of New York.* New York, 1868.

Hovey, Alvah, *A Memoir of the Life and Times of the Reverend Isaac Backus.* Boston, 1859.

Howard, Simeon, *Election Sermon, Preached . . . . . May 31, 1780*. Boston, 1780.

Howell, Robert B. C., *The Early Baptists of Virginia*. Philadelphia, 1876.

Howison, R. R., *History of Virginia*. Richmond, 1849.

Huntington, Joseph, D.D., *National Justice: A Sermon Delivered . . . . May 13, 1874*. Hartford, 1784.

Inglis, Charles, *The True Interest of America Impartially Stated, in Certain Strictures on a Pamphlet intitled Common Sense, by An American*. Philadelphia, 1776.

Inglis, Charles, *Letters of Papinian, in which the Conduct, Present State and Prospect of the American Congress are examined*. London, 1779.

Jacobs, H. E., *History of the Evangelical Lutheran Church in the United States*. New York, 1900.

James, Charles F., *Documentary History of the Struggle for Religious Liberty in Virginia* Lynchburg, 1900.

James, E. L., *The Character and Career of Francis Asbury, Illustrated by Numerous Selections from his Journal, Arranged in Chronological Order*. 1872.

Jefferson, Thomas, Writings of. Washington edition, 9 vols. New York, 1861,

Jefferson, Thomas, Writings of. P. L. Ford edition, 10 vols. New York, 1892-1899.

Johnson, Samuel, *Taxation no Tyranny; An Answer to the Resolutions of the American Congress*. London, 1775.

Johnson, W. F., *America's Foreign Relations*, 2 vols. New York, 1916.

Jones, R. M., *The Quakers in the American Colonies*. London, 1911.

Jones, R. M., Sharpless, Isaac, and Gummere, *The Quakers in the American Colonies*. New York, 1911.

Journals of the Continental Congress. Library of Congress edition by W. C. Ford and Gaillard Hunt. Washington, 1904—in progress.

Journal of the Federal Convention by James Madison, edited by E. H. Scott. Chicago, 1893.

Journals of the House of Delegates of Virginia, 1776, 1777. Richmond, 1827-1828.

Journals of Each Provincial Congress of Massachusetts in 1774 and 1775. Lincoln edition. Boston, 1838.

Kempshall, Reverend Everard, *Caldwell and the Revolution, a historical sketch of the First Church of Elizabeth prior to and during the war of the Revolution. Being a discourse delivered on Sunday, January 25, 1880 . . . . .* Elizabeth, New Jersey, 1880.

Kohler, Max J., *Phases in the History of Religious Liberty in America* in *Publications of the Jewish Historical Society*. vol. 11.

Langdon, Samuel, *A Sermon before the Congress . . . . . at Watertown, May 31, 1775*. Watertown, 1775.

Lauer, P. E., *Church and State in New England* in *Johns Hopkins University Studies*, series 10, number 10, Baltimore, 1892.
Lee, Jesse, *A Short History of the Methodists in the United States of America.* Baltimore, 1810.
Lee, Leroy, M., *Life and Times of Jesse Lee.* Richmond, 1848.
Leland, John, Writings, edited by Miss L. F. Green. New York, 1845.
Leonard, Lewis A., *Life of Charles Carroll of Carrollton.* New York, 1918.
Lincoln, C. H., *The Revolutionary Movement in Pennsylvania, 1760-1776.* Philadelphia, 1901.
Livingston, E. B., *The Livingstons of Livingston Manor.* New York, 1910.
Livingston, M., *Letter to . . . . . John, lord bishop of Llandaff.* Boston, 1768.
Loyalist Poetry of the Revolution. Philadelphia, 1857.
Loyalist Verses of Joseph Stansbury and Doctor Jonathan Odell, relating to the American Revolution. Albany, 1860.
Madison, James, Writings of. G. Hunt edition. 9 vols. New York, 1900-1910.
McMaster, J. B. and Stone, F. D., *Pennsylvania and the Federal Convention.* Lancaster, 1888.
Mains, George P., *Francis Asbury.* New York, 1909.
Mann, William J., *Life and Times of Henry Melchoir Muhlenberg.* Philadelphia, 1887.
Mayhew, Jonathan, *A Discourse concerning Unlimited Submission and Non-resistance to the Higher Powers, with some Reflections on the Resistance to King Charles the First, and on the Anniversary of his Death,— in which the mysterious Doctrine of that Prince's Saintship and Martyrdom is unriddled.* Boston, 1750.
Mayhew, Jonathan, *The Snare Broken, A Thanksgiving Discourse, preached . . . . . May 23, 1766, occasioned by the Repeal of the Stamp Act.* Boston, 1766.
McConnell, S. D., *History of the Americqn Episcopal Church, from the Planting of the Colonies to the End of the Civil War.* New York, 1890.
McIllwain, Charles H., *The American Revolution: A Constitutional Interpretation.* New York, 1923.
McIlwaine, H. R., *Religious Toleration in Virginia*, in *Johns Hopkins University Studies in History and Political Science.* 10th series, number 4, Baltimore, 1894.
McSherry, James, *History of Maryland*, Baltimore, 1849.
McTyeire, H. H., *History of Methodism.* Nashville, 1914.
Meade, William, *Old Churches, Ministers and Families of Virginia.* 2 vols. Philadelphia, 1857.
Memoirs of the Historical Society of Pennsylvania. Philadelphia, 1864.
Meredith, W. H., *Jesse Lee, A Methodist Apostle.* New York, 1909.

Merrill, J. H., *Memoranda relating to the Mifflin Family.* Philadelphia, 1890.

Miller, Samuel, *Memoir of the Reverend John Rodgers.* Philadelphia, 1840.

Minutes of the Annual Conferences of the Methodist Church for the Years, 1773-1823. New York, 1840.

Minutes, Methodist, British. Edition of 1812. London, 1812.

Minutes of the (Provisional) Synod, 1771-1793 and of the (First) Particular Synod, 1794-1799. (Dutch Reformed).

Minutes of a Convention of Delegates from the Synods of New York and Philadelphia and from the Associations of Connecticut, held annually, 1766-1775. Hartford, 1843.

Minutes of the Presbytery of New York. Edited by D. R. Fox in *New York State Historical Association Journal.* Vol. i, pp. 22-43.

Minutes and Letters of the Coetus of the German Reformed Congregations in Pennsylvania, 1747-1792. Philadelphia, 1903.

Minutes of the Synod of New York and Philadelphia (Presbyterian).

Morris, B. F., *Christian Life and Character or Civil Institutions of the United States, developed in the official and historical annals of the Republic.* Philadelphia, 1864.

Morse, A. E., *The Federalist Party in Massachusetts to the Year 1800.* Princeton, 1909.

Morse, Jedidiah, *Annals of the American Revolution.* Hartford, 1824.

Moss, Lemuel (editor), *Baptists and the National Centenary.* Philadelphia, 1876.

Muhlenberg, H. A., *Life of John Peter Gabriel Muhlenberg.* Philadelphia, 1849.

Muzzey, D. S., *Thomas Jefferson.* New York, 1918.

Myles, William. *A Chronological History of the People Called Methodists of the Connexion of the Late Reverend John Wesley, from their rise in the year 1729 to their last conference in 1802.* London, 1803; fourth edition, London, 1813.

Narrative of the Organization and of the Early Measures of the Protestant Episcopal Church in the United States in the *Pennsylvania Register,* vol. iii, pp. 405-406, June 27, 1829.

Neuman, A. H., *History of the Baptist Churches in the United States.* 3rd edition, New York, 1900.

Notes and Queries: A Medium of Intercommunication for Literary Men, General Readers, etc. 92 vols. London, 1849-1895.

Novanglus et Massachusettensis: or Political Essays, published in the Years 1774 and 1775, on the principal points of Controversy between Great Britain and her Colonies. The former by John Adams, late President of the United States; the later by Jonathan Sewell, the King's Attorney General of the Province of Massachusetts-Bay. To which are Added a number of Letters lately written by President Adams to the Honorable William Tudor, some of which were never before published. Boston, 1819.

O'Brien, M. J., *A Hidden Phase of American History: Ireland's Part in America's Struggle for Liberty.* New York, 1920.

O'Gorman, Thomas, *A History of the Catholic Church in the United States.* New York, 1895; 3rd edition, New York, 1900.

Overton, J. H., *John Wesley.* New York, 1891.

Payson, Phillips, *Election Sermon, Preached . . . . . May 27, 1778.* Boston, 1778.

Perry, W. S., *A Half-century of Legislation: Journal of the General Convention of the Protestant Episcopal Church in the United States, 1785-1835; With Historical Notes and Documents.* 3 vols. Claremont, New Hampshire, 1874.

Perry, W. S., *A Handbook of the General Convention of the Protestant Episcopal Church giving its History and Constitution, 1785-1880.* 2nd edition, New York, 1881.

Perry, W. S., *The History of the American Episcopal Church, 1587-1883.* 2 vols. Boston, 1885.

Perry, W. S., *Influence of the Clergy in the War of the Revolution.* Pamphlet, New York, 1891.

Perry, W. S., *The Faith of the Signers of the Declaration of Independence* (N. P., 189?)

Perry, W. S., *Bishop Seabury and Bishop Provoost.* (N. P., 1862.)

Perry, W. S., *Historical Collections Relating to the Episcopal Colonial Church, Covering Virginia, Pennsylvania, Massachusetts, Maryland, and Delaware.* 4 vols. Hartford, 1870.

Peters, M. C., *Justice to the Jew: the story of what he has done for the world.* New York, 1908.

Philadelphia Ledger, January 27, 1776.

The Reasons of Dissent. Philadelphia, 1787.

Records of the General Association of the Clergy of Connecticut, 1738-1799. Hartford, 1888.

Records of the Presbyterian Church in the United States of America, etc. Philadelphia, 1904; earlier edition Philadelphia, 1841.

Reformed Dutch Church, Minutes of the General Synod, vol. i, 1771-1812. New York.

Report of Committee of Revisors appointed by the General Assembly of Virginia in 1776. Richmond, 1784.

Robin, Abbe, *A New Journey in North America.* Philadelphia, 1782.

Robinson, W. A., *Jeffersonian Democracy in New England* in *Yale Historical Publications.* Miscellany, vol. iii. New Haven, 1916.

Rodgers, John, *The Divine goodness displayed in the American Revolution, A Sermon Preached December 11, 1783, a day of Public Thanksgiving.* New York, 1783.

Rodgers, John, *The Faithful Servant Rewarded. A Sermon delivered at Princeton, May 6, 1795, occasioned by the death of the Reverend John Witherspoon.* New York, 1795.

Rowland, Kate Mason, *Life and Writings of George Mason.* 2 vols. New York, 1892.

Sabine, Lorenzo, *Biographical Sketches of Loyalists of the American Revolution, with a Historical Essay.* 2 vols. Boston, 1864.

Sanderson, John, *Biography of Signers of the Declaration of Independence.* 9 vols. Philadelphia, 1823-1827.

Schaff, Philip, "Church and State in the United States" in *American Historical Association Papers,* vol. ii, number 4.

Schaff, Philip, *The Creeds of Christendom.* New York, 1877-1884.

Schlesinger, A. M., *The Colonial Merchants and the Revolution* in *Columbia University Studies,* vol. lxxviii. New York, 1918.

Schmucher, S. S., *Retrospection of Lutheranism in the United States.* Philadelphia, 1840.

Seabury, Samuel (2nd), *A Brief View of the Origin and Results of Episcopacy in the United States of America.* New York, 1836.

Seabury, Samuel, *Free Thoughts on the Proceedings of the Continental Congress, held at Philadelphia, September 5, 1774: wherein their Errors are exhibited, their Reasonings confuted, and the fatal Tendency of their Non-importation, Non-Exportation, and Non-Consumption Measures are laid open to the plainest Understandings; and the only means pointed out for preserving and securing our present happy Constitution . . . . . By A W. Farmer.* New York, 1774.

Seabury, Samuel, *The Congress Canvassed: or an Examination into the Conduct of Delegates at their Grand Convention in Philadelphia, Sept. 1, 1774, addressed to the Merchants of New York. By A W. Farmer, Author of Free Thoughts.* New York, 1774.

Sedgwick, Theodore Jr., *Life of William Livingston.* New York, 1833.

Seidensticker, Oswald, *First Century of German Printing.* Philadelphia, 1893.

Semple, Robert B., *A History of the Rise and Progress of the Baptists in Virginia.* Richmond, 1810. Revised and extended by G. W. Beale, Richmond, 1894.

Sharpless, Isaac A., *A History of Quaker Government in Pennsylvania.* 2 vols. Philadelphia, 1899.

Sharpless, Isaac, A., *Political Leaders of Provincial Pennsylvania.* New York, 1919.

Sharpless, Isaac A., *Quakerism and Politics: Essays.* Philadelphia, 1905.

Shea, John Gilmary, *The Catholic Church in Colonial Days.* New York, 1886.

Shea, John Gilmary, *History of the Catholic Church in the United States.* 4 vols. New York, 1886-1892.

Shea, John Gilmary, *Life and Times of Archbishop Carroll.* New York, 1888.

Smith, G. G., *Life and Labors of Francis Asbury.* Nashville, 1896.

Smith, Samuel S., *Life of John Witherspoon, D.D., Prefixed to his Works.*

Smyth, Thomas, "Presbyterianism, the Revolution, the Declaration, and the Constitution" in *The Southern Presbyterian Review,* March, 1848, vol. i, no. 4, pp. 33-79. Columbia, South Carolina, 1848.

Smyth, Thomas, "The True Origin and Source of the Mecklenburg and National Declaration of Independence", in *The Southern Presbyterian Review,* June, 1847, vol. i, no. 1. Columbia, 1847.

Smyth, Thomas, *Works.*

Smith, William, *The Works of.* 2 vols. Philadelphia, 1803.

Sprague, William B., *Annals of the American Pulpit.* 9 vols. New York, 1859-1869.

Staples, W. R., *Annals of Providence to 1832.* Providence, 1843.

Staples, W. R., *Rhode Island in the Continental Congress, with the Journal of the Convention that Adopted the Constitution, 1765-1790.* Providence, 1870.

Stevens, Abel, *History of Methodism.* 3 vols. New York, 1858.

Stevens, Abel, *History of the Methodist Episcopal Church.* New York, 1864.

Stevens, Abel, *Memorials of the Introduction of Methodism into the Eastern States.* Boston, 1852.

Stillé, C. J., *The Life and Times of John Dickinson, 1732-1808.* Philadelphia, 1891.

Stillman, Samuel, *A Sermon, Preached . . . . . at Boston, May 26, 1779.* Boston, 1779.

Strickland, W. P., *The Pioneer Bishop: or, The Life and Times of Francis Asbury.* New York, 1858.

Story, Joseph, *Commentaries on the Constitution of the United States.* 3 vols. Boston, 1833. Text edition, Boston, 1833.

"Stuart, Reverend John, Memoir of" in *Documentary History of New York.* vol. iv. Albany, 1851.

Thom, W. T., "The Struggle for Religious Freedom in Virginia: The Baptists" in *Johns Hopkins University Studies.* Series xviii, numbers 10-12. Baltimore, 1900.

Thomas, A. C. and R. H., *History of the Friends in America.* 5th edition, New York, 1919.

Thomas, David, *The Virginia Baptist: or a View and Defense of the Christian Religion, as it is professed by the Baptists of Virginia. In three parts; containing a true and faithful account, 1. Of their Principles. 2. Of their Orders as a Church. 3. Of the principal Objections made against them especially in this Colony, with a serious Answer to each of them.* Baltimore, 1774.

Thompson, J. P., *Church and State in the United States.* Boston, 1873.

Thomson, R. E., *History of the Presbyterian Churches in the United States.* New York, 1890.

Thornton, J. W., *The Pulpit of the American Revolution:* or, *The Political Sermons of the Period of 1776.* New York, 1860.

Thorpe, F. N., *The Federal and State Constitutions* . . . . . 7 vols. Washington, 1909.

Tiffany, C. C., *A History of the Protestant Episcopal Church in the United States of America.* New York, 1895.

Tigert, J. J., *A Constitutional History of American Episcopal Methodism.* Nashville, 1894.

Tigert, J. J., *The Making of Methodism: Studies in the Genesis of Institutions.* Nashville, 1898.

Tipple, E. S., *Francis Asbury, The Prophet of the Long Road.* New York, 1916.

Tipple, E. S., *The Heart of Asbury's Journal, Being the Substance of the Printed Journals of the Reverend Francis Asbury, Forty-five Years Itinerant Preacher in America and Thirty-two Years a General Superintendent of the Methodist Episcopal Church.* New York, 1904.

Todd, J. A., *Centennial Discourse.* New York, 1876.

Transactions of the Moravian Historical Society.

Trent, William P., "The Period of Constitution-Making in the American Churches" in *Essays in the Constitutional History of the United States in the Formative Period, 1775-1789.* By Graduates and Former Members of the Johns Hopkins University. Edited by J. F. Jameson. New York, 1889.

Tyerman, L., *The Life and Times of the Reverend John Wesley, M. A., the Founder of the Methodists.* 3 vols. 6th edition, London, 1890.

Tyler, M. C., *The Literary History of the American Revolution, 1763-1783.* 2 vols. New York, 1897.

Usher, R. G., *The Pilgrims and their History.* New York, 1918.

Wales, Samuel, D.D., *The Dangers of our National Prosperity: A Sermon delivered . . . . . May 12, 1785.* Hartford, 1785.

Ward, Julius H., *The Life and Times of Bishop William White.* New York, 1892.

Washington-Duché Letters: Now Printed for the first time from the original manuscript, with an introduction by Worthington Chauncey Ford. Brooklyn, 1890.

Washington, George The Writings of. Edited by W. C. Ford. 14 volumes. New York and London, 1889-1893.

Washington, George, The Writings of. Edited by Jared Sparks. 12 vols. Boston, and New York, 1834-1847.

Webster, Richard, *History of the Presbyterian Church in America from its origin until the year 1760, with Biographical Sketches of its Early Ministers.* Philadelphia, 1857.

Webster, Samuel, *Election Sermon, Preached . . . . . . May 28, 1777.* Boston, 1777.

Wesley, John, Works.

West, Samuel, *Election Sermon, Preached . . . . . May 24, 1776.* Boston, 1776.

Wetherill, Charles, *History of the Free Quakers.* Philadelphia, 1894.

White, William, *A Sermon on Duty of Civil Obedience, as Required in Scripture.* Philadelphia, 1799.

White, William, *A Sermon on the Reciprocal Influence of Civil Policy and Religious Duty: delivered . . . . . Philadelphia . . . . . February 19, 1795.* Philadelphia, 1795.

White, William, *Memoirs of the Protestant Episcopal Church in the United States.* Edited by B. F. De Costo. Philadelphia, 1820; 2nd edition 1836; New York, 1880.

White, William, *The Past and the Future: A Charge on Events Connected with the Organization of the Protestant Episcopal Church in the United States of America and the Lessons they Inculcate.* Philadelphia, 1834.

White, William, *The Case of the Episcopal Churches in the United States Considered. "To Make New Articles of Faith and Doctrine No Man thinketh it lawful: new laws of government, What Commonwealth or Church is there which maketh not at one time or another," Hooker.* Philadelphia, 1783. Reprinted, 1827 and in the *Protestant Episcopal Quarterly Review,* vol. vi, 1859.

Wiernik, P., *History of the Jews in America.* New York, 1912.

Wilberforce, Samuel, *A History of the Protestant Episcopal Church in America.* New York, 1849; 3rd edition, London, 1856.

Wilson, Bird, D.D., *Memoir of the Life of the Right Reverend William White, D.D., Bishop of the Protestant Episcopal Church in the State of Pennsylvania.* Philadelphia, 1839.

Windsor, Justin, *Narrative and Critical History of America.* 8 vols. Boston, 1886-1889.

Wise, John, *Democracy is Christ's Government in Church and State.* Republished, 1772.

Witherspoon, John, *The Dominion of Providence over the Passions of Men: A Sermon, preached at Princeton the 17th of May, 1776.* Philadelphia, 1776.

Witherspoon, John, *Essay on Money, as a Medium of Commerce: with remarks on the advantages and disadvantages of paper admitted into general circulation: by a citizen of the United States.* Philadelphia, 1786.

Witherspoon, John, Works of. To Which is prefixed an account of the Author's life, by Reverend John Rodgers. 9 vols. Edinburg, 1815.

Wolf, Simon, *The American Jew as Patriot, Soldier, and Citizen.* Philadelphia, 1895.

Woodburn, J. A., "Causes of the American Revolution," in *Johns Hopkins University Studies,* series 10, number 12. Baltimore, 1892.

Zeisberger, David, Diary of, translated and edited by E. F. Bliss. 2 vols. Cincinnati, 1885-1888.

Zollmann, Carl, "American Civil Church Law" in *Columbia University Studies,* vol. 77. New York, 1917.

Zubly, John Joachim, *An Humble Enquiry into the Nature of the Dependency of the American Colonies upon the Parliament of Great Britain and the Right of Parliament to lay Taxes on the said Colonies, by A Freeholder of South Carolina.* Not printed, 1769.

Zubly, John Joachim, *The Law of Liberty: A Sermon on American Affairs preached at the opening of the Provincial Congress of Georgia.* Philadelphia, 1775.

Zubly, John Joachim, *The Stamp Act Repealed: A Sermon preached at Savannah, June 25, 1766.* Charleston, 1766.

INDEX